THE LIFE OF

GENERAL ELY S. PARKER

LAST GRAND SACHEM OF THE IROQUOIS AND
GENERAL GRANT'S MILITARY SECRETARY

BY
ARTHUR C. PARKER
STATE ARCHAEOLOGIST OF NEW YORK

BUFFALO, NEW YORK:
PUBLISHED BY THE
BUFFALO HISTORICAL SOCIETY
1919

Windham Press is committed to bringing the lost cultural heritage of ages past into the 21st century through high-quality reproductions of original, classic printed works at affordable prices.

This book has been carefully crafted to utilize the original images of antique books rather than error-prone OCR text. This also preserves the work of the original typesetters of these classics, unknown craftsmen who laid out the text, often by hand, of each and every page you will read. Their subtle art involving judgment and interaction with the text is in many ways superior and more human than the mechanical methods utilized today, and gave each book a unique, hand-crafted feel in its text that connected the reader organically to the art of bindery and book-making.

We think these benefits are worth the occasional imperfection resulting from the age of these books at the time of scanning, and their vintage feel provides a connection to the past that goes beyond the mere words of the text.

As bibliophiles, we are always seeking perfection in our work, so please notify us of any errors in this book by emailing us at corrections@windhampress.com. Our team is motivated to correct errors quickly so future customers are better served. Our mission is to raise the bar of quality for reprinted works by a focus on detail and quality over mass production. To peruse our catalog of carefully curated classic works, please visit our online store at www.windhampress.com.

OFFICERS OF THE
BUFFALO HISTORICAL SOCIETY
1919

HONORARY PRESIDENT, ... ANDREW LANGDON.
PRESIDENT, ... Hon. HENRY W. HILL.
VICE-PRESIDENT, ... CHARLES R. WILSON.
SECRETARY-TREASURER, ... FRANK H. SEVERANCE.

BOARD OF MANAGERS

Term expiring January, 1920

ALBERT H. BRIGGS, M. D.,   LEE H. SMITH, M. D.,
JOHN G. WICKSER,   EDWARD S. HAWLEY,
WILLIAM A. GALPIN.

Term expiring January, 1921

HOWARD H. BAKER,   DR. G. HUNTER BARTLETT,
G. BARRETT RICH,   HENRY W. SPRAGUE,
WILLIAM Y. WARREN.

Term expiring January, 1922

HON. HENRY W. HILL,   HENRY R. HOWLAND,
GEORGE R. HOWARD,   CHARLES R. WILSON,
EVAN HOLLISTER.

Term expiring January, 1923

ANDREW LANGDON, ... LORAN L. LEWIS, JR.,
FRANK H. SEVERANCE, ... GEORGE A. STRINGER,
CARLTON R. PERRINE.

LIST OF THE
PRESIDENTS OF THE SOCIETY

FROM ITS ORGANIZATION TO THE PRESENT TIME

*MILLARD FILLMORE, ... 1862 to 1867
*HENRY W. ROGERS, ... 1868
*REV. ALBERT T. CHESTER, D. D. 1869
*ORSAMUS H. MARSHALL, ... 1870
*HON. NATHAN K. HALL, ... 1871
*WILLIAM H. GREENE, ... 1872
*ORLANDO ALLEN, ... 1873
*OLIVER G. STEELE, ... 1874
*HON. JAMES SHELDON, ... 1875 and 1886
*WILLIAM C. BRYANT, ... 1876
*CAPT. E. P. DORR, ... 1877
*HON. WILLIAM P. LETCHWORTH, ... 1878
*WILLIAM H. H. NEWMAN, ... 1879 and 1885
*HON. ELIAS S. HAWLEY, ... 1880
*HON. JAMES M. SMITH, ... 1881
*WILLIAM HODGE, ... 1882
*WILLIAM DANA FOBES, ... 1883 and 1884
*EMMOR HAINES, ... 1887
*JAMES TILLINGHAST, ... 1888
*WILLIAM K. ALLEN, ... 1889
*GEORGE S. HAZARD, ... 1890 and 1892
*JOSEPH C. GREENE, M. D., ... 1891
*JULIUS H. DAWES, ... 1893
 ANDREW LANGDON, ... 1894 to 1909
 HON. HENRY W. HILL, ... 1910 —

*Deceased

PREFACE

THIS volume is in the main a narrative of Indian life, by an author who, perhaps because of his own Indian ancestry, perhaps because of his family associations and his peculiar educational equipment, is better qualified to present the red man's case from the red man's viewpoint, than could any chronicler of purely Caucasian blood. The why and wherefore of the case really matters little. The essential and important thing is, that we have here a study of Iroquois life and character from the pen of one who is not merely exceptionally well-informed in his subject, but who treats it with an inborn, native sympathy and certainty of interpretation.

It is a fine thing, a happy thing, to be able to picture for the reader of to-day, the home life and social status and relations of a typical though perhaps exceptionally endowed Seneca family. The Parker family, judged by inherent qualities, would have been notable in any community. Fortunately, where the white strain came in, it came from clean, honest, capable stock. Who that knew her, or knows only by tradition and record, of Martha Hoyt, devoted missionary to the Senecas when Buffalo was near its beginnings, would question that in taking her to wife, Nicholson Parker, the Seneca, found a helpmate as loyally devoted to his people as though she were of their race. In the long record of white and Indian dealings, usually so full of fraud and iniquity, of wrong and evil of every sort, it is refreshing to find an instance like this.

Mr. Parker's sketch of his great-uncle is, obviously and successfully, an attempt not merely to trace that worthy's creditable and unique career, but to do justice to his memory, and through him, to his people. But our author does much more than this. He pictures old-time conditions known for the most part only to the Indians themselves. He shows that the Senecas on their reservations had better standards of living—remembering their ancestral forms and traditions—than were held to by many of their white neighbors. Now and then—as in Mrs. Laura Parker Doctor's recollections of her grandmother—he gives us a glimpse of more remote days, which is like the recovery of a lost page of history.

Of the author of this volume, the editor may say in his Preface what Mr. Parker could not—or would not—say for himself. To a large circle of students his work has made him so well known that any sketch of it would be superfluous; but there are others, into whose hands this book will come, who may be grateful for some glimpse of the personality and achievements of our author.

Arthur Caswell Parker was born on the Cattaraugus Seneca reservation April 5, 1881. His father, Frederick, a graduate of Fredonia Normal School, is a son of the late Nicholson Henry Parker, for many years Secretary of the Seneca Nation. Nicholson H. Parker was a brother of General Ely Samuel Parker, Grant's Military Secretary and the co-worker with Lewis H. Morgan in writing "The League of the Iroquois." The mother of Arthur C. Parker was Geneva H. Griswold, of Scotch and English descent. She was a teacher for five or six years on the Allegany and Cattaraugus reservations.

Mr. Parker's grandfather's grandfather was Handsome Lake, the Seneca prophet. His paternal grandfather six generations back was Old King or Old Smoke (Gaiengwatoh), the supposed leader of the Senecas at Wyoming, Pa., and the friend of the Rev. Samuel Kirkland. The great-grandmother of Mr. Parker was a descendant of a Neuter captive and a lineal descendant of Jigonsaseh, "the Peace Queen" of the Neuters. She, with Haiowentha and Dekanawida, was a founder of the Iroquois League. Nicholson Parker's sister, Caroline, was given this name, Jigonsaseh, as a right of heritage. She was the wife of Chief John Mountpleasant of the Tuscaroras.

Arthur C. Parker was educated in the reservation schools, in White Plains (N. Y.) High School, and in Dickinson Seminary; and later studied under Frederic W. Putnam, Peabody Professor of Anthropology at Harvard University, then Curator of Anthropology in the American Museum in New York City.

In 1904 he made contributions of folklore manuscripts to the State Library of New York. He previously, 1901-1902, had been a field assistant in archaeology for the American Museum. In 1903 he was, with Mr. Raymond Harrington, jointly in charge of the Peabody Museum Archaeological expedition to Western New York. In 1906 he was appointed by the Civil Service Commission (after competitive examination) as the Archaeologist of the New York State Museum which office he still holds.

Mr. Parker has practically created a new archaeological museum; he has installed special exhibits along new lines, and since his appointment has brought in collections of Iroquois material totaling about 50,000 specimens. The Iroquois habitat groups, which are a chief attraction of the New York State Museum, are of his conception and execution.

The list of his principal writings, already a long one, will be found with the "Editorial Notes" following the Appendix to this volume. Also, long is the list of his activities in various learned societies and other organizations. For four years he was the secretary-treasurer of the Society of American Indians, having been one of its organizers at Ohio State University. He is the founder and editor-general of the *American Indian Magazine* (Washington), formerly the *Quarterly Journal* of the Society of American Indians. He is a Fellow of the American Ethnological Society, the American Anthropological Society, the American Association for the Advancement of Science; and was one of ten American archaeologists appointed to represent the science of archaeology at the Pan-American Congress. He is a member of the American Sociological Society, the Wisconsin Archaeological Society, a life member of the Buffalo Historical Society; founder and past president of the Society of American Indians; founder and past president of the Philosophical Society of Albany; and active and distinguished in many another organization. By the University of Chicago he was awarded the Cornplanter medal, for research. He was the originator of "American Indian Day." It is an imposing and honorable list, not by any means exhausted in the foregoing enumeration; but it is not the present purpose to forestall the encyclopaedia. Let this suffice, with the following, which perhaps he alone, of all living scholars and loyal Americans, can say with pride and truth:

"I am a Seneca Indian, whose ancestors from the beginning have been connected with our history—and all of whom have left an indelible impress upon our State and Nation."

The Buffalo Historical Society feels justified in devoting this volume largely to a review of General Parker's career, for he was one of its most distinguished members—in a membership, we may be pardoned for recalling, which has included two Presidents of the United States, Cabinet officials, diplomats and others of high distinction. But the notability of Ely S. Parker was and is unique, for he embodied in his life and career the best traits of a race always imperfectly understood and usually unfairly judged by their white neighbors. He was a high type of the Iroquois in transition—a connecting link between the days of more primitive conditions and institutions, and a later period, woefully slow in coming, when the strong, good qualities of the Iroquois shall not only be recognized but encouraged by juster and more sympathetic social and governmental conditions.

This volume, in its principal narrative and in its appendix, brings together numerous letters and other documents, many of them hitherto unpublished, of certain historical value. We commend it to our readers as by no means the least in interest and historical worth in the lengthening series of the Buffalo Historical Society Publications.

F. H. S.

Historical Building, Buffalo, June, 1919.

CONTENTS

		PAGE
EDITOR'S PREFACE,		vii
AUTHOR'S INTRODUCTION,		3

CHAPTER		
I.	THE MEASURE OF THE MAN,	7
II.	THE VALLEY OF THE RAPID WATER,	12
III.	HOW THE SENECAS MADE WAR UPON GREAT BRITAIN,	24
IV.	THE GRAND-DAUGHTER OF THE PROPHET,	40
V.	BOYHOOD DAYS ON THE RESERVATION,	50
VI.	THE WAY THE TWIG WAS BENT,	71
VII.	LEWIS H. MORGAN AND THE "NEW LEAGUE OF THE IROQUOIS,"	79
VIII.	EARLY EXPERIENCE AS AN ENGINEER AND MASONIC CAREER,	91
IX.	HOW PARKER'S ENLISTMENT WAS REFUSED BY SECRETARY SEWARD,	99
X.	A SACHEM BECOMES A WARRIOR,	105
XI.	THE FALL OF THE CONFEDERACY,	117
XII.	THE INDIAN IN THE DRAMA AT APPOMATTOX,	129
XIII.	THE WARRIOR AFTER THE WAR,	142
XIV.	AN INDIAN COMMISSIONER OF INDIAN AFFAIRS,	150
XV.	A SACHEM'S LETTERS TO A POETESS,	162
XVI.	THE GETTYSBURG SPEECH OF GRANT'S MILITARY SECRETARY,	181
XVII.	THE HOUSE OF BROTHER NICHOLSON,	189
XVIII.	THE BONES OF RED JACKET,	202
XIX.	THE LAST GRAND SACHEM,	221

APPENDIX

A VISIT TO THE PARKER HOMESTEAD,	231
THE BOY WHO DARED TO TRAVEL WEST,	238
HANDSOME LAKE THE PEACE PROPHET,	244
THE RELIGION OF HANDSOME LAKE,	251
ELY S. PARKER'S SCHOOL DAYS,	262
"THE AMERICAN RED MAN,"	263
"TRAITS OF INDIAN CHARACTER,"	270
"INDIAN DANCES AND THEIR INFLUENCES,"	279
LETTER OF ELY S. PARKER, ON LAWS AFFECTING INDIANS,	286
THE SACHEM AT CHATTANOOGA,	292
HOW THE QUAKERS FOUGHT A LAND CONSPIRACY,	296
GENERAL PARKER'S REPLY TO CHARGES AGAINST HIS ADMINISTRATION,	304
SECRETARY SEWARD'S INTEREST IN THE INDIANS,	309

EDITORIAL NOTES

	PAGE
THE KENJOCKETYS,	313
WAS THE SLOCUM CAPTIVE A PARKER ANCESTOR?	317
"A PROPHECY FULFILLED,"	320
GENERAL PARKER'S NAME,	320
THE MOUNTPLEASANTS,	321
MRS. HARRIET MAXWELL CONVERSE,	323
"THE TRIAL OF RED JACKET,"	325
THE RED JACKET MEDAL,	326
IROQUOIS ADOPTION,	329
MR. ARTHUR C. PARKER'S WRITINGS,	333
MEMORANDA,	335
INDEX,	337

ILLUSTRATIONS

ELY S. PARKER AS GRANT'S SECRETARY,	*Frontispiece*
FALLS OF THE TONAWANDA,	Op. page 32
ELY S. PARKER'S PARENTS,	Op. " 40
OLD FARMHOUSE, TONAWANDA RESERVATION,	Op. " 48
RELICS OF EARLY DAYS,	Op. " 60
FACSIMILE FROM E. S. PARKER'S DIARY,	Op. " 76
LEWIS H. MORGAN,	Op. " 80
CAROLINE G. PARKER,	Op. " 88
GRANT'S HEADQUARTERS, 1864,	Op. " 110
GRANT AND STAFF, COLD HARBOR, VA., 1864,	Op. " 128
GEN. PARKER AND MISS SACKETT AT TIME OF MARRIAGE,	Op. " 146
ELY S. PARKER AS BRIGADIER GENERAL,	Op. " 162
NICHOLSON H. PARKER AND WIFE,	Op. " 188
FREDERICK E. PARKER AND ARTHUR C. PARKER,	Op. " 200
GENERAL PARKER'S HOME, FAIRFIELD, CONN., 1879,	Op. " 220
SCENE AT REBURIAL OF GENERAL PARKER, BUFFALO,	Op. " 226
GENERAL PARKER IN 1869 AND IN 1894,	Op. " 228
HANDSOME LAKE'S CREDENTIALS,	Op. " 250
NICHOLSON HENRY PARKER,	Op. " 262
POSTER, NICHOLSON H. PARKER'S LECTURE, 1853,	Page 277
PHILIP KENJOCKETY,	Op. page 314
JOHN AND CAROLINE PARKER MOUNTPLEASANT,	Op. " 320
"THE TRIAL OF RED JACKET,"	Op. " 326
THE RED JACKET MEDAL,	Op. " 328

THE LAST GRAND SACHEM OF THE IROQUOIS

INTRODUCTION

In a great steel vault in the New York State Museum there reposes a long purple wampum belt. It is the record of a great sachemship, the title of the historic Iroquois Indian Confederacy. To the expert Indian annalist this woven belt of purple shell beads has a hidden meaning and preserves in its mysterious strands the story of the rulers of a mighty American Empire.

Not every "reader of the wampums" would tell the same story as he handled that sacred belt, but each reader would undoubtedly tell his story with accuracy. Outlined in white beads made from the columella of the Busycon, five hexagons display themselves on that belt, each hexagon symbolizing the council of a nation in the confederacy of nations that formed the "Empire" of the Iroquois. The white beads are emblematic of purity, peace and integrity and teach those qualities to the nations. The dark purple beads, softly clicking as you handle the belt, and glittering in the light like the scales of a black snake's skin, symbolize royalty, dignity and determination that no adverse influence can weaken. The name of that belt is Do-ne-ho-ga-wa. That word means "The Door Keeper," and it is the title of the last national sachem in the roll of Iroquois sachems. Ordinarily it is translated, to reveal its true significance, "The Keeper of the Western Door." Its "holder" was the guard of the Confederacy, the sentinel before the door of the emblematic Long House of the Five Nations.

For many years up to 1852, this belt was the seal of office, the badge of title, of Blacksmith, the Tonawanda Seneca sachem. Blacksmith died and at the condolence ceremony the Ho-ya-neh women of the Five Nations in 1852 confirmed the nomination of the nations of the Wolf clan and bestowed the title and name upon an Indian youth, named Ha-sa-no-an-da, or Ely Samuel Parker. From that time until his death in 1895 this man held the title. He was the sentinel-sachem of a crumbling empire and the last to use his office as his forefathers would have wished.

It is as difficult to make a beginning of this true story as it is to end it. It has many beginnings. It is impossible to describe all of them for a shifting of the kaleidoscope will give us another view. Our plan is to reveal the manner of man this Indian was, and to analyze the elements that produced him. After all, in our contemplation of great men (or even lesser men after we have learned of their deeds), do we not search first for the secret of their successful efforts, and then review the results of those efforts, as a matter of secondary importance to us? After we have learned what a man has done, if we are ambitious, do we not then ask how he managed to do it, and why? Is it ancestry that makes the man, is it environment, or is it a combination of both with the individual determination to win? Perhaps herein at least may be found the solution to one man's life effort.

An Indian boy became angry at the insults of an English lieutenant. It was not ordinary savage madness, but a choking anger that drained the blood from the boy's face and left him trembling and speechless. Then, with the return of the pulsing blood came hot tears and a resolution to revenge the insults of that English officer.

The Indian boy was driving mules; the lieutenant was in charge of an outfit of horses, mules and drivers. As a first means of revenge the boy left his job and walked nearly a hundred miles. Then he went to school. His pride had been touched, it had awakened his slumbering spirit and his contemplated revenge was not to be of the ordinary kind. In his plan he had no desire to do injury to the English lieutenant. Indeed, in later years, he totally forgot the man who hurt his pride. There is pain in the birth of many emotions, but that natal pain, forgotten as real consciousness comes, indicates the creation of a new force that dies or lives according to the creative power of its sire.

This book is the story of the result of the resolution and will power that came when pride was awakened in Ha-sa-no-an-da, the Indian boy, and it tells how it brought to him a spirit and a determination that lived until the last drop of blood had been pumped from the chambers of his heart.

Great resolutions are the result of strong emotions, and the struggle to attain those resolutions makes men.

The Indian boy whom we have mentioned was the son of Jo-no-es-sto-wa, Dragon Fly, otherwise known as William Parker, a Tonawanda Seneca chief. Indians, though they use their native names among themselves, realize that they must have names that English-speaking people can pronounce and remember without difficulty. The Indian boy was therefore called Ely because everyone knew the distinguished Mr. Ely of Rochester.

It has for some time been the author's ambition to write the life of this man. For twenty years he has gathered the meager data that go into the make-up of this volume. As a biographer of incidents the author confesses his failure; the aim is not to write of events for the sake of recording history, but to mention events as the cause of action, and as the elements that went forth to determine the character of a man. There are many men whose lives are filled with countless thrilling incidents, but here is a man whose life is so strange in many of its phases as to be almost tragic. With ambitions constantly balked he rebelled not, but philosophically rose above his obstacles. No defeat was accepted as a blow, but as a lesson from which to profit.

THE LAST GRAND SACHEM OF THE IROQUOIS

OR

THE LIFE AND TIMES OF GEN. ELY S. PARKER

CHAPTER I

THE MEASURE OF THE MAN

In the character of Ely Samuel Parker we have a unique American. It is not entirely because he was a Seneca Indian of pure lineage, or that he was a citizen of the United States and a general in its army that he is called unique. He was indeed a successful and distinguished military officer in the Civil War and later a Federal official in civil service. Likewise, he was a successful sachem of the historic Iroquois League of the Five Nations, and for many years, its foremost defender. But the special honor that we wish to give him is that he is the only American Indian who rose to national distinction and who could trace his lineage back for generations to the Stone Age and to the days of Hiawatha. First and last he was an Iroquois. In any sense or viewpoint he was an American. There is a sense in which he was the first American of his time and an embodiment of all the heroic ideals that enter into our conception of American manhood.

His life is the story of a man's struggle against adversity —of an effort to achieve; but he was a warrior as well as a statesman and found honest philosophy in the fight. However we may look at him, we must not lose sight of the fact that he was a red man, a native product of the soil. It is not especially because we wish to emphasize race differences, but because we are writing history.

There have been many heroic figures in the annals of the American Indian—dignity, poise and native wisdom combined with intense patriotism have characterized these superb men whose history we know but know so imperfectly. American history would lose the peculiar luster of its early pages without such names as Philip of Pokanoet, Powhatan, King Hendrick, Captain Brant, Tecumseh, Dekanisora, Garangula, Black Hawk, Pontiac, Osceola, Red Jacket, and Logan.

We know these men by names, we know something of their achievements; but what produced them? Who were their sires, their mothers, and what is their background in heredity? We cannot answer.

How grateful we would be to know the genealogy of that incomparable hero, Tecumseh, that nobleman of the forest, that fiery patriot, that fighter for his people! We should welcome the insight into the knowledge of the forces that produced him; but the curtain is drawn and we may never know.

The great men of the red race did not vanish with Tecumseh and Osceola. They continued to appear and even now, in this modern day, there are red men whose names are indelibly written in the records of this nation; but among the American Indians of the last century none perhaps rose to the height of Ely Samuel Parker, this Sachem of the Senecas. Of pure Indian lineage on both sides, both history and tradition unite in affording us a glimpse of his forefathers and mothers who lived in the generation before him. We may know his ancestral setting and the hereditary forces that produced him. In this, then, he is unique.

When James F. Kelly, the sculptor of military men, had General Parker in his studio in New York, posing for his bust at the request of Mr. Kelly's mother, the sculptor remarked, "General Parker, in my estimation you are the most distinguished Indian who ever lived."

"That is not so," was the laconic reply. "Better and wiser red men lived before me and now live."

"Who are they?" asked the sculptor.

The Indian looked at him curiously and flashed back, "Can it be that you fail to recall Brant and Tecumseh, both military men, and a host of others?"

"Ah, General," said Mr. Kelly, as he worked on the plastic clay, "I see you have not caught my meaning. I do not intend to flatter you; I would not stoop to that—I mean that you are a man who has 'pierced the enemy's lines.' You have torn yourself from one environment and made yourself the master of another. In this you have done more for your people than any other Indian who ever lived. Had you remained with your people, and of your people alone, you might have been a Red Jacket, a Brant or a Tecumseh, but by going out and away from them you added to the honor that you already had and won equal, if not greater, honors among the white people. You proved what an Indian of capacity could be in the white man's world. The heroes you name did not. We have no way of measuring their capacity in our own standards. We do not even know exactly what they said; their speeches were all translated by interpreters. But we know what you have said as we know what you have done, and that measured by our own ideals."

"That may be true," answered the General to the sculptor, "but why should you test the capacity of the red man's mind in measures that may have an improper scale? Do you measure cloth with a balance or by the gallon?"

It was Mr. Kelly's delight to draw out, in his ingenious way, the thoughts of his many distinguished sitters. A large box filled with note-books of quarto size attest his genius, and from that box came the note-book that has given many valued facts about General Parker's army career.

It always pained the General to have men discuss his achievements. The testimony of his many friends is that he almost never talked about what he had done, unless forced by circumstances. His ears were deaf to praise and adulation.

In a confidential letter to Mrs. Harriet Maxwell Converse he wrote:

"I am credited or charged by you with being 'great,' 'powerful,' and finally crowned as 'good.' Oh, my guardian genius, why should I be so burdened with what I am not now and never expect to be! All my life I have occupied a false position. I have lost my identity and look about me in vain for my original being."

Modesty is an attribute of true greatness, and General Parker in spite of his dislike of being "talked about" and his disavowal of having done exceptional things, is eminently deserving of the laurels of greatness. He was great because he was a man who labored unselfishly for his brother man. In this he was not unlike the great culture heroes of the famous Iroquois league, Ji-gon-sa-seh, De-ka-na-wi-da, and Hiawatha, who in the misty centuries before, had established the Iroquois Empire State and created a government that in its day ruled half of North America. Each of these great personages about whom have clustered many invented tales, was a living person and not a myth. Each was a great constructive force and each was modest and unassuming.

Ely S. Parker was a descendant of Ji-gon-sa-seh, the Great Woman, "the mother of nations." His sachemship name was Do-ne-ho-ga-wa, and bearing that name, by right of descent, he held the honored office of "Keeper of the Western Door" of the historic "Long House of the Iroquois."

Colden, Hale and Morgan have written well of the League of the Five Nations of the Iroquois, and the strength of the League in its glory is well known to historians. Suffice for us to say that it had a strongly centralized constitutional government, ruled by fifty hereditary ho-ya-ne, or civil sachems. Its object was to establish universal peace and to make the Iroquois the arbiters of the great "earth-island."

The wampum codes of De-ka-na-wi-da and his helper, Hiawatha, furnished an almost ideal code for the ethnic culture with which it was designed to cope. By holding to their old laws the Iroquois became the dominant power east of the Mississippi and during colonial days exercised an immense influence in determining the fate of English civilization on the continent. As allies of the British they fought for it and in the end they destroyed all the hopes of France for colonization. They cast their lot with the British and at a critical period saved the Atlantic seaboard for an English-speaking people.

From the beginning, the ancestors of Ely Samuel Parker had fought for progress and enlightenment and fought as strenuously with mind as with muscle.

CHAPTER II

THE VALLEY OF THE RAPID WATER

The story of this red man does not begin with his birth. His race, his country, his ancestral and geographical setting, all have much to do with it. These things all determined the beginning of the man. His birth only determined his individuality. To know the elements you must learn, as he learned, of the extirpated Neutral Nation and of the Tonawanda.

The Neutral Nation (so called because it would war upon neither the Wyandots, Hurons, nor the Iroquois), was a populous tribe, having many towns on the Niagara peninsula in Ontario and four or five villages in the region we now know as the Niagara frontier in New York. Their eastern boundary line was probably the Genesee, and the western line probably Buffalo creek, though some say it extended to Eighteen-mile creek. To the west of their dominion in New York and stretching westward in Pennsylvania, lay the land of the Eries. Near them were two sub-tribes, known as the Wenroes [1] and the Kah-Kwas. All these tribes were an industrious agricultural people, living in large palisaded towns with bark houses of considerable size. They were expert hunters and skilled craftsmen in flint working and pottery making. Their pots and pipes were famous for their beauty and on the sites of their ancient towns the broken pieces of their cooking vessels may be found in enormous quantities. The Eries, the Neutrals and the Five Iroquois nations all belonged to the same cultural stock, known as the Huron-Iroquois. They spoke a common stock language and had a common origin. Except in minor details their religion, their myths and traditions

---

1. Wen-roh-ro-non, People-of-the floating-scum.

were the same. Their name for themselves was Ongwe-oweh, meaning Real Men. Thus every member of the Huron-Iroquois stock considered himself "Oweh" or truly human; other races were of "uncertain origin." Certain it was the Iroquois creation myth did not account for them. Inasmuch as they could understand each other's tongue and had common traditions, they had more or less racial sympathy, but there were disputes over boundaries, and political rights that eventually brought trouble—and no enemies can be more bitter than those who have once been friends or who as relatives have turned against each other. The Iroquois for generations hated the Hurons because of their alliance with their enemies on the St. Lawrence, and so the Hurons and the Iroquois fought, but the Neutrals would fight neither, for in their tribe lived a woman who was a direct descendant of the "sky mother" who came to earth from heaven. Moreover, in their territory were the towns of refuge where enemies or fugitives might find shelter and where exiles might stay until the time came for them to return home for execution or for forgiveness.

In 1651 the Iroquois charged the Neutrals with treachery and violation of the ancient compact. The first result was the capture and destruction of the Neutral town near the present site of Buffalo. The tale was often related at the Parker fireside, for the old chiefs who came to feast and council with the grandfathers oft would tell how the war was pushed with all the customary energy of the Iroquois, and the Neutral Nation was speedily conquered. Hundreds of captives were brought into the Seneca towns and adopted. The Jesuit "Black-robes" in 1669 had found some of their old Neutral converts in one of the Seneca towns in the present Ontario county, their records say.

Students of history, especially Iroquois history, should have clearly in their minds that when the Iroquois "exterminated" or "annihilated" another tribe they did not destroy the entire body of people. Quite the contrary, surrender meant clemency and a subsequent adoption into the Iroquois clans. The warriors of the enemy who had fought fiercely were sometimes singled out for torture, it is true, but those who manifested their "good will" toward the Iroquois by quietly submitting, were treated well. They became in a sense slaves, but their children were free-born and had every right of an Iroquois.

One fact, too, that historians have neglected to appreciate, is that the Senecas often left little towns of their conquered vassals and placed over them an Iroquois governor. There were several of these settlements west of the Genesee after the Neutral-Erie wars. It will be remembered that in later days Shikellamy was made governor of the conquered tribes in the Susquehanna valley. Many of the conquered Neutrals were not absorbed for several generations and as late as 1800 Sken-dyuh-gwa-dih or Beyond-the-multitude, whose Indian name had been anglicized to John Kenjockety, lived with his family on Kenjockety creek within the present limits of the corporation of Buffalo. Kenjockety was a Neutral and the fact was well known. His loyalty to his adopted people was intense, and Rev. Samuel Kirkland, in 1788, called him "the second man of influence and character among the Senecas at Buffalo." Kenjockety protested to Governor George Clinton in 1789, remonstrating against a sale of Seneca land which he deemed unauthorized. Later he was a joint agent with Red Jacket for the Senecas in determining the boundaries of the Seneca dominion, going with the Hon. Augustus Porter who surveyed for the State of New York, the Buffalo "gore."

But if Kenjockety's ancestors had escaped the arrows of the Senecas and the fiery torture, he did not escape the white man's fire-water. He died at an advanced age in 1808 while on a spree. He had just been to Buffalo village, and, leaving town under the influence of liquor, died on the way home. He left numerous descendants and a farm on Squaw Island—and thus passed the last great Neutral to the quiet realms "beyond the multitude."

Opposite Grand Island on the American shore, is the mouth of a considerable stream. It rises in two branches, and flows with various windings westwardly and a little south, through a fertile region. It is the "Swift water stream," Tonawanda creek. Tonawanda creek was the route of the mid-country trail from the Genesee country to Niagara. From time immemorial its valley had been occupied by forest dwellers of various tribes. Early it had been the home of mound-building Indians who journeyed, no doubt, up from the Niagara River. Indeed its mouth, being near the great falls, must have invited the visits of many aboriginal adventurers. In later centuries the Neutral Nations had claimed it and built their scattered villages on its pleasant banks.

Some of the most interesting tales, told at the fireside of the Parker family in the old days, were these stories of the Neutral Nation and its destruction. One tale to which the writer as a boy listened with great glee, told how a few young warriors had frightened an entire town of Neutrals and driven them into the forest after burning their bark houses and plundering their stores. Now and then old warriors of the Senecas would come in to smoke a pipe and listen to the tale the grandfather told, just to see that he was telling it right to his grandchildren. They would all nod and say, "Heh!" to show their interest when he told of the little band of Seneca warriors, who paddling almost noiselessly down the river until within sight of the Neutral town, had captured it by a single war-whoop. The river had a sharp bend and formed a loop curving directly around the town. Thus canoe after canoe would float down and by the town, and, when a little way below, the warriors would steer for shore, port across the tongue, re-embark and float down again. To the frightened Neutrals it seemed as if the Iroquois had filled the river from end to end and were sending thousands of warriors against them. So they sorrowfully abandoned their homes at the first war-whoop and retreated into the forest without even giving battle. It is little wonder that the potency of the Iroquois war-cry became famous. It is little wonder that the cry of "the Mohawks!" set all New England in a panic.

The Senecas early had a village near the mouth of the "Swift Water" but later abandoned it for a town farther up stream. When the French anchored at the mouth of the creek they named it "La rivière aux bois-blancs," meaning "the white-wood river," but on some of the earlier maps it is known as Maskinongez, after the famous game fish, the muskalunge. The stream once abounded with these gamy, under-water people and it is not to be thought strange that the sport-loving Seneca carefully bated his bone fish-hook with a frog and drew it up and down the "swift water" stream, in the pools where the muskalunge made his nest. Thus we may readily believe that the creek and valley attracted many a bronzed aboriginal and indeed large parties of explorers and home-seekers. All along the valley, whether the plain is wide or the cliff over the stream is high, one will find broken flints, fragments of crushed pottery and now and then protruding bones.

The great village of the Neutral Nation had been near Lewiston. It is recorded in our documentary histories as Kieuneka or Ga-o-no-geh. There had been the home of the "mother of the nation"—the "fire woman," as some have called the female ruler of the nation. Another important town was on Grand Island. Tradition makes it one of the towns of refuge. The secret of its existence long remained obscured until Frederick Houghton, principal of a public school in Buffalo, and archeologist of the Buffalo Society of Natural Sciences, sought it out in 1910 and dug up many of its buried relics.[2] The Senecas had long had traditions of Grand Island, some vague and some fanciful, but all indicating that they had a certain reverence for it.

Likewise the Tonawanda valley to them was a chosen region, and after the bloody war of 1651, in which the Five Nations triumphed over the Neuters and adopted the survivors, all this fair country fell into the keeping of the Senecas. The western end of the "Long House," as they called their confederacy, was then extended from its original location on the Genesee and placed against Lake Erie. Small settlements began to be made and the Tonawanda land and water trail became a commoner highway than before. With the destruction of the Erie Nation three years later all the western New York country, the Allegheny and the territory west into the Ohio became Seneca dominion.

The Tonawanda valley was not entirely wooded; there were ancient clearings here and there, but in general there were thick forests of basswood, of pine and hemlock, together with tracts of hardwood timber, such as oak. The "swift water" runs over broken beds of slate with here and there a little fall. Midway, however, is a beautiful cascade of some height, and on either side below it, high cliffs with mossy sides. Along the creek for several miles west of this point the Tonawanda Senecas have their modern reservation. It is fertile country in general with rolling uplands above the limestone escarpment and sandy loam that in denuded spots show stiff clay.

The Senecas did not gain this country without a struggle nor did they retain it after the white man came, without another. They won it in a fair fight in the field against a hostile, treacherous foe; and they again fought for it, this time in courts and with brains and wit instead of arrows and war clubs—but the foe as before, was a treacherous one, and hostile.

2. *Vide*, Bulletin, Buffalo Society of Natural Sciences, Vol. X, No. 2.

With the sale of the Genesee country and its loss in part through fraud, many of the Genesee Senecas removed to Tonawanda. It was the nearest refuge. Others pushed on to Buffalo Creek, while still others went to Cattaraugus or down the Allegheny.

As a reserved tract Tonawanda was set aside by the treaty of Big Tree in 1797. It then covered seventy-one square miles. Today, however, only 6,550 acres remain. The red man still clings to the tenth of his original holding, and it is to be hoped that the possession of that shrunken tenth will mean at least a "nine-tenths right" to hold it for many generations more.

One of the most distinguished families of Seneca Castle on Seneca Lake, the present site of Geneva, moved to the Allegheny country, settling at Dyo-ne-go-no, or Cold Spring. Later they moved farther down the river and built their homes at Dyo-no-sa-de-ga or Burnt Houses, later known as Cornplanter's town. About this time when the Senecas were demoralized and broken, there arose a prophet. He was Handsome Lake or Ga-nio-dai-u, one of the Sachems of the League. With great vigor he proclaimed his revelations and there rallied to his support a considerable number of converts. Like many prophets of old he was inclined to do eccentric things, and this was more than even the benighted Indians could stand. They arose and drove him out, he and his family, his converts and his friends. A "revelation" pointed the way to Tonawanda. Therefore, Handsome Lake, with Joi-e-sey, Ga-wa-so-wa-nch and a host of others who believed, took up their journey over the hills and valleys to the land of the "swift water." The prophet probably did much thinking as he traveled and no doubt determined not to have any more visions about big snakes under the river. At Allegany he had such a revelation and set hundreds of the work-shirking warriors digging frantically into the bottom lands. They threw up great banks of earth and penetrated below the bottom of the river but not a sign of the monster snake could they find. When the prophet explained that the creature had crawled under the mountains and was eating out the heart of the earth like a worm in an apple, the Allegheny people arose in wrath. They half suspected the prophet was going to order them to dig down the mountains. It was hard enough to hoe corn and hill up the beans without looking for reptiles inside the limestone spurs of the Alleghenys. They hoped the beast would fill himself with rocks and then choke to death. He could die that way for all they cared. The reptile was allowed to eat his way through the hills but the prophet found that it would not be easy for himself. He had to pack up and depart for regions where he could no longer penetrate the earth with his enchanted eye and see snakes a mile long and with teeth that would crush boulders like chestnuts. But then, there are always persons who are skeptical of signs and wonders. How comforting it was to have a few who believed and would sacrifice to uphold their faith! Why should we of today smile in our superiority when many other people in the days gone by followed prophets with far less to commend them than Handsome Lake? Do we not, even now, expend our energies seeking shadows and build our hopes on idle dreams? Handsome Lake had a great end in view and accomplished it. He was no self-seeking imposter, but a prophet with an unselfish purpose.

Among those who went with him were three brothers who had acquired the English surname of Parker. The boys were named Samuel, Henry and William. Not much is known of Henry but Sam was a stalwart young warrior and hardened to the chase, while William at this time was a small boy of eight or nine. The journey to them was an excursion and they basked under the favor of the prophet, ejected though he was. The family settled at

Tonawanda and Sam and William grew up together there. Whether William became tired of the prophet's teachings or not or whether he commenced to see through it all, we do not know. However, in later years he became a Baptist and married the prophet's great grand-daughter, a young woman of wondrous beauty.

His mother had chosen as their new home a commanding location near the beautiful falls of Tonawanda creek and indeed their little farm sloped down to its very banks. The Parker homestead was built of logs.[3] It was large and roomy, for a log dwelling, and with its several additions became a real "establishment," and the stopping place in later years of many distinguished visitors both red and white. Their names are well known to the student of history, for they were men who made history.

The Parker home as rebuilt in later years was set well back from the road. Log dwelling though it was, its size made it more than a cabin, while the tall poplars and other trees carefully trimmed about it gave the place an air of permanence.[4] The land about it was cleared, for William was a worker and his wife, Ga-ont-gwut-twus, a woman who inspired him to do his utmost. She was ho-ya-neh, that is, of the noble families, the company of women who held the sachemship titles. It was therefore not for him to shirk. His home, his farm and its surroundings should be the finest. It was indeed fine in its day and its setting as romantic as it was picturesque. There were deep woods filled with game, flowing streams filled with fish, and below the booming falls were deep fishing holes.

The years have passed, but a portion of the old log house remains. It is, however, now on white man's land, for the Senecas lost a large portion of their Tonawanda country—

---

3. The first house was a roomy one-story cabin used afterward as the kitchen of the larger establishment of later years.

4. This house was 40 by 50 feet with one large room below, a second story with four rooms and a garret above. The first cabin served as a kitchen addition.

nine-tenths of it, as we have said. With the change, the dress of nature changed. Its geography remained, it is true—the falls, the creek, the hills are there, but the forests, the game, the romances have gone.

It may seem strange that an Indian with little or no associations with the whites and no European blood should take the name of Parker. There have been many inquiries as to the origin of this name. In General Parker's notes the answer is found. An English officer had been captured and in the Iroquois way adopted. This was back in the Revolutionary days just before Sullivan's destructive raid through the Seneca country. The Englishman's name was Parker. He lived for some time with the family of his adoption, was given a Seneca name and adopted into the Hawk clan. He became very fond of the two boys who then constituted the family and was a cordial and helpful companion to the old father. When the time came for his return to Canada he bestowed his surname, Parker, upon his adopted father and foster-uncle. [5] To the two boys likewise he gave English names. One he named Samuel and the other Henry; William was born later. This bestowal of English names was a great advantage but the family still preserved its Seneca names and always used them among themselves. The father never used the English appellation. The only English names used by William's father, as far as can be discovered, was Little Smoke, but he was known to the Senecas as Joy-e-sey. His brother was the well known leader, Young King. Their father was the celebrated Gai-yen-gwa-toh, or Disappearing Smoke, whose history is as thrilling as that of any character in Indian romance. The story of his part in the raid at Wyoming is a stirring one and one that his loyal and patriotic descendants in later years spoke very lightly of, if they spoke of it at all. It was not a war record to make an

---

5. This brother of the "original Parker" married the offspring of the captive Slocum woman and a French military officer from Canada.

American unduly proud; but the old man had only done his duty and fought as an ally of Great Britain. His home town was known as Ga-nun-da-sa-ga, or to the whites as Kanandesaga or Old Town. This ancient village was surrounded by a palisade and an earthen wall and was a village of the ancient Iroquois type. It was sometimes called Seneca Castle by the English traders who wandered in from Fort Johnson. Disappearing Smoke or Old King was known to Rev. Samuel Kirkland and to Sir William Johnson, as the foremost leader of his nation, a friend to be sought and a foe to be feared. Col. Stone in the "Life of Red Jacket" tells us: "Old Smoke was the most powerful, as he was deemed the wisest sachem of his time. He was the principal sachem, or civil chief of the nation, and his word was law. When he thought proper to convene a council it was only for the purpose of announcing his intentions and none said nay to his behests. His infallibility was never questioned."

The older men of the Senecas who remembered his influence described him as a man of great stature and of commanding presence. He seemed to be a man who loved justice for its own sake, and even though he was a savage whose glimpse of civilization was slight indeed, he opposed any plan for the Iroquois to take part in the Revolutionary War. It is said, too, that his defense of Rev. Samuel Kirkland, whose life was in peril at the hands of the Senecas who had accused him of bewitching the man who had sheltered and fed him, was a wondrous example of native eloquence. It bore down all opposition, cleared Kirkland and brought forth a burst of cheer-cries that made the council house ring with their vehemence. And this same man led his warriors into the Wyoming Valley and massacred the white inhabitants there. So contrary is human nature! Let is be said, however, that Old King was under the direction of the English Tories—these savage white men who murdered their own kin—but so far as known at the Wyoming "massacre," not a single woman or child was killed. Of the two forces the Seneca Indians showed far greater humanity than "the envenomed hate of their Tory allies that showed no relenting." Little Smoke and his noted brother, Young King, fled to the British Fort at Niagara during the heart-breaking, nation-breaking, raid of Major John Sullivan. Later he settled at Buffalo creek and then moved down on the Allegheny. After his wife's journey to Tonawanda with Handsome Lake he built a lonely cabin and died shortly after. He would neither follow the prophet nor his family who followed the prophet's teachings. In his life he had been taciturn—in habit a hunter and wanderer, but from the faith of his fathers he would not wonder, not even when his wife and his boys followed the "new light" into the valley of the "rapid water." Rather he would follow the paths of his fathers to the happy hunting-ground and discover the true light there.

CHAPTER III

HOW THE SENECAS MADE WAR UPON GREAT BRITAIN

The first decade of the Nineteenth century was one of readjustment for the Senecas. The victory of the American colonists had proved the power of the "Thirteen Fires" and the weakness of the British as allies and as a continental power. The years that followed the destructive raid of Major General John Sullivan, in which he burned nearly every town of the Iroquois, west of the Oneidas, gave the Senecas time for much serious thinking. White men could be as savage as they, they well knew, but that this fury would turn to fire and blast their dominion as it did, they never dreamed. They learned the power of the whites and their defenseless condition when attacked at home. The tables were turned and Sullivan's men played the savage, even to skinning a young Seneca to make leather for leggings. Their ancient farms were devastated and thousands of bushels of corn burned and thrown into the rivers. The Senecas abandoned their old home-land and fled to the protection of the British at Fort Niagara. Never as a people did they resume their old seats on the "river beautiful," the Jen-nes-see-u. They settled at Buffalo or wandered off into Ohio with their broken vassals, the Eries and Neuters, who in small numbers camped there. Those who remained dwelt in bitterness of spirit and stalked about like dead men, dreaming, meditating, but only half seeing or hearing.

Then came the secret word from Ohio. It roused the restless young men to life. It spread like the wind and fanned to a flame the patriotism of the young Senecas who had been but babes when the boom of Sullivan's cannon spoke the doom of Seneca power. The word which came was whispered into the ears of the young men lest the old become hostile. It told of a great leader who had arisen, who had proclaimed that if all the red men of the continent would unite and fight, the invading white man could be driven out. The great "earth-island" again should belong to the red man alone as their supreme possession. The name of Tecumseh became a watchword to the young men who regarded him as the hero of the race. His plan for a mighty league of the tribes who should unite to resist further encroachment of the invading whites appealed to their natural love of country. It made them aspire for great things and served to revive their hopes as a people.

True, the Iroquois of New York lived in tracts of country entirely surrounded by white settlers and had been at peace since the Revolutionary War. The chiefs were friendly with their white neighbors, but notwithstanding all this the young men had not yet seen that their salvation lay in learning all the good things the settlers had to teach and eschewing the evils they brought. They felt a consciousness that their race had been wronged and thought it patriotism to revenge it and seek to make the land the red man's undisputed own. Many of the younger men hurried west to join the forces of Tecumseh and the prophet or ally themselves with Little Turtle, the Miami. This bold idea was opposed with vigor both by Red Jacket and Handsome Lake. The latter used his influence to dissuade his converts from having anything to do with the affairs of the western tribes against the Americans. Handsome Lake was a "peace prophet" and urged his people to obey the precepts that he claimed to have received from the "four messengers" from the land above the sky. In this respect he was directly opposed to Elskawata, the "war prophet" of the Shawnees who was fostering, by convenient revelations, the plans of his brother Tecumseh. In other respects, however, there are strange similarities between the moral teachings of the two prophets, and their ideas of the hereafter are quite identical.

Red Jacket, that vigilant guard of the Senecas, went to the various councils in the West which were held in the interests of Tecumseh's confederacy, and was particularly conspicuous at the council of Detroit. The largest intertribal council held for generations had met there. With Red Jacket were many of the finest examples of Seneca manhood to be found in the nation. The Senecas, haughty in their demeanor, manifested a keen consciousness of their glory. Upon the first day a spirited debate arose as to the right of precedence in debate. This was a delicate point of honor. The Wyandots claimed it but Red Jacket, ignoring their able chiefs, arose and with such a brilliant oration argued for the Senecas that no one afterward disputed him. The intimate knowledge that he displayed of the history and traditions of all the tribes gathered before him was too profound, and some of it too galling to be disputed. Not one wished to argue against Red Jacket's assumption of the superiority of the Senecas. Then, as his turn came to voice the ideas of the Seneca nation, he argued for peace and afterward consistently worked to prevent the members of the Iroquois League from entering into conflict with the whites under the leadership of Tecumseh.

Just to digress, suppose that the gallant leader had succeeded in getting the solid support of the Six Nations, embittered as they were by the suffering and humiliation they had endured through Sullivan and Brodhead? Suppose the Iroquois, stung with their former ignominious defeat, had again taken up the tomahawk and wielded it with their ancient vigor, might not Tippecanoe have been won by the red man and that battlefield be described differently in the pages of history? But Tecumseh was not there and the Six Nations as a unit held back their experienced warriors.

Perhaps there was a reason for delaying or refusing to engage in such a momentous undertaking. Perhaps there was another and more poignant reason than the bans of the prophet and the logic of Red Jacket. Every Iroquois today knows the reason why the tomahawk lay buried deep and why they continued friendly with the whites.

The Iroquois were grateful to Washington. It was he who had shown them mercy and preserved for them at least a portion of their ancient domain in New York, when the entire country clamored for their removal into the West. The treaty at Fort Stanwix in 1784 gave the Six Nations a guarantee of their lands, diminished though they were. Many of the people were not satisfied but as Cornplanter in 1790 expressed the general thought of the nation to Washington: ". . . When you gave us peace, we called you Father because you promised to secure us in the possession of our lands. Do this and so long as the lands remain, that beloved name will live in the heart of every Seneca." The name was Town Destroyer, the Seneca name for George Washington.

Six or seven months after the mid-winter war council of the Senecas called to discuss the impending war with Great Britain, a general meeting of the Onondagas and Senecas was held at the residence of Hon. Erastus Granger, then superintendent of the Senecas. Judge Granger pleaded with the Senecas to remain neutral and reminded them of Washington's advice, "That you take no part in the quarrels with the white people." Even Red Jacket deplored that the Canadian Mohawks of Brant's party were bound to fight as British allies, even as they had done before. This embittered the two divisions of the Iroquois and caused a breach that even yet has not entirely healed. Both Judge Granger and Red Jacket made impressive speeches.

and the outcome was so important in the minds of the people that the first book published in Buffalo was a record of the speeches of Granger and Red Jacket.[1]

The rumblings of the war disturbed many of the inhabitants of the village of Buffalo. They were in a position exposed on all sides to danger. The British were opposite and the Indians swarmed all around them. Many left the village and sought refuge beyond the frontier. Fears were entertained that the New York Indians were in reality under the influence of the British, through the Canadian Mohawks who were constantly visiting them. It was under this apprehension that Judge Granger called the council to explain the reasons of the war. Red Jacket afterward alluded to the fear of the residents of Buffalo and said as he unrolled the great George Washington treaty belt that the whites should never regard an Indian Council as serious, nor regard it as a dangerous thing unless the national wampums were brought forth and displayed. He scoffed at the panic that resulted from a fisherman's fight on the banks of the creek.

On June 6, 1812, the British were reported to have taken forcible possession of Grand Island, the property of the Seneca Nation. The Senecas would now no longer promise neutrality. A council was called at Buffalo reservation, "the old council fire of the nations" was kindled and a general proclamation was issued. Red Jacket, who but a few days before had argued for peace and who had displayed the famous Washington treaty wampum, now argued for war. The British had seized the lands under the dominion of the Senecas! War should be declared! As allies of the United States the Six Nations of New York

---

[1]. "Public Speeches, delivered at the village of Buffalo on the 6th and 8th days of July, 1812, by Hon. Erastus Granger, Indian Agent and Red Jacket, one of the principal chiefs and speakers of the Seneca Nation, respecting the part the Six Nations would take in the present war against Great Britain. Buffalo: Printed and sold by S. H. and H. A. Salisbury—Sold also at the Canandaigua and Geneva bookstores—1812."

would punish the invaders. The declaration of war read as follows:

"We the chiefs and councillors of the Six Nations of Indians residing in the State of New York, do hereby proclaim to all the war chiefs and warriors of the Six Nations, that war is declared on our part against the provinces of Upper and Lower Canada. Therefore we hereby command and advise all the war chiefs of the Six Nations to call forth immediately the warriors under them, and put them in motion to protect their rights and liberties, which our brethren the Americans are now defending."

The call was generally respected and later on, September 28, 1812, a memorial was sent out from the ancient capital of the League of the Iroquois at Onondaga in which it was said, "We are few in number, and can do but little, but our hearts are good." They might have added, "likewise our weapons, too, are good and our aim unsurpassed."

When the council at Buffalo on August 4th was called, Red Jacket mentioned the rumor of the British occupation of Grand Island. In addressing Judge Granger, he said:

Brother! Our property is taken possession of by the British and their Indian friends. It is necessary for us now to take up the business and defend our property and drive the enemy from it. If we sit still upon our seats and take no measure of redress, the British according to the customs of you white people, will hold it by conquest, and should you conquer Canada, you will claim it upon the same principles, as conquered from the British. We therefore request permission to go with our warriors and drive off these bad people and take possession of our lands.

Little Billy, one of the wise councillors of the Senecas, on September 8, 1812, at Buffalo, made a stirring address in which he explained most logically the situation of his people:

Brother! I have spoken of the pains we have taken to preserve peace. Your agents have done the same, but in vain. We went to

Grand river, [Canada] lately, to keep peace, but in vain. The path of peace is broken in every part. We find no place to flee to, where there is peace now. Upon this subject we have been deliberating.

Brother! I have said we have come with all the others to seek the path of peace. We find there is no path left for us, but between us and the United States. It is cut off in every other direction.

Agreeably to your communication we, the Senecas, shall now prepare to defend ourselves against the common enemy. It is true we have friends on the other side, but we are exposed to the blow as well as you and must prepare to meet it.

We know of no other way to preserve peace but to rise from our seats and defend our own fire-sides, our wives and our children.

We hope you will not ask us to cross over. Those who go, must go voluntarily. We wish to act only on the defensive. Part of the Onondagas and Cayugas who live with us, agree with us.

We volunteer; we must act under our own chiefs, according to our own customs; be at liberty to take our own course in fighting; we can not conform to your discipline in camp. So far as we can we will conform to your customs.

We volunteer for this service. We wish you not to place us in forts, where we can not act. You know what took place at Detroit; an army was sold; we wish not to be sold!

Among the Senecas were many whose ancestors of a century and a half before had been captured and adopted in the war with the Neuter Nation. Although the laws of the League commanded its adopted members to "forever forget their own tribal origin and to know themselves henceforth and forever as Iroquois," yet in actual fact the people so adopted seldom forgot, and the knowledge of their tribal origin was passed down to their children. Thus it was that there were many Senecas who felt an interest in defending Grand Island, besides that of protecting their nation's dominion. To the descendants of the Neutral Nation's captives, it meant the defence of the graves of their forefathers. To be sure there was no loud discussion over the matter. It was contrary to convention and besides it was not etiquette to mention the dead, especially to mention them in connection with trouble. It was a belief that their spirits heard such things and would be disturbed.

One of the descendants of these Neutral captives was Elizabeth, the grand-daughter of Sos-he-o-wa. Her mother held as her birthright the ancient title of the Ye-go-wa-neh, the "Fire woman," and the "Mother of Nations." This was the most honored hereditary title any Iroquois woman could have. Elizabeth and her mother were therefore concerned with the coming struggle for Grand Island, captured by the insolent British, for it was ancestral domain.

William Parker was otherwise concerned. It was enough to know that his people had been insulted and that there was a glorious chance to fight. He was young and had never yet had a chance to battle. He longed to redeem the honor of the Senecas and the weak retreat of his fathers from the Genesee country before the army of Major Sullivan.

The call to arms gave rise to great industry among the Iroquois. They had arms and equipment to get and many of them spent hours carving out war-clubs and hammering out iron spear-heads. Some of these war-clubs are now in the State Museum at Albany. They were not used, for the Iroquois agreed to fight under "civilized rules" and to "take no scalps and murder no captives." This pledge they sacredly kept.

The call to arms brought all the war chiefs together. They mustered their troops in companies, each under its own captain and several companies were placed under the leadership of a colonel. Among these Indian military leaders not one outranks Colonel Farmer's Brother. Though a man of eighty years, he gathered together his captains and warriors and led them on to battle. He was a true nobleman, morally clean, physically perfect and intellectually the peer of Red Jacket. Unlike Red Jacket, he was never addicted to the use of rum. Had it not been for his great modesty the name of Farmer's Brother, today, would be known far more widely than even Red Jacket's.

Other leaders were Major Henry O'Bail, or Young Cornplanter, as he was called. It was he, who with 400 Senecas, took part in the defense of Buffalo.

William Parker was the first Tonawanda to enroll, and he chose as his Captain, Little Billy and followed Farmer's Brother as his colonel.

The roster kept by the Parker family records, besides the names given, the following captains: Captain John Kennedy, a Cayuga, who is on the record as being exceedingly brave; and Captains Sundown. King, Peter Kenjockety, Isaac, Jonas, Joeh, Snow, Jackson, Bone, Shongo, Cold, Heegan, and Tommey. Others are Colonel Lewis, Colonel Smith and Major Berry.

In the battle at Fort George, Colonels Farmer's Brother, Smith, Billy, Captains Halftown, Pollard, Red Jacket, Black Snake, Johnson, Silverheels and Captain Cold of the Onondagas, were in command of the Indians. This is from the official report of General John N. Boyd, who speaks well of the behavior of the Indian allies.

Crossing over into Canada, the Iroquois troops fought at Chippewa and at Lundy's Lane under General Scott. At the former battle, while fighting under Captain Pollard, William Parker was wounded in the shoulder. So splendidly did these Indians fight that General Boyd, who noticed their action in particular, said: "The bravery and humanity of the Indians were equally conspicuous."

And here, truth again appears stranger than fiction. So thoroughly aroused were the Iroquois, to such a fervent pitch was their patriotism wrought, that more than a score of their women donned uniforms, shouldered muskets and fought like the patriots they were. Most of them were

Oneidas and went to war with their husbands. The Oneidas had long been a tribe faithful to the American cause.

In the old army register kept by William Parker, and later his son Nicholson, we find a list of these patriotic women. Lest we forget, let us doff our hats at the names of Annie Metoxen, Usena Reed, Polly Antonine, Margaret Adams, Susan Hendrick, Dolly and Mary Schenandoah, Salmo Adzquette, Margaret Stevens, Polly Cooper, Mary Williams, Margaret John, Mary Antonine and Susan Jacobs. They wore sometime the rough garments of men, they fought like men, they bled and died like heroes. What more patriotic heroes indeed does our history record than these!

Some of the warriors were mere boys just in their "teens," among them Saul Logan the Squawkie Hill Indian, the sentry at Black Rock. He was fourteen years old. Even William Parker was only seventeen. Others were white-haired old men. There we have it. The whole people fought—men, women and youths!

There are many stories of gallant service, of courage, of daring. Ga-uch-so-wa of the Beaver clan clung close to the front at the redoubt at Black Rock. It was he who bayonetted the first red-coat to appear. White Seneca was hailed by his people as the "bravest of the brave." There were men like Sho-a-go-wa, of the Turtle clan. It was he who volunteered to run in front of the enemy's line, in order to get them to discharge their guns. Then immediately our troops poured upon them. Yet brave Sho-a-go-wa was not even scratched. Like his patron totem, "he lived long and died hard." Other men were eager and fearless, like Do-sa-ga-ni-yak, of the Bear clan. In his eagerness to get at the enemy he crossed the Niagara on a raft, and in the rapids just above the Falls. John Street (Ho-wa-yok-se) did not even have a raft. He tied his gun to his long hair, let it rest upon his back and then swam the river, making directly for the red-coats when he landed. Native strategy was shown by Captain Isaac who was shot in the neck and taken to the British camp. Regaining consciousness, he slowly opened his eyes, kept quiet and when he had located himself as in the enemy's lines, he waited his chance and escaped to the American encampment. Jo-ho-a-hoh was captured in the Buffalo fight, but mixed with the crowd calmly and when he was ready he simply "disappeared," and entered his own ranks again. Some of the older men having greater faith in the arms of their ancestors used their ancient weapons, the tomahawk and bow. Peter Halfwhite (De-gai-i-da-goh, of the Deer), was one of these and carried his bow, arrows and quiver all through the war. William Parker carried a tomahawk, but kept it mainly as an ornament.

Even the captives of the Iroquois fought with them, the Delawares, Squawkies, Cherokees, Shawnees and Chippewas. The record shows them to have been as daring as the Iroquois themselves. Thus it was that the Six Nations of Indians became the allies of the United States of America. Indian Americans, they were, and defending with the pale-faced Americans, "their land, their wives and their children," they had a common cause. All through the war they fought, at Buffalo, Black Rock, Youngstown, Fort George, Lundy's Lane, Chippewa and Fort Niagara. William Parker, with his brother Samuel who was eleven years older than he, took part in all these engagements. His commanders had been Young King, Red Jacket and Little Billy. Nearly all the Seneca captains operated under orders from the venerable Colonel Farmer's Brother, who in turn was subject to the general orders of Generals Scott, Boyd and Porter.

We cannot leave the discussion of the brave Indian, Farmer's Brother, without relating an incident that occurred at Buffalo. It is a familiar tradition in the

Parker family and is found recorded in the life of Red Jacket, by Stone.

At Lundy's Lane several of the American officers were severely wounded, among them General Scott, Major General Brown and his aide-de-camp, Captain Worth. The genial nature of the latter made him popular with the Senecas, who delighted to do him small courtesies. Farmer's Brother especially was constantly at the bedside of the captain.

The British were anxious to discover just how conditions were in the American camp, and sent over a Chippewa Indian to mingle with the Senecas who were in the village of Buffalo, and get all the information he could. He claimed to have deserted the British, to have swum Chippewa river and crossed the Niagara in order to join the American army. This was a little more than the Indians could swallow, and it being an exceedingly hot summer's day, they proceeded to imbibe a little freely of the army rum. Perhaps it was to wash down the improbable tale. As their spirit was awakened they commenced to boast of their exploits; how many red-coats they had killed and how they had defied and outwitted the enemy. The Chippewa spy then forgot his character and began to boast of the Yankees and Senecas he had killed, and scalped. Twenty Senecas sat around him and heard his confession. A dispute arose and the Chippewa was told just what the Senecas thought of him.

Farmer's Brother, who had been sitting at Capt. Worth's bedside, heard the commotion and came out to ascertain the cause. He listened a moment and then stepping up to the spy gave him a blow upon the head with his war-club. The Chippewa staggered and then fell, and lay stunned. Then, suddenly leaping up he burst through the circle and took mad flight.

The Senecas then jeered at him, calling him a coward and a man afraid to die. The taunts struck home. Not even in this moment of crisis would he allow any man to call him a coward. Though he was a spy he was not that. He turned and walked back into the circle. Drawing his blanket over his head he stood facing his foes. Then conscious of his crime he lay down on a log from one of the burned buildings near Main and Swan streets and covered his face. He knew that his punishment was but a question of a few moments. Farmer's Brother lifted up his rifle, pressed it against the culprit's head and shot him dead. This was the Indian way, and it left every man's honor clean.

It has been stated that there were 1,200 Iroquois allies of the Americans in the war. The Parker record book gives the names of only 600, and records their tribe, clan, and Indian name, as well as giving the place of enlistment and discharge. It is certain in any event that the Senecas supplied two-thirds of the total number engaged. In the old battles of the League they had done the same.

The names of the gallant Iroquois allies of the United States do not appear on the regular muster rolls of the army or even upon its pay-rolls. These facts made it difficult in after years for them to obtain pensions and land bounty warrants.

With the success of the American cause, the home country was preserved. The mouth of the Tonawanda creek opened out safely to an American Niagara. The mysterious island was saved, but only later to be relinquished. The passing of years make newer generations forget. And so from the minds of the Senecas, with the passing of the old sages, passed the knowledge of the graves of the forgotten Neuter villagers.

Though the entire Niagara was ceded to private land owners by the Senecas, one long forgotten fact remains:

The Seneca Nation never gave up their title to the bed of the Niagara River! Today they own it and a strip along the shore. It is theirs, and some day the State of New York must reckon for its payment. The State may wriggle and squirm, it may balk, and prune down, as it did in the tardy justice it has given the Cayugas, but even as the 118-year fight was won by the Cayugas and the 60-year fight of the Six Nations for payment for their Kansas lands, so some day must the land and the river defended by the Senecas in 1812-15 be paid for by the sovereign State.

The War of 1812 estranged the two branches of the Iroquois. For many years there was a bitter feeling between them. The Canadian branch, uniting all their tribes in a general council, continued to govern themselves in the ancient way and under the laws of De-ga-na-wi-da, and Hiawatha. They claimed to be the true confederacy and to have shown the right spirit in clinging to their British allies. The Iroquois that remained, they pointed out, were broken, scattered bands without coherence or spirit. On the other hand the New York Iroquois claimed that the Canadian branch had seceded, thereby violating the constitution of the Confederacy and automatically cutting themselves off from its forms and rights. They accused them of abandoning their ancestral domain, of allowing their "heads to roll away." There had been no actual break until the War of 1812, but when arrayed against one another they fought on opposite sides, then bitterness was gall, indeed! Cordial relations were not soon again established, although there were journeys to and fro soon after the close of the war.

The lingering prejudice manifested itself at the last council on the Genesee in 1879, when William Pryor Letchworth dedicated the old Caneadea council house. Representatives of all the Six Nations were there, among them Colonel Simcoe Kerr, a Mohawk of the Canadian army, and his sister, Kate Osborn. The Colonel refused an introduction to the Seneca chiefs, Parker, O'Bail and Jacket, but later at his sister's entreaties, grasped their hands and pledged his friendship. Thus was that council a memorable one.

For the sake of historical accuracy it will be interesting to record a description of the uniforms and clothing worn by the Iroquois allies. Many of them took the regular uniforms of the army, but others clung to the Indian attire of the day. Some wore buckskin leggins and fringed leather hunting-shirt. Others used broadcloth leggings neatly beaded in designs of various patterns. The shirt was always worn outside like a coat, and was never "tucked in." Sashes of native weaves were worn by the chiefs or captains. These were strung across the shoulder and over the chest diagonally to the left hip, where the long-fringed ends were tied. Most of them were woven of red worsted but a few were of buckskin with moose hair, or quilled in porcupine. The Seneca moccasin was made of one piece of leather with a seam in the heel and over the top of the foot.

The Iroquois did not wear the plumed feather bonnet of the Sioux, but wore round caps that covered the head. From the middle of the crown was suspended a cluster of downy feathers five or six inches long and from a spindle in the center arose an eagle plume that whirled as the wearer moved. A decorated band or a silver crown encircled the cap which was of leather, fur or cloth. Sometimes the entire breast was bare and only leggins, breech clout and moccasins worn. Some of the older men, conforming to the ancient custom, shaved their heads by burning off all the hair except the scalp lock at the crown. Many too had slit the rims of their ears and wound silver foil around them. In the small socket in the top was placed a fluffy plume or a woodpecker's feather. Between the

Indian costume and the military uniforms were all gradations, but in most cases every Indian carried or wore a "match-coat" or blanket. Sometimes these blankets were only cotton sheets. The leaders often wore military coats and carried sabers but one can readily imagine that their feet were moccasin-shod. It is a belief that the moccasin on the feet of the dead helps find the way to the Indian heaven.

In this manner appeared the Iroquois army, the last time it was ever called as a unit to the front. We need not smile at their garments or deplore the fact that they knew nothing of the "Macedonian phalanx" or of forming hollow squares. This knowledge does not make a soldier. A half-starved sick and vagabond army in tattered raiment eventually won the independence of this nation. Like them the Iroquois were loyal and good shots. Those qualities have helped maintain the gloried independence of this nation.

Nearly all of the Senecas who fought in the war took the oath of allegiance to the United States. This circumstance, coupled with the fact that they felt that they were actually resisting an invasion of their own territory, did much to estrange the Senecas from the English and to render void the overtures of the British agents that had been made continually since the close of the Revolution. More than anything else, the War of 1812 cemented the Iroquois to the United States and left them a loyal people, confident in the integrity and justice of the nation. Their hopes were high and they believed that a new era of good fellowship had dawned. Alas, how falsely they were deceived! In fifteen years' time this hope snapped like a bubble.

CHAPTER IV

THE GRAND-DAUGHTER OF THE PROPHET

And so William Parker the young warrior, came home. The war was over and the scars attested to his valor in the fight. He remained a short time with his aged mother and then began to clean up a farm that he could call his own. His experience during his three years' service had taught him several valuable lessons. It had taught his people as many. They were the value of concerted action, industry, order and progress. Whatever may have been William's early training he now resolved that the old days had passed and that neither he nor his nation could live on memories or succeed by lamenting the events that had gone by. So he shouldered his ax as bravely as he had his gun and whistled "Yankee tunes" as vigorously as when he felled the British on the banks of the Niagara. For a while he worked in his saw-mill, but later as his learning grew he developed one of the best Indian farms along the valley. It is not strange that the Senecas should have fine farms, for the Genesee Valley only in his father's day had been one great garden, with thousands of acres of waving corn, twining beans, squashes, and melons. To charge these Indians with only being hunters is incorrect. There was this difference, however; under the old regime it was William's mother who tilled the fields; it was his father who cleared them. It was in those days considered fair that each sex should share the burden of providing food; the man, the meat; the woman, the bread. Nor was it any easier to carry a deer ten miles than it was to hoe ten rows of corn. But William had learned the new way. He both shot the deer and hoed the corn. His mother had more leisure. The example of industry that he taught inspired many of the young men, who like him had fought in the war. Others affected to despise him and looked with jealousy upon his cleared fields with their winding rail fences. However, his counsel was sought even by the older men, and his good judgment compelled respect.

It was not until five or six years after the War of 1812 that William married. It was plainly seen by Sos-he-o-wa that William was the favorite of Elizabeth, his grand-daughter, and thus Elizabeth's mother one day took a basket filled with wedding bread and placed the loaves at the door of William's mother's cabin.[1] They were accepted and the prospective mothers-in-law held a council. In those days the mother of the girl "proposed" to the mother of the boy. It was so much less embarrassing for the lad, when he liked the girl; but when he did not and his mother did, it is still not recorded that he ever objected.

In this case William offered no objection and the wedding was arranged with all its solemn lectures by the old "experienced" women, and the joy songs of the warriors. Then William went with his bride to his mother-in-law's house, where he dwelt a year. Elizabeth's grandfather was the noted Jemmy Johnson or Sos-he-o-wa, a sober chief who was preparing to become Handsome Lake's successor as the expounder of the "new religion." William seems to have been a successful son-in-law for after he had provided meat and corn for the old folk for twelve moons, he was pronounced worthy of Elizabeth's hand. The watchful eyes of her parents could detect no flaw and he was allowed to take her to his own house at the Falls of the Tonawanda.

William had one fault; he was too kind to his friends and too hospitable to strangers. His home became the stopping-place for every traveler over the road. For years he kept an open door and a table filled with food for the travelers

---

1. William and Elizabeth were cousins, but since their respective mothers were of different clans, were eligible to marry.

who passed; and he never asked for a "thank you" or even a *"nyah-weh"* as the Indian would express it. He strictly obeyed the ancient laws of hospitality, to the great discomfort of Elizabeth, though she never complained. Arduous as were her labors in preparing the tasteful corn foods, she always had them ready and many a weary paleface sat with delight at her table and ate the strange dishes she prepared after the native fashion.

Elizabeth, as has been intimated, was a descendant on her mother's side of a captive of the Neuter Nation. Ordinarily this would have caused some social disability in spite of the attempts of the Iroquois to claim their captives just as much Iroquois as one of unbroken lineage. However, Elizabeth was in direct line from the famous Wolf clan family of the Neuters in which had rested the exalted title of Ye-go-wa-neh, a name that goes far back into the days of tradition. She had been well schooled in this family tradition and as a child she had sat by her mother's side and listened to tales of the olden days. She knew how the earth rested on the back of a great turtle and how it was the duty of all Iroquois who called themselves Ongweh-oweh, or real men, "to spread their peace and extend their power throughout the entire earth." She knew of the Neuter Nation, known to the Senecas as Kah-gwa-onoh and to the Wyandottes as Atiwandaronk. Many of these traditions were told her and she passed them down to her children. If she ever forgot a single one, Sos-he-o-wa, or James Johnson, her father, took good pains to inform her. Some of these tales were later put in writing by her boys, of whom we shall speak later.

Gathered about the fireplace in the family loghouse, her mother would tell her the story of the Ongwe-oweh, the Iroquois. We can imagine the effect of the tale as she related the tradition, so well known to the family.

"The Ongwe-oweh, they are the men of men, lived on the highest portion of the Great Island. Their territory stretched over the shoulder ridge of the Turtle's back and great rivers ran down the slopes from all sides, on the Turtle's scales lay long pools of pleasant waters.[2] The Ongwe-oweh could quickly travel by canoe to all parts of the Great Island. By canoe they could go to the source of a stream, port a short way over a ridge and then re-embark to float down and onward on the bosom of another stream, the Ka-nyen-geh.[3]

"The country of the Ongwe-oweh was favored by the Sky Holder and he watched over the Ongwe-oweh, for they were the Men of Men. Mountains, great lakes, and impassable marshes lay between the Ongwe-oweh and their enemies to the north, the Tree Eaters (Hadion-das)[4] The Crooked Tongues (Ha-dia-no-sa-tci-gwads),[5] and the Men of Fire.[6] To the west and to the south deep dark forests intervened and it was not easy from without to reach the country of the Ongwe-oweh.

"So were they favored, for they were the Men of Men.

"To the north in the flinty country flowed the River of Many Rapids[7] and beyond it to the east lived the fierce Tree-Eaters. The Ongwe-oweh had long sought to destroy this hostile people and wars had gone on for generations. Warriors bands of the Ongwe-oweh went at every season to the country of the insolent Tree-Eaters and harassed them continually. So also did they war upon the Crooked-Tongues who should have been brothers but were traitors to the traditions of the Ongwe-oweh, for their blood was common. So again in another thing the Crooked-Tongues were traitors and allied themselves in battle with the Tree-Eaters.

---

2. The finger lakes. 3. This refers to the portage at Wood creek. The river is the Mohawk. 4. The Adirondacks or Abenakis. 5. Probably the Hurons. 6. Probably the *"gens de feu"* of the French writers. 7. The St. Lawrence.

"From the favored country of the Ongwe-oweh the Wanderers (Shawano)[8] had been driven and also a strange people who lived in little clusters and possessed great skill and patience.[9] So here in possession of the country on the shoulder ridge of the Turtle's back lived the Ongwe-oweh, and though there were wasteful wars they increased their numbers and the westward settlements of the Flint Nation (Kanyen'ge)[10] seceded and became known as the Nation of the Stone.[11] So then this nation lay between the Nation of the Flint and the Nation of the Many Hills.[12] Westward about a pleasant lake lived the Nation, Drawn-up-from-the-Lake[13] and the sons of the Nation of the Great Hill (Nundawa'ga).[14] Beyond the populous towns of the Nation of the Great Hill[15] dwelt the Cultivators (Hadiyent'togeo'no),[16] brothers of the Crooked-Tongues and cousins of the Men of the Great Hill. In their villages by the Great Fall, Oniagara, was the Peace House where dwelt Yegowaneh, the Mother of Nations and her name was Ji-kon-sa-seh.[17] Beyond the Cultivators lived the Raccoon Nation[18] also claiming to be Oweh and the allied brothers of the people of the Great Hill. South of these nations of the River Wide Flats[19] and the River of the Big Bay[20] lived the tribes of the Sunken Pole[21] and they were scattered hunters. To the east and south of this nation were the Wolves,[22] a great nation and the Grandfathers of many small nations. Toward the southwest of the Great Hill in the mountain country lived the Nation of the Caves,[23] and they were Crooked-Tongues (Tadi-wen-no-de), but stammered more. They had united with small bands of the Skillful Nation and built hills for their council houses and fires issued from the hills. To the southeast

---

8. The Shawnees. 9. Mound Building Indians. 10. The Mohawks. 11. The Oneidas. 12. The Onondagas. 13. The Cayugas. 14. The Senecas. 15. Bare Hill on Canandaigua lake. 16. The Neutral Nation. 17. Meaning fat face or wild cat. 18. The Eries. 19. The Susquehanna. 20. The Chesapeake. 21. The Conestogas or Susquehannocks. 22. The Delawares. 23. The Cherokees.

surrounded by nations speaking a tongue much like the Wanderers, lived the Nation of the Sunken Tree.[24] They were Ongwe but their heads had rolled away when the Ongwe-oweh were small and scattered. Their speech was much awry, for their throats were sick.

"So lay the nations about the Ongwe-oweh, they were the Men of Men, when our Founder [25] came. It was he who gave peace and strength to the Men of Men and they alone are the Men of Men. All others lost their blood as Men of Men when they failed to grasp with their arms the Council Tree.

"The Mother of Nations, Yegowaneh, the Great Woman, lived in a Long-House in the territory of the Cultivators. Her house was at Oniagara. The Cultivators were Crooked-Tongues and cousins of the Ongwe-oweh. In the dim distant past when the Turtle's back was small and the world was new all the Crooked-Tongues had been Oweh, even as the Ongwe-oweh and as the nations grew and divided it was found that the first family and the Mother of the Nations fell to the Cultivators, the Atiwandaronk. So then thereafter the nations of them who were Oweh called the Great Woman, Yegowaneh, but through all generations the Great Woman's name was Ji-kon-sa-seh, the Lynx. Now in the territory of the Cultivators there was no war. Bands of warriors passed from east to west and from west to east through the paths of the Cultivators and delivered Peace Belts to Yegowaneh. So likewise, bands of warriors passed from south to north and from north to south through the territory of the Cultivators and delivered belts of peace because the Great Woman was the Mother of Nations. She would provide food for the War Captains and then exhort them to follow the paths of peace since all men are brothers who are Oweh.

---
24. The Tuscaroras. 25. Dekanawideh.

It was therefore said, 'The path of war runs through the House of Peace.'

"Thus were the Cultivators a peaceful people and no one made war upon them lest the Great Mother be killed and the line cut off, so it was said in the old time.

"But at length war was made and after several years of struggling the Nation of the Cultivators (they who had corn and tobacco), was broken and the people who remained were taken beyond the Genesee and scattered through the Seneca villages. So was captured the Ye-go-a-neh, of the Ongwe-oweh, and thus the Mother of Nations was made a Seneca."

In writing the story of those early days Cusick, the Tuscarora historian, tells much about this "Fire Queen," as he called her, and the part she played in the contest between the Neutrals and the Five Nations. Likewise in the wampum codes of the Six Nations of the Iroquois, we are told that both Hiawatha, the Onondaga, and Dekanowideh, the Wyandot, made their journeys to the tribes with the "Great Mother," Ji-gon-sa-seh, the Ka-kwah, and consulted her in every important detail. Without the approval of this "mother of nations" and her sanction of Hiawatha's plans the integrity of the principles of the confederacy of the Five Nations could have been assailed. But Ji-gon-sa-seh, who was regarded as a descendant of the first woman who came to earth, and as the direct descendant of the first Ye-go-wa-neh, the woman who was the mother of all the first *ongwe* was sacred to her people, for her word was law and her sanction was necessary in all political measures of inter-tribal importance. Elizabeth, the descendant of this honored line of "hoyaneh" women, held an honored place among the favored, and William was proud of his wife so gifted by ancestry. His clan, the Turtle, was glad to have him unite with her.

William and Elizabeth were blessed with five sons and one daughter. They named them Levi, Nicholson, Caroline, Ely, Spencer, and Isaac Newton. Each seems to have been a healthy normal youngster. They were brought up on the old-fashioned baby-board in strict accord with the ways of their fathers and mothers of ancient days.

Elizabeth was a woman of such remarkable beauty and charming manner that travelers who stopped at the Parker home wrote the fact in their note-books. Of course she had never been to a white man's school and indeed had little knowledge of the English language. Nevertheless in the purely Indian way she was considered most accomplished. She had a very sensitive nature but good control of her emotions. Many times she had strange, incomprehensible impressions and there were times when she seemed able to foretell events.

William Parker was a hunter by instinct and had several fine guns. When the autumn's harvest had been gathered each year he would take his knapsack, shoulder his rifle and go off into the frosty October for a hunting trip. As Ely once wrote of his father, "he never lost his love of hunting until many years after this. He was fond of furnishing his table with juicy bear steaks and tender venison chops together with the plump quail and dry partridge."

Likewise he never quite lost his love of a satisfactory horse deal, and it is even said that he once traded off a colt that could hardly stand because of a defect in its legs for a fine mare. This he did much to the chagrin of a rival horse fancier, who lost out in the bargain. He seemed to enjoy the deal as a good one and laughed heartily afterwards, for he had once been cheated by this same horse trader.

Traditions among the Tonawanda Indians tell us that before Ely was born his mother had a strange vision.

Mrs. Harriet Maxwell Converse, who was adopted by the Senecas, found the tale and recorded it. Likewise, John Habberton, sent by the New York *Herald* to investigate the condition of the New York Indians in 1891, found it and placed it with the newspaper biographical material relating to General Parker.

About four months before the birth of her son Ely, so the tradition runs, Elizabeth had a strange dream. It so impressed her that she consulted one of the "dream interpreters," or as the Senecas call them, "djis-ga-da-ta-ha." She related to him that she had dreamed that she was in Buffalo Reservation and near the Granger farm. It was winter, but strangely the sky opened from the middle, and, though it was snowing, a rainbow spread out, then it broke in the middle; from one side were suspended signs with letters, like those seen over white men's stores."

The man who could see inside dreams then told Elizabeth the meaning of her dream. It was a prophecy, he said. Then he added:

"A son will be born to you who will be distinguished among his nation as a peace-maker; he will become a white man as well as an Indian. He will be a wise white man, but will never desert his Indian people, nor 'lay down his horns,' (sachem's title) as a great chief, his name will reach from the east to the west, the north to the south, as great among his Indian family and pale-faces. His sun will rise on Indian land and set on white man's land. Yet the ancient land of his ancestors *will fold him in death.*"[26]

Elizabeth had already two children, Levi and Carrie; Nicholson was born later. With Carrie came the girl of the family, the future "name bearer" for the mother line of ancestry. The titles, clan and national rights of the

---

26. See a full account of this tradition in the Buffalo *Express*, Jan. 24, 1897, entitled "A Prophecy Fulfilled."

Iroquois, as every student knows, descend through mother to daughter. Thus with the girl child was the fulfillment of the clan requirement. But what of the future son who was promised and of whom the strange prediction is said to have been made?

CHAPTER V

BOYHOOD DAYS ON THE RESERVATION

The trading store, where William Parker obtained the white man's staples used in his home and on his farm, was near the town of Buffalo, though Batavia was nearer and was a town larger than Buffalo.[1] It was nearly thirty miles from his dwelling to the post, but what was thirty miles! His horses were good, indeed the best that any man had for miles around. When it came to a horse he was an expert. He often traded horses and was known as an expert judge. Thirty miles for his team was a holiday.

Upon a certain occasion (it is not known even now what time of the year it was) it became necessary to journey to the trading post. It was thirteen years after the war and Buffalo had grown into an important center of trade. It had become a great center for the Indians, at least, and in its way, a wicked center. When William and Elizabeth with their "lumber"-wagon and team drove in they stopped at the agency where they were well-known and welcome guests. It must have been a tedious ride for Elizabeth over the rough uneven roads and in a springless wagon. It was the custom for the women to sit in the back of the wagon-box and upon a pad of blankets placed on a pile of hay.

It is not recorded how long a visit was made at the agency but during the stay Elizabeth urged a sudden journey home. When home was reached a little son was born. He was named Ely after a prominent white citizen of the day. It is certain that had the sudden journey not been made that the future sachem would have been born near Buffalo town and upon the Buffalo Creek reservation,

---

1. In 1825 Buffalo had a population of 2,412, and Batavia, 3,352.

the loved Do-sho-wey, "the place of basswoods," but the facts record his birth near Indian Falls, town of Pembroke, Genesee County, in the year 1828.

When the young couple returned bringing a new baby brother to their three children there was great rejoicing at Tonawanda—and little Carrie had a new playmate.

The Parker home was commodious enough for all the children that came, as well as for the many white travelers who stopped, ate and slept freely. Then too there were the prominent Indians, the chiefs and headmen, not including just regular neighbors who happened to drop in to see the newest baby. There was but one word spoken at a sound of a footfall at the door—it was "da-djoh," enter. To support so large a table William had to be a mighty worker and so his acres grew until they extended on both sides of Tonawanda creek at the Indian Falls and crept eastward until they adjoined Elizabeth's own estate. The saw-mill which he owned and occasionally worked was just east of his farm on the south bank of the creek.

And thus it was that the Parker home became the meeting place of the chiefs and warriors. Samuel Parker was one of the fourteen chiefs of Tonawanda and so also was old Jemmy Johnson. Inasmuch as both were relatives it made William's home most convenient for them.

Red Jacket was a frequent visitor, since he was a member of the same clan as Elizabeth—the Wolf. Little Billy, Silver Heels, Blacksmith, Captain Pollard, Black Squirrel, Big Fire, Blue Sky, Black Chief, Black Snake, Sky Carrier, Tall Chief, Half Town, Twenty Canoes, Powder Horn, Two Guns, Big Kettle, Big Deer and Tall Peter, Sundown and many more all came and knew a welcome awaited them.

It is interesting to note the characteristic of the Indians in their native expressions, their ideals and instincts are so different from those of the pale-face who came and urged his "virtues" as superior. The uncultured Seneca believed that food like air was the gift of the Creator and should be as free to the visitor as the spring water at the wayside. His religion taught kindness and hospitality to the peaceful stranger and to the neighbor less fortunate; it required that every adult or child who entered the door should have food placed before him. Every convenience of the home was at the disposal of those who entered the door. Then, the red man who claimed this hospitality had a knowledge of his own obligation not to claim more than the giver could easily give. Every man trusted the honor of the other and so no doors were locked. The simple expedient of placing a broom before the main entrance was the sign that the family was absent and the house not to be approached. There were no house-breakers. It may seem strange to modern man that with every temptation to get things easily and freely that some men did not fall. But they did not because it never occurred to them that one should possess the objects belonging to another any more than one man should steal another's arm or head. This arose out of the old communistic life and had its basis in the fact that the Indian has developed no "acquisitive instinct." The fifty sachems of the League were its poorest men, in worldly goods. They were hard workers and set an example of wisdom and industry to their people, but the religious law required that to be ho-ya-neh, or "noble," one must give all he possessed to those who had less ability. Thus the rich man, the noble man, was the poor man. He felt that it was right to give of himself and of his ability that his people might benefit. A man might hold his sacred "medicine" charm as a means of power but he never used his wealth of material substance as a lever to crush other men. The instinct was to give, not to get; to serve, not to be served. It was because of these inbred principles that William was willing and glad to use his strength and ability to produce for his friends and visitors. They would do the same for him. His good wife felt the same; she was "ho-ya-neh," and the proof of her nobility lay in her willingness to serve.

Civilization has almost absolutely crushed out these finer native instincts. The white race has over-developed its desire to acquire until in modern America it amounts to madness and brings only misery.

Ely was reared in this old atmosphere and early imbibed every fine principle of his people. His grandfather, Sos-he-o-wa, had become the successor of Handsome Lake, and therefore the chief priest of the Senecas. This fact had some disadvantage for it made the Parker family a member of the "progressive party," the "new religionists" who were opposed to the ancient religion of the Iroquois. But by the time of Ely's birth the new religion of Ganeodaiu or Handsome Lake, the brother of Cornplanter, had almost absorbed the older party.

The Senecas were in a critical stage. Everything was uncertain. The steady inrush of white settlers brought a feeling of hopelessness. Nothing seemed true or certain any longer. The settlers were Christians but violated every rule the missionaries taught the Indians as Christianity. This led to confusion. Confusion came when it was seen that no great calamity came from changing from the old religion to the new. Confusion came when some of the Indians dropped their "paganism" for Christianity. Nothing seemed certain. The old law said "give;" the new law said "get." The old law said "talk with one tongue and trust thy neighbor;" the new law was, "say one thing and artfully mean another, use two tongues and distrust your neighbor." So, demoralization grew. Then came the loss of native industries. The Senecas became dependent largely upon articles which they either did not or could not produce. Even their arts became demoralized to a certain extent. Their basketry and bead-work was commercialized. It was made to sell to the whites in the surrounding towns. Every move and every relation that the Senecas had with the whites seemed only to bring greater demoralization to the Indians in all lines, civic, social, moral and industrial. The simple ethics of the red man were overwhelmed—asphyxiated, in the new atmosphere.

The Senecas had long been farmers on an immense scale, as is attested by all the French and English explorers who came among them. Their extensive cornfields were described by every writer and military invader who visited them. Every one of the journals of Sullivan's campaign records the large agricultural lands of the Iroquois. Sullivan's campaign, with all the misery it brought, carried with it also a destruction of the old agricultural pursuits. The Senecas wandering down the Allegheny or Cattaraugus, became for a time hunters and the garden patches were small, just large enough to support the family and no more. The land was not well cleared as it had been in the Genesee country and beyond. They had lost that now.

True, Broadhead found some remarkable fields on the Allegheny settlements when he made his raid on the settlements there. In his report to General Washington he reported the destruction of $30,000 worth of corn and said that with the burning of the towns it took him three days. He added, "I never saw finer corn."

After these destructive raids the Senecas relied more on the chase for a livelihood. Broken-hearted, the men penetrated the heavy forests and fought for existence in the wilds. The Allegheny country was the great hunting-ground and hundreds of hunting parties swarmed both sides of the valley from Bradford to Warren. Many went down as far as Pittsburg but there was no legitimate excuse for going so far unless it was because rum by the barrel was cheaper there.

The Parker boys were reared in the old Indian way. At birth they were plunged in cold water and then wrapped or rolled in a blanket. Each was reared upon a baby board such as Indians use. Ely's cradle-board for many years was shown in the New York State Museum but was burned in the Capitol fire, March 29, 1911.

During their youth each boy was compelled to bathe often, summer or winter. During cold weather they were compelled to do this even if they had to break the ice to take a dip. In the summer they took what is known as the sweat bath. A small dome-shaped tepee was erected of bent saplings, covered with blankets. In a fire built outside, "hard head" rocks or fossiliferous stones were heated. These were raked inside with a hooked stick and dropped in a little pit. The bather than dipped water from a pail or bark receptacle and poured it on the stones. This caused cloud after cloud of steam to rise and the "bather" would sweat and steam until he thought himself perfectly clean. Companions would rub his skin with a brush or with sand and then all would suddenly burst from the sweat lodge and jump into a near-by stream. After swimming for a few moments they would emerge, roll up in a blanket and take a nap. The Parker boys often did this on the banks of the Tonawanda.

Visitors in western New York, who saw such practices, thought the pile of stones were altars, and the sweat lodges, shrines for worship. One missionary left an interesting account of his idea of what in reality was only a group of Indian boys taking a bath.[2]

There had been little change in the costumes of the people since the War of 1812. When Ely went to the little Baptist Mission School at Tonawanda, the Senecas were still wearing blankets. Most of the men wore long hair,

---

2. See Publications of the Buffalo Historical Society, Hyde; Vol. VI, p. 248.

divided into two braids. A few of the warriors still shaved or burned the hair from their heads with the exception of the scalp-lock. The picturesque cap, covered with feathers, was still in vogue, though now the material was oftener red or blue broad-cloth or a fancy silk handkerchief, fastened over a wooden frame. The head-band was often of quill work in chaste colors or more often fretted in design from beaten silver. The more progressive wore tall beaver or "plug" hats over the tall crown of which they placed band after band of silver, the number indicating the wealth of the individual, in silver crowns, at least. Even the women wore these tall beaver hats, crowns and all. Fancy the appearance of Elizabeth Parker, direct descendant of Ji-gon-sa-seh, compeer of Hiawatha, dressed in a "stove-pipe" hat! And yet it is said she had one.

The Indians early held that a thing was valuable only as it could be used. Gold and silver meant nothing when in the form of money, in the earliest days of pristine ignorance. So they beat them into plates and fretted out brooches and buckles. The custom continued many years after they had been taught the white man's use for his round pieces of white and yellow metal. The silver brooch fad had a firm hold on the Iroquois and they kept many native silversmiths busy in making them. The women used them as dress ornaments and as buttons. A wealthy woman often had a peck or more.

It is interesting to note that the leggins worn by the men in times of peace were not fringed at the side at all. The seam was in front and a decorated band ran along the seam and around the bottom. Only the warriors wore fringed leggins, but more often they merely twisted their peace leggins around and tied a garter below the knee. A breech clout was worn, being either of buckskin or broadcloth, but sometimes a doeskin or broadcloth kilt was worn instead. This was usually the case when men went bare-chested. The skirt at this period was either of cloth or of light cotton, according to the season. In general form it followed the pattern of the earlier buckskin garments, but was without fringe. There was one material difference, however. The more modern shirts had sleeves. The broad sashes were still worn and decorated bags or pockets had not gone out of fashion. The men had a *negligé* habit of dressing for comfort and no one among their own people, at least, thought any convention violated by such a natural desire. Often they wore only the long shirt that reached nearly to the knees, a cap and a pair of moccasins. As often they wore only a pair of leggins and a kilt, leaving the chest bare. Still if a man appeared in a breech clout and a blanket and a cotton *e-yuse* (sheet), it was merely thought that he was keeping cool, if anything was thought at all. The day had not yet dawned for these simple-minded folk when it was to be learned that the human body is a thing disgraceful, shocking, immodest! They saw no wrong in the form that the Creator had molded as His supreme expression. If they wore more clothing when they went to the trading posts or to the towns it was because they knew it was the style and not because they thought it immoral to reveal their bodies.

When the cap, the gus-to-weh, was not worn by the men, the hair was neatly brushed and parted and a feather or two placed in the crown where the braids united. Married women wore a single braid, doubled up and tied. There was a fastening barette used, made of a piece of wood, covered with decorated buckskin. It resembled the object called by archeologists the gorget. It had two holes for fastening and was worn up and down, though when silk ribbons came into vogue it was worn across so as to resemble the extended ends of a bow. Unmarried women wore two braids and were careful to color the scalp where the parting of the hair revealed it. They considered it good etiquette to paint their cheeks red, providing everyone could see the paint. And here is a toilet secret not found in any book on Indians, notwithstanding the vigilant researches of ethnologists. It is about the face powder the Seneca women used. It was not white, you may be sure. It was red and made from the pulverized, dry-rot of the inner portion of the pine. It had a delicate fragrance and gave the skin a smooth velvety finish, absorbing all the natural oils and mosture. Milady was vain, even in those simple days, but it was only natural.

No Iroquois woman, or any other Indian woman, ever wore a war bonnet or a feather in her hair. Sometimes she wore a simple headband or a tight cap, but an upright feather, never. She would as soon shave her head and deny her sex as "stick a feather in her cap." It was purely a masculine prerogative. The feather in an Indian woman's hair is a creation of the Wild West show. The real Seneca woman of old wore a head-throw of doeskin, a cap or more often only her shining black tresses, well oiled with sunflower oil or bear's grease.

When Ely Parker became of school age he was named Ha-san-no-an-da, meaning The Reader.[3] His youngest brother Nicholson was named Gai-e-wa-gowa or Great Message. Their sister Carrie was known as Ga-ho-na, meaning the Blue-bell. Then there was the older brother Levi, and Isaac Newton. From the very beginning these children manifested their own individuality. Each developed naturally in his and her own way. The only direction they had from their parents was, "Learn all you can." Their father at least was a progressive in his desires for his children, but his own talents were used mostly in raising wheat and horses. He never had had the opportunity for attending school. Thus it was that Ely early acquired a primary

---

3. Sometimes translated, "The Name that leads."

schooling, and was grateful for the help the missionaries gave him. He was a keen observer, and the things of his time impressed him indelibly, young as he was. He saw the bark houses gradually giving way to substantial log cabins and the buckskin garment supplanted by cloth. This was the result of civilization's mad on-rush.

The bark cabins in his early days were at least well ventilated; the log cabins were not always so, unless a big fireplace yawned up an equally large chimney. There were many bark houses along the Allegheny and a few at Cattaraugus.

The old custom of burial had not entirely given way to the white man's method. The body was wrapped in blankets and tied in a covering of bark. Some of the older people even requested to be doubled up in their graves, on one side as if sleeping, others wished to be placed in a tree for a year. There were tree "burials" at Cattaraugus and Allegheny at late as 1838.

The social and religious side of the Senecas was interesting and varied, and of this we shall later speak.

The region about the falls of the Tonawanda is full of the mysteries of the old days. There are strange ledges of rock, ghostly clumps of trees, places where ancient people seem once to have dwelt; and there was the mysterious spirits' pond.

All the Parker boys had visited that strange lake of spirits, whose waters seemed to glisten with enchantment. Indeed, it lay only a short way from their home at the falls, and at the foot of a high cliff, that rises almost fifty feet in places. Not only have Indians looked with awe upon this little sheet of water, but white men as well have felt the terrors suggested by its uncertain depths. No less a Christian than Rev. Samuel Kirkland looked at it and recalling the traditions, shrunk from touching it, and hurried on. This was a century and a quarter ago. The story he had heard was that the pond was inhabited by a great serpent, known to the Indians as Sais-tah-go-wa. It disgorged balls of fire and required a constant tribute of sacred tobacco.

The Parker boys knew a better tale and their mother in warning them away from its dangerous shores told them the legend of Spirit Lake. She told the story of the maiden who was offered as a sacrifice to this under-water monster. Her lover, that he might be with her in death as in life, entered the canoe and pushed it from the shore, flinging aside the paddle and folding his arms when the great horned serpent lifted his head above the water. Some hostile Indians who had come to attack the Tonawanda's village saw the situation and tried to kill the underwater dweller, but failed. Their arrows only broke against its scales. So it bore the lover and the maiden far down beneath the waters; and even now, on certain evenings, their voices can be heard as they rise above the waters as spirit people. Even now the horned monster lifts his head to survey the landscape and claim his sacrificial herb. In the boyhood days of Ely Parker, oftentimes the old men offered their tokens and the Society of Charm Holders held dark dances in the night, lest Sais-tah-go-wa become angry.

This pond might become a source of a fine water supply to the town of Medina, but the villagers there, affected by the traditions of the red men, seem inclined to turn elsewhere for this element.

There are many strange traditions hovering over this region and all of them have been faithfully handed down by the story-tellers of the family. Sos-he-o-wa was insistent that his children and grandchildren learn them all; and so Elizabeth told them to her boys.

We should like to repeat some of these traditions but perhaps they ought to be told in a book of legends, rather than in a simple biography. One story, which was news in those days, however, should be related for it was gossiped about the Parker fireside in the years of the early '30's, and its dramatic incidents happened but a little way from their own doorstep. It is of importance, too, to those who live there today, for it explains the ghosts that hover about the haunted corners.

A little below the village of Akron runs a picturesque stream known as Murder Creek. It was a stream frequented by the Indians, who appreciated its beauty. One of their trails led across it at the Sulphur spring. In later years a mill-dam was erected just above the spring, but the locality with the Senecas always kept its ancient name, De-on-go-te, "the place of hearing." It was so named because the roar of Ga-sko-sa-dah, the falls at Falkirk, could be heard with great distinctness. The banks of the stream and the tall forsets seemed to wall in the thunder and hold it there to rumble on the ears of the traveler. Here another trail ran on to another stream two miles farther west. Like its larger brother, this stream had a waterfall, and a hidden waterway beneath its bed. It was called Wai-out-hah Gahonda, sometimes translated, "Stream with the beautiful falls."

In the spring of the early '20's a white man named John Dolph came from the Mohawk country and built his cabin a stone's throw from the Wai-out-hah. Here Dolph with Peter Van Deventer intended to build a saw-mill.

On a certain October evening, Mr. Dolph spread his mill plans on his kitchen table in order to discuss them with his good wife, who was rocking the baby boy in a cradle near the fire. Suddenly a piercing shriek was heard in the woods outside. The agonizing cry was repeated again and sounded nearer. Flinging open the door Dolph saw the figure of an Indian girl rushing toward his cabin. Dashing in, she fell to the floor moaning breathlessly, "Oh, save me, save me!"

Dolph closed and barred the door and had no sooner done so than the burly voice of a man was heard and then the clamor of his fists on the door. "Let me in! Let me in!" he cried as he threw his weight against it.

"You can't come in by trying in any such way," called out Dolph, at the same time motioning his wife to conceal the Indian girl.

Mrs. Dolph lifted up a trap door and led the trembling girl into the mouth of a cavern. Dolph, with musket in hand, then advanced to the door and asked the intruder what business he had.

"My name is Sanders," said the man, "and that girl is a prisoner, whom I am to deliver to the authorities at Grand river, Canada. Her father, a chief placed her in my hands, because she is wayward and wishes to marry a bad Indian. Now let me in, gentleman, please."

Mr. Dolph unbarred the door and the stranger entered, looked around but saw no sign of his prey. Glancing upward he saw an attic opening and a ladder leading to it. Dolph handed him a lighted candle and somewhat nervously Sanders went up but soon came down, angry and excited.

"Give up that girl, she's here, I saw her come in," he snarled. "Where is your cellar?" he asked, glancing down at the floor.

Dolph removed a bit of carpet, handed the stranger a candle and bade him descend, but he found no trace of the girl and no visible outlet of escape, save to the room above. He flew into a rage and muttering threats as he came up the ladder, "she shall not escape me; I shall find her yet," he exclaimed as he walked out into the darkness, to watch if he could any suspicious actions at the house.

It was not long before he saw Mr. and Mrs. Dolph creep down the side of the gorge and enter a clump of bushes.

Sanders had said that he was going to Canfield Tavern on the Buffalo road, and thus Dolph did not believe he was watched. He scanned the path, the woods and stream, but saw no one. A dark figure in the shadow of a great pine escaped his eye. So together the Dolphs went out and crept into the outside entrance of the cavern, which lay a few rods north of the falls, part way down on the right bank. Looking around again in the darkness they satisfied themselves that they were unobserved. The October moon, though bright, could not pierce the depths beneath the autumn foliage. They entered the chamber, stooped low and crept on until they came to a high-arched cavern. There they saw the Indian girl, asleep from pure exhaustion. At the sound of a foot-fall she awakened and in wild-eyed alarm exclaimed, "Where is he?" Mrs. Dolph allayed the girl's fears and drew from her the story of her unhappy adventure. Mr. Uriah Cummings, long the local historian of Akron, relates this strange tale as he found it in Mr. Dolph's own records. We draw upon his version for the girl's story.

"My name," said the girl, "is Ah-weh-hah, which in the language of the pale-face is Wild-rose. My home is near Spirit Lake, under the cliff about a mile below the Tonawanda Falls. I live there with my aged father, who is a chief of the Senecas and his name is Go-wah-na, meaning 'The Great Fire.'

"My mother has been dead several years, and my poor old father has just been murdered by that dreadful man Sanborn, from whom I had escaped when you opened your door and allowed me to enter.

"For more than a year this dreadful man has been hovering around Spirit Lake trying to get a chance to talk with me. He has urged me to marry him, but my Gray Wolf, my Tah-yoh-ne, is very dear to me and I was to become his wife very soon. But this man Sanders declared to me, that sooner than see me the wife of the

Seneca brave, he would murder me and all who stood in his way.

"My father, thinking to avoid trouble, said he would take me to the Cattaraugus nation where I would be among friends and Tah-yoh-ne could join me there, and thus could we be free from the annoyance of Sanders' threats and entreaties.

"I have had much to do to restrain Tah-yoh-ne from meeting this vile man Sanders. By much entreaty I have induced Tah-yoh-ne to do no harm to the wicked monster, for should they meet and should the pale-face fall, the authorities would not listen to anything we might say in defense of my brave Tah-yoh-ne. They would say he was guilty of murder and must be punished.

"It was this morning that my dear father came to me and told me to prepare for a journey to Cattaraugus.

"Soon all was ready and we started on foot, taking the old trail, the Wah-ah-gwen-ne, leading on to Te-os-ah-wah, a place called 'Buffalo' by your people.

"We had reached the De-on-go-te Gah-hun-da and had sat down to rest and listen to the wondrous Gah-sko-sah-dah, when suddenly we saw the man Sanders close upon the trail behind us.

"My poor aged father trembled with fear and apprehension, for he saw the look of wicked triumph in the hard face; and the offensive manner of the cruel intruder boded nothing but evil for us."

After a brief interval in which the young Indian girl had indulged in paroxysms of grief and anguish, Mrs. Dolph had taken her hand and endeavored to soothe and quiet her, she at last continued her painful story.

"Suddenly the entire manner of the man was changed. He seemed to have relented, and was sorry for his past conduct.

"He smilingly came forward and extending one hand to my poor old father and his other hand to me, he said he wished us to banish from our minds entirely all thoughts of evil intent on his part; that he had made up his mind to cease trying to persuade me to marry him; that he hoped I would be happy with the brave Tah-yoh-ne.; that he had decided to leave all behind him, and seek a home in the far West and there try to forget his great love for me; that he hoped all would be forgiven and forgotten; and that even now he was on his way to the great unknown West; he had not thought of seeing us again, but now that we were going in the same direction, he would do all he could to make us remember this journey with pleasure.

"The man spoke so pleasantly that we were deceived as you shall soon learn.

"My father was so pleased at the turn of affairs that he invited Sanders to journey as far as On-tar-o-ga, today; he said that as soon as we reached that 'place of hills and rocks' we would build our campfire, prepare our evening meal and there rest until morning. To all this Sanders readily assented.

"And now as the details were settled, we lingered long at the De-on-go-te Ga-hun-da.

"The moon came up bright and clear; the thunder of the Gah-sko-sah-dah came rolling down the valley and the time passed pleasantly, as Mr. Sanders can be very entertaining whenever he chooses to be.

"Finally we resumed our journey. We followed the Wah-ah-gwen-ne westward and came on up through the valley of the Wun-ne-pa-tuc and on up the trail leading westerly out of the valley, and on to the hills of On-tar-o-ga. Presently we came to the accustomed camping-place and soon we had a fire started and our evening meal disposed of, and my dear father sat before the fire contented and happy.

"I had arisen and was looking eastward when I thought I saw a light across the head of the valley and not far away. At that instant I heard a blow struck, followed by a groan, and quickly turning I saw my poor father lying prostrate on the ground, face downward, with that fiend Sanborn standing over him with an uplifted club in his hands.

"With the look of a demon the brute sprang toward me intent upon murdering me also. With a shriek of despair and desperation I fled into the forest with the mad man close behind me, brandishing his club and vowing he would brain me. As I ran, it came to me about seeing the light through the trees, and as well as I could I fled in the direction of the light. I ran until I came upon the bridge over the Wun-ne-pa-tuc and there your light was in plain view, and I gathered up all my remaining strength and as I ran I cried, 'Save me,' when your door was suddenly opened for me with the fiend not ten steps behind me. You know the rest."

Ah-weh-hah was a beautiful maiden, so the Dolphs thought, so during her story, they resolved to keep and protect her. She was tall, and her perfect teeth, her soft-reddish brown complexion, her expressive black eyes and her long black hair betokened an Indian maiden of the finest type. Her refined manner and soft voice indicated that she had been carefully trained as a woman of the ho-ya-neh class.

Mr. Cummings, who gives her conversation from the Dolph records, says it may seem incredible that this young Indian girl should have a command of English but he believes that Mr. Dolph's records must be correct. The real answer is that Ah-weh-hah was a student in the mission school at Tonawanda, where the Seneca youth obtained the rudiments of an English education.

The old chief, whose name no previous historian has given, was Big Fire, a veteran of the War of 1812. His body was found by Mr. Dolph in exactly the same spot as described by the girl. There too, he found the smouldering remains of the campfire. Ever since the day of his murder the cross-trail there has been known as the Haunted Corners. The spot is at the east side of Cumming's Park.

Dolph after his horrible discovery took the trail for his partner's tavern. When morning came Van Deventer and Dolph buried the remains of the victim of Sander's treachery. The murderer had taken the Buffalo stage at midnight.

When Dolph returned home he found the Indian girl delirious. The news of the tragedy and of Ah-weh-hah's escape had reached the ears of the Indians and Tah-yoh-ne hastened to the refuge of his unhappy sweetheart. Ah-weh-hah was overjoyed at seeing Gray Wolf and begged that he go with her to the grave of her father. So together they journeyed over the trail until they stood by the newly-made mound. Here, together they chanted the death song, as a last token of their affection. A grave fire was lighted and the sacred tobacco incense rose to lift the burden of their prayer to the Maker-of-All.

While thus absorbed in their funeral devotions, a sudden step was heard and Sanders jumped from the underbrush, ax in hand. Wolf grabbed his tomahawk and then began a terrible struggle. Losing their weapons in the fray each grabbed their hunting-knives and tore each other's flesh until the blood ran down in gushing streams. Then came a pause and the white man fell backward, dead.

Prostrate, and sickened by the awful sight, lay the girl. Wolf tried to speak but his lips were sealed. He was too weak to comfort his horrified sweetheart, and she too weak from the shock to rise to go to him. He staggered forward and fell. He too had perished at the graveside of her father. With an agonized cry that pierced the forests depths she gave vent to her horror and grief. Mr. Dolph heard the cry and ran the quarter mile to find what new tragedy had occurred. There he found the unhappy Wild Rose, on her knees, swaying back and forth as she moaned between her sobs the death chant. As she looked upward at Dolph her grief-stricken expression revealed such a depth of sorrow that he records that he felt her mind must soon give way.

As she followed him back to his cabin his fears he found were realized. She was incoherent and dazed. Dolph, with the help of a neighbor, buried the two bodies, the Wolf near the Chief and the white man's a little to one side.

Often the Wild Rose would visit the graves of her father and lover to weep and to chant her grief. Mr. Dolph recorded her song as he heard it:

> "Oh, my Gray Wolf, my Tah-yoh-ne,
> Do you hear the Wild Rose calling,
> Hear the song of your Ah-weh-hah,
> Hear her tell you how her heart aches?
> Why did not the brave Tah-yoh-ne
> Take his lonely Wild Rose with him.
> O, come back, my own Tah-yoh-ne,
> For my heart is breaking, breaking.
>
> You will wait for me, my Gray Wolf,
> For I soon shall come to join you.
> O, my Gray Wolf, my Tah-yoh-ne,
> Hear the voice of your Ah-weh-hah,
> Only wait a few days longer
> And I then will walk beside you."

When one day the Dolphs missed the Wild Rose they went out to the graveyard so tragically called into existence and there they found her, lying upon the grave of Gray Wolf, lying cold and lifeless. And so beside his grave they buried her. Many were the sincere tears they shed as their tender sympathies reached out in grief for the unhappy Ah-weh-hah.

Now as in former days the lover of midnight strolls may hear the voices of the two lovers as they wander over the modern dust of the ancient trail. The ghosts of the father and the murderers never come back to earth—they who come are only the spirits of the lovers whom destiny forbade a marriage in the earth life, but whom death united in a bond that the years have not broken.

For many years the story of Big Fire's murder was told at the Parker fireside and the tale of the unhappy Ah-weh-hah never failed to bring tears to the eyes of those who heard it. It had one moral to the Indians; it was: "Look out for white man." But as ever, the warning was in vain, for as the traditions run, "White man very cunning, he get you pretty soon."

The tragedy of Ah-weh-hah was the tragedy of the people. The white man was on their trail. The "land sharks" had found them, and a life and death struggle for their homes was in progress. The child Ely passed quickly from the old stories, the ancient traditions of his people, to these new stories of wrong. As a child the need of a decisive action had often to be met, and it seemed to have found him ready.

Because of the unhappy conditions among his people Ely, when ten years old, decided to run away. The whole nation was in the utmost confusion. By a system of highhanded fraud every foot of land the Senecas had was signed away and the order came, "March West." The stoutest heart felt the clutching of emotions that could not be concealed. There were bickerings and quarrelings and the people were in a pitiful situation. Ely did not wish to stay in a country where confusion, deceit and trickery existed. He resolved to go to Canada where the followers of Brant lived, and to join the Six Nations band on the Grand river. His father consented and he went, accompanied by an older man, a friend of his father.

Every chief of the Tonawanda band of Senecas had refused to sign the treaty, had refused to accept the bribes of the Ogden Land Company's agents and had spurned every overture. Only a single name of a Tonawanda chief appeared on the fraudulent treaty, that being forged.

The story of this effort of the Ogden Land Company to obtain the lands of the New York Indians is a sad one, and the results did much to stimulate Ely Parker and other young men of his time to acquire an education and fight for their people. Among these were Maris B. Pierce and Peter Wilson, both of whom graduated later from Dartmouth College.

CHAPTER VI.

THE WAY THE TWIG WAS BENT.

Grand river in ancient times was one of the great water routes of the Neuter nation. On its banks once lived branches of the Hurons and later the Mississaga Chippewas. It was a tract of land on either side of Grand river, from its mouth to its source that Captain Joseph Brant selected for his followers when he led them across the Niagara line and back under the British flag. He selected a garden spot and his followers soon settled down to the work of re-establishing the League of the Five Nations—or six, as there were then.

He concentrated the gathered tribes about the site of his town, now known as Brantford, Ontario. Here later was built his church to which Queen Anne gave a solid silver communion service and the hand-carved coat-of-arms of England.

This gathering of the Mohawks with the Onondagas, the Oneidas, the Cayugas, the Tuscaroras, and a few hundred Senecas, together with the broken captive tribes, such as the Tutelos, the Brothertowns, the Delawares and Nanticokes, made possible a new "Long House" of the Iroquois. They still remembered their old laws and traditions and under Brant's inspiration soon had a closely knit and centralized government patterned upon the laws of Hiawatha and Deganowideh. New sachems were "raised up" and the council fire of the "great peace," as the league was called, was kindled afresh. It was a new country and gave abundant promise for the fulfillment of the old hopes.

In pitiful contrast stood the broken dissipated tribes in New York whose government had been wrested from the civil sachems and seized by the war chiefs. Their attempt to maintain the ancient League seemed only a pretense.

It is little wonder that many of the New York Iroquois stepped away to Grand river and became members of the new council fire. It is little wonder that the tales of the "new hope" sunk deeply into the mind of the boy Ely and that he too wished to live as his fathers had lived before him. After an ardent plea to his parents, he was allowed to go. He was ten when he made the trip. An older friend went with him and promised to teach him all the mysteries of woodcraft and hunting.

He learned many other mysteries than hunting. He learned the lore of his ancestors. He visited all the long houses, for each nation had one or more, and thus became thoroughly acquainted with the rites and ceremonies of each tribe. The beginning which his early training at Tonawanda had given him thus expanded and he early became an adept in interpreting one Iroquois dialect into another. Indeed he gave so much attention to his hunting and woodcraft and his learning of the old ways that he straightway forgot all he had learned at the mission school at home!

During his stay at Grand river he had an opportunity to go to an Oneida settlement on the river Thames, where his uncle Samuel's wife had relatives. There he had an opportunity of going out on trips with horse-buyers. Soon he had a job of driving horses to the Canadian military post at London. For nearly a year he worked as a hostler's boy. Then came an order at the fort to deliver a number of horses to the military post at Hamilton. These were to be delivered under the charge of two or three English officers. Ely went along as one of the party. It was a long, wearisome journey despite the shifting scenes and adventures by the way, and thus the officers, no doubt duly impressed by their superior English ancestry, sought to amuse themselves at the expense of the Indian boy, who understood the king's English" so imperfectly. They knew nothing of his ancestry nor dreamed him of far more royal blood than themselves. They indeed were petty officers in a provincial regiment and gloated in their superior rank. He was an Indian boy, indeed, but the heir to a sachemship in the League of the Iroquois. But he felt no vanity because of it. He once told the writer about one of his boyhood journeys to Hamilton, and told how the rude jests galled him. Later, too, he mentioned the subject in a brief autobiography which he left in manuscript form in his desk.

He could not reply or "get back" at his tormentors, who as he says, jested from good nature and from pure desire for fun, rather than malice. These jests and sharp thrusts they gave him were of highest importance in determining his character and did much to arouse his ambition. In the long lonesome ride he did a great deal of thinking. He tells us that he resolved not only to continue his education but to become a master of the English tongue. More than this, he resolved to know that language so well that he could talk as brilliantly as any Englishman could. Who knows but that there was a latent resolution to become an army officer some day, in rank far above the jesting subalterns who drove horses? Thus with these new-born ambitions to achieve glory, that he might show white men what he could do he resolved to return to his home in the Tonawanda valley and begin his struggle for achievement.

He walked all the way from Hamilton to Buffalo and thence to Tonawanda. He was a broad-shouldered strapping boy and thought nothing of the trip, except perhaps that he wished he could make greater speed. When he eagerly related his hopes to his father he found that while he met with warm encouragement he could expect no financial help from him. Nevertheless he told the good missionaries what he desired and found them in sympathy with him. He reviewed his old studies and pushed forward until he outgrew their ability to teach him more. He had then qualified himself to enter an advanced school. He entered the Yates academy of which he wrote appreciatively in later years:

"Here I progressed irregularly but well in all my studies, and having no Indian companionship, I advanced perceptibly and rapidly in the use of the English language. The school was eminently respectable and the association was therefore good. It was non-sectarian and permitted freedom of religious thought and action. It was a mixed school and the association of the sexes had a refining, elevating tendency. I can recall my stay here as among the happiest days of my youthful existence."

At this time his brother Nicholson and his sister Carrie, almost equally ambitious, were studying in Pembroke, Genesee county.

There are many records of the progress of the Parkers in their school careers, in the form of essays and other papers written during their school days, and through these documents it is easy to see that absence from home sharpened their devotion to their race and gave them a higher viewpoint than they ever could have had by remaining on the reservation. There is little doubt, too, that their ardent arguments in behalf of their fated race did much to mold the minds of their fellow students in their opinions of the Indian and his capacity.

Cayuga Lake in ancient days was a favorite region for the wandering tribes that passed through the country of the Finger Lakes. The many sites of ancient camps and Indian villages attest this. Later the Cayuga Nation clustered about it and many silent tokens of these people are still found there to tell the story of other days.

The beauty of this region as seen by the Revolutionary soldiers under Major Sullivan attracted them and despite solemn treaties which assured the Cayugas that they might live there "forever," the land was gradually purchased for small sums until the Cayugas had left only a 64,000-acre tract at the foot of the lake.

The country was thus opened to settlement and the first town to be founded was Aurora on the east bank, midway. A beautiful spot, Aurora is associated with many interesting facts in our history of minor things. It was here on November 21, 1818, that Lewis Henry Morgan, historian of the Iroquois, was born. The most famous academy in Western New York was situated at Aurora and it was at this Cayuga Academy that Morgan received his early training.

After a two years' course at Yates, Ely Parker entered Cayuga Academy, already famous for the number of its successful students. He was then about seventeen years of age and more than usually ambitious. He came as a "son of the forest," as he says, to compete with white boys from the finest families in the land.

In passing it may be said that nearly every Indian who has achieved a high position in business or commercial life has been educated away from his people and amid surroundings that compelled him to keep on his mettle. It is competition with keen intellect that awakens and develops greater intellect, generally speaking. The Government school where hundreds of untrained Indian youths are brought together can never accomplish the good that might be accomplished if the same students had the opportunities and could meet the requirements of the common schools of the land. It is the culture that one gets by good associations and the standard one must rise to in order to be regarded as "par," that keep ambition alive and keenly active.

Certain it is that the opportunities that the Parker boys had at the schools among the whites were not lost. They felt that it was incumbent upon them to live up to all the higher ideals men had of the red race and to disprove all the current tales that the Indian was lazy, drunken and inferior in intellect. Their life at the academy gave them two great opportunities. The first was that of reading the then recently published works of Thatcher and Drake. Here they found recorded the proof of the fine qualities possessed by the old leaders of the race before the time when contact had caused too great corruption. They read with the joy of discoverers of Tecumseh and Pontiac, or Philip of Pokanet and of Garangula. This not only awakened a healthful race pride but spurred on ambition. The second opportunity that came was that of delivering in oration and essay, heroic defenses of the Indian. Once they had declaimed the virtues of the red man's way they were compelled to live up to those virtues, and they did this to the last detail.

This endeavor to emulate the virtues of the old regime led to many interesting arguments, and both Nicholson and Ely felt compelled to deliver orations explaining why they were seeking a white man's education if the Indian way was so superior.

Nicholson was ever Ely's favorite brother; at least they had more elements of common interest and were oftenest together. While they were at school—Ely at Cayuga and Nick at Pembroke—they devised a way of utilizing their literary productions to mutual advantage. Each would send the other his essay or oration, as it had come from the teacher's hands for correction, and then the other reviewed, rearranged it to suit himself and used it as his own. This mutual interchange did much to keep their thoughts in the same general channel and led each to read the books the other read. It is quite possible that this fact would never have been known if their school essays had been lost or burned. However, on looking over the papers one can see the date on the essays; on one, "E. S. P., Nov., 1847," and on another, "N. H. P., Dec., 1847." Then on another set, "N. H. P., Jan., 1848;" "E. S. P., Feb., 1848." This was at least brotherly reciprocity even if it had some suspicion of a lack of ethics. It was a secret between the brothers that a biographer has unearthed for the critic which may not be quite fair. But sinless heroes would be mummies, things that neither Nick nor Ely would exactly care to be. They were boys and very much alive. If they did "crib" from each other it did not destroy their individuality or dull their ability to originate. On the contrary it did help mightily in winning prizes in oratory. One of these orations had as its title, "Original Thoughts Impossible to Man."

The confusion in tribal affairs caused great distress. The Senecas between 1838 and 1850 were in a constant state of agitation and it was necessary for them constantly to send messengers and attorneys both to Albany and to Washington.

Ely Parker was often sent on such errands. His first trip to Washington was made when he was fifteen years of age. His polished manner and keen wit quickly won him many friends and he at once became a favorite in the elite circles of both state and national capitols. The affairs of the Tonawandas demanded the attention of some earnest advocate and it was this demand that led to Ely's leaving school at the age of eighteen.

Durings his schooldays Ely had already met many of the distinguished men of New York, and he had dined at the White House as a guest of President Polk. Later on he met with Webster, Clay and Calhoun, and was a favorite with them, though his costume was of buckskin and his hat of doeskin and feathers.

He was a great admirer of Mrs. Polk, and related with evident pride how Mrs. Polk had stopped her carriage in the streets of Washington when she saw him crossing and invited him to a seat by her side. The Indian boy thus associated with the best men of his day, always convinced that it was the right due to an heir of a sachemship of the Senecas.

CHAPTER VII

LEWIS H. MORGAN AND THE "NEW LEAGUE OF THE IROQUOIS."

The situation of his people had naturally turned the mind of Ely Parker to the study of law, and with the gradual settlement of difficulties he began his career as a student in the law office of Angel & Rice in Ellicottville, Cattaraugus county. Here again he was thrown into competition with other clerks and the fact that he was an Iroquois gave him greater ambition. He spent three years reading law, drawing up forms, preparing arguments and listening to court proceedings. Then came a discovery that would have crushed many a lad.

Competent though he was and able to meet every requirement, he could not be admitted to the bar. A Supreme Court decision had ruled otherwise, making it possible only for a male white man and a citizen to enter. He had one great disability, and neither learning nor capacity could avail against it. He was an Indian, a native of the soil. Therefore he could not be admitted to the bar for he was not a citizen of the country. There was no way by which he could become one. He was a man without a country, a victim of legal injustice and popular prejudice. No Seneca could curse in his own tongue. He had to talk "white man" to do that, and it is said Ely for once talked "white man" curses, though ever after he abjured the use of such language.

Disappointed in his ambition he drifted into Rochester to consult his friends. He had made up his mind to become a civil engineer. He took a short elementary course in the Rensselaer Polytechnic Institute in Troy and then joined one of the parties sent out to improve the Erie Canal.

During Ely's endeavors to acquire a profession he had become acquainted with Lewis H. Morgan, who some years before had attended Cayuga Academy and later graduated from Union College. The two men developed a strong liking for each other and this friendship was accentuated by events to be related later. Perhaps it was Morgan who helped Parker to gain admission to Cayuga.

When Morgan attended Cayuga Academy he was instrumental in organizing a school fraternity known as the Gordian Knot. The Masonic Order had received a severe setback through the so-called exposé of another "Morgan" who lived but a few miles away on Canandaigua lake. Popular fury, ignorant of the beautiful teachings of Masonry, led to such persecutions, that the Masons, rather than foment civic discord, abandoned their lodges and even returned their charters in some cases. The school club found the Masonic hall, therefore, an ideal meeting-place, and arrayed in the white lamb-skins of the fellow-crafts, or in the silken robes of Solomon or Hiram, King of Tyre, the academy boys held their secret sessions and initiated candidates into the mysteries of the Gordian Knot. The club filled the members with a youthful enthusiasm to do something useful as well as amusing and each member as he returned home was commissioned to establish a branch society. Lewis Morgan appears to have been the leading spirit and the society lived and prospered.

Morgan's study of the Iroquois began with his acquaintance with Ely Parker. As Charles Talbot Porter, a friend to both men, wrote in later years, "Parker was an invaluable find for Morgan." Parker's influence was soon felt, for soon after his initiation into the Gordian Knot the society completely changed its name and character. It was reorganization on the principles of the League of the Iroquois and indeed became known as the Councils of the New Confederacy of the Iroquois. To its members it was known by the mysterious name of We-yo-ha-yo-de-za-de Na Ho-de-no-sau-nee, a Seneca phrase meaning, "They who live in the home of the dwellers of the Long House." The society became popular and branches were established as far east as Utica. Conventions were held at the place of the parent chapter in Aurora, and in the old Masonic lodge room. The members developed a wholesome interest, not only in the social features of the organization but in the study of Indian customs. Thus such men as Henry R. Schoolcraft and Alfred B. Street were initiated and read papers and poems on Iroquois life.

Morgan's interest was doubly sincere and later the society served most useful purposes. It used the forces it could influence to defeat the aims of the Ogden Land Company and poured forth to the State Legislature such a mass of evidence of the dishonest characters of the Land Company's agents that the legislators were astounded. Mustering their forces, the members of the Grand Order of the Iroquois sent in petitions and did much to defeat the crooked schemes of the land sharks. Both Morgan and Parker went to Washington to bring about a defeat of the fraudulent treaty. Morgan thus became widely hailed as a champion of the Iroquois. The society did much to place Ely's brother Nick and his sister Carrie in the State Normal school in Albany and finally led Morgan with Parker to write "The League of the Iroquois," a book that has become a classic wherever Indian books are known. This work was the first detailed description of an Indian tribe ever written and has made the name of Lewis H. Morgan imperishable.

Morgan's interest in the Senecas was of a variety that won the respect of these people and he was honored with an invitation to come and be one of them. He responded and was adopted as the brother of Jimmy Johnson and made a member of the Hawk clan. It has sometimes been said that he was made a son of Johnson, but that is not so. He would have been a son of Johnson's wife which would have made him a Wolf. The adoption took place on October 31, 1847, and he was named Ta-ya-da-o-wuh-kuh, meaning "One lying across," or "Bridging the Gap," referring to him as a bridge over the differences that lay between the Indian and the white man. With Morgan at this time were Thomas Darling and Charles T. Porter, both of whom were given family adoptions. Mr. Porter has written a fine account of the occasion in the Lloyd edition of the "League."

One of the unique testimonials given Morgan was a wampum belt of white background, showing the outline of eight purple diamonds. This was the pledge of the entire nation through its eight clans to Morgan. This belt, made especially for him by the matrons of the Senecas, is now in the State Museum of New York where so many other rare relics of Morgan's gathering are to be found—though he kept many in Rochester, apparently also having a private collection. [1]

Mr. Morgan interested many of his personal friends in the Senecas and their needs. Among these was Charles Talbot Porter, whom we have already mentioned. He became deeply interested in Indian affairs, and although his view of the red man was not as optimistic or as sympathetic as Morgan's, he was nevertheless a staunch friend. In Mr. Porter's recollections of Morgan, published in Mr. Lloyd's edition of the "League," [2] he gives an interesting account of his visit to the Tonawanda reservation.

"Not long after the rejection of the treaty, probably in 1847," says Mr. Porter, "Mr. Morgan was invited to visit the Indians on the Tonawanda for the purpose of being

---

1. Many years later this collection, which was made for Morgan's son, was given or sold to the University of Rochester. Morgan was married in 1851.

2. Lloyd, Herbert M., new edition of "The League of the Iroquois" (by Morgan), Dodd, Mead & Co., N. Y., 1901, vol. II, p. 157.

adopted. I had the honor, together with Mr. Thomas Darling of Auburn, New York, to accompany him. No date was fixed. The Indians were always at home. We went in a pleasant season, and when we knew we should find Ely Parker there."

There seems to have been no reception committee provided for Mr. Morgan and his party, and after a four-mile walk, Mr. Porter describes the attempt to cross the Tonawanda creek. Mr. Porter waded, for the water was only eighteen inches deep at the ford. Mr. Darling and Mr. Morgan wished to pass over dry-shod, so they hunted up a dug-out canoe and arranged their passage by craft. Porter stood on the farther shore, impatient, no doubt, at the ceremonious delay. Darling entered the canoe, wrapped himself tightly in his shawl and then Morgan, famed student of Indian lore, grasped the paddle, shoved off the canoe and leaped into it. But alas, he no sooner leaped in than he leaped out, for his "shoving out" was also a shoving over. This was a sad plight for Mr. Darling, for he was wound in his shawl like an Egyptian mummy. He rolled into the water and soaked out of his wrappings. Thus baptized in the waters of the "swift water stream," the candidates for adoption entered the domain of the Senecas "wet shod," all save Porter who had watched the whole proceeding with merriment.

Mr. Porter writes:

> Our visit lasted ten days. The forenoons were devoted by Mr. Morgan to filling his note-books; the afternoons to witnessing games and dances got up in our honor, and the evenings mostly to hearing Indian traditions, in which I remember feeling deeply interested at the time, but of which I do not now remember a word.
>
> The ceremony of adoption was a very simple one. In fact, all of it that I now can recall was a long address by old Jimmy Johnson, the religious teacher of the Indians; each of us received a name and was made a member of a particular tribe; a different one in each case, and learned who were our brothers, and who were only our cousins—all long forgotten.

The morning sessions with the oldest Indians, held with them in their own houses, were very interesting. A number of these were devoted by Mr. Morgan to obtaining geographical names, Parker, as always, acting as interpreter. I was full of admiration of these old men, who in their youth had hunted over all Western New York and who showed such wonderful acquaintance with every river and stream. In fact the whole map appeared to exist in their minds. They seemed to have developed another sense, which we who depend on books and maps, do not possess. They were men of the woods, who, with nothing to depend on but their powers of observation and memory, in trackless forests could never lose their way.

Our initiation was followed by a dance in the council house, in which we were allowed to participate, and were provided with partners. This was the only dance we witnessed in which the women took part. Then for the first time my ears were regaled with Indian music. Two young men were seated on opposite sides of a drum, which looked to me very much like a nail keg. On this they pounded violently with sticks, as an accompaniment to the most discordant howling. The Indian has no conception of musical intervals. The performance had therefore the attraction of complete novelty. But they kept good time, and the dancing was animated.

This was followed by a curious feast. A bullock had been killed and cut up in Indian fashion; that is, all the flesh had been cut in small pieces and made into a stew. The large kettles in which this had been boiled were taken into the council house, and set in a row in the middle of the floor, and the dancing was in a procession around them. The dancers were in pairs, facing each other, about six feet apart, one moving forward and the other backward, with a shuffling step. Every minute or two, on a signal from the leader, all changed places. I remember that my partner by a sudden exclamation saved me from dancing backward into a kettle of hot stew. Every family had brought a pail, and at the conclusion of the dance these pails were filled, and the stew carried home to be eaten.

I was much impressed on another afternoon by a grand thanksgiving dance performed by thirty or forty young men, attired in full Indian dress, that is, in head-feathers and breech-cloth. The dance was really inspiring. It was a slowly advancing processional dance, in single file. Each dancer seemed to follow his own inspiration and all appeared to vie with each other in the vigor of their steps and the stateliness of their postures. This exhibition of animated statuary, with the varied and majestic character of their movements, had a grandeur which to my mind was most suggestive of the sentiment of worship which it was intended to express. Just in this manner, doubtless, King David "danced before the Lord with all his might."

We were entertained at several houses, different families taking us in turn, and apparently proud to do so. The entertainment, however, was everywhere the same. We enjoyed most the hospitality of Parker's father, who was a rather progressive Indian of the Christian party and who spoke a little English. His daughter Caroline whom the Society was having educated in the State Normal School in Albany was then at home, and helped much to make it pleasant for us. She seemed quite as exceptional as her brother Ely.

We were naturally interested in what we should get to eat. The reader may be amused by a description of our breakfast. Corn was kept on the cob. The inner husks were turned back and braided together, the ears being arranged like a bunch of Chinese crackers. The first thing every morning, some of these were unbraided and the corn was shelled by rubbing two ears together. The corn was then boiled a few minutes in a kettle with ashes. This completely removed the skin and cortex from every kernel. The former floated and were poured off with the water. The latter softened sufficiently to be pounded into a meal, were washed in clean water and placed in the mortar, which was a tree-stump, hollowed out. The women, standing on opposite sides of the mortar with their pounders soon made the corn fine enough. We were awakened every morning by the sound of the pounders all over the reservation.

The meal was then mixed with black beans and made into cakes about an inch thick and six or eight inches in diameter, without salt or leaven. These cakes were set on edge in a pot of water and boiled for perhaps half an hour, when breakfast was ready. Our beverage was hemlock tea, without milk or sugar. Dinner was the same, except that the corn and beans were made into succotash, instead of cakes; and sometimes we had beef stew.

When we left, a brother of Ely Parker [Levi], a lad about twelve years old, drove us over to the village where we were to take the train, and we invited him to dine with us. At dinner he stared at us with distending eyeballs, and at last exclaimed: "How you eat! You made me think of the appetite I had once, after I had been a week with the white folks and could hardly eat anything."

Mr. Porter describes in his letter the disturbed mind of the good Baptist missionary who occupied the Mission station at Tonawanda. The preacher had endeavored to discourage the "old time" ways as things that carried the minds of the Indians backward, while his gospel and his school bade them look forward into a different life. Mr. Porter defends the Indians, however, from the imputation of having done anything wrong. They were not idolators, he says, and then he asks, "And who ever heard of any Christians who were more grateful to the Giver-of-all for so little?"

The idea of writing a book on the Iroquois must have occurred to Morgan soon after his acquaintance with Parker. One of his earliest papers was read before the New York Historical Society in 1846 under the title: "An Essay on the Constitutional Government of the Six Nations of Indians." The paper was never printed but it gives evidence that Morgan had a knowledge of the "Great Law" or constitution of the Confederacy, at which no other writer for many years has even hinted. [3]

Later, in 1847, Morgan prepared a series of "Letters on the Iroquois" and published them in the *American Whig Review,* under the pen name of *Schenandoah.* Then came his activities in collecting for the New York State (Cabinet) Museum. His constant companion was Ely Parker and his collecting headquarters was at the Parker house. Ely went with him to Grand river, and piloted him through the wilds. Their stopping-place there was with a Mohawk family named Loft. The mother of that family still remembers the visits of Parker and Morgan and tells what she gave to help them in their efforts.

Many of their traditions were recorded by Ely Parker, who also took down translations of his grandfather's speeches on ceremonial occasions. Nicholson and Ely both contributed their boyish essays on Indian life and the

---

3. This ancient code of Iroquois law edited by the present writer has been published by the State Museum under title of "The Constitution of the Five Nations."

description of the Seneca dances found in the "League" is mostly from their joint labors.

Morgan had a rare mind for a man of his time, and in collecting the specimens of native workmanship for the New York State Museum, did so, not with the idea of getting curiosities but with the studied purpose of illustrating in a detailed way the material culture of a people. He gathered utensils of domestic life, weapons, and ornaments and fabrics in a methodical manner so as to illustrate, not only the use of the object, but the method of its manufacture through various stages. This paved the way for detailed inquiry into the civic laws of the people. His principal informants were William and Elizabeth Parker, the parents of his collaborator, Ely Parker. Here he tapped a fount of knowledge, for Jimmy Johnson was the high priest of the Confederacy, and a reciter of its old laws. William was familiar with many of the old hunting laws, and the geography of the Indian country; and with his wife Elizabeth gave Morgan descriptions and models of the ancient long-houses. In later years Morgan, in writing of this, says:

> An elderly Seneca woman, Elizabeth Parker, informed the writer, thirty years ago, that when she was a girl, she lived in one of these joint houses (called by them long-houses), which contained eight families and two fires, and that her mother and her grandmother, in their day, had acted as matrons over one of these large households. This mere glimpse at the ancient Iroquois plan of life, now entirely passed away, and of which remembrance is nearly lost, is highly suggestive. It shows that their domestic economy was not without method, and it displays the care and management of woman, low down in barbarism, for husbanding their resources and for improving their condition. A knowledge of these houses, and how to build them, is not even yet lost among the Senecas. Some years ago Mr. William Parker, a Seneca chief, constructed for the writer a model of one of these long-houses, showing in detail its external and internal mechanism.

Finally after much patient inquiry Lewis H. Morgan produced his book, "The League of the Ho-de-no-sau-nee of Iroquois." It was published in 1851 by Sage & Brother of Rochester. The dedication reads as follows:

TO HA-SO-NO-AN-DA (ELY S. PARKER)

A SENECA INDIAN

This Work, The Materials of which are the fruit of our joint researches, Is inscribed; In Acknowledgment of the Obligations, and In Testimony of the Friendship of The Author.

This book is recognized today as being the first methodical treatise along scientific lines ever written of an ethnic group of mankind. At least it was the first account of this character, relating to an Indian tribe. It won for Morgan the title of "the father of American anthropology." Notwithstanding its great value it contains a number of errors both in statement of fact and in the viewpoint of certain matters, but these circumstances do not detract from the fact that the book is a valuable guide and a classic. Certainly it immediately created a host of students and stimulated inquiry into the institutions and conditions of the red race.

Many of the choicest heirlooms of the Iroquois were procured for the State Museum of New York by Ely Parker and turned over to Morgan. The choicest native textiles, rare embroideries in dyed moose-hair and porcupine quills, had been the work of the women of the family. Even several of the pieces of bead-work were made by Caroline Parker and the costume represented in the plate just preceding Morgan's "Spirit of the League" was made by her. Ga-ha-no the maiden who is shown as wearing it is none other than Caroline, who holds her head just to one side—a characteristic pose.

Among the rarer relics in the State collection is Cornplanter's tomahawk. This beautiful relic of the days now gone forever, has an interesting history, for it is only by accident that it did not share the fate of many other historical objects destroyed by the old chief.

Cornplanter had left his tomahawk at the cabin of a relative and so did not destroy it. Later it was sent to a friend of his known as Canada. When Canada died his widow preserved the heirloom which was widely known and often looked at by the curious among the tribes. When her cabin burned it was Ely Parker who rescued it from the flames. To him it was a part of family history, for Cornplanter was the half brother of his great grandfather.

Once again the tomahawk was threatened by fire. When on March 29, 1911, the State Library and the archæological collections were destroyed by a disastrous fire, the writer tore the tomahawk from the case where it hung. The blade was too hot to hold in the hand and the varnish on the handle was blistered. In that fire perished ten thousand specimens of Iroquois handiwork, including more than one hundred of the implements and textiles collected by Morgan.

The Parker home was in a measure the spot where a new American science was born. The family has ever felt responsible for recording and preserving the fame of its race. The store of old-time lore held by the older members of the family was made available by the education of Ely. Morgan and Parker, each in his turn, and using what opportunity he had, did his best to stimulate wider inquiry. The task undertaken by them has not yet been finished. The complete story of the Iroquois is yet to be written.

In after years other books were written in Nicholson Parker's home, among them, "The Iroquois, or the Bright Side of Indian Character," by Minnie Myrtle, and "Our

Life Among the Iroquois," by Harriet Caswell, not to speak of translations of hymn books, the Bible and a newspaper known as the *Mental Elevator*, published in the Seneca tongue.

Nicholson lectured through central New York for several years on the subject of the Iroquois, and his sons and grandchildren following his example have done what opportunity has called them to do in spreading the fame of the League of the Iroquois.

CHAPTER VIII

EARLY EXPERIENCE AS AN ENGINEER AND MASONIC CAREER

For several years Parker stayed near his home and was soon able to purchase a large estate near his father's land. His chief occupation, however, was that of superintending the improvements on the western terminal of the Erie Canal. This was invaluable training.

There are several persons who recollect having seen him engaged in running lines, laying out new feeders and carrying on his office work in Rochester. One man tells how Ely Parker could recognize a man's voice without seeing his face. "I was often sent down with verbal messages to deliver to Ely Parker," one informant says, "and would call out the message to him. He would keep his eyes riveted on his work and without ever turning to look at me would talk over the requirements, calling me by name. I always thought it strange that he could talk with his back to me, but he seemed to know what was going on behind him."

Parker's proximity to his people gave him an abundant opportunity for helping them in their national affairs, and he was rewarded for saving his people by being given, before he reached the age of twenty-one, the sachemship of the Senecas, when he became known as Do-ne-ho-ga-wa. This name means "Open Door" or "Keeper of the Western Door," and alludes to the fact that his office was to guard the western door of the Long House and mark well those who entered and passed out. The ancient laws required him to place, metaphorically, of course, the slabs of slippery elm bark at the threshold as the mat for the undesirable. Thus he became the most important officer in the Seneca council and one of the fifty civil sachems of the Iroquois confederacy.

For five years he held the office of resident engineer at Rochester, where he had many friends. During this time he kept up an active interest in his farm, raised his colts and looked after his parents. To add to his many duties he was appointed United States interpreter, and always accompanied the agent on his trips. The office had previously been held by Dr. Peter Wilson.

Nicholson and Carrie in the meantime were completing their courses in the Albany Normal School, where Nick won some little fame as an orator. Many of his essays and orations remain to tell of his attempts at platform-speaking. He discussed many subjects, but his longest discourses were always on Indian topics. After graduation he returned to Tonawanda to manage his farm and to look after his brother Ely's estate. Ely's special injunction was always, "Take care of the colts." He had inherited his father's love of horses and always wanted a fine span of lively colts for his personal use.

The Tonawanda Indians at this time were in a most peculiar position. By the "treaty" of 1838, which was obtained by fraud and bribery, the New York Senecas had parted with every foot of ground they had in New York. The Tonawandas had steadfastly refused to consider any treaty and had no part in the transaction. Later, in 1842, a compromise treaty was signed by President Martin Van Buren. The earlier treaty compensated the Senecas for their 114,862 acres of land at the rate of about $1.67 an acre and gave them certain tracts of land in Kansas. The treaty of 1842, however, allowed the Indians to stay in their old home country, providing they would accept the Allegheny and Cattaraugus reservations and give up Buffalo and Tonawanda. All the chiefs signed the treaty except those at Tonawanda. They refused to a man, either to be bribed or bought out. Moreover, when their kinsmen signed away their land they refused to acknowledge the right, asserting the doctrine of "state rights." The order came for them to move on, either to Kansas or to one of the other reservations that still had the yoke of the Ogden "claim" hitched to it. Their hearts were bitter and they refused to move from their homes. They were allowed to remain, since it was thought some means for ejecting them could be found. With this threat of sudden ejectment hanging over them the Tonawanda Senecas lived in constant fear. It was a fear that paralyzed effort and gave but scanty encouragement to industry or improvement. They lived in an atmosphere of constant suspense. But one ambition animated them. It was to get a deed by purchase for the land that was theirs. In that lay their only salvation.

The Tonawandas had learned several things and one was that the usurpation of their government by the war chiefs had brought great harm. They therefore repudiated the military chiefs and gave their government into the hands of the ancient *ho-ya-neh* or sachems, together with their assistants. To illustrate how far the Senecas had departed from their ancient laws it is only necessary to show the entire nation situated on the four reservations, submitted to an unstable rule by eighty-one chiefs; instead of the eight constituted by the ancient law of the confederacy. Any man who would get out and by power of fist, bribery or through force of personality, collect a following could be a "chief." This was veritable anarchy and was made good use of by the "land-grabbers." The Tonawandas alone were conservative and clung to the higher ideals of the old way.

In 1855 Ely Parker, or Do-ne-ho-ga-wa, as he was known to both the whites and Indians, was appointed chief engineer on the Chesapeake & Albemarle canal. He left his home and went to his southern post. His brother Nick, or Gai-wa-go-wa, had married Martha Hoyt, the niece of the Wrights who were the American Board missionaries at Buffalo and later at Cattaraugus.

Ely Parker laid out all the preliminary surveys for the new canal, made the final draft, and even chose the final location for the canal. His success kept him active as superintendent of the construction for several months longer. It did not hold him, however, for the Government needed engineers, and the Secretary of the Treasury, Guthrie, offered him the position of constructing engineer for the Lighthouse District composed of Lakes Huron, Michigan and Superior. This work was a new variation, but he was uniformly successful in the new task, holding the title Major, since the task was for military purposes.

These isolated positions in a rough country and amid crude surroundings were not always to Parker's taste. He loved occasional society and would frequently attend local social functions where he could mingle with cultured people. At one time while on the Chesapeake & Albemarle assignment, he had an office at Fortress Monroe, Virginia. The monotonous evenings palled on him and when some of his companions proposed that they all go to the grand ball at Norfolk, he was one of the first to push the proposition. When the uninvited party was about to enter the ball-room the floor manager stepped before the door and refused them admission. In vain did they argue—all except Parker; he acted. Stepping up to the offending manager he grasped him by the seat of the trousers and by the nape of the neck; carrying him a few steps to the stairs he held the terrified man over the abyss and then dropped him. Turning quietly as if nothing had happened, he entered the ball-room and had an enjoyable evening with his party. "The gentlemen as well as the ladies were very courteous," he confessed in later years when he was pressed for the story.

Parker was phenomenally strong but seldom used this power to injure anyone. He was as gentle as he was strong when made indignant by insult that concerned others more than himself. His great expanse of chest gave him lung power as well as muscles to sustain his arm action.

During his stay in Illinois it is said he was pounced upon by a hotel-keeper who sought to push him into the street. The inn-keeper's wife who tells the story says the Indian shook her husband loose and grabbing him by the shoulders swung him around in a circle until her husband's body lay straight out in the air like a rope and his heels swept over the bar or knocked against the wall. She interceded and Parker set the inn-keeper down. Later they became good friends but whenever Parker came to see them he would laughingly grab his new friend and give him another swing, "just for old time's sake."

Parker once said he was afraid to use his strength for he did not know what the results would be. "A man came up to me in a hotel in Buffalo," he once related by way of illustration, "and after looking at me a moment made a grab for me as if he wanted to wrestle. I did not want to hurt him and so I grabbed him by the upper arms and held them firmly. Suddenly he let out a peculiar yell, so strange that I let go of him. A few days later he came back to the hotel and asked for me. I met him in the lobby and he said, 'I want to speak to you.' I thought he wanted to fight and so I loosened my neckerchief so he could not twist it and choke me. He started to take off his broad-cloth coat. The old cloth was torn in a few places where I had pinched him and both his arms were black. He said, 'I want to show you how you abused me. I could not move my arms without great pain for two days. I think you ought to give me something.' I felt sorry for him for his arms looked very bad, and I had spoiled his coat. I made up my mind to be careful after that."

In 1857 Parker was appointed superintendent of construction for a custom-house and a marine hospital in Galena, Illinois. Here he became acquainted with the clerk in the harness store and often had long "talks" with him, though the clerk did most of the talking. They became quite friendly especially after Parker had rescued the clerk from a serious predicament due to the "overflowing bowl." The harness shop clerk was Captain Ulysses S. Grant.

Parker found great comfort in his love of Free-masonry. Back in 1847, he had been "raised," as Masons say, in Batavia Lodge, No. 88. Later he affiliated with Valley Lodge, No. 109, of Rochester. This was on May 6, 1850. He became immediately active in Galena and with a few Masons that he found there, he became one of the founders of Miners Lodge, No. 273. He demitted from his home lodge September 6, 1858, and became the first Worshipful Master of Miner's Lodge in Galena. He was a member of both the Royal Arch and of the Knights Templar and his love of Masonry as well as his popularity with his fellowmen is shown in that he was Worshipful Master of Miner's Lodge in 1858-'59-'60, and M. E. High Priest of Jo Daviess Chapter of the Royal Arch in 1859-'60-'61. He was elected Grand Orator of the Grand Lodge of Illinois in 1861 but his duties as a Government engineer prevented his accepting the honor. In 1860, he was, however, grand representative near the Grand Lodge of Illinois.

Among the distinguished men of his time who were initiated into Masonry by Parker was General J. C. Smith. General Smith in writing of this in the *Masonic Chronicle* says:

May 25, 1861, Brother Parker as Worshipful Master of Miner's Lodge, No. 273, raised the Venerable Chief of this Masonic Veterans'

Association to the sublime degree of Master Mason, having previously made him an Entered Apprentice and a Fellow Craft Mason. March 15, 1860, having at various dates conferred other degrees as High Priest of Jo Daviess Chapter, No. 51, he exalted the venerable chief to the Holy Royal Arch; hence, Do-ne-ho-ga-wa, the Six Nations Brother Ely S. Parker, was my father in Free Masonry.

Brave and eloquent as was Red Jacket, so was our veteran brother. Of the bravest of the brave, tender and loving as a woman, courteous as a Chevalier Bayard, the soul of honor and integrity, he, too, was an orator who would have been deemed worthy of Grecian prizes. [1]

General Smith refers to the oration delivered by Parker at the Masonic banquet in Chicago in 1859. Ely Parker spoke of himself as almost the last of what once was a powerful and noble people, of his struggle in early manhood of seeing his race disintegrating; and he asked:

Where shall I go when the last of my race shall have gone forever? Where shall I find home and sympathy when our last council fire is extinguished? I said, I will knock at the door of Masonry and see if the white race will recognize me as they did my ancestors when we were strong and the white man weak. I knocked at the door of the Blue Lodge and found brotherhood around its altar. I knelt before the great light in the Chapter and found companionship beneath the royal rock. I entered the Commandery and found valiant Sir Knights willing to shield me here without regard to race or nation. I went further. I knelt at the cross of my Saviour and found Christian brotherhood, the crowning charity of the Masonic tie. I am most happy to meet you in the grand councils of this gathering. and sit with you at this festive board to share these greetings and hospitalities.

I feel assured that when my glass is run out and I shall follow the footsteps of my departed race, Masonic sympathies will cluster round my coffin and drop in my grave the evergreen acacia, sweet emblem of a better meeting. If my race shall disappear from this continent, I shall have the consoling hope that our memory will not perish. If the deeds of my ancestors shall not live in story, their memories remain in the names of your great lakes and rivers, your towns and cities to call up memories otherwise forgotten.

---

1. Vol. 16, No. 2, Columbus, Ohio, Nov., 1896.

His address concluded in a like strain and one of his auditors[2] records: "Silence reigned as our brother sat down, eyes were dimmed and hearts were too full for speech."

Later Parker became a charter member of Akron Lodge, No. 257, near his birthplace, and became its first Worshipful Master. A portrait of him hangs in the lodge room today.

---

2. Gen. J. C. Smith.

CHAPTER IX

HOW PARKER'S ENLISTMENT WAS REFUSED BY SECRETARY SEWARD

When the first rumors of a clash between the North and the South were heard, Ely Parker was interested. His country was in trouble and his natural instinct was to fight for it. However, he could not easily abandon his work on the levees of the Mississippi and he was prevailed upon to stay for "the war would last but a few months at most."

His friend, Captain Grant, however, recruited a regiment and was later ordered to the front. He was commissioned Brigadier-General and much was heard about his work below Cairo, especially his capture of Fort Henry. The war dragged on and Parker resolved to resign his position and go back to Tonawanda, get his father's consent to "go to war," and then tender his services to the Governor of New York. He resigned absolutely in 1862 and went back home. His father was glad to see him but was worried when he told why he had come.

"Father," he said in his native tongue, "I think I ought to fight for my country just as you did years ago. I want you to let me go."

"My son," said the old man, "I have only my children now, since your mother has gone. I will think it over and tell you tomorrow."

In telling about the incident later Parker said, "The next morning my father told me to go, he said that I ought to go. I don't think he slept much, judging from his looks."

It is related that when Ely showed his father a picture of the army officers and a drawing of one of the battle scenes, as illustrated in *Harper's Weekly*, that William, his father, looked at the portraits carefully and then placing his finger on that of Grant's said: "Here is the man who will be the great general who shall lead his army to victory. You follow him and you will be a great war captain, too."

It is interesting to note that both Newton, who already had enlisted, and Ely asked their father's permission to go into battle. They were men and independent of their father, yet they respected him, and like dutiful sons of the Seneca, asked their sire's blessing on their project.

There was a great deal of talk about Ely's going to war. Some of the old women thought he ought to lay aside his title as sachem, for no Iroquois sachem of the "Great Peace" could ever enter battle, bearing his title. Others thought it was a white man's war and that he need not abdicate his sachemship. So they feasted him and made speeches in his honor and sent him on to the Governor of the State.

He arrived in Albany full of ambition and high in hopes. In full confidence he went to the Governor and asked for a commission, mentioning his experiences as an engineer. The Governor looked at him and said that he had no place for him and that he had much better go home. Parker was stunned at his rebuff but went back to Rochester to consult his friends there. He was still determined to go to the front. While there he met Mr. W. W. Wright, an old acquaintance who in after years recorded his impression of him at this time. Mr. Wright's statements are not entirely correct in some instances but in general his narrative is good. It runs as follows:

> Some seven or eight years before the commencement of the Rebellion I met Colonel Parker at the old Mansion House, Albany, which stood upon the ground now occupied by the crockery store of Van Heusen Charles & Company. It so happened that this gathering included some of the most noted politicians and brilliant orators of the State. Among others I remember Judge Church, Attorney

General, and ex-speaker Levi S. Chatfield, ex-Senator Orville Clark of Sandy Hill, and the man of all others most at home on such occasions, General James W. Nye. It was a happy affair and a great success. Its incidents were remembered and discussed for years afterwards by those who participated in this "feast of reason and flow of soul."

All the distinguished men I have named, and many others, were called out, and delivered appropriate and entertaining speeches, but the speech of the evening that called forth on its delivery the most vociferous applause, and was best remembered after the event has passed, came from an unexpected quarter. It was made by Ely S. Parker, the Indian, and everybody was surprised and delighted. He had just come from some school (which I do not remember),[1] and this was probably the first occasion for airing his oratory. It was certainly his first appearance in such distinguished company, and he might well be proud of his triumph in such a place. But his modesty and good taste were as conspicuous as the wit and intellectual features of his speech.

He had just chosen the profession of civil engineering, and was already employed upon the construction and enlargements of our canals. At that date the railroads attracted little attention, and engineers almost universally sought employment upon the canals of New York, Pennsylvania and the newer states of the West, like Ohio, Indiana and Illinois. Nobody then believed that the railroads, which then occupied but a few hundred miles leading to and from our most populous cities, through the richest and most densely settled portions of the country . . . would ever so completely supersede our waterways . . .

Of course I was attracted to Parker by his extraordinary speech, and watched his career with special interest. But he did not happen to be employed where I often met him, and we barely kept up a speaking acquaintance, and after a few years he disappeared from our canals altogether.

I had almost forgotten him till the first or second year of the Rebellion when I met him in the streets of Rochester. I asked where he had been and whether he had abandoned his profession. He informed me he had not, but left the service of the State to take a position under the Government, on the Mississippi, and that he had located at Galena.

---

1. Parker had been "out of school" for several years and had considerable experience in public speaking. He had many times before appeared in Albany as well as in society circles in Washington. Mr. Wright errs therefore, in assuming this as the entrance of Ely Parker into polite society.

After a pleasant chat he asked me if I had ever known Captain Grant, and I replied in the negative, but said that there was such an officer, a few years earlier, in command of the barracks at Sacketts Harbor. I owned and occupied a farm a few miles from that post, and generally knew the officers, but this one I never met, though I had often heard of him. Colonel Parker said he had become well acquainted with him, that he had rejoined the army, and he added in substance, "I shall go with him. He is a most extraordinary man. We are about the enter upon the most gigantic war in history. The country has many experienced and able military leaders, and most of them will be found on the Union side, but not one of them will be found capable of dealing successfully with this terrible rebellion unless it be this Captain Grant. Now recollect my prophecy:

He will come forth as the great central figure of the loyal states and will win a name and a fame which has no parallel in modern times."[2]

Writing from casual conversation, I can hardly do justice to the manner and the matter of Parker's singular estimate of the coming hero. But in view of General Grant's subsequent career and achievements, I never forgot his prediction, which if not inspired, deserved to be recorded as a singularly correct estimate of those qualities required of the great leader of the Union armies, and the discovery that they were all to be found in the then obscure ex-Army Captain.[3]

From Rochester, Parker went down to Washington to offer his services as engineer to the War Department. He was yet full of enthusiasm and filled with high hopes of becoming a real help in a time of trouble. All his education and training had fitted him for an army engineer.

In full confidence, therefore, the young engineer called upon Secretary William H. Seward and offered to give his services to the Union. Parker later records his reply.

"Mr. Seward in a short time said to me that the struggle in which I wished to assist, was an affair between white men and one in which the Indian was not called to act.

---

2. This was his father's prophecy made to Gen. Parker when he went home to ask his parent's consent to enlist.

3. From a letter from Hon. W. W. Wright, dated Geneva, N. Y., June 15, 1888.

'*The fight must be settled by the white men alone,*' he said. 'Go home, cultivate your farm and *we will settle our own troubles without any Indian aid.*'" (The italics are the author's because of later developments.)

Parker does not record how he felt, but it is easy to imagine his feelings after having lost his old home through a fraudulent treaty; after having been denied admission to the legal profession and after having been rebuffed by the Secretary of War—all because he was an Indian. Many a man would have said: "The white man's country can go to Liberia if it wants to. I won't worry over it." But he did not say even that though he had resigned a splendid position and staked his all on getting a commission.

He simply obeyed what seemed the only recourse. He went back to the farm, heard the jeers of his rivals, heard of the success of other Indians. of Dr. Wilson who had become an army surgeon, and of three hundred Seneca volunteers who had gone to the front. And yet *he* was not wanted because this was a white man's war that could be settled without Indian help!

So he donned his blue jeans, cleared his land, pulled stumps, painted his barns and plowed his fields. It must not be forgotten that he planted a flag pole, too, and floated a big starry banner.

He never talked much except when he had something important to say and thus he settled down to the routine of farm life and breeding horses. His father was glad to have such help, but sorry to hear his son called a failure by his people. This did not matter, for he stood an upright man before God and man. A man naturally proud and accustomed to honors, who knows what emotions raged in his breast? Who knows of the tumult there? Or who knows but that in his native philosophy he was as inwardly calm as he was outwardly? Iroquois philosophy is strange philosophy to modern Americans in our day and it may be safe to say that his spirit was at peace with itself, whatever ambitions it might have had.

"The fight must be settled by white men alone," must have been a sentence that sounded strangely in his ears as it rang in his memory again and again. With three hundred of his kinsmen in the smoke of the 'white man's war' it seemed as if he alone were not a white man and he alone the only Indian. And it may be that he inwardly gloried in the apparent fact that he alone was the Indian.

The weeks came and went and he worked with his ponies and his wheat fields, his corn and his repairing. For recreation he hunted and fished as when a boy and it is believed he actually enjoyed it, for it was the life he loved most of all—the life on the farm, in the open, on the soil of his fathers, and amid simple surroundings. The only bitterness, if there were such, was the whispered insult, "He can't be much of a man to be refused by the army." He heard this but said nothing, looking only sadly at the thoughtless comrade who taunted him.

As he was plowing for the spring planting, a horseman was seen galloping down the road. It was a military officer. He stopped a moment at the house and then cantered down the road to the field where Parker was plowing. Those who peered curiously down the road saw the officer hand Parker a document which when opened showed a big red seal that was plainly visible at a distance.

CHAPTER X

A SACHEM BECOMES A WARRIOR

During the progress of the Civil War, *Harper's Weekly* was a most eagerly read news source in the Parker home. Three or four times a week those who went to Akron or Batavia brought the newspapers and other periodicals, and thus Parker, once constructing engineer, and now farmer, gleaned the news and viewed the pictures of the war. He had watched the career of Grant from the time he won the first great victory of the war at Fort Donaldson, winning the name "Unconditional Surrender Grant." He had read of Bull Run and of Father Abraham's call for volunteers, but he felt he at least was denied the right to join the chorus of the army song, "We are coming, Father Abraham, three hundred thousand strong." Father Abraham's secretary had turned him away. Fredericksburg and Murfreesboro had passed into history and the Emancipation Proclamation had been hurled at the South. The city of New Orleans had been taken and war and adventure were everywhere making men martyrs or heroes. Then came the campaigns in the East, when Hooker crossed the Rapidan to march on to Richmond. News came of the disastrous fight at Chancellorville, in which Stonewall Jackson fell and Hooker was wounded and unable to command his ranks. Here were chances for trained men. Why didn't they want one more engineer? Had Grant forgotten him, and where were the rest?

The Indian nodded at the flag that flapped at the top of the pole in front of his home and then went to the barn to hitch his horses for plowing. Chief, though he was, he grasped the plow and with a farmer's skill and an engineer's eye he turned over furrow after furrow of the good brown sod, in lines as straight as a rule. After all, if there were no cornfields there could be no battlefields. The farmers had to grow the food that soldiers ate; and so with his native philosophy ever ready, Parker simply plowed as an expression of his patriotism and duty.

It would be interesting to know what he was thinking about when the horse galloped down the road. It would be interesting to know what he thought when he saw the military costume of the rider. We do not know. We only know that he stopped his horses in the furrow, took the document that was handed him and read it. The paper must have been full of interest and brought with it a denial of the galling words of Seward.

"Then came to me in my forest home a paper bearing the red seal of the War Department," wrote Parker of the incident afterward. "It was an officer's commission in the army of the United States."

This commission is said to have been signed by Lincoln himself, and transmitted through the Secretary of War. It brought with it the rank of Captain. "It seemed odd," Captain Parker once wrote, "that an Indian was now desired and that the Government wished to confer honors for which I had not served an apprenticeship, nor even asked."

On June 4, 1863, the commission was formally accepted and the newly-made army officer made ready to go to war. It was then that the Indians held a great council and asked their chief to remain to guide and protect them. A great feast was made in his honor and Do-ne-ho-ga-wa was commended to the care of the Great Spirit. A public thanksgiving was offered, thanking the Ruler of the Great-World-Above that the Keeper-of-the-Western Door had indeed guarded it well. The "Proclaimers of the Law" chanted the *Adoweh* ritual and the Keepers of the Faith invoked the spirits to guard the sachem who was to go to battle.

Scoffers were silent and rivals were glad to sound the common praise.

Nothing has been said of an Indian maiden who was to wait until the war was over, but there was one who listened to the praise of the sachem, but as the war wore on did not wait. Like many things the soldier lost through sacrifice, Parker lost that which perhaps was best for anyone to lose before it is too late to lose—a faithless sweetheart. But even this philosophy has never brought comfort for violated faith, trust and confidence; every balm but irritates the open wound. Perhaps it is well we can not foreknow the acts of our friends; it would make us bitter many times.

Captain Parker reported to General J. E. Smith as assistant adjutant general. The army record shows that he acted as division engineer of the 7th division, 17th army corps, until September 18, 1863, "And," said General Smith, "he was a good engineer."

He joined Grant at Vicksburg, and entered that terrific long-drawn-out contest raw but eager and as stoical as any of his ancestors would have been. Vicksburg and its surroundings were anything but similar to the peaceful valley and the quiet farm "up North" that he had so suddenly abandoned only a bare month before. He faced the bullets, apparently with the disregard of a seasoned veteran. He followed Grant closely, he stood quietly under fire and rode with the troops where bullets were thickest. When the steamboat explosion occurred he stood as unconcerned as Grant himself, though in mentioning the event in later years he said, "Though Grant acted as if he never heard it, I noticed some appeared greatly startled and that even 'old Baldy' walked a little faster than usual."

In writing to his brother Nicholson he said: "I fear no rebel bullet shot or shell in a fair fight, and to tell you my honest conviction, I do not believe I am to be killed in the war."

Then to explain how he was received in the army he tells his brother Nicholson of his commission:

"My official experience in the army as an adjutant is checkered, or as some would say, singular. When I received my appointment, the Secretary of War ordered me to report to General John E. Smith. He was delighted to receive me, and made it very pleasant for me. I was getting on swimmingly when orders came for me to report to Major-General Grant, and he put me on his staff."

Just why Parker was placed on Grant's staff is explained by General Horace Porter, who says in his book: "He commended himself to Grant by his conduct in the Vicksburg campaign and was then placed on his staff and served in the Adjutant General's Department."

Parker had the power of concentrating his mind on the plan immediately before him and thus although often in the thickest of the fight he rode his horse as easily as if he neither heard nor saw the things that make war so hideous. Whether lack of fear is true bravery or not is a question, but like Grant, whom he so much admired, Parker would face the music of battle as if it were all a game.

At Vicksburg he caught the fever and ague and tried to break it with the usual remedy of whiskey and quinine, and quinine sometimes was scarce even in headquarters. However, the remedy gave temporary relief but not until he had suffered severely with the malady. In the journey by gunboat from Vicksburg to Cairo, Parker was constantly under an army physician's care and the doctor told him afterward he "sure was a sick Indian."

The Vicksburg campaign gave him a taste of real war and he proved his mettle. Then followed the campaign of Chattanooga with its bloody battles and thousands of slain. All through the campaign he was with Grant and in one of his letters he tells of riding with the commander for half a mile directly under the enemy's fire. A delay had cut the staff from headquarters.

The transfer from one division to another was full of incidents for the Indian warrior who was acting in the capacity of adjutant. Of one he writes:

"In October, 1863, in going from Bridgeport, Alabama, to Chattanooga, Tennessee, to assume command of the Military Division of the Tennessee, General Grant halted for lunch on the summit of the mountains he was crossing. A sleet-storm was raging, compelling him to step into a log cabin for temporary shelter. This cabin had one large square room, used for sleeping-room, sitting-room and dining-room, and also as a kitchen, or cooking-room. Here he found two or three women and several young children. They were all poorly and scantily clad; the furniture was mostly home-made, the bedding was scarce and the larder apparently empty. When asked where the husband and men folks were, the simple reply of the women was, 'Hiding in the mountains.' Alas for them, they were Unionists and to live at home was not safe. When asked if they had any provisions in the house the women replied, 'Yes, a little meal, but no meat.' The General's heart was touched; and although supplies were low and his soldiers were as his own children, he left them an order on any train-master passing on the way to Chattanooga with provisions, to leave for this family a barrel of flour and one-half barrel of pork."

At Lookout Mountain and Missionary Ridge Parker acquitted himself with honor, but like his forefathers, was silent when in the presence of others, unless he had something of value to communicate. Captain Beckwith in his memorial address [1] mentioned this quality and said that in

---
1. Publications, Buffalo Historical Society, vol. VIII, p. 515.

riding with him to the summit of Lookout Mountain, Parker scarcely uttered a word.

While at Nashville during January, 1864, the chills and fever came on again and the usual remedy was prescribed. Brady, the photographer, who was a good friend of Parker's, told with a great display of amusement just how the army "ague" remedy affected him. He is the authority for saying that after the medicine had taken effect, a series of loud war-whoops rang out and the Indian was seen chasing Bowers, one of the other adjutants, who was fleeing in apparent fear of his life. However, there was no bad feeling between the two, who were in fact great friends. In army days when medicine was not practiced as now, this effect of the ague remedy was common. In the years following the war Parker became an absolute teetotaler. During a severe illness his physician told him to take a dram of whiskey at certain intervals. "I will not use it," he said emphatically. "You must use it or you may die," said his doctor. "Well, if that is the case," he answered, "I shall still refuse. I do not have to take whiskey but I do have to die sooner or later." And so he refused—and lived, despite his doctor's warning.

Parker was often called upon to lay out a line of entrenchments and often made the surveys directly under fire. He was known everywhere in the Army of the Potomac as "the Indian" and as he rode upon his great black horse he was a conspicuous figure. In the operations about Richmond he was constantly engaged in the engineering.

The appointment of Grant as Lieutenant General in February, 1864, drew the army together and gave it new strength. Then began the operation of the Army of the Potomac which on April 30, 1864, numbered 92,000 men and 274 field guns. Against this force Lee opposed with only 64,000 men and 224 guns. Then began the campaign of the Wilderness and the endeavor to capture Richmond and the grimly determined announcement: "I propose to fight it out on this line if it takes all summer." Thus commenced the struggle in the tangled wilds. The country had been stripped of its virgin forest and had become a desolate region of stumps, underbrush and pitfalls.

On one of those rare occasions when he could be prevailed upon to talk of his army career, the General told of his adventures in the wilderness:

"As a matter of fact I was never concerned about getting killed in open battle," he said. "Bullets were flying through the air constantly but I got used to them. I even grew hardened to the sight of the dead and wounded on the field. I did not believe I was to be killed by a bullet and though I was under fire many a time I came through the war without a wound. My coat and hat got a few holes.

"When I was a young man I was fond of hunting and learned the art of woodcraft in all its minute details. I could track a deer even over the leaves. I developed the instinct to feel the presence of game or danger. Perhaps I had the good will of the spirits. This was useful to me oftentimes during battle or in the presence of danger. I distinctly remember the time while we were riding together —the whole staff, at Spottsylvania. It was one day when General Grant led out for a ride with General Meade; Rawlins and I were in the rear and Comstock was leading. I noticed that we were riding into the rebel line. I said to Rawlins, 'Where is the General going?' He answered, 'I don't know.' 'If he doesn't look out,' I told him, 'he will be in the rebel lines.'

"Then Rawlins roared out: 'Hey! General, do you know where you are?' (He always treated Grant like a dog.) 'No,' he replied, 'Comstock, do you?' 'No,' answered Comstock, 'but Parker says if you don't look out we will ride plumb into the rebel lines!'

"'Parker,' called Grant, 'do you know where we are?' I answered, 'Yes, General.' Grant then quickly said, 'Well, then lead.' I put spurs to my black horse and galloped off in another direction and they full tilt after me.

"After the battle I met a rebel captain whom we had captured and he said to me, 'Colonel, I wish to ask you about a certain incident. The other day I saw General Grant with General Meade and a party of which you were one riding into our lines. My men wanted to fire on you, but I said, 'Hold on, they will ride in and we can capture the whole lot.' Then I saw you ride up and say something to Grant and then your whole party galloped off in haste. You were within forty rods of us and we hoped to get you all in the next five minutes..[2]

"No, Grant did not give me credit for this incident. He got the circumstances mixed and gave the credit to Comstock in his memoirs. Never mind, I did not care to dispute about it. It was enough for me to know how the incident really happened. He did not write about it until twenty years later and during his last illness.

"At one time I was the commander of the Army of the Potomac. Every staff officer except myself was away from headquarters and all matters were left to me. There was no fighting yet. While I was stuck in my tent the rebels came over and made a raid on the cattle on the outposts. You see I made a poor General.

"Grant never cared much how he looked, but he did take care of his hat while riding. If a twig hit it and made a dent he would take it off and smooth it out. I think General Grant was a little proud of his riding. He would gallop off to meet some officer and dashing up would sud-

---

2. Related by Gen. Parker to Mr. J. F. Kelly, Mr. F. E. Parker and Mr. and Mrs. Frank Converse.

denly rein his horse and dismount before the horse had stopped.

"People seemed to have many queer recollections of Grant. I went with Grant on his tour after the war. I was often photographed with him. I remember a man coming up to me in a theatre. He said, 'I remember Grant when he worked in a tanyard, he worked as a clerk in his father's store.'

"General Grant was not a man who would stand profanity. He did not curse and often rebuked those who did."

Mr. J. T. Lockwood of White Plains, New York, often observed Parker during the Wilderness campaign and relates the following story:

"It was on May 30, 1864," says Mr. Lockwood, "when I was with my battery, the 4th New York Artillery, at Mechanicsville near Richmond. We arrived there early in the morning and were at once ordered to stack arms. This we did, the place being the Shelton farm.

"Orders were to grab a rail either from the fence or those piled in stacks, and to follow the officer on horseback and to drop the rails in the horse's tracks. This we did to outline the entrenchments. He simply galloped off in a straight line, made a turn or two and came back to the brick farmhouse. There was an orderly riding in his rear. The officer was Colonel Parker, whom we always called 'the Indian.' He was on Grant's staff and did much of the engineering work. When the Colonel returned I spoke to him for the first time, though I had often seen him. A strange battalion was only 500 yards in front of us and I asked a very natural question.

" 'Colonel,' I said, 'What corps is that over there?'

" 'Those are the Johnnies,' he replied. 'Take your shovel and get as busy as they are. They are doing the same thing we are. Better get some dirt in front of you.'

"I was only a common soldier but when I saw the Johnnies as near as that I worked that shovel uncommonly fast.

"Our battery supported the 4th United States Artillery and we were generally very close to Grant's headquarters. I had ample opportunity to observe Colonel Parker.

"When we were commencing the entrenchments some of the officers entered the Shelton house and requested the ladies to vacate. One of them had a small boy. 'We refuse to go,' they said emphatically and with a certain gleam of haughty arrogance. Then Mrs. Shelton came to the door and said, 'We shall not leave this house for my husband is in command of the troops over there and there is no danger of this house being fired upon.'

"Colonel Parker then said politely, 'Stay as long as you please, ladies, we shall not harm you.' Then turning to his officers, he roared, 'Throw up a redoubt directly back of this house and plant a battery there!'

"It was a clever bit of strategy for that battery did unmerciful work and it was a long time before the rebels sent a shell in our direction.

"When Colonel Parker laid out breastworks or entrenchments he always rode alone except perhaps with an orderly. Whenever we saw him laying out fortifications we knew there was to be a big fight. We also knew that there was an event ahead when he or Meade began riding over the field from one headquarters to another.

"We always supposed 'the Indian' was one of Grant's chief engineers. Of course I didn't know because I was only one of the rank, although we always stuck to Grant's headquarters."

The many records show that during the movements of the Army of the Potomac, while Grant was at City Point, Colonel Parker was exceedingly busy. This is especially true after his appointment on August 30th, as Military

Secretary to Grant. As assistant Adjutant, however, he had his hands full and followed Grant very closely in all his moves.[3]

Much of Grant's correspondence was transcribed by Colonel Parker and during times of great pressure Grant entrusted the preparation of important letters, orders and reports to him, merely signing them with his name. Parker's command of English and his handwriting as well as his intimate knowledge of the campaign, eminently fitted him for these important tasks.

General Horace Porter in his book [4] writes of Colonel Parker's activities and tells among other incidents an amusing tale.

"Colonel Parker, the Indian," says General Porter, "had been diligently employed in these busy days helping take care of General Grant's correspondence. He wrote an excellent hand, and as one of the military secretaries often overhauled the General's private correspondence and prepared answers to his private letters. This evening he was seated at the writing table in the General's tent while his chief was standing at a little distance outside talking to some of his staff. A citizen who had come to City Point in the employ of the Sanitary Commission, and who had been in Cairo, when the General took command there in 1861, approached the group and inquired, 'Where is the old man's tent? I'd like to get a look at him; haven't seen him for three years.' Rawlins to avoid being interrupted said, 'That's his tent,' at the same time pointing to it. The man stepped over to the tent, looked in and saw the swarthy features of Parker as he sat in the General's chair. The visitor seemed a little puzzled, and as he

---

3. Some of his correspondence as found in the archives of the War Department shows the character of his work and its responsibility. The letters show the matter-of-fact way in which disaster or death was reported. Some of the letters, as paragraph sketches of the days of the last campaign are included in the appendix of this volume.

4. "Campaigning with Grant," page 207.

walked away was heard to remark: 'Yes, that's him; but he's got all-fired sun-burnt since I last had a look at him.'"

The General was greatly amused by the incident, and repeated the remark afterwards to Parker, who enjoyed it as much as the others.

The order for Colonel Parker's appointment came on August 30, 1864, and was announced by the War Department as below shown:

WAR DEPT., ADJT. GENERAL'S OFFICE.
WASHINGTON, D. C., August 30, 1864.

General Orders.
No. 249.

Capt. Ely S. Parker, assistant adjutant-general, U. S. Volunteers, is announced as private secretary on the staff of Lieutenant-General Grant, with the rank of Lieutenant-Colonel, vice W. R. Rowley resigned.

By order of the Secretary of War.

E. D. TOWNSEND,
Assistant Adjutant-General.

Colonel Parker from this time until long after the war ended was intimately associated with Grant and constantly at his side to receive and transmit his orders. His intimate knowledge of Grant's desires and policies made it possible for him to offer many suggestions. The fighting about Petersburg and the naval operations on the James river drew the enemy closer to the headquarters of Grant at City Point, which had no heavy guns to defend it. This led Colonel Parker to seek to bring about the adequate protection of Grant's immediate headquarters. Thus, Col. George H. Butler says, "It is suggested by Colonel Parker, of Grant's staff, that the same be reported to you, that a request be made to have such disposition made of the gunboats as will remedy the want of artillery here."

CHAPTER XI

THE FALL OF THE CONFEDERACY

During the years that followed the war Parker was often called upon to relate the incidents that came to his notice. To strangers and acquaintances he would uniformly reply, "Those who know nothing of war may like to hear of it in all its awful details, but to a man who has gone through it some visions are too shocking to recall. I had rather not discuss it with you."

It was only to the long-time friend that he would tell his war experiences, to his brother Nicholson or to an acquaintance who won his confidence and who could play billiards well. Parker was a great lover of the game and would seek to meet the best players wherever he went.

In the old farmhouse back on the Cattaraugus belonging to his brother he would, when visiting there, sometimes tell a tale or two to his nephews, grand-nephews and nieces. He would tell some of these stories in his native language which he mostly talked when he "went back home, to loosen up my tongue," as he would say. Thus it is from the tales he told there, about the hearth of his brother's home, for the recollections of his intimate friends and from the few papers that he left that we relate the story of Appomattox.

No attempt is made to picture the entire scene, for that work belongs to the historian. Our task is merely to examine the fragments that Colonel Parker left in writing or imprinted on the minds of his friends, and then to fit these fragments like a mosaic into the picture. If parts are missing it is because we cannot find them. And now we take up our task. Where we can quote exactly we shall do so.

The moral support given by one's countrymen counts much in giving a leader of men inspiration. Leaders often deport themselves upon occasions to draw the admiration of the men or people whose confidence they need in order to carry out their plans successfully, but this is a thing that Grant never did. Notwithstanding his successful campaigns Grant was not the idol of the North to the same degree that Lee was of the South. His very modesty, his simple manner and lack of demonstration caused many to think him dull and unappreciative. His dress was often disarranged and he preferred to take the labors given him like a soldier rather than to simulate the dignity of an officer. No one could deny, however, that Grant was a grimly determined leader, who from the beginning, had shown great capacity and resource. The months after the battle of Chattanooga had taxed every faculty and all through the severe trials that he underwent he exhibited great fortitude and skill. Indeed, his great tenacity during long seasons of disaster when his ranks were thinned by rebel shot, won the admiration of the country. He was the directing force of the army and planned many battles that his generals fought to success. Even Meade was constantly under his orders, though Meade commanded the Army of the Potomac.

Meade manifested many of the unselfish qualities of his leader and would have resigned his commission for lower rank if Grant would have allowed it. But Grant knew Meade. He understood his generals and knew their capacity. He also knew most of the Confederate leaders and knew how to oppose each at his weakest point. His career at West Point had given him an insight into their character and habits that was invaluable. But with all this he was not the hero of his nation as Lee was of the seceding states. Lee's fame was heralded all over the world and to the South he was the idol that it swore by. The North had yet to learn to swear by Grant.

From his headquarters at City Point, Grant continued to direct the campaign against Richmond, and his uniform success combined with the desperation of the Southern army, which was in an almost famished condition, began to cause grave fears throughout the South. There were many abortive plans to send spies into the Union lines to assassinate Grant and throw the army into disorder by removing its leader.

The headquarters camp was directly on the edge of the bluff that overlooked the Appomattox river on the south side at its confluence with the James. Grant's tent was simply arranged and his winter quarters were built of logs. He lived as simply as any of his officers and mingled freely with them. Rough benches were placed in a square about the front of Grant's hut and a cheerful camp-fire was kept blazing. About this fire the officers clustered, and here Colonel Parker was to be found always ready with his pen and manifold to take down dispatches. It was here that Colonel Parker mingled closely with the leaders of the Federal forces, and met the civil officials who came from Washington. Even Lincoln himself came down for long visits during the winter of '64 and '65. Often he would sit near Colonel Badeau or Colonel Parker and eagerly read the dispatches as they came in.

The entire military family of Grant shared a common table and both Grant and Lincoln dined together with the staff officers. Both Grant and Lincoln were absolutely frank and outspoken. They discussed with great freedom the dispatches that came in and the plans of the campaign, listening with courtesy to the suggestions or remarks of the officers of the staff.

It was during his stay during the winter at City Point that Parker had opportunity to discuss Indian affairs with both Grant and Lincoln. He outlined his plans for the betterment of conditions, condemned the treaty system and pleaded for the education of the young. Lincoln was most sympathetic, and said that he knew the red man had suffered awful injustice which he hoped the nation some day would requite.

Grant's men were absolutely loyal to him and were greatly concerned with his welfare. During the winter months early in '65 they often did sentinel duty outside his door in order to minister to his needs and guard against spies and assassins.

Colonel Parker relates that there was a feeling that the rebels would attempt either to assassinate or kidnap Grant, as they had Crook and Kelly. Often, therefore, Parker watched outside the door of the hut with his revolver ready for any suspicious character. Colonel Badeau has written in a detailed way the story of the precautions taken by the staff. Nevertheless the Confederates had once smuggled a spy into the camp armed with a clock-work bomb which was placed on the ordnance boat in the river below Grant's headquarters.

The war had reached its crisis and every precaution was taken to prevent panic of any sort in the Union ranks. The two armies, almost within speaking distance of each other's lines, faced in the last great struggle along the Appomattox. The closing days of March saw the beginning of the end. Sheridan had arrived from the South, Sherman came up the James from his quarters in North Carolina and President Lincoln came down from Washington, as if to see for himself the close of the fratricidal struggle. The City Point Headquarters were the scene of ceaseless activity. Every plan was laid to catch Lee like a rat in a trap. Grant's plan was to force Lee from his fortified position and then send Sheridan with his cavalry to hound his heels.

"I mean to end this business here," said Grant. And Fighting Phil smiled as he replied, "That's what I like to hear you say, General. Let's end this business here."

On the morning of March 29, Colonel Parker dispatched the following order to Gen Sheridan:

HEADQUARTERS, ARMIES OF THE UNITED STATES,
CITY POINT, VA., March 29, 1865.

Special Orders
No. 64

Maj. Gen. P. H. Sheridan, commanding Middle Military Division, will order the detachment of Company D, Fifth U. S. Cavalry, now serving with him to report immediately to these headquarters, wherever they may be, in the field.

By command of Lieutenant General U. S. Grant.

E. S. PARKER,
Acting Assistant Adjutant-General.

Sheridan's orders were to get at the enemy's rear and "force him out if possible. Should he come out and attack us," wrote Grant, "or get himself where he can be attacked, move in with your entire force in your own way and with the full reliance that the army will engage or follow as circumstances will dictate. I shall be on the field and will probably be able to communicate with you."

Colonel Bowers was then advised of the situation and the location of the corps commanders:

HEADQUARTERS, ARMY OF THE POTOMAC,
March 29th, 1865. (Recd. 9: P. M.)

Lieut. Col. T. S. BOWERS:

The two corps moved out, meeting with no serious opposition until quite late in the afternoon, when Griffin's division, of Warren's corps, struck the enemy and had quite a fight. Griffin captured about 100 of the enemy. His loss not reported. Warren promptly brought up his whole corps, and upon advancing he found that the enemy had retired to his main works. Humphrey met with no opposition in his advance. Warren's left is across the plank road. Humphrey's right is on Hatcher's. Sheridan is at Dinwiddie and no enemy to oppose him.

E. S. PARKER,
Lieutenant-Colonel, etc.

The Union forces now held without dispute the country from Appomattox to Dinwiddie Court-house. The heavy rains of the night, however, made traveling difficult. It did not dampen the ardor of the National army, though some minor plans were changed. Grant drew his generals into concert and then with a masterpiece of team play flung them at the Southern ranks. "We will all act together as one army until we can see what can be done with the enemy," wrote Grant to Sheridan.

On the 30th Sheridan was at Five Forks, a most important position. If Sheridan's cavalry could hold it Lee would be forced to retreat from his position at Petersburg. Dispatches soon came in that Lee was holding the roads about Five Forks; and to inform General Rawlins, Parker dispatched the following note:

HEADQUARTERS, ARMIES OF THE UNITED STATES,

March 30, 1865, 12:10 P. M.

Brig. Gen. JOHN A. RAWLINS:

GENERAL: A messenger just in from General Merritt says that the reconnaissance sent out from near Boisseau's encountered the enemy in considerable force. They went to about two miles of the Five Forks, and found the enemy occupying the road. Those going north proceeded to about a mile of the White Oak road, and found the road also occupied by the enemy. Nearly all the forces met were cavalry. All the roads leading toward the White Oak Road are covered by the enemy. No engagement reported.

E. S. PARKER,
Acting Assistant Adjutant-General.

The engagement at White Oak road came later. With the Union army pressing from every point Lee continued to resist as he retreated. Wright of the Sixth Corps and Parker of the Ninth, on April 2d expressed their confidence of breaking through Lee's lines. At daybreak with Ord they engaged the Confederates and carried Five Forks. Warren was ordered to advance following the cavalry and the Fifth Corps was to take a position at the enemy's left. The battle was a terrific one, and the Union cavalry suffered heavily. Sheridan won out, however, capturing 6,000 prisoners. Fitz-Hugh Lee and the brave Pickett were beaten. The good news was dispatched throughout the army. Petersburg had fallen! A letter to Meade from Parker tells of the vigilance and eagerness with which each move was regarded:

GRANT'S HEADQUARTERS,
April 2nd, 1865.

Major-General MEADE:

The following just received:

"*Brigadier-General* RAWLINS:

"General Sheridan desired me to inform you that the Second Corps is marching up the Boydton road toward Petersburg, and that Lee and his forces are moving in this direction. We have come up to their rear guard, about two miles on the Claiborne road from their works in front of that road, probably; but few stragglers.

P. T. HUDSON, *Aide-de-Camp*, 11 A. M.

"Miles has carried all the main work on the Claiborne road. We are following the enemy up that road. The enemy evacuated the works about 10 o'clock. Will send particulars as soon as heard.

P. T. HUDSON, *Aide-de-Camp*."

(Signed) E. S. PARKER,
Lieutenant-Colonel and Acting Assistant Adjutant General.

Events followed fast upon one another and on the morning of April 3d the Union Army entered Richmond and once again the starry banner floated over the rebel capitol. Bands played Yankee airs and the city rang with the shouts of the successful army. Then the city was brought to order by Grant and all plundering and rioting stopped.

Grant now arranged his divisions to tighten about the Army of northern Virginia. Sheridan was in the advance, then came Meade with Wright and Humphreys, who had been detailed by the following command:

HEADQUARTERS, ARMIES OF THE UNITED STATES,

SUTHERLAND'S STATION, April 3, 1865.

Major-General HUMPHREYS,
Commanding Second Corps:

You will hereafter report to Major-General Meade, commanding Army of the Potomac, for orders. On the morrow, however, you will follow the route of march designated for you by General Sheridan.

By Command of Lieutenant-General Grant.

E. S. PARKER,
Lieutenant-Colonel and Acting Assistant Adjutant-General.

HEADQUARTERS, ARMIES OF THE UNITED STATES,

April 3rd, 1865.

Major-General MEADE,
Commanding Army of the Potomac:

You will furnish to General Humphreys the rations called for by him at the earliest moment possible, in accordance with your suggestion of 9.15 this evening. Inclosed are orders for General Humphreys to report to you hereafter, except that on to-morrow he will follow the route of march designated for him by General Sheridan.

By Command of Lieutenant-General Grant.

E. S. PARKER,
Lieutenant-Colonel and Acting Assistant Adjutant-General.

P. S.—Please forward to General Humphreys the order by one of your officers.

The Southern Army, routed at Five Forks, Petersburg and Richmond, was fleeing with fifty thousand troops. Lee hoped to draw Grant after him and cause the Union Army to abandon its entrenched position and pursue from the rear. Grant, however, sent his army to the south side of the Appomattox to head off Lee and hem him from further advance. Lee's hope was to unite with Johnson. But Sherman was pressing close and that brave leader, ordering the Fifth Corps to entrench across the railroad, cut off all supplies from Lee's famished army.

Grant was marching with his army and Colonel Parker followed his chief and saw the high spirits of the men who everywhere cheered the Commander-in-chief as he rode through the lines. The cordon was rapidly drawing about Lee and the men were enthused at the successful moves that moment by moment were putting the rebel army in sore straits. Finally there came a dispatch from Sheridan telling of Lee's distress at Amelia Court House. The next day Lee fled from Amelia and took up flight on the roads leading to the southwest. The Confederate soldiers were actually starved out and their horses famishing, the spring grass not yet being sufficient for forage. Blow after blow was delivered by the Union corps and each time a victory was won. Lee's army was depleted fifty per cent. by the battles of the first seven days of March, and nearly a quarter of his troops had deserted. Lee held to the last hope but his officers pressed him to surrender. Further resistance only meant unnecessary bloodshed and needless suffering. That the power of the Army of Northern Virginia was gone was seen only too clearly. Even the discipline of the troops was relaxed and the line straggled along in disconnected, discouraged groups; but when the Union bullets sang into their ranks they doggedly turned and blazed back as only desperate men can.

Grant saw their pitiful plight on April 7th and dispatched a letter from Farmville to Lee. The message was in these words:

GENERAL:—The results of the last week must convince you of the hopelessness of further resistance on the part of the Army of Northern Virginia in this struggle. I feel that it is so, and regard it as my duty to shift from myself the responsibility of any further effusion of blood, by asking of you the surrender of that portion of the Confederate States' army known as the Army of Northern Virginia.

U. S. GRANT, *Lieutenant-General.*

Lee in his reply denied that further resistance on his part was useless, but agreed that further bloodshed should be avoided if possible. Lee inquired for terms, but Grant did not allow this parley to interfere with his strategic movements, for no truce had been declared or sought. Sheridan pushed across the Appomattox, carrying his cavalry with the Army of the James and the Fifth Corps. Humphreys and Wright kept hammering at the fleeing Southern lines, but on the 9th of April halted at Appomattox Court House, where Lee displayed a white flag. Custer in the previous day had captured the supply trains of the enemy and Sheridan was opposing the rebel front. Lee was in a desperate position and must have been in a disturbed mental state when he wrote Grant explaining his stand. "In mine of yesterday," he wrote, "I did not intend to propose to surrender the Army of Northern Virginia but to ask the terms of your proposition. To be frank, I do not think the emergency has arisen to call for the surrender of this army. . . . I can not therefore meet you with a view to surrender the Army of Northern Virginia. . . ." The day before he had asked the terms of surrender, but this was when he was pursued by Crooks and his baggage trains were burning in his rear. With the open country before him, as he thought, there was hope, and supplies ahead, for he did not know he was marching directly into Sheridan's cavalry lines.

Grant saw through the entire situation and ignoring Lee's illogical stand simply wrote: "The terms upon which peace can be had are well understood. By the South laying down their arms they will hasten that most desirable event, save thousands of human lives and hundreds of millions of property not yet destroyed."

Grant then hastened to join Sheridan while Ord marched his men for twenty-one hours. Lee began attacking Sheridan, who moved back gradually giving Ord a chance to form his line and march forward to attack. Then the Union armies closed in on Lee. His broken but defiant army was completely hemmed in and at the mercy of the grimly determined Union forces. Then Sheridan seemed to give way and the rebel ranks gave their last battle yell as they rushed into the opening. Then a fresh infantry line burst upon them. The Southern lines broke. Sheridan swung to the left and drew up for a charge upon the disorganized ranks before him. The men were ready, but the charge was never made. Lee sent forward a white flag and requested that hostile action cease, pending a conference with General Grant. Sheridan was suspicious and feared treachery, since Lee had previously declined to discuss terms. The truce seemed like a plan to refresh the rebel troops or await re-inforcements. Sheridan rode over to the Court House where he found that negotiations for surrender were pending.

Lee saw his position plainly. Sheridan with Ord and Griffin opposed his advance; Meade with Wright and Humphreys attacked his rear and there was no avenue for flight. Lee's message to Grant was: "I received your note of this morning on the picket line whither I had come to meet you and ascertain definitely what terms were embraced in your proposals of yesterday with reference to the surrender of the army. I now ask an interview in accordance with the offer contained in your letter of yesterday, for that purpose."

Meanwhile, Lee sought to inform Meade of the proposal and to expedite matters allowed a Union officer to be escorted through the Confederate lines. Grant was with Sheridan and received Lee's letter ten minutes before noon. He immediately wrote out his reply, agreeing to meet Lee and discuss the terms of surrender. Colonel Babcock hastened back with the reply, going through the rebel lines under escort by a Confederate officer.

Grant had "made good." "He was closing this business right here."

The jubilant officers forgot their fatigue, their travel and battle stains and galloped off to meet the Southern general who had eluded them so long.

CHAPTER XII

THE INDIAN IN THE DRAMA AT APPOMATTOX

General Lee had chosen the McLean farm-house, which stood on one side of a knoll that overlooked the valley where both armies lay stretched out for miles. Parker often spoke to his friends of that vision that stretched out before him as he rode up to the McLean house with Grant and his staff. There was a word or two of explanation from Sheridan who still doubted Lee's sincerity and then Grant approached the house. Lee came to the door and greeted Grant. Lee had with him his Military Secretary, Colonel Marshall; and with Grant were Bowers, Babcock and Parker. There followed the other officers of the Union forces, among whom were Sheridan, Ord and Porter; Meade was twenty miles away.

In describing the room chosen for the interview General Parker said that most of the furnishings had been removed, such as pictures and bric-a-brac, although some brass candlesticks were on a small table. "There were two stands, a mantle-piece, a book-case and several chairs, perhaps five, of the old-fashioned hair-cloth style. On the long sofa sat General Porter; Colonel Badeau sat to his right, then Williams and General Rawlins, who occupied the right end. Grant sat at a small oval table and Lee took his seat at a square-topped stand. The rest of us sat, or stood where it was most convenient. We had no form about it. I went to one side because of the light. Not everyone could find seats. General Lee sat near the front window to the left and near Colonel Marshall, who was the only Confederate besides Lee in the room.

"Everyone removed his hat upon entering and Grant placed his upon the floor or perhaps the table. Lee was dressed in a splendid new uniform and wore a handsome saber. Marshall was dressed in a similar way. Colonel Marshall was a rather fine-looking gentleman with light hair. He wore spectacles, as also did General Lee.

"Grant wore boots and had on a belted blouse, beneath an army coat. He wore no sword and apologized to Lee for not wearing it, as he was afraid he might think it a discourtesy. No, he did not lose his sword, but it had been mixed with the baggage and sent off.

"Lee began talking about the Mexican War and other reminiscences. He seemed composed but was quite stiff in his dignity. Grant seemed relaxed but as he smoked he was thinking hard. Then Lee said he presumed that both he and Grant had carefully considered the terms suggested by Grant. Grant then looked at Lee and said, 'Do I understand, General Lee, that you will accept the terms?' Lee answered that he would if Grant would write them out for signing. But General Grant simply wrote a letter. There was no formal contract.

"Grant then called for his manifold order-book, which I brought him, together with the oval table. The manifold book is about twice the size of a business letter sheet and has a sort of a stencil that will imprint about six copies at a time. The book was prepared for three copies."

General Porter in his book [1] describes the writing of the letter and says: "When he (Grant) had finished the letter he called Colonel Parker to his side and looked it over with him and directed him to interline several words."

"The letter as written in the manifold book was handed by General Grant to Lee. Both half rose and leaned over their tables. Porter reached out for the book and passed it

---

1. "Campaigning with Grant," page 476.

to Lee, who cleared his table and put on his spectacles to read the terms in the open book before him.

"General Grant then said unless Lee had some further wish he would put the terms in ink and submit his final copy. Lee said that he would like to have a statement inserted allowing the horses and mules to be retained by the men, but Grant said he would not change his letter, but would grant this request by special order, because he thought the war was over and the men would need their animals for farming. Lee handed the book back to Grant.

"General Grant then called over Colonel Bowers and told him to write out the terms in ink. Colonel Bowers, who was senior adjutant, took the book and came over, but was so nervous he could not write."

That historic moment, with all its lack of ostentation, was in reality quiet only because of its very tenseness. Men were outwardly calm, but inwardly greatly agitated. The nerves of the Anglo-Saxon tingled with suppressed emotion, but Parker, the red man, whose life's discipline had steeled him for composure during times of crisis, was as calm inwardly as outwardly. Porter relates that Bowers took the book "and turned the matter over to Colonel Parker, whose handwriting presented a better appearance than that of anyone else on the staff. Parker sat down to write at the oval table which he had moved to the rear of the room." There was no ink in the farm house, but "Colonel Marshall now came to the rescue," continues General Porter, "and took out a small boxwood inkstand which he placed at Parker's service."

"Having finished it," says General Parker, in telling his friend, Sculptor Kelly, of the transcription of the terms, "I brought it to General Grant, who signed it, sealed it and then handed it to General Lee. When I made the copy in ink, I put the original in my pocket. I then came back here (pointing to a diagram of the room). The original, which I still have, reads as you see in this frame:"

HEADQUARTERS, ARMIES OF THE UNITED STATES,

APPOMATTOX COURT HOUSE, VA., April 9, '65.

General R. E. LEE,
  Commanding C. S. Army.

GENERAL: In accordance with the substance of my letter to you of the 8th instant, I propose to receive the surrender of the Army of Northern Virginia on the following terms, to wit: Rolls of all the officers and men to be made in duplicate—one copy to be given to an officer to be designated by me, the other to be retained by such officer or officers as you may designate; the officers to give their individual paroles not to take up arms against the Government of the United States until properly exchanged, and each company or regimental commander to sign a like parole for the men of his command. The arms, artillery, and public property are to be packed and stacked, and turned over to the officers appointed by me to receive them. This will not embrace the side-arms of the officers, nor their private horses or baggage. This done, officers and men will be allowed to return to their homes, not to be disturbed by United States authority so long as they observe their paroles and the laws in force where they may reside.

Very respectfully,

U. S. GRANT,
Lieutenant-General.

"General Lee consulted with Colonel Marshall, who came over here," said General Parker, referring again to his sketch, "and asked me if I had any paper without a printed heading. He had none as their baggage wagons had been burned. I had nothing but note-paper which I gave him. He wrote the note of reply."

"Was he standing?" asked his artist interviewer.

"No, he sat by the table or piano with his elbow on it and wrote his reply and handed it to General Grant, who received it."

Lee's reply of acceptance was short and pointed. It reads:

HEADQUARTERS, ARMY OF NORTHERN VIRGINIA.

April 9, 1865.

GENERAL: I received your letter of this date containing the terms of surrender of the Army of Northern Virginia, as proposed by you. As they are substantially the same as expressed in your letter of the 8th instant, they are accepted. I will proceed to designate the proper officers to carry the stipulations into effect.

R. E. LEE, *General.*

Lieutenant-General U. S. GRANT.

During the letter-writing and the time consumed by Marshall and Parker in copying the terms, General Grant introduced to Lee the officers of the Union Army who were in the room. Lee was especially cordial to Seth Williams, who had been an adjutant under Lee when he was the commanding officer at West Point Academy. Lee greeted each staff officer and then being introduced to Colonel Parker, who was busy with his papers, he looked at him searchingly. Porter writes of this incident: "Parker, being a full-blood Indian, when Lee saw his swarthy features, he looked at him with evident surprise, and his eyes rested upon him for several seconds. What was passing in his mind no one knew, but the natural surmise is that he first mistook Parker for a negro."

This remark also occurs in the Century Company's Warbook, but it is an inference that Parker indignantly denied. "After Lee had stared at me for a moment," said Parker to more than one of his friends and relatives, "he extended his hand and said, 'I am glad to see one real American here.' I shook his hand and said, 'We are all Americans.'"

This brief conversation occurred in the rear of the room and as Lee had his back to the rest in the room except Marshall, no one of the several eye-witnesses of the surrender who wrote of the incidents seemed to have noted it. This personal version of the incident was heard by the writer of this sketch and was related several times to Mrs. Harriet Maxwell Converse, who in the years after the war was an intimate friend of Parker's. The writer has recorded the story also from the lips of Mr. Kelly, who copied many of his interviews with General Parker immediately after they happened. We thus seek to make the record straight.

After the conversation and introductions, each General signed his letter. Grant used the oval table, which Parker again carried over to him. Then Parker handed the transcribed copy to Colonel Marshall, who in turn handed Lee's acceptance to Parker. Most of the officers then went out of the room, but Parker remained at the oval table and wrote out the directions for carrying into effect the final terms. This he did in his own words, being familiar with Grant's wishes. These messages, so significant in importance, are entirely in Parker's handwriting, and indeed signed by him. They are reproduced below:

(Special Orders)

HEADQUARTERS, ARMIES OF THE UNITED STATES,

IN THE FIELD, April 9, 1865.

Major Gen. John Gibbon, Bvt. Maj. Gen. Charles Griffin, and Bvt. Maj. Gen. Wesley Merritt are hereby designated to carry into effect the stipulations this day entered into between General R. E. Lee, commanding C. S. Armies, and Lieutenant-General Grant, commanding Armies of the United States, in which General Lee surrenders to General Grant the Army of Northern Virginia.

Bvt. Brig. Gen. George H. Sharpe, assistant provost-marshal-general, will receive and take charge of the rolls called for by the above-mentioned stipulations.

By command of Lieutenant-General Grant.

E S. PARKER,
Lieutenant-Colonel and Acting Assistant Adjutant-General.

HEADQUARTERS, ARMIES OF THE UNITED STATES,

APPOMATTOX COURT HOUSE, April 9, 1865.

General MEADE:

GENERAL: The Fifth Corps of the Army of the Potomac and the Twenty-fourth Corps of the Army of the James will remain here until the stipulations of the surrender of the C. S. Army, known as the Army of Northern Virginia, entered into by General R. E. Lee and the lieutenant-general commanding, have been carried into effect, and the captured and surrendered public property has been secured. All the other forces will be moved back to Burkeville, starting to-morrow where they will go into camp. The chief ordnance officer of the Army of the Potomac will collect and take charge of all captured and surrendered ordnance and ordnance stores and remove them to Burkeville. The acting chief quartermaster of the Army of the James will collect and take charge of all the captured and surrendered quartermaster's property and stores and remove them to Burkeville. You will please give such orders to your troops and officers of the staff departments as will secure the execution of the foregoing instructions. The troops going to Burkeville will turn over to those remaining here all the subsistance stores—they may have a bare sufficiency to take them back.

By command of Lieutenant-General Grant.

E. S. PARKER,
Acting Assistant Adjutant-General.

During the entire proceedings Grant had smoked a cigar which he half chewed. This fact was strongly impressed upon Parker, for in looking over Kelly's picture sketched for Bryant's history he said as he smiled, "If you want to make the thing historically correct, though I don't know that it will improve it, you will have to show Grant with a cigar in his mouth." Mr. Kelly adds in his notes, "I put the suggestion in the finished picture." In later years Parker told in a series of recollections, published in *McClure's Magazine,* how Grant once lost his cigar because of his own strict orders. His story is:

"All military men know that orders emanating from proper authority must be obeyed and executed without question, and that officers and men entrusted with them must obey and execute them irrespective of the station or rank of the person or persons they may affect. President Lincoln once experienced the rigidity of military orders, when, late in the fall of 1864, he attempted to enter General Grant's Headquarters camp at City Point, Virginia, by crossing the sentinel's lines. He was promptly halted by the sentinel and informed where the entrance to the camp was. He told the sentinel who he was, and explained his right to pass anywhere within the lines of the army. The sentinel was inexorable, simply replying that he might be all he claimed to be, but that the orders were positive not to let any one pass his line, and he would not. Lincoln was perforce compelled to go a little farther, and enter the camp at the proper entrance.

"About the same time General Grant had an experience not similar, but which was another example of the inflexibility of military orders. After lunch one day, he asked me to accompany him in a walk along the Quartermaster's wharves. Accordingly, lighting our cigars, we descended the stairs to the Appomattox river, the foot of the stairs being about three hundred feet from the head of the wharf, on the James river. We walked leisurely to the wharf, enjoying our cigars. We had not gone far on the wharf when a sentinel halted us, saying: 'Gentlemen, it is against orders to smoke on the wharf.' Nothing more was said, but our cigars went into the river. A few moments later the General remarked: 'I am sorry to lose my smoke, but the order is right.' I can not say whether or not the guard knew the General, but he knew his duty, and doubtless would have arrested us had we disobeyed him.

"Smoking seemed to be a necessity to General Grant's organism, rather than a luxury. With him it antagonized nervousness, and evidently was an aid to thought; for I often noticed that he smoked the hardest when in deep thought, or engaged in writing an important document. After the terrible battles about Spottsylvania in 1864, and when the second flank movement toward Richmond was in process of execution, he asked for paper on which to write a report to Washington of the battles, and of his future plans. As I sat only a few feet from him I noticed that he was smoking very hard, at times completely enveloping his face in the smoke. Finally, blowing it all away from him, he wrote his dispatch, in which occurs the epigrammatic phrase, 'I will fight it out on this line if it takes all summer'—a phrase that infused new life and confidence into the Northern mind. He smoked in the same manner when, near Appomattox, he received General Lee's last note asking for a meeting with a view to surrender; and again when sitting with Lee in McLean's parlor arranging the terms of surrender.

"Before Lee left the McLean house he asked one more favor. His men were suffering from lack of food and if possible he wished Grant to issue rations to them.

" 'General Grant,' said Lee, 'I want to ask you something. If our positions were reversed I would grant it to you. My men are starving and I wish to ask if you will give them rations.'

" 'How many men have you got?' asked Grant.

" 'About twenty-five thousand,' answered Lee.

" 'General Grant came over to me and said, [and here Parker smiled, interpolates Mr. Kelly] 'I guess you had better make out an order for thirty thousand.' He knew, and did not propose to have any one suffer."

At nine o'clock on the morning of April 10th Grant and his staff rode out and took their station on a knoll overlooking both armies. It was attempted to pass through the Confederate lines, but the pickets had not been instructed to permit the entry of the Union officers. Notice, however, was sent to Lee who at once rode forward and greeted Grant, when both raised their hats. The subordinate officers gave similar salutes and grouped themselves about their commanders.

Parker came with his leather portfolio slung over his shoulder, ready for taking notes; and then, he tells us, "I used to carry a little wooden ink-bottle with a screw top and when I would write I would tie it to my button-hole. I always carried my portfolio slung over my shoulder." In describing the incidents of the morning of April 10th, General Parker told his artist friend, Mr. Kelly, that he was much impressed by the picturesqueness of the scene.

"There is one scene that would make a good picture," he said. "The affairs at the McLean house were the preliminaries of the surrender. The next day General Grant and his staff went down here," and he drew the diagram of a stream. "General Lee came down this way"—drawing another line and making a dot opposite Grant. "They sat on their horses and discussed the final terms of the surrender, while the officers of General Lee mingled with ours who instinctively drew back and formed a half circle in the rear of Generals Grant and Lee. General Grant sat here"—making a dot; "General Lee sat here. As they would come to a decision on any point I would write it down."

"Did they have any writing or signing there?" asked the artist.

"No, I would write it down, and sign it by order of General Grant. I was over here"—pointing to a dot at the right of Grant. "There was an old stump and I would stoop over it while I wrote.

"I remarked at the time to a couple of rebel officers that it was a pity an artist was not here to make a picture of the scene. Looking from here"—indicating the sun coming from the left and rear of General Grant—"the sun came from behind them and made a very pretty sight."

"As he started to make this diagram," records the artist, "I asked him to make it in my book, but he said, 'No, I will make it here,' and he made a diagram of the scene on his writing-pad. I then, on the margin of his pad, made the composition which he said was correct. Pointing to the group of officers in the rear of the Generals I asked him if he would name the officers who were in the crowd.

" 'All of our principal officers, and a great many of the Confederates,' he answered. Looking at my sketch he said, 'That is a first-rate scene. I think it would make a good picture. It would make a better picture than the interior of the house.' I said, 'I think I will get the editor to use this picture instead,' but Parker said, 'No, that scene is more interesting historically, while this is only the culmination of the agreements that were entered upon the day before; it was only finishing up the business, as it were.' To which I added, 'Filing up the casting.' 'Yes, that is so,' he acceded."

During the conference of Grant and Lee, Parker wrote out the orders for the parole of the officers and men in Lee's army. It was glad news for the Confederates, who at first feared harsh terms. The magnanimity of Grant at first surprised them; then it overwhelmed them with gratitude and they gladly signed their paroles, not one refusing. The order as posted, read as follows:

Special Orders,
No. 73.

HEADQUARTERS, ARMIES OF THE UNITED STATES,

IN THE FIELD, April 10, 1865.

I.—All officers and men of the Confederate service paroled at Appomattox Court House, Va., who, to reach their homes, are compelled to pass through the lines of the Union armies, will be allowed to do so, and to pass free on all Government transports and military railroads.

II.—Bvt. Gen. R. H. Jackson, U. S. Volunteers, is hereby assigned to duty according to his brevet rank, by authority of the Secretary of War.

By command of Lieutenant-General Grant.

E. S. PARKER,
Lieutenant-Colonel and Acting Assistant Adjutant-General.

It was then echoed through the Confederate lines in the form given below:

Special Orders,
  No. . . . . . .

HEADQUARTERS, ARMY OF NORTHERN VA.

April 10, 1865.

The following order is published for the information of all parties concerned:

Special Orders,
  No. . . . . . .

HEADQUARTERS, ARMIES OF THE UNITED STATES,

IN THE FIELD, April 10, 1865.

All officers and men of the Confederate service paroled at Appomattox Court House who, to reach their homes are compelled to pass through the lines of the Union Armies, will be allowed to do so, and to pass free on all Government transports and military railroads.

By command of Lieutenant-General Grant:

E. S. PARKER,
Lieutenant-Colonel and Assistant Adjutant-General.

By command of General R. E. Lee,

C. S. VENABLE.
Assistant Adjutant-General.

Thus the Indian whose enlistment had been refused because the war was "a white man's war," after all was called upon for service. Thus it happened that the words of Secretary Seward came back, "It is an affair in which the Indian is not called to act. The fight must be settled by the white men alone. Go home, cultivate your farm and *we will settle our own troubles without any Indian aid!*"

And yet the Iroquois Indians alone sent three hundred of the flower of their race to battle in this white man's war. They gave men whom the army records show, "for stature, physical fitness and endurance had no equal in the entire army." The Iroquois Indians gave two army surgeons to the Union cause, and provided the military engineer, the adjutant-general, the military secretary whose record we have related. Thus, after all, it must be said that it was in the handwriting of an Iroquois sachem, and an *Indian* that the two warring factions of the white race were finally united. And as a reward for his services, he was declared competent, even though an Indian, to become a citizen and a voter.

CHAPTER XIII

THE WARRIOR AFTER THE WAR

Colonel Parker followed Grant back to Washington, where he continued his office as Military Secretary. No sooner had he taken his desk at headquarters than he was presented with a document which conferred upon him the brevet title, Brigadier-General of United States Volunteers, "for gallant and meritorious services during the campaign terminating with the surrender of the insurgent army under General Robert E. Lee." The document was dated April 9, 1865, the day Lee surrendered.

The labor of administering the affairs of the army after Grant's return to Washington was an arduous one. The war was not entirely over. Johnson had not finally surrendered, but when cornered by Sherman began adroitly to dicker for terms. Then came the assassination of Abraham Lincoln and the grief of a nation. General Parker was a great admirer of Lincoln, whom he knew, and his grief was deep and sincere.

General Parker, and indeed the entire staff, were alarmed lest Grant also be murdered. and redoubled the vigilance with which they had watched his safety. Grant only escaped the aim of the coward by his absence from Washington. It was fully expected that he would be at a box at Ford's Theatre but his fatherly heart, lonely for his children, caused him to change his plans and he had taken the train for Burlington, N. J., where his children were at school. He returned immediately, and controlling his sorrow he left for the South to adjust the difficulties into which Sherman had fallen in treating with Johnson. These were busy days for General Parker. From that time on he labored at the War Department, resigning April 26, 1869.

On July 1, 1866, he was honorably mustered out of the volunteer service and was appointed as Second Lieutenant of U. S. Cavalry. On June 1, 1867, he was promoted to First Lieutenant. Then in the service of the regular U. S. Army, he received the brevets of Captain, Major, Lieutenant-Colonel, Colonel; and on March 2, 1867, the brevet Brigadier-General, U. S. Army, "for gallant and meritorious service during the war."

He had faced the rebel minie-ball, the cannon shot, grape and canister, saber and bayonet at Vicksburg, at Lookout Mountain, at Missionary Ridge, about Chattanooga, at Ringgold, Georgia, in the Wilderness, at Spottsylvania, at Cold Harbor, and in all the battles and operations about Petersburg and Richmond in '64-'65, and in the campaigns that terminated at Appomattox. The target of many a bullet as he rode his great black horse, slashed at by rebel saber, and the mark of bursting shells, he never received a wound that left more than a harmless mark. His prediction was fulfilled. As he wrote to his brother, he did not believe that he was to be killed in the war.

General Parker accompanied General Grant and the staff during the tour of the great leader after the war. Many of the photographs taken at the time show him at Grant's side. General Parker, Colonels Bowers and Babcock, watched Grant with the eyes of hawks lest some harm befall him. It was feared that some crank might yet send a bullet into him even as was done to Lincoln. Captain Beckwith in his address at the grave of General Parker in Buffalo[1] alludes to the care with which Grant was guarded.

General Parker left one or two stories of his tour with Grant, among them the following:

---

1. See Publications, Buffalo Historical Soc.: Vol. VIII, p. 515.

"In 1865, as Grant was returning from a visit to West Point, New York, accompanied by his Assistant Adjutant General, Colonel Bowers—a man greatly beloved by all who knew him—was killed at Garrison's Station by the cars. The next morning the staff found General Grant at Army Headquarters on Seventeenth Street, Washington. He looked haggard and nearly distracted with grief at the loss of a favorite officer. He said to the staff: 'Gentlemen, Colonel Bowers was accidentally killed at Garrison's yesterday. I wish as many of you as can to go to the funeral. I can not go. The loss has come very near to me.' To us this determination did not seem strange. We knew how devotedly he was attached to Colonel Bowers, who had been on his staff since the battle of Shiloh, and we knew, besides, how very fatigued he must be, having traveled all night to reach Washington. Nearly all the staff decided to go to the funeral and left Headquarters to make the necessary preparations, agreeing to meet again in the railroad station. What was their surprise, on coming to the station, to find General Grant there, and to learn that he also was going back to the funeral."

Long before the war the administration of Indian affairs had been a serious problem to honest citizens and legislators. The entire system was corrupt, Indians not only were massacred upon the slightest provocation, but even when peaceful they were encroached upon and robbed. There was a powerfully entrenched machine back of this system of murder and robbery. Each thief had his lobbyist.

General Parker kept up his interest in his own people and several years before the war, in 1859, had been successful in saving the Tonawanda Senecas their home land. The tract of country set aside for them in Kansas was sold and he had arranged that the proceeds be used for the purchase of the Tonawanda Reservation, and that the nation as a corporation hold it by deed of purchase. In this manner the Tonawandas bought back their domain and today hold it more securely than any corporation of citizens holds its property. In 1867 General Parker, to still further protect his nation, drafted "an Act for the protection and improvement of the Tonawanda band of Seneca Indians residing on the Tonawanda Reservation in this State." Afterward he drew up the national laws of the tribal council and made his people secure in their happiness.

In financial affairs he was likewise successful and soon had a comfortable fortune. He had never cared especially for wealth, but as he moved about in the circles of Washington society he met a lady who all unknowingly led him to seek to increase his fortunes.

During the fall of 1867 Washington society received the announcement of the engagement of Miss Minnie Sackett, to General Parker. Later the wedding invitations announced the ceremony on December 17th. The *élite* of the nation's capitol were invited, for General Grant had been chosen to give the bride away. The church was filled with guests and flowers, but no groom appeared.

Printed accounts say that a few days later General Parker appeared. He never made any public explanation of his conduct but his private apology to his *fiancée* was apparently successful for the date was set ahead to Christmas. It was expected that the wedding would take place at the Church of the Epiphany. Thither flocked the invited guests and the rank and fashion of Washington were once more met with closed doors and all absence of preparation. In the meantime the bride and groom had skipped off to "a little church around the corner" and had been privately joined in wedlock. It is probable that the fuss and feathers of a "civilized marriage ceremony" had proven too much for the simple nature of the red man; so reads the account as the public knows it.

The real fact, which has never been related, is that one of his friends was his rival. On the day of December 17, 1867, General Parker was drugged in hopes that it would not only spoil the wedding, but change the mind of the bride. Then later came a more sinister threat neatly veiled. No one knows what might have happened if there had been a wedding at the Church of the Epiphany. Washington society might have had more sensational topics to discuss. No one now knows the exact story of the circumstances attending the marriage. Suffice it to know that they narrowly bordered on a tragedy. But then, many a tale of love and war brings into view many things that appear abnormal and strange when viewed in ordinary lights.

The routine of office work following the reduction of the army, kept General Parker busily engaged. His knowledge of Indian affairs was constantly increasing through the various visits which he made in the West in behalf of the Government. He often met and discussed Indian affairs with western Indian delegates and did his utmost to assist them to obtain justice. More and more he felt that their outbreaks against the settlers in the West were due to a lack of care and understanding in dealing with them.

Several grand councils were held in Indian Territory in which General Parker addressed the assembled representatives of the various tribes. Nor have the older Indians entirely forgotten these meetings with the Government commissioners.

During January, 1913, the writer, together with Professor M. Raymond Harrington of the University of Pennsylvania Museum, met at the home of Comanche Jack for a council. Our plan was to stimulate the interest of the chief in the Society of American Indians and to explain the plans of the organization for the uplift of the race. The writer made a lengthy speech to the dozen of men present and listened as it was interpreted. Comanche Jack made a splendid reply, giving his reasons for believing that the Indian should now know how to walk over the white man's road. Then a surprise was sprung. Old Cabeyo, the medicine man, arose, and looking at the writer as he sat on a roll of blankets on the floor said: "See how black his hair. He is an Indian. What he says is true. I heard those statements nearly fifty years ago at a big council. There were several white men who were commissioners and one Indian. He spoke. He said: 'In the East are Indians who live like white men. They have houses and barns, they send their children to school. Some day one of them will come and tell you what you must do to save your people from destruction.' For many years I have wondered if that man would come. What you have told us is true. This day have my eyes seen him. You are that man." And Old Cabeyo the Comanche pointed his finger, his arm extended at full length.

This plan of General Parker's, of meeting the Indians half way, did much to suggest the "Peace Policy" later inaugurated by President Grant. It had been in Parker's mind for many years.

During Grant's busy campaign in 1868 for the Presidency both Parker and Rawlins were kept busy furnishing information and answering the numerous letters that came in. Parker was an ardent Grant man as were all who knew the great military leader. A letter written by General Parker to his brother's children explains in his own words his life during this period:

HEADQUARTERS. ARMY OF THE UNITED STATES.
WASHINGTON, D. C., Oct. 1st, 1868.

To My Nephews Freddie, Frankie, Albert and My Niece Minnie.

DEAR CHILDREN:—It is a long time ago since I received from each of you, nice little letters, transmitted by your kind teacher Miss Clark. I have been a great bear for not answering you sooner, and I hope you will tell me so the next time we meet, should it please

Providence to grant us that privilege. Your letters were very nice indeed, they pleased me much and gave me ocular proof of the progress you have all made in your studies. I hope that you have improved much since you wrote to me, and that you have always been good, kind and obedient to your teacher and to your parents as well as to your estimable uncle and aunt, Mr. and Mrs. Wright.

I am very busy looking after and attending to the interests of the great army of the United States, as well as the interests and wants of her citizens generally and that I suppose is the main reason why my little people are neglected. Yet I have thought of you often.

Congress was in session until July and it kept myself and others very busy in answering and attending to all their questions and demands for information. Then General Grant went away to the Rocky Mountains early in July and nearly all his officers left the city soon after, leaving only myself and General Rawlins, the Chief of Staff, at these headquarters to do all the work and represent General Grant, and this I can tell you is no easy work to do. The work was too much for General Rawlins and he was taken sick. Last Monday he left the city to be gone perhaps a year. This has left me almost alone for besides the Assistant Adjutant General there is only one officer here to keep me company.

General Grant you know is the Republican candidate for President of the United States, in opposition to Seymour of your State, and this fact has made my work a great deal heavier, as we are compelled to see and talk with politicians from every part of the country. I want to see Grant elected, because I think he is the best patriot and that he only can bring peace to the country. He is a very nice man indeed. He is a great general and has a good heart. He loves his country and greatly desires to see it enjoy the blessings of peace and prosperity. He has a very pleasant family. He is father of four children. The oldest is named Freddie, he is now at West Point Military Academy studying to become a soldier. The next is named Ulysses S., after his father, but he is generally called "Buckie" or "Buck," because he was born in Ohio, the Buckeye State of the Union. The next child is a daughter named Nellie—she is about 12 years old and is a very sweet, pretty and smart girl. The youngest child is a boy, named Jesse, and he is very smart and bright. He owns a pair of Shetland ponies not quite as large as some Newfoundland dogs I have seen, and with these he drives about our streets in his little buggy, which his father had made for them, or he rides pony-back. They go very fast and can really worry a large horse in point of speed. You may also recollect my ponies, that your Pa kept for me. I have them yet and they are very beautiful and very fast. I enjoy driving them very much. I shall probably go North in two or three weeks with your aunt Minnie, but I don't know as I shall have time to come and see you. I shall be at Aunt Carrie's only a day. I cannot be gone long from here, and that is the reason I cannot promise to see you. Give my love to your Pa and Ma. Your Aunt Minnie sends love to all. She has gone to Baltimore today and left me alone.

From your

UNCLE ELY.

CHAPTER XIV

AN INDIAN COMMISSIONER OF INDIAN AFFAIRS

After General Grant was inaugurated as President of the United States one of his first appointments was that of General Parker to the office of Commissioner of Indian Affairs.

General Parker entered upon his new task with a strong determination to lift the people of his race from their unhappy condition. Two ideas controlled his policy. The first was to make the Indian himself see his duty in becoming a useful and constructive member of society, to make him economically independent, contributing his share to the sum total of human welfare. The second idea was to impress the various departments of the Government with the idea that the people of the United States owed the Indians a clean administration of their affairs, and not only that, but that they must take upon themselves the burden of rescuing the Indian from the unhappy state into which he had been thrust and of lifting him up into an understanding of civilization and Christianity.

He knew how the old Indian looked upon civilization and the church. Civilization to the Indian had meant a conflict with a thousand evils that were only elementary in his original state. It meant an abandonment of many of his old ideals and a crushing out of native virtues. It meant an entirely different economic life. Frequently it meant the entire destruction of the tribe through disease and rum.

Two great departures occurred in the administration of Indian affairs, when General Parker was appointed. One was the creation of the Board of Indian Commissioners and the other the institution of the "Peace Policy." A new day had dawned for the Indian and for the first time the Government began its duty to save and uplift at all cost, the people whom its citizens had robbed and debauched. The Board of Indian Commissioners was a body of highly conscientious men, some of them almost supersensitive.

The whole "bureau system" was graft-ridden. The goods placed in Government warehouses for Indians were stolen or replaced with inferior material. Contractors who had no conscience were continually foisting upon the Government worthless cloth and food. Cattle-dealers who were paid for delivering "beef on foot" reaped a rich harvest of gold. One of the schemes which they successfully worked was to drive their consignment of cows onto a reservation, get the agent's receipt, wait until the beef had been distributed to the Indians and then either steal, or buy them back for a trinket or a few pennies—twenty-five cents in most cases; then drive them on to the next agency and deliver them there, only to repeat the operation. Men like this had money to defend themselves with and were seldom caught. The need of a competent board of citizens to watch these scoundrels and to check up the warehouses was imperative.

To fulfill this need President Grant appointed the Board of Indian Commissioners whose duty should be to bring the public, the Indian and the Government into close terms of accord and sympathy. General Parker felt that this board would be of great service and he at once sought its co-operation. The first letter of instruction from the Indian Bureau to the Board was written by Commissioner Parker and is reproduced below:

                    DEPARTMENT OF THE INTERIOR,
                       OFFICE OF INDIAN AFFAIRS,
                          WASHINGTON, May 26, 1869.

To the BOARD OF INDIAN COMMISSIONERS.

GENTLEMEN:—You have been solicited by the President, under the provision of the fourth section of the act of Congress, approved

April 10, 1869, entitled "An act making appropriation for the current and contingent expenses of the Indian Department," etc., for the year ending June 30, 1870, for the purpose of enabling the President to exercise the power conferred by said act. And I being authorized by the same act to exercise, under the direction of the President, joint control with the Secretary of the Interior over the disbursement of the appropriations made by said act, or any part thereof that the president may designate (and you having been convened in the city for the purpose of organizing for the execution of your duties), and believing that, in common with the President and other officers of the government, you desire the humanization, civilization and Christianization of the Indians, I very respectfully, after consultation with the honorable Secretary of the Interior, submit the following questions, which with a view of proper and intelligent action in the future relation of the government with the Indians, I deem it important should receive your early consideration and suggestion, viz.: A determination or settlement of what should be the legal status of the Indians; a definition of their rights and obligations under the laws of the United States, of the States and Territories and treaty stipulations; whether any more treaties shall be stipulated with the Indians, and if not, what legislation is necessary for those with whom there are existing stipulations, and what for those whith whom no such stipulations exist; should the Indians be placed upon reservations, and if so what is the best method to accomplish this object; should not legislation discriminate between the civilized and localized Indians and the roving tribes of the plains and mountains; what changes are necessary in existing laws relating to purchasing goods and provisions for the Indians, in order to prevent fraud, etc.; should any change be made in the method of paying the money annuities and if so what? Great mischief, evils, and frequently serious results follow from friendly Indians leaving the reservations, producing conflicts between the citizens, soldiers and Indians. At what time and point shall the civil rule begin and the military end? Is any change required in the intercourse laws by reason of the present changed condition of the country? I respectfully suggest that inspection should be made by your commission of as many Indian tribes, especially the wild and roving ones, as the time of the honorable commissioners will permit, and their conditions and wants be reported on, with any suggestion that each case may seem to require. Also, the accounts of superintendents and agents should be examined, and the efficiency or inefficiency of those officers should be reported upon. All suggestions, recommendations and reports from the commission should be made to the honorable Secretary of the Interior, to be by him submitted, when necessary, to the President and Congress.

Very respectfully, your obedient servant,

E. S. PARKER,
Commissioner.

It will be noted that General Parker at the very beginning of his administration saw the vital need of determining the exact legal status of the Indian together with an exact definition of all their rights and disabilities as laid down by the many complex laws and treaties. This suggestion was never carried out, and, because of this lack of definiteness, the Indian and the Government have been forced to pay millions of dollars in legal fees, in seeking to adjust details. The Indian has suffered more than the loss of money; his flesh and blood and his very soul have been sacrificed upon the altar of neglect. Only now is the public awakening to the need of a re-codification of Indian law and a determination of the legal status of each tribe, band and division of Indians.

In the first annual report submitted by Commissioner Parker in 1869 were many important suggestions.

The difficulty of enforcing the law on the frontier caused much expense in property and life. In concluding his report for 1869 the Commissioner in this connection says:

I deem it my duty in closing this report to invite attention to the insufficiency, or the want of means to enforce existing laws and to remedy evils which are common throughout the entire service. Acts of a criminal character are often committed in the vicinity of Indian agencies, or upon Indian reservations, by both whites and Indians, no notice of which is taken for want of adequate power at hand, and frequently when authority is asked from Washington to arrest the offenders, they in the meanwhile escape, so that the effect prompt action would have had is entirely lost, and crimes go unpunished, to be renewed again with impunity. To make the uncivilized Indian respect law and observe his treaty obligations, the power to punish must be present, and the penalty of violated law promptly enforced. The same may also be said of the whites, who would not so readily commit wrongs against the Indians if they knew that punishment would follow close upon the commission of the crime. To the end therefore that it may be made apparent to the Indians as well as to the whites in any way connected or dealing with them, that the Government intends to execute the laws applicable to such cases and treaties, it is respectfully recommended that Congress be asked to pass a statute requiring the military to station at the agencies, whenever requested by proper authority, a sufficient number of troops to assist the agent in charge to make prompt arrest of all persons offending, that they may be handed over to the civil authorities for trial.

In achieving the office of Commissioner of Indian Affairs, General Parker had reached the highest goal which his dreams of usefulness could bring to his mind. The great desire of his life—to serve his race—had reached its fulfillment. Friends of the race rejoiced in the fact that an Indian was administering the affairs of his people and rendering the Federal Government a unique service.

For the first time there was an Indian Commissioner of Indian Affairs, and needless to say *that* Commissioner loved his people, and they trusted him and looked to him with hope. It was the first faint hope of permanent self-government, freedom, and a new day of life for the red race in America.

For the first time in the history of the Indian Department, Indian affairs were being cleaned up. The numerous councils held in the West by Commissioner Parker and the various members of the Board of Commissioners had a salutary effect upon the Indians who had reason to believe they had been injured. A new era had come for the Indians, and also for the grafting contractors. The latter were losing their customary profits, for many eyes were directed toward them. Their schemes therefore became shrewder than before and with great subtlety they put in vogue new operations to defraud both the Government and the Indians. If they could then throw the blame upon the head of the Commissioner, they wanted to do so.

Then there fell like a thunderbolt upon General Parker an accusation lodged by William Welsh, one of the members of the Board who had resigned. He accused Parker of scheming to defraud the Government of the United States and to mulct the Indians out of their just dues. His venom was such that he scornfully remarked about General Grant and libeled the Indian race itself by exclaiming that the President had put into office "one who is but a remove from barbarism." When good men go "wild" they sometimes do many damaging things and slander without thought men who may be entirely innocent. The battle waxed so fiercely that General Parker was in February, 1871, tried before a Committee of the House of Representatives.

Mr. Welsh's charges were that General Parker exceeded his authority and had responded to measures requiring immediate attention by prompt action without consulting the Board. He was charged with neglecting rules, with violating the law and with wasteful use of public money. Thirteen charges were brought.

General Parker welcomed an investigation into his administration. His files were open, but even this did not satisfy his accusers. They looked into his bank account to find the grafted millions that their suspicion had scented, but found the Commissioner a poor man indeed. No millions and no thousands could be found. Every one of their charges was disproven by the records of the Interior Department or the Indian office. The "bad Indian" could not be roped and branded with the title "bad."

The trial was held during the first winter months of 1871. There was a steady purpose seen throughout the trial to ruin General Parker if possible. The General, however, answered all questions freely, opened up his records and invited critical inspection of all his official acts. His attorney was General Chapman, and the entire proceedings were ordered published in the House Documents of 1871.

The House Committee reviewed the evidence, and found that the incompetence and neglect which had been charged were not of the Commissioner, but of his subordinates. Many an Indian Commissioner has since seen all his good plans set at naught by the scheming or neglect of an assistant or a dishonest superintendent. The committee after a long investigation summed up the trial by saying:

> But your committee have not found evidence of fraud or corruption on the part of the Indian Commissioner. With much to criticise and condemn, arising partly from a vicious system inherited from the past and partly from error in judgment in the construction of statutes passed to insure economy . . . we have found no evidence of any pecuniary or personal advantage sought or derived by the Commissioner or any one connected with the bureau.

In the end General Parker was found without a stain, but his heart was broken. He had done his utmost unselfishly and with the single idea in his mind of doing immediately what should be done instead of dragging around his work the tangled coils of "red tape." But one thing could not be undone entirely. He had started reforms and new methods. These lived and the Indians benefited. "Barbarian," though he was called by the Philadelphia shopkeeper, he was yet a gentleman, and among all the documents that he left not one slur is cast against Mr. Welsh, or one derogatory reference having a personal element is made toward his accusers. Though he was assailed he never lifted his voice to imitate his enemies. They were good men, without doubt—every one—but it is to be feared they were misguided in their zeal to discover crime's stain on innocent hands.

Under Parker's administration all Indian wars ceased. Under Parker there was an era of peace, for Indian bloodshed had been shown to be unnecessary. The Indians were beginning to develop a new confidence in "the Government." Christian men and women of all denominations were sent to the tribes as missionaries and teachers. For the first time a systematic effort had been made to do a real service to the wards of the nation.

Then came the onslaught: *"The Indian must be put out!"* But every effort was defeated. Parker was cleared, but as he says in one of his letters, "I gave up a thankless position to enjoy my declining days in peace and quiet." He resigned in August, 1871. What now was before him?

Ten years before, General Parker had been a successful civil engineer, entrusted with important undertakings. When the Government had wanted difficult pieces of work done Parker had been the man for the job. When lighthouse, levee or canal was wanted and there seemed to be grave difficulties in the way, problems to solve and dangers to avoid, men in official position knew whom to choose. Even the railroads knew the man to select when a roadbed must be laid across a swamp. It was always Parker, the man with a reputation for making good. He was the man to work night and day on a scheme for success; he was the man who could figure out details, and best of all he was the man who could stick until the work was finished.

As an engineer he was a success, his life's labor seemed assured. Then he heard the call of his country and responded. He stayed until the war was over and in his own handwriting had written out the terms of settlement. Continually he had stayed in the War Office and helped clear the way for the reconstruction.

Event after event followed as a natural sequence. Grant, the idol of the North, was announced as the candidate for the Presidency. Parker clung to his leader and did his share to make the campaign a success. Grant was elected and again Parker heard the call to service. It was a double call in which there mingled the voices of two races—his own and that of the sovereign nation—the Indian's and the pale-face's. Both were troubled, each misunderstood the other. Each had paid the penalty of that misunderstanding, in bloodshed; but of the two, the red man had suffered most, lost most, sacrificed most. The call which Parker heard was the call to a most difficult service.

During the last days of his term President Taft said to me, as I talked over the resignation of Commissioner Valentine, with him: "The office of Commissioner of Indian Affairs is the most difficult appointive office in the country to fill," and then he sighed. This has always been so since there were such entities as Indian Commissioners. It was this difficult office that General Parker was called upon to fill. He took the office, filled with high hopes and visions of a better day for the men and women and children who were crying for an understanding friend, for a helping, healing hand to lift them from the sod where they had been trampled upon and wounded with the hoofs of many horses. There they lay almost plowed under the sod, as the plowshare of civilization cut its way into the West; there they lay prostrate beneath the ax-hewn trees of their own loved forests; there they lay cemented to earth by the clots of their own wounds. Who was there to help them? It was the idea that it might be he, that led General Parker to accept this difficult task.

We have seen what difficulties he met. We have seen that there were men who did not wish the man "but one remove from a barbarian himself" to serve in this position. We have discussed the charges brought against him and seen that he was clear of guilt.

But was it actually true that General Parker was honest, or did the investigation of his affairs merely fail to convict him of criminal action because of technicalities? We have only to seek the answer in his later life. Was he honest? Did not his barbarian blood, his "undeveloped" nature, make him inclined to cheat when he had the chance and to evade responsibility where it was too heavy? Did it not make him say, "Oh, well, I'm only an Indian—men must not exact as much of me as of Anglo-Saxons"? How these questions irritate the friends who know the real qualities of Parker's character! They irritate because they are not honest questions, but implied crimination and imputation of inferiority.

General Parker was honest, more honest than his accusers; in ability he was the peer of any of his associates and far superior to his enemies, as to real manhood. He never "crawled," never begged, never stooped to that which was mean. He took what came with the demeanor of a true gentleman and a philosopher.

It is not strange, therefore, that when Commissioner Parker found himself clear and his reputation unscarred by his trial he should have prepared to resign his office. He would not stay where he was not wanted or where he had made himself, even though unintentionally, a rock of offence. Six months after his vindication by the Congressional committee he handed in his resignation. He gave his critics ample time to find new flaws, to lay out a new line of prosecution; and they failing, he felt that he could honorably hand over the work to others. This he did in August, 1871. To what was he now to turn?

General Parker went to New York, where he found that keen competition left him but few opportunities in his profession as an engineer. He found occasionally a project worthy of his efforts, but found it easier to build a fortune in Wall Street. Out of the proceeds of his investments he built a country home in Fairfield, Connecticut.

General Parker moved in the best social circles wherever he went; his friends must be men of brain and standing. He chose them as he had chosen his books. He never lost his host of friends, but he did lose his fortune, and how he did this will answer the question, "Was he honest?" He was a bondsman for a bank cashier. The cashier defaulted and General Parker was called upon to make the bond good. It was a rude shock to have a trusted friend turn out a thief, almost as bad as making up for his embezzlements.

General Parker's attorneys hastened to him with advice. "You won't have to pay," they said; "You are an Indian, and the law does not hold you to it. You can not be compelled by law to live up to that bond. It is not worth the paper it is written on." Here was a loop-hole that would save the accumulation of a lifetime. The elements of escape were few and simple; "Indian, do not have to pay, law can not compel—contract void."

But General Parker gave a single answer, "I fully intend to make that bond good," he said. "I executed it in good faith. I am a *man* and if the law does not compel me to pay, my honor does." And he paid, though his fortune was wrecked. Years after the defaulter became wealthy and respected, but he never repaid a penny.

Again an effort was made to repair the loss of funds, and another small fortune was accumulated, only to be swept away in the crash of the Freedman's bank. More money flowed out in the failure of an insurance company and still more in a publishing venture. This left a man past middle life in a position where he must struggle again for new footing and new resources. What do most men do amid such discouragements? What did he do? He went to work. And herein lay the secret of his life's success. It is well embraced in the family maxim—it is Iroquois in its origin: "Spend no time in mourning the failures of the past.

Tears make a bitter throat. Look ahead, there is more work to do. Unstop your ears and listen. Hear the call."
More than a quarter of a century he had heeded this advice of the stone-age sages of his nation, when he had swung from his study of law to the study of engineering. When he had most to discourage him he listened and heard another call. He most thoroughly believed there was some place in the world for him and a place where he could do, upbuild and be useful as another man could not. He was not a fatalist who idly sat and took the shower or the sunshine as it came. He stood upright and active and used the shower or the sunshine as suited him best. It was an opportunity for service. He would use the shower to make good things grow and the sunshine to make them blossom.

CHAPTER XV

A SACHEM'S LETTERS TO A POETESS

General Parker was essentially a home-loving man. His family and his home were first in his thoughts. His devotion to his wife, who was much of an invalid, revealed his great tenderness and the true depth of his affection. These qualities manifested toward others made him a true friend, if he was a friend. He had many friends, from coast to coast. He could hold his friends because he knew the full meaning of the word.

One of these friends was Mrs. Harriet Maxwell Converse, the daughter of Hon. Thomas Maxwell, of Elmira. Mrs. Converse was a poetess, a magazine writer and the wife of Frank M. Converse, the musician, known as "the father of the banjo." Through her father her interest in the Iroquois was an hereditary one. It became an active first-hand interest when in the course of the social life of the metropolis she met General Parker. The knowledge he gave her brought with it the inspiration for a deeper study of Indian life, and resulted in many years of devotion on her part to the Indians of New York State. In a certain measure the archæological museum of New York at Albany, owes its new beginning to her influence.

Mr. and Mrs. Converse and General and Mrs. Parker became true friends. The mind of the poetess was especially attracted to that of the sachem, and he found in her a pleasant sympathetic companion. Indeed, General Parker never really knew or thought much about his real self until he met Harriet Maxwell Converse. This was probably about 1881, when she first began to take an active interest in Indians. Their acquaintance ripened into a deep friendship that continued without abatement until the

General died. In a letter to her he once wrote that had it not been for her sympathetic interest in him and his people he should almost have forgotten his ancestry. True, he had ever been plied with questions regarding his race, and called upon to give his opinion in Indian matters, but this was simply because he was an authority on such matters as any man might have been; it did not serve to draw him to himself. The matter-of-fact world of civilization has a tendency to drive from the mind the memories, the theories and longings of long ago, and it was in the matter-of-fact world that General Parker lived, toiling day by day for a livelihood. Constant business pressure left but little time for reflection and introspection. The mind of the Indian had been turned into the channels of the white man and the Indian thought of himself not as much, but simply as a man among a million fellow-toilers, struggling for bread and dollars. It was then that the poetic mind of Mrs. Converse drew back to its old channels the mind of General Parker. He felt himself an Indian again, he remembered his boyhood, he endured again the dream fast, he plunged into the deep forests and brought back pelts of wildcats and bears, he heard the tall pines sighing in the forest and saw beneath them the long-house where his red brothers were wont to meet and sing to the Great Spirit and dance before him; he thought of the fireside tales of the old storytellers, of the medicine men of the secret societies that met in isolated lodges in the forest's depths—the Society of the Bear, the Society of the Birds and the Society of the Otter. All these things flashed as in a vision before him and he was in the midst of all. He was an Indian again. A sympathetic friend had brought it all back and he was ever grateful. Then were the poetess and the Indian friends in truth, confessing and confiding to each other the innermost secrets of their souls.

When Mrs. Converse died, among her papers was found a number of letters—only a few of many, that General Parker had written her. These letters reveal the writer, not as the engineer, the architect, the diplomat, the military commandant, but as the Indian, the friend and the man. As I have said, a man may best be known by what he confides to his friends, and it is hoped that something of the true General Parker may be learned from a perusal of what he said, criticized, lamented, praised and confessed in these letters.

The General addresses Mrs. Converse as "Gayaneshaoh," this being her Seneca Indian name, or as the "Snipe," her clan insignia, while he signs himself "Donehowaga," his sachemship title.

The letters, it is hoped, will tell their own story. They were written in confidence to a friend and not intended for the eyes of anyone else. Hence, they may be considered as revealing the true inner man better than any other means. Were General Parker and Mrs. Converse alive today both would protest against these letters being published, but no apology is offered in presenting them. Both were prominent and influential in their generation, and to the host that knew them these letters will serve as an interesting sidelight, to others they will record the thoughts of an Iroquois sachem.

[*Without date*]

DEAR GAYANESHAOH:—On reading your last note I was greatly amused—and why? Because what I have written heretofore has been taken *verbatim et literatim* and a character given me to which I am no more entitled than the man in the moon: I am credited or charged with being "great," "powerful," and finally crowned as "good." Oh, my guardian genius, why should I be so burdened with what I am not now and never expect to be: Oh, indeed, would that I could feel a "kindling touch from that pure flame." That a fair and ministering angel would endow me with the exuberance of prejudiced enthusiasm. . . .

And why all this commotion of the spirit? Because I am an ideal or a myth and not my real self. I have lost my identity and I look about me in vain for my original being. I never was "great," and never expect to be. I never was "powerful," and would not know how to exercise power were it placed in my hands for use. And that I am "good" or ever dreamed of attaining that blissful condition of being, is simply absurd.

All my life I have occupied a false position. As a youth my people voted me a genius and loudly proclaimed that Hawenneyo had destined me to be their saviour and they gave public thanksgiving for the great blessing they believed had been given them, for unfortunately just at this period they were engaged in an almost endless and nearly hopeless litigated contest for their New York homes and consequently for their very existence.

For many years I was a constant visitor at the State and Federal capitals either seeking legislative relief or in attendance at State and Federal Courts. Being only a mere lad, the pale-faced officials, with whom I came in contact, flattered me and declared that one so young must be extraordinarily endowed to be charged with the conduct of such weighty affairs. I pleased my people in eventually bringing their troubles to a successful and satisfactory termination. I prepared and had approved by the proper authorities a code of laws and rules for the conduct of affairs among themselves and settled them for all time or for so long as Hawenneyo should let them live.

They saw all this and thought it was good. They no longer wanted me nor gave me credit for what had been done. A generation had passed and another grown up since I began to work for them. The young men were confident of their own strength and abilities and needed not the brawny arm of experience to fight their battles for them, nor the wisdom brought about by years of training to guide them any longer. The War of the Rebellion had broken out among the pale-faces, a terrible contest between the slaveholding and non-slaveholding sections of the United States. I had, through the Hon. Wm. H. Seward, personally tendered my services for the non-slaveholding interest. Mr. Seward in short said to me that the struggle in which I wished to assist, was an affair between white men and one in which the Indian was not called on to act. "The fight must be made and settled by the white men alone," he said. "Go home, cultivate your farm, and we will settle our own troubles without any Indian aid."

I did go home and planted crops and myself on the farm, sometimes not leaving it for four and six weeks at a time. But the quarrel of the whites was not so easily or quickly settled. It was not a wrangle of boys, but a struggle of giants and the country was being racked to its very foundations.

Then came to me in my forest home a paper bearing the great red seal of the War Department at Washington. It was an officer's commission in the Army of the United States. The young Indian community had settled in their untutored minds that because I had settled quietly, willingly and unconcernedly into the earning of my living by the sweat of my brow, I was not, therefore, a genius or a man of mind. That they were in truth correct, they did not know, jealousy and envy having prompted the idea and utterance. But now this paper coming from the great Government at Washington offering to confer honors for which I had not served an apprenticeship, nor even asked for, revived among the poor Indians the idea that I was after all a genius and great and powerful. . . . They pleaded with me not to leave them but to remain as their counsellor, adviser and chief; they said that they would be powerless and lost without my presence. They tacitly acknowledged my genius, greatness and power, which I did not. When I explained that I was going into the war with a splendid prospect of sacrificing my life, as much for their good as for the maintenance of the principles of the Constitution and Laws of the United States, and upholding of the Union Flag in its purity, honor and supremacy over this whole country, they silently and wisely bowed their heads and wept in assent as to the inevitable. I bade them farewell, commended them to the care and protection of Hawenneyo and left them, never expecting to return.

I went from the East to the West and from the West to the East again. They heard of me in great battles and they knew of my association with the great commander of all the Union armies and how I upheld the right arm of his strength, and they said, "How great and powerful is our chief!"

The quarrel between the white men ended. The great commander with his military family settled in Washington, where the great council-fire of his nation was annually lighted and blazed in all its glory and fury. As an humble member of this military family I was the envy of many a pale-faced subordinate embryo-general who said in whisper, "Parker must be a genius, he is so great and powerful."

In a few years my military chieftain was made head and front of the whole American people, and in his partiality he placed me at the head of the management of the Indian Affairs of the United States. I was myself an Indian and presumably understood them, their wants and the manipulation of their affairs generally. Then again went out among the whites and Indians the words, "Parker must be a genius, he is so great and powerful."

The Indians were universally pleased, and they were all willing to be quiet and remain at peace, and were even asking to be taught civilization and Christianity. I put an end to all wars either among themselves or with their white brothers, and I sent professed Christian whites who waxed rich and fat from the plundering of the poor Indians, nor were there teacherships enough to give places to all the hungry and impecunious Christians. Then was the cry raised by all who believed themselves injured or unprovided for, "Nay, this Parker is an Indian genius; he is grown too great and powerful; he doth injure our business and take the bread from the mouths of our families and the money from out of our pockets; now, therefore, let us write and put him out of power, so that we may feast as heretofore."

They made their onslaught on my poor innocent head and made the air foul with their malicious and poisonous accusations. They were defeated, but it was no longer a pleasure to discharge patriotic duties in the face of foul slander and abuse. I gave up a thankless position to enjoy my declining days in peace and quiet. But my days are not all peace and quiet. I am pursued by a still small voice constantly echoing, "Thou art a genius, great and powerful," and even my little cousin, the restless Snipe, has with her strong, piping voice echoed the refrain, "Thou art great, powerful and good."

Your cousin,

DONEHOGAWA, *The Wolf.*

NEW YORK, 12, 24, 85.

DEAR GAYANESHAOH:—I know well that the Snipe is a restless, uneasy, harmless little bird, hence I was not surprised to find that my Uncle's gray uniformed, lightfooted messenger had today left another note on my table from you. Yet notwithstanding the known character for rapacity and cruelty of the Wolf in mythological lore in all countries and among all peoples, it is yet a noble animal. It was the father and mother of the founders of ancient Rome, and it deceived poor little Red Riding Hood. I am not certain whether the fidgety Snipe figures in either ancient or modern history. I hope it does since you desire it. I promise that the restless flighty, prodigal, but good little Snipe, shall receive nothing but kindness and protection from the wild, ferocious, untamable Wolf of North America, for it is very probable that the two are cousins. There must be no "Kilkenny" business in our relationship, nor any such foolish affairs as is reported to have occurred between the parrot and the monkey. . .

NEW YORK, 1, 8th, 86.

MY DEAR COUSIN GAYANESHAOH:—You have asked me a hard and perhaps an unanswerable question, viz.; when does *"the New Year begin with the Indians?"* To tell the truth, I do not believe that any such thing as New Year's is or was ever known or recognized among the Indians. They calculated time by moons, seasons, flower, berry, planting and harvest times and by all other annual occurring events, also from one annual or quarterly feast to another. Literally speaking, they termed their years, cycles, being reckoned from one event to the same recurring event, *i. e.*, a return to the same point, and this is commonly styled one snow or winter.

If your question refers to the annual Iroquois festival when purifications take place, shortcomings confessed, old fires put out, and new fires started, during which time also the immaculate white dog is sacrificed and which is now generally called by writers the "New Year's Festival," then I can answer, that it usually takes place in midwinter, which by them is fixed and corresponds to the second moon in the Christian year. The Festival might, and perhaps often does, occur in the latter part of January and sometimes in early February. No particular day is established, the moon is the only guide, together with the whims and convenience of the "Keepers of the Faith."

Hoping that my explanation may be satisfactory,

I remain your Cousin, *The Wolf,*

DONEHOGAWA.

NEW YORK, 1, 12, 86.

MY DEAR COUSIN:—Many thanks for permitting me read Mrs. Wright's interesting letter. It is very singular that those who know the Indians the best, either by being one of them or by having intimate relations with them, should almost always entertain similar views. Mrs. Wright says it is greater to Christianize than to civilize a nation, "Especially when they are surrounded by the vices of civilization, and I had almost said of Christianity and perhaps I might as well, for is not nominal Christianity flooded with vices?"

When I read this I was reminded of a sentence I had written to a lady in Lawrence, Mass., a short time ago who had plied me with nearly a score of questions on Indian matters. In answer to one question, I remarked that "the vices peculiar to Christian civilization are enveloping the remnants of this interesting people and strangling the life out of them with an Archimedean force." To this sentence she very sweetly replied, "Call it rather a *Christless civilization*. The blessed Christ had not 'where to lay His head.' And surely most dear to His heart are those to whom He gives the privilege of so entering into His earthly state through sympathy with like suffering; His many mansions will infinitely repay them all the moneys and losses here."

This lady is doubtless a good Christian, philanthropic in a useless way and evidently impracticable. Mrs. Wright is also a good, philanthropic Christian, thoroughly practical, and she knows of what she writes. I prefer her sentiments, and honor her for making a plain statement of the truth. A few more equally conscientious missionaries among the Indians would be of more benefit than all things else.

This matter is interjected here simply to show you what variety of view may or can be entertained by good people who are working for the same result. One of these ladies is a member of the "Indian Aid Association," the other is a practical, personal "*aider*" and has given her life, thus far, to the thankless task of civilizing and Christianizing the Indians, a result that after many years of labor, now seems to her an almost hopeless possibility, for she thinks the tendency of the race is "*downward*."

Respecting your own note, I can only say that I am happy, if I can by writing or by my presence bring the least bit of sunshine into your soul. I bury the fact that

"The melancholy days are come, the saddest of the year.
 Of wailing winds and naked woods, and meadows brown and sere,"

and only remember and revel in the thought that "A friend should bear his friends' infirmities," that " 'Tis only noble to be good," and that "Kind hearts are more than coronets."

Semper Idem,
The Wolf,
DONEHOGAWA.

To GAYANESHAOH,
The Snipe.

NEW YORK, 3, 12, 86.

MY DEAR COUSIN GAYANESHAOH:—I should have answered your note of yesterday the moment it was received but I was unusually busy and was in my office only for a very few minutes during the whole day. You wonder at my long silence and absence. 'Tis easily explained. You know that for some time past my wife has not been well. I made it a point to be with her just as much as I could. I was compelled to forego all social obligations and pleasures and went nowhere except where imperative necessity demanded. Thus all my friends were neglected and many found fault with me. Duty with me however was paramount. My wife did not improve and last Tuesday she took to her bed. The doctor has attended her closely since, and promises now to have her about again in a few days. My whole time therefore has been divided between the discharge of my official duties and my home. By this you will understand why I have not sought admission at your door. It was my intention to have gone to your house last Tuesday evening to lay before your consideration a letter from Mr. Tripp and my answer thereto. But the sickness at home broke up my well-laid plans and you were saved from a bore. Mr. Tripp's letter related to the same matter which has made your heart sick, *vis.*, the Sessions scheme. It was a pathetic appeal to me to do or write something, or go to Washington and help to break up this infamous plan to sink forevermore the Seneca's individuality as well as his nationality. It was almost like the Macedonian call to Paul to "come over" and "help us." My sympathies, feelings and every fibre of my soul are for my people. Yet I do not think Mr. Tripp will like my letter. It was too practical. The fact is that the Indian question. in Congress and with the American people generally, is no longer one of humanization, but is now purely political and all interested persons must treat and look at it as such.

Messrs. Jemison and John Seneca, delegates to Washington, called at my house on last Monday, but as I was still at my office I missed them. I was sorry for I wanted to find out the prospects.

As requested I return you my brother's letter. He writes a good letter. I wish I could do as well. Do not look for me at any stated time. I will appear when least expected.

As ever truly yours,

DONEHOGAWA,
The Wolf.

To My Cousin, Gayaneshaoh,
  The Little Snipe.

Your note of today seems to have been written in a spirit of vexation. And why? Because callers interfered with or interrupted the pleasant chat we were having. That was all right and proper, for society has its demands upon its votaries which cannot be avoided or evaded without offense. I am glad I did not know that it was your day, though had I known I would have called all the same, as it was the first loose time which had fallen to me since my return from the great West. Some time in the near future we may have another talk about our great country, &c. Tomorrow p. m. I go to Philadelphia to spend Sunday with a sick friend.

As ever truly yours,
DONEHOGAWA,
  The Wolf.

N. Y., 8, 27, 86.

NEW YORK, Dec. 7th, 86.

DEAR GAYANESHAOH:—I shall never attempt to criticise the work of your pen or pencil because I have not the magic spell over either which you possess. Besides I am fearful of exciting the ire of your watchful and powerful muse if I fail to grasp every idea and word she inspires. I am very glad though to know that the drooping spirit of the restful Snipe has been revived and that the smouldering embers of her lodge-fire have been revivified into a cheerful blaze by the fitful glimpse of a prowling Wolf "down the distant valley." The "foot-tracks of a wandering wolf on the fallen snow imprinted," I must ignore, for it is too near akin to "tracks on the sand," the one so suddenly disappearing at the dictation of the most gentle zephyr, and the other yielding so readily to the slightest basilisk or glance of the sun-god. A distant view of the reality even if the view be but fitful and uncertain is, to my "untutored mind," more satisfactory, Little Snipe. Keep your watch and wait for the reality of the substance whose shadows the eye of your imagination hath seen in the "far and distant valley," for remember that where a shadow is seen there is some substance to make it.

I beg you not to tell me that because the beautiful snow has fallen and covered the lovely bosom of Mother Earth, and because the North Winds howl and scream into every crack and crevice of man's shelter, I should be revelling in legendary and forestry lore.

No, dreamland, fairy-land and story-land are all good and charming for those who have time and talent that way. For me there is but one world to deal with at present, viz., the world of stern reality, and all other fancies are pushed aside for life's actual strifes. Do you know or can you believe that sometimes the idea obtrudes itself into my obtuse and lethargic brain, whether it has been well that I have sought civilization with its bothersome concomitants and whether it would not be better even now (being convinced by my weakness and failure to continue in the gladiatorial contest of modern life) to return to the darkness and most sacred wilds (if any such can be found) of our country and there to vegetate and expire silently, happily and forgotten as do the birds of the air and the beasts of the field. The thought is a happy one, but perhaps impracticable. I mention it only as a stray *ignis fatuus* of a bewildered and erratic brain.

Once more I bid the Snipe *au revoir* until circumstances decree favorably to my inclinations of visiting your tepee.

Sincerely and truly,

DONEHOGAWA,

THE SNIPE. *The Wolf.*

NEW YORK, Jany. 7th, 87.

DEAR COUSIN:—I have yours of yesterday which gave me some pleasant reading. I am pleased to know that the "New Year" just past was so satisfactory to you. I hope also the approaching New Year and the annual recurring "milestone" in your life may bring nothing with it but the most pleasant reflections, reminiscences and beneficent and healthful resolves to live the life to which an all-wise Creator has predestined you. I sometimes envy people who are gifted with birthdays and who can proudly point to some day of the year that passes over them as the day of all days most consequential to them. For remember, I am nearly akin to Topsy who never had a birthday, never was born, and only growed up; my birthday which occurred sometime "in the course of human events" was never recorded in any book of man, hence I take the liberty of being neither elated nor depressed on any special day of the year and I know not whether I am old or young. I love all the days of the year alike, and can claim any one or all of them as my birthdays. Can any one be more blessed, and also more unfortunate? I am afraid if I knew the day I should always be dreading its return or live in fear of its never returning. But as it is I am in the most gifted state of "innocuous desuetude" and consequently always happy. Pardon this wild digression but the thought flitted through my erratic brain, I caught it on the wing and impose it on you. Your literary shoulders are broad and can bear it. I can never tell whether to congratulate one for the return of a birthday. Life may have been a misery and burden to them so far, and to congratulate such and wish them many returns of the happy day would only be the most bitter mockery and sarcasm. Again with others, the pathway of life may have been strewn with roses and lighted with the brightest sunshine; congratulations to such would be an empty superfluity. In your case, however, while I know nothing of your past and much less of your future, I can sincerely congratulate you in safely nearing another important epoch and "finger-post" in your journey of life, and I can truly wish that your future roadway may be made easy and charming by every blessing which a kind and good Hawenneyo can bestow upon you.

Do you know that your use of the word "milestones" struck an uncanny chamber in my cerebrum? It brought vividly to my mind's eye those old-fashioned milestones once so numerous and important in country districts and which always reminded me of those marble slabs placed at the head of a grave in rural cemeteries, or "grave-yards," as they were called. To some they marked the buried loves and hopes of families and sometimes of peoples; to others whose fancies run free and unbridled, they mark the entrance gate to a life of which we know nothing, but which is said to be fraught with happiness or misery according as one has planted on earth. I wonder if the "milestones of life" has any philosophic semblance to the funeral or "grave" stones. I pause not for a reply, but for sober reflection and thought.

Your note respecting Mr. Clark's visit is also received. It will make Jemison's heart glad to know what Mr. Clark says. I am also delighted, and thank you very much for the aid which you have given me in this matter.

My contemplated call on you is still an uncertain event of the future. I was coming last evening, your "night at home," but a flood of company pouring in and staying prevented the execution of my plans. It is I who should apologize for writing, as you say, "so often." Your letters are solid business, my replies are "airy nothings." Then, whose is the apology? A "word to the wise . . ."

Your cousin,

DONEHOGAWA,
The Wolf.

NEW YORK, Jany. 11th, 1887.

DEAR GAYANESHAOH:—As requested I return you herewith friend Hutchinson's good letter. I also thank you for the pleasure you give me in sending me that excellent, well digested, thoughful letter of your own. I must though, right here, disclaim all knowledge of my dear mother's dream, or vision, at a certain period of my pre-existence, or advent, into this world of trouble. The "rainbow" business was rather an indiscreet interjection at so early a period of my affairs, and its influences and effects cannot with any degree of positiveness be explained or interpreted at this distance of time. It is possible that I may then have been impressed with that variegated and kaleidoscopic character of mind and fortune which thus far in my life has been my lot. That the mysterious hieroglyphics on the beautiful face of the bow of the covenant was an assurance to her that the son to be born of her would "be learned and great" is beyond my ken. The vision was beautiful and heavenly divine, but the "romance" you put into my life and attainments, in consequence, is too incongruous and unhallowed. Pardon me for using this last word, but it seemed to be so *apropos* to my abhorrence of being suspected as a "child of fate" that I could not help using it as it strikes hard at the root of the matter. You know that I mean no reflection on you or on your convictions and beliefs, for I only wish to express in the most emphatic manner my disbelief in the doctrine of fatalism. However we will let this drop and remain what we have so far been, and expect to be in this "vale of tears," cousins and friends. The past is gone never to return, the present alone is here and in it we can pluck the fruits that the gods give us, remembering, for our future that Christly injunction, to "take no thought for the morrow, for the morrow shall take thought for the things of itself." Is this fatalism? I hope not.

In your note you remark, "*I know you.*" From the bottom of my heart I wish you did. There are so many sides to my nature that I sometimes fancy myself like a chameleon, ever changing color in thought with every varying circumstance. If you do know me, you have a far deeper insight into dark mysterious human nature than I possess over my own earthly kingdom.

Now I will cry *peccavi;* I will cease to wrangle, I will restore my tomahawk to my belt, my scalping knife to its sheath and unstring my bow. These primitive weapons are no match for your electrical pen. Like Scott's coon, I say, "Don't shoot." I will come down and resume the manner and custom of civilized mankind and the rest of the world, and look only at the surface of things, which is all I generally submit to the outside world. What you read above, are only the meteoric flashes of my nomadic, ethereal brain and are harmless.

Your Insentient Cousin,
DONEHOGAWA.
THE WOLF.

NEW YORK, Jany. 22nd, 1887.

DEAR COUSIN:—I received and perused with interest the introductory "Ode" to your contemplated "Festivals," on which I dare not pass judgment, primarily because I have not the literary capacity and finally because it meets my hearty and unqualified approval. The ancient League is legitimately entitled to great praise and honor among the expiring peoples of the earth. It possessed moral and physical courage in a remarkable degree, equal perhaps to any example that the most civilized people ever recorded of themselves. Naturally, their intellectual qualities were of a marked and higher order. In the organization of the League, they attempted the unification of the contemporaneous occupants of this country on a plan worthy of the wisest and most sagacious statesmen of any age, or country. In their simplicity they early discovered, adopted and exemplified the incontrovertible and wise political doctrine, that in union there is strength.

Your exordial lines to the "Clans" to cling closer and stronger one to the other because their day is passing and night falling fast, are grand and sublime. Further comment is superfluous.

I am as ever &c.
DONEHOGAWA.

TO THE GIFTED SNIPE.

NEW YORK, Oct. 4th, 1887.

DEAR COUSIN:—The outpourings of your terrific wrath against certain Christian practices, beliefs and propositions for the amelioration and improvement of certain unchristian people who live on reservations where the English language is not spoken, and where "vice and barbarism" are rampant, was duly received yesterday. The Bishop is right in his reference to the remnants of the Six Nations being yet deplorably subject to individual disability, disadvantages and wrong arising from their tribal conditions," in all except the last proposition.

The disabilities, disadvantages and wrongs do not result however either primarily, consequently or ultimately from their tribal condition and native inheritances but solely, wholly and absolutely from the unchristian treatment they have always received from Christian white people who speak the English language, who read the English Bible and who are pharisaically divested of all the elements of vice and barbarism. The tenacity with which the remnants of this people have adhered to their tribal organizations and religious traditions is all that has saved them thus far from inevitable extinguishment; when they abandon their birthright for a mess of Christian pottage they will then cease to be a distinctive people. It is useless though to discuss this question already prejudged and predetermined by a granitic Christian hierarchy from whose judgments and decisions there seems to be no appeal.

I hope you are well. Tomorrow evening I am booked for a meeting of the Loyal Legion. Hope to call ere long.

Your Cousin,

THE SNIPE.   THE WOLF.

NEW YORK, Nov. 19th, 1888.

MY DEAR COUSIN:—Yours of the 18th received. I sympathize with you in the loss of your whilom friend, Mr. Perry. I can easily imagine that he must have been of essential and material service in spurring you on in the development of your natural instincts. I only hope that although he has gone to join the great army in the unknown land you may not lay aside the weapons with which you are armed and wrap yourself in a mantle of despair.

I do not think I am very well either mentally or physically, but I attend to my work the same as if every thing was lovely and serene, and life were worth living. The reading of "Robert Elsmere," the detestable agnostic, (which by the way I have not yet waded through) may have something to do with my imaginary or fancied depression. So far, I don't like the book,—it is probably too deep metaphysically, psychologically and religiously for me.

I have business in your neighborhood about 3 p. m. tomorrow, and I may run in and greet you. Until then, *au revoir.*

As ever,

To THE L. S.   THE WOLF.

NEW YORK, May 23rd, 88.

DEAR COUSIN:—The old saying that man proposes and God disposes is only too true. I know a lady who once wrote that on a certain afternoon she was always at home, but it seems that sometimes Providence thwarts her plans. I have always voted myself a victim of circumstances, and outside of business, I never make plans and I go and come as the ever-shifting winds, and if my impulsive schemes miscarry or disjoin, I do not nurse a feeling or thought of disappointment, and do not lose hope of better luck next time; besides I call to mind the words. "Try, try again."

Grand Army affairs and other peremptory duties command every minute of my well time, for you must know that I am far from being well, though I never speak about it to any one and I go along in the even tenor of my ways, discharging my business and other obligations like one in a trance. Twice I have called at your house because I had a few spare moments. I did not find any one at home, but I shall not give it up so, I will come again when time admits of it. Your lament received. By the way, will you and Mr. C. accept seats on the G. A. R. reviewing stand on Memorial Day? If so I will send or bring you tickets.

Yours,
THE WOLF.

THE SNIPE.

N. Y. 2, 15, 89. 12.M.

MY DEAR COUSIN:—Your two notes of yesterday, with enclosures, just received, as I have only this moment made my first call at my office.

Between your overpowering love and Mr. Bryant's fulsome adulations I am about ready to surrender the ghost. I am not aware that I have done anything either for you or for him to deserve that such commendations should be heaped like coals of fire upon my poor defenceless head. One remarks, "I never loved you so much as yesterday," and the other says "the General is the most consummate flower of all the Iroquois." Surely nothing can be sweeter and more exquisite than to have the love and flower of two dear friends thus combined and so tenderly expressed and consecrated. I thank you both with all my heart, but all the same, I am like Simeon of old, now ready to depart in peace.

I sincerely hope that when friend Bryant reads the typewritten copy of my "inspiration," as he is pleased to call it, he may like it more and give it his Samsonian support. I ask no more, and if, after all, it fails we shall fall together.

Sincerely,
THE WOLF.

POLICE DEPARTMENT OF THE CITY OF NEW YORK.

No. 300 MULBERRY STREET.

NEW YORK, March 24th, 1890.

DEAR COUSIN:—Thanks for yours of the 20th from Buffalo. The R. J. business looks encouraging, all owing to your perseverance and courage. You have had awful weather for your work, yet I hope your labors will be crowned with success, and that you have kept well through it all.

Last week I was miserable and stayed at home nearly the whole week. It is all in the foot. The sore spot is constantly enlarging and of course it is very painful. I am continuing the diet of beef and hot water. I see the Doctor often. He is very kind and good. I cannot conjecture what the issue of my trouble will be. Hoping for your success, good health and safe return in the Great Spirit's good time.

I am as ever,

THE L. S.   THE WOLF.

NEW YORK, June 23rd, '91.

MY DEAR MRS. C.—I was extremely delighted to get your brief note and learn how bountifully honors have been showered upon you by the remnants of the Iroquois, both in New York and Canada. You deserve these honors, empty and shadowy though they be, and a great deal more for the service you and yours have rendered them.

I got your card from Brantford and Mr. Converse transmitted to me from Syracuse a telegram of the proceedings there. Accept please my hearty congratulations on your triumphal tour among these simple but honest-hearted children of our ancient forests. That the Great Spirit may bless you and them always is my constant prayer.

We high-minded New Yorkers are sweltering in a temperature tinctured with suggestions of the infernal regions and consequently cooling drinks are in constant and unceasing demand. Mrs. P. and I have spent three days at Manhattan Beach and found it charming. Mrs. P. is now talking of making a visit to Chicago. Have called twice at your house and each time Mr. C. was absent. I am expecting to visit Philadelphia this week, but not for sure. I am making the same slothful advance towards recovery of good health that I have so long struggled with. If I live long enough, I may possibly get well!

You are having such a nice time, I would not by any means hurry back to New York but let the Snipe rest its little wings and fish and flutter and twitter its notes on the streams of Central New York. It will be most welcome back to New York, when it can go nowhere else.

Semper Idem,
WOLF.

L. S.

NEW YORK, July 6th, '93.

MY BELOVED SNIPE:—Yours of the 2nd was duly received and I thank you very much that you remember me and speak to me from your quiet and lovely retreat. I am very, very sorry to say though that judging from your brief note that you are much worse, in mind at least, if not in body, than when I saw you last. Every line of your note is as blue as indigo, and you picture humanity, as if they were all demons or devils, conspiring on burdening you with every misery mortal flesh is heir to, even to the unsettling of the mind, and forever darkening and damning even the soul.

Now why is this? You say yourself that you are in a most lovely country with beautiful views all around you; the silent, but peaceful, murmuring of the babbling brooklet near by inducing quiet repose, the heavenly music of the feathered songsters constantly in your ear, the almost intelligible prattle and scolding of the pretty tiny red squirrel to amuse you, the endless grinding of the cricket on the hearth encouraging reflection, and the unceasing hum of thousands of insects, seen and unseen, in the grass and shrubbery about you,—all this, I say, would seem unmistakable aids to drive dull cares away, and to bring rest, peace and happiness to the weary body and soul, and yet they evidently only increase your misery, depress your spirit, make you gloomy and morbid and your soul heavy. This is all wrong and should not be. They say that when you are in Rome you must do as the Romans do, therefore if every thing about you, animate and inanimate, is peaceful, restful and speaks of happiness, then you, who are so susceptible, impressible and imaginative should drift into the same mood and spirit of your environment, and thus disperse the gloom, desolation and inky darkness in which you are attempting to enshroud yourself, and which is by no means conducive to the recovery of good health or an even balance of the mind. Don't think for one moment that I am scolding you.—no, I never could do that; but I only want to speak plainly, honestly and truthfully to you, and end my homily. Forgive my errors.

I am in my usual health and enjoy everything around me. Mrs. Parker has again changed her mind and, with Maud, has gone back from Western New York to Denver, to stay until she again changes her mind to come home to me. Our summer weather so far has been invigorating, delicious. I am more than gratified to know that my Snipe will write me at least once a week, but don't write unless it is perfectly easy and in harmony with your mood. The Great Spirit will protect and watch over you and in his own good time, restore you in health and vigor to us who love you.

From THE WOLF.

NEW YORK, July 10th, 94.

MY DEAR SNIPE:—To say that I am busy would not be news, yet it is high time to acknowledge the receipt of your good letters, one from Buffalo and one from Bath rec'd to-day. I am happy to know that you enjoy yourself so much. You deserve it and are entitled to all the happiness you can extract from your well-earned outing.

On the 15th ult. I started or commenced a letter, (but never finished it) to you expressing my disappointment at not finding you home when I called to say good-bye and to bless you for a good journey and a safe return. I say also that you have already heard and seen things, which you had never before "dreamed of in your philosophy." The people you have been visiting, have never yet been understood, not fully comprehended. I say that "to study them satisfactorily needs a lifetime, and at the end of life one has hardly begun the study. The study of a race is like the study of a single character, both are extremely kaleidoscopic." Your opportunities have been grand and rare; you have improved them well, and to-day you are the best posted woman on Indian lore in America.

I do not feel as well or as strong as when you left; perhaps I have done too much, for business crowds me hard, or the hot weather may be too exhausting, but I am very tired and care not how soon the end comes.

My family are well. Maud is in Jersey and wife at home. When I can get away, we shall all go together somewhere, the *where* not yet determined.

I have missed you greatly, and shall continue to miss you until your return next fall.

Sincerely and Ever Yours,

TO THE WANDERING SNIPE. THE WOLF.

CHAPTER XVI

THE GETTYSBURG SPEECH OF GRANT'S MILITARY SECRETARY

Among the papers of General Parker, but one has been found having the character of an address to his military comrades. It is his speech at Gettysburg on September 26, 1891. In it we catch a glimpse both of the soldier and the sachem. The speech follows, copied directly from the first draft of his own manuscript:

GENERAL PARKER'S ADDRESS AT GETTYSBURG

"Twenty-eight years ago last July many of you were here under very different circumstances and for a totally different purpose than that which recalls you here today. Then you came to maintain the doctrine of the indivisibility of the Union of the American States, whose organic law was the liberty and equality of all men. You came to maintain the integrity of the American flag and the right that it alone should float over the free icy regions of the North to the tropical country, extending from climes of the South and East and West and from ocean to ocean. But you then came here more especially and directly to repel an invasion that was being made in this free state by a hostile army whose avowed object was the dissolution of the Union you were seeking to preserve, and which strove to perpetuate the institution of human slavery which your success would abolish and destroy forever. Here by your courage, skill, bravery and heroic determination, the rebel schemes were defeated, and today you have returned to commemorate this sad but important event by the erection and unveiling of a monument to the honor and memory of your comrades whose dust mingles with the dust of this ground.

"I can hardly comprehend how, or why, I am honored with the privilege of addressing you on this occasion, for

I can say nothing but what has been better said before by somebody else, except it is that one of the prominent features of your monument is the figure of Tammany, the Delaware Indian chief, who is said never to have had his equal as such. During the Revolutionary War his enthusiastic admirers among the whites dubbed him a saint and he was established under the name of St. Tammany, the Patron Saint of America.

"The Delaware Indians, of whom Tammany was chief, were once a numerous and powerful tribe and were masters of and occupied the whole territory lying between the Hudson and Susquehanna rivers. They were a warlike race, and, like all other primitive people who existed on the face of the earth, were at perpetual war with their neighbors and were ever ready to battle for the lands they claimed, and for the graves of their ancestors. They and all the other Indians of this continent, whether living in the dense forests, on the vast prairie plains or in the fastnesses of the mountains, enjoyed liberty in its largest and most liberal sense. They loved their freedom and believed that when the Great Spirit made this country he made it free and placed his red children here to enjoy it.

"The power of the Delawares was finally completely broken and the people subjugated by the more powerful and proud Iroquois of New York. I am not here to give you a lecture on the Indian problem, the solution of which agitates so many good minds of the present day, or to enumerate the causes which have led to their gradual extinction, or to excite your sympathy by rehearsing the wrongs, cruelties, injustice and many violations of faith they have endured and suffered at the hands of the palefaces, although as one of them I naturally and emphatically sympathize deeply with them. The two races have ever been antagonistic, though all writers agree that the Indians always received the new comers with the most open-handed hospitality. At first also the Indian looked upon the paleface as a god from another world. Soon through the antagonism of the two races, hatred revealed itself and true friendship and brotherly confidence ceased to exist. Then deadly hostilities commenced, continuing ever since, almost without cessation. In the Indian bosom was then planted to grow fiercer and fiercer with time, an implacable and unconquerable aversion, amounting almost to hatred, for the civilization and Christianity of the new-comer. Their hostility was so persistent that it soon became apparent that their continued presence constituted an almost insurmountable barrier to the advancement of the eastern progressive and aggressive civilization and the successful planting and dissemination of that religion which teaches "peace on earth and good will toward all men," but which, alas, was not to extend to the Indian until the lamp of their national life was nearly extinguished.

"To this doomed race did the chief Tammany belong. He was a brave warrior, a mighty hunter and a wise councilor. Very little indeed was known of him. Yet it is written of him that 'He was in the highest degree endowed with wisdom, virtue, prudence, charity, affability, meekness, hospitality,' in short with every good and noble qualification that a human being may possess. He was then supposed to have had intercourse with the 'great and good spirit,' for he was a stranger to everything that was bad.

"It is not known when or where or how he died, but presumably in one of the wars in which his people were engaged. His memory was ever reverenced among his people, and his name is still perpetuated among the whites by the powerful society in New York which bears his name. I believe that if ever there was a good Indian he was one, and that, too, before he was a dead one. This monument, too, while it transmits the memory of heroes who fell here, also perpetuates his name, in this beautiful monumental field, where was fought perhaps the most earnest battle of the war, and one which nearly decided the fate of the Union. This field and this beautiful valley were indeed the Thermopylæ of America—defended not by the Spartan king and his unconquerable heroes who never turned their backs to the invading millions, but by American patriots, as brave, daring and as fully imbued with a healthful, lofty and patriotic martial spirit, as any warrior band that ever marched to a field of slaughter. Their watchwords were, 'Union, Liberty and the Starry Flag forever!' They contended stoutly, with masterly constancy and unyielding tenacity, for the maintenance of the principles enunciated in the imperishable Declaration of Independence, the godlike truths of which their fathers had established after many years of doubt and suffering and many hard-fought battles. These wise fathers had electrified and horrified the civilized world when they announced their political belief, unheard of before, 'that all men are created equal,' and endowed by their Creator with certain 'inalienable rights,' among which are 'life, liberty and the pursuit of happiness.'

"On this field upon which we this moment stand, not only were the lives and liberty of the immediate participants in danger, but the lives and liberty of millions of human beings not here; and what was more important than all, the life and liberty of the Nation was imperiled and at stake. Here and yonder you stood like a wall of adamant and resisted the vast hordes who would have done all this wrong. At every point you met them with a firm, unshaken determination to do or die. Your serried ranks were thinned and broken by the savage minie, and the howling, shrieking and screeching shot and shell, whose infernal noise mercifully deafened the cries of the wounded and dying around you. The earth moaned and groaned as it swallowed the blood of the contestants. Yet, as if Mother Earth had here a plantation of the mythical dragon's teeth, other soldiers and comrades seemed to spring out of her bosom, refilling your depleted ranks and reforming your shattered lines, reviving your nearly exhausted energies and strengthening your hopes of final success. But so oft repeated were these scenes of bloody carnage on that eventful day, it appeared at times as though every man must march into the jaws of Death before the dreadful contest could be decided. Physical endurance has its limits; bright hopes had almost succumbed to black despair, Liberty was about to shriek even louder than when brave Kosciuszko fell, when the Supreme Arbiter of Nations and the God of Battles dropped his wand and gave to you the field of battle. Peace forever be to those who fell!

"The battle of Gettysburg has been written of by many as the most important and decisive of the war. Perhaps it was—I cannot judge; but on the same day that you were executing on this field such wonderful and unparalleled feats of military strength, courage and dauntless heroism, equally as important and exciting transactions were being enacted in and about the Gibraltar of the West, on the Mississippi. There that invincible strategic warrior, General U. S. Grant, was closing his anacondian coil on the City of Vicksburg, resulting the next day, the ever memorable 4th of July, in the surrender of Lieutenant General Pemberton with his entire army and the city of Vicksburg. Then, as has been beautifully expressed, 'the waters of the Mississippi again flowed unvexed by hostile forces from its source to its mouth'—the would-be confederacy severed and the field of future operations circumscribed."

"This, too, was virtually important. Yet, neither Gettysburg nor Vicksburg closed the war. The battles of Lookout Mountain, Missionary Ridge, Atlanta, Nashville, the

Wilderness, Spottsylvania, Cold Harbor, Five Forks, and Petersburg, and Sherman's March to the Sea, were yet to be executed ere the field of Appomattox Court House could loom up to witness the closing act of the gigantic conflict. At many of these points, you my comrades, were actively engaged. Upon many of these fields you have left companions who had stood shoulder to shoulder with you in battle, shared with you the danger and responsibilities of the picket-line, tented and bivouacked with you, in winter and summer, in storm and sunshine, and who did not return with you, when the war closed, to the homes they had left. It is to their memory and honor, to their unselfish, patriotic virtue, that these monuments are properly erected, dedicated and consecrated. To the survivors on any field they are speaking reminders of struggles endured, not for glory, but for their country's good; reminders of the principles they contended for, and of the necessity burdened upon them, of indoctrinating into the minds of their children as they grow up, and of their neighbors who come from other lands, the sacredness of the charge and the inestimable inheritance they have left at so great a cost of life and treasure.

"I have a foolish belief that all true and honest patriots, whether they labor in the civil or military service who die in their career, do not cease their connection with the onward march of their country. Hence, as a matter of honor and justice to all such, I would that every American child could be taught thoroughly the history of his country from its discovery and settlement onward. They should be taught to comprehend and understand how first the pioneers and early settlers grappled in a deadly conflict with the aborigines of this continent to wrest from them their country, and to make it a land 'flowing with milk and honey' and the wilderness 'to blossom as the rose.' How again, while yet in the infancy of their growth towards a national manhood, they battled with their own mother country for the causes so eloquently and clearly set forth in the immortal Declaration of Independence to which I have already referred, and for the maintenance of which declaration they placed their 'reliance on the protection of Divine Providence,' mutually pledging to each other their lives, fortunes and sacred honor.'

"Passing from that time through minor though important wars, we may gradually bring them to the last great struggle in which you, my comrades, were prominent actors, to preserve the unity of the republic, maintain the sanctity of the flag, save the life of the nation and to make a truth of the theory long since announced to the world, 'that all men are created equal;' for you freed four millions of slaves who were held in bondage to their fellowmen and made them citizens equal with you. Fully understanding and comprehending all this, it will be their plain duty to preserve the country and government you helped to save, and by their wisdom to carry forward its aims by every means consistent with justice and the general Constitution."

"The present commercial industrial and agricultural prosperity of the whole country, the universal spread of education and the consequent diffusion of general knowledge, the freedom of speech and of the press, the free and untrammeled discussion on all political subjects and theories of government, the unprecedented development and growth in every branch of the arts and sciences, and the unrestrained and unrestricted exercise allowed in all civil and religious liberties, unknown in any other country of the world, are so many safe guarantees that these United States will never again seek to indulge itself in fratricidal blood.

"I will now close by repeating with your permission a few lines written of Tammany a long time ago:

" 'Immortal Tammany of Indian race,
Great in the field and foremost in the chase,
No puny saint was he, with fasting pale.
He climbed the mountain and he swept the vale,
Rushed through the torrent with unequalled might;
Your ancient saints would tremble at the sight;
Caught the swift boat and the swifter deer with ease,
And worked a thousand miracles like these.
To public views he added private ends,
And loved his country most, and next his friends;
With courage long he strove to ward the blow;
(Courage we all respect even in a foe)
And when each effort he in vain had tried,
Kindled the flame in which he bravely died;
To Tammany, let the full horn go round;
His fame let every honest tongue resound;
With him let every generous patriot vie,
To live in freedom or with honor die.' "

CHAPTER XVII

THE HOUSE OF BROTHER NICHOLSON.

The written life story of Ely S. Parker will always remain incomplete. Probably no one now living can supply the missing fragments that would be so full of interest to us of the present day. Much of value would be lost, however, by omitting to mention briefly the other brothers and the sister, all of whom were ever dear to the General, despite his broader interests and his continued absence from his home reservation.

Isaac Newton Parker seems to have been of a roving disposition. He had a polished education, and was a keen student of fine literature. He was generally spoken of as Newton or "Newt." He served in the Union Army during the Rebellion and afterwards became a teacher in the West. His great failure was intemperance, that brought with it unreliability. His fault was ever a source of sorrow to his family and a constant element of annoyance to Ely, to whom generally fell the task of "getting him a job." His last labors were in Montana, where he contracted a fatal malady. He fell dead from his horse as he journeyed over the prairie and was buried on the plains near the spot where he died.

Levi always was a farmer and remained on his farm at the Tonawanda reservation. He was well respected and industrious to the day of his death. His children were Frank, Fred, Laura and Otto. All are living today at Tonawanda and all have large and productive farms. Otto is a chief, and Laura married Jacob Doctor, one of the head Tonawanda sachems. Laura Doctor or Ga-a-gwi-de, Sun Follower, is the "name bearer" of the family at the present time. She is "ho-ya-neh."

Besides Ely, the children of William Parker who achieved most perhaps were Carrie and Nicholson. Both were graduates of Albany State Normal School and both were ambitious to maintain the ancient ideals of the family and of the nation. Perhaps they had better opportunity than Levi and Newton. Spencer, because of a tribal political blunder, exiled himself but was restored in after years through the pleas of his father.

Carrie Parker married John Mount Pleasant, for many years the leading mind of the Tuscaroras. Her commodious home was on the Tuscarora reservation near Niagara Falls. Her fame as a hostess was hereditary. Her mother had bred the gentle art of gracious entertainment in her daughter. Carrie Mount Pleasant's home was for years a place where honored guests were cared for. Tourists, men and women of culture and refinement, noblemen and titled ladies from Europe, American men in public life, generals, congressmen, and citizens in all the humbler walks of life, came to the Mount Pleasant home when they came to Niagara. She was long known as the "Queen of the Senecas," or the "Peacemaker."

Her native name was at first Gahona; her husband's name was Dagayahdont, "Falling Woods." At a tribal ceremony after her marriage, Carrie Parker Mount Pleasant was given a new tribal name and title. She received the ancestral name, that had of right been transmitted through her mother's line for generations. It was none other than Ji-gon-sa-seh, commonly spelled Ge-go-sa-seh, and meaning "The Wild Cat" or "The Lynx." It was rightfully her mother's name and title, though Elizabeth Parker was commonly called Ga-i-ya-kuh, though her official name was Ga-ont-gwut-twus. We have told the story of Ji-gon-sa-seh in a former chapter. General Parker in writing of his sister's name said: ". . . It was once borne by the last ruler of the Neutral Nation, who was a woman. It was during her reign that the Hurons proposed to violate the neutrality of her territory in their wars with the Iroquois Confederacy. She disclosed the conspiracy to the Senecas who punished the Neutral Nation by exterminating it. Wild Cat they adopted and made her the equal of their sachems and chiefs and when she died they retained her name among them. I have, however, never heard of it being borne by any woman since her day, until it was bestowed upon my sister by the sachems and chiefs of the Seneca nation on account of her conspicuous character, connections and abilities."

Of all the lives of members of the Parker family of the grandfather generation, I am most familiar with that of Nicholson, for he was my grandfather. From his books and records and from his lips I have learned most about "Uncle Ely" and "the old days."

Nicholson, or "Nick" as grandfather was known to his intimate friends, passed the greater part of his life on the Cattaraugus reservation. He was a man of great energy, and worked with method and regularity. He never allowed Sunday work on his farm and never would permit a drop of liquor on his premises. He was a true "son of the prophet" in this respect. His industry and sobriety, too, may have been due in some measure to the influence of Rev. and Mrs. Asher Wright, the sainted missionaries who gave their very lives to the Senecas. He was first employed as an interpreter, printer and clerk by Dr. Wright. With him he translated the Bible into Seneca.

Dr. Wright wooed his wife by correspondence. She was a Vermont Sheldon and her appearance on the Buffalo Creek reservation was the first sight Dr. Wright ever had of his bride. Both had been convinced, however, that they had been called to the same great work, and both were content in the love that came with the first meeting. With Mrs. Wright came her niece Martha Hoyt, of Massachusetts stock. Then began another romance. The Indian interpreter, my grandfather, wooed and ,won the niece. During Dr. Wright's lifetime my grandfather and grandmother lived at the Mission House at Cattaraugus, where all their children were born. Soon after Dr. Wright's death in 1876 Mrs. Wright moved across the farm line and into the newly built house, occupied by grandfather Nicholson.

It was a wonderful home in many ways and until their maturity the boys and girls of the family found a happy home there. Three of the boys had helped build the house. Frank, and Fred, my father, were old enough to use a hammer, saw and square with accuracy, while Albert, though a small boy, was able to help considerably. Minnie, at this time, went away to a "select school" in Rye, New York, as the protégée of her Uncle Ely. Sherman was then but a tiny lad.

The farm, part of which had been purchased of an Indian named Two Guns, was an ideal "boys' farm." It had—and yet has—a fine orchard that produces the best kind of apples; it has good garden soil, good pasturage, and a brook where you can catch trout, if you are a trout fisherman and patient. The farm is divided by the main or Lake road, and lies between two large creeks, though each is beyond the farm line. Cattaraugus creek is "across the road" and "under the hill." Everything is handy on the farm there. Next door is the Mission House where good missionaries live; on the other side is the national fair ground. A stone's throw down the road is the Government medical dispensary, while across the road is the tribal cemetery. A stage route traverses the road. Members of the family by this rare situation get the daily paper; can be married and preached to, attend the fair, get sick, call a doctor, die and be buried, with all the rites of the church, without even leaving the neighborhood,—so "civilized" has the reservation become.

Adjoining the dispensary property is the Thomas Indian School, which was started by my grandmother years ago. I like to give her credit for its foundation, for the trials and cares of looking after seventeen Indian orphans in her own busy home led her aunt, Mrs. Wright, to enlist the sympathy of an eminent Quaker named Philip Thomas. He gave one hundred dollars to start a real orphan asylum, so in gratitude it was named after him, by my grandmother. His example induced others to give of their means. Today a magnificent State institution stands as a monument to my grandmother's compassion and confusion in caring for seventeen children who could not talk, nor eat, English style, but who could cry in all languages.

It was to this farm house that Uncle Ely made a visit once or twice each year. Over the mantel in the sitting-room, in his honor, hung his picture in full military uniform as Colonel. Over it hung his sword. The room was remarkable in other ways. In it hung the heirlooms of the family, that is, such as could be exhibited. There were quaint Indian trophies, beaded sashes, tomahawks, scalping-knives that had seen service, old flint-locks and pictures of famous members of the family all in Seneca regalia. There were large oil paintings of my grandmother's ancestors, a crayon portrait of Asher Wright and near it a wonderful engraving of "Christian, the Pilgrim." All the events of "Pilgrim's Progress" were illustrated in small circular engravings all around the picture.

I want to describe this room because I first remember seeing "Uncle Ely" there. He always sat in a big walnut arm-chair by the front window. My grandmother always kept a crash towel with roses embroidered on it over the back of the chair, because the gold thread in the brocade "got into people's clothes." It was the "best chair," and came from Boston. She always rubbed off the claws of the bottom of the chair's legs, too. I remember the claws clutched wooden balls, because I once dreamed the chair chased me and threw all those balls at me—and more too.

I always called it "Uncle Ely's chair." He was brave to sit in that chair, I thought. I never did.

In one corner of the room near the dining-room door was a "what-not." It was my grandmother's set of curio shelves. On the top shelf was the "winter bouquet" of autumn plants, leaves and grasses. Rising above all was a tall sheaf of wheat. At the bottom of the sheaf were sprays of bitter-sweet, everlasting, milkweed stalks and sprays of oak and maple leaves, colored by the frost. The lower shelves held minerals from the farm and neighboring creek gorges. There were fossils, concretions and freaks, a horse-shoe or two, knots, gnarls and vegetable monstrosities. On one shelf were coins from many countries, medals, ores and Indian silver ornaments. On another were the largest ears of corn, mingled with bird nests and fancy Indian beadwork and baskets. On the lowest shelf of all were Indian arrow and spearheads, stone axes, polished stone gorgets, fragments of broken pottery, pipes and a piece of skull, all picked up on the farm.

All the boys and girls, brothers, sisters and cousins, would lie on the bear-skin rug and look at that wonderful "what-not." We would wonder if we would ever know as much as grandma, ever be as good hunters as "Gramp" or be as great as Uncle Ely, and wear a sword like that on the wall. That room was my grandmother's to rule. Nicholson, my grandfather, might receive his honored guests there, but his own room adjoined the big kitchen. There he had his tall "secretary" filled with papers and books. He never forgot his books with all his busy farm life, and although for many years he was a "chief" in the capacity of "clerk of the Nation," or as the greater republic would say, "Secretary of State," he was ever a student. The Seneca nation, be it known, is a republic, self-governing and recognized by the State of New York and by the United States. It had revolted from the "chiefs' government" in

1848 and set itself up as a democratic state. However, the older system of aristocracy continued as an undercurrent, and grandfather was honored by having his name changed from Gai-e-wah-gowa to Gyantwaka, a name and title once borne by his celebrated half-great-grandfather, Cornplanter, of historical fame.

Grandfather every evening would refresh his mind with some classical volume. Before I was nine years old he had read Milton's "Paradise Lost" to me and had done his best to make me understand it. He read to me "King Lear," and "Midsummer Night's Dream," and had even tried to teach me algebra. At the age of seventy he went through his mathematics again. There was some rivalry between my grandmother and my grandfather in this early attempt to educate me. "Don't put such useless ideas in that child's head," she would say, "read him something sensible." Then she would take from her own shelves, "Common Things We Should Know," "The Book of Why," and "The Primer of the Stars." When it came to Scriptures grandfather would read Isaiah and Proverbs to me, while grandmother always recited the Psalms from memory. She knew most of them but years after at the age of eighty, started learning some she had neglected.

The big kitchen with its cheerful fire was the general meeting-room for the Indian neighbors who "just dropped in." Real callers of course got in the immaculately clean sitting-room. The old men who did not meet grandfather at the barn or on the big "horse-block" platform came in that big kitchen. A kitchen floor of fiction is always snowy white; this real kitchen floor was not. It was my grandfather's fault and he never heard the last of it. He laid it of elm timber and then to make it look nice had rubbed coal oil, linseed and whale oil into it. The result was a floor that always looked brown and stained. The discoloration never could be scrubbed out and I sometimes have thought that grandfather learned his algebra over again just so he could figure out how much it had cost him in brooms, hired girl help, pails, soap, sal-soda and mops to remedy his oil idea of treating floors. It was always clean, but never looked so.

It was in this big kitchen that I heard much of the lore of my ancestors. From his bedroom grandfather would take out the family records that told how his father had fought in the War of 1812. He would show me Uncle Ely's war letters, and once he showed me an envelope full of newspaper clippings about himself. Once he said he had been a lecturer and to prove it he read an old lecture and showed me the handbills he used at Victor and Canandaigua, way back in 1854. Years afterwards I found those old documents; some others had been destroyed by unappreciative hands.

To this home of his brother, filled with sons and grandchildren, would come our great Uncle Ely. Usually when he came he would bring a suit of clothes for my grandfather, made in exact pattern of his own; and a big satchel of presents for every one else. I must have been seven years old when I first saw Uncle Ely. I did not know he had come, and rushing into the sitting room, I called out "Gramp!" Then I fell back in dismay, for there were two "Gramps," dressed alike and to my startled eyes, each an exact counterpart, but when they spoke I noticed that their voices were slightly different.

While our distinguished uncle was there, all the Indians of note would come to greet him. Then there would be a time of story-telling and reminiscences, that grandfather would relate to me when all the guests had departed, or when later we would drive together with Flora or Nell, the faithful old mares.

All the Parkers of the "grandfather" generation had an hereditary love for fine horses. Uncle Ely never was without a fine span of dashing colts, and for many years, up to about 1875, my grandfather trained or bred his steeds for him. Sorrels, blacks and bays were the favorites. In many of Uncle Ely's letters to grandfather he expresses his solicitude for his "colts." There were always good horses on the farm in the grandfather days, and a pair of mules that could do some wonderful endurance work in plowing or haulage—also kicking and balking.

The prestige of being a good family of horse-traders was lost by my Uncle William, the son of Spencer Parker who married my aunt Minnie. He never made a good horse trade. The horses he got in trade always looked fine on first sight, but that in buying them Uncle William lacked the powers of second sight, was quite evident. The doughty steeds were halt, maimed or blind. Some of them had a gait like a rabbit and others walked with their front feet and dragged their rear limbs after them like the wooden teeth of a corn row-marker. It took my cousin Carl to drive those balky, walky, stalky steeds. At the first sign of eccentricity they got a series of hickory hints that came as rapidly as if shot from a gatling gun. Soon, very soon, those abnormal animals learned to behave—for Carl. Yet the horse-trading instinct had gone. Civilization does eliminate lots of judgment—and as a blind orchardist with a relentless pruning-knife trims the branches of the family tree, to shape it without considering the virtues or the products of the new twigs that project beyond the line of convention.

My grandfather was ever a pioneer of progress among his people. He, with Noah Two Guns, had the first stump-puller, and they formed a stock company. The first Deering self-binder used on the reservation was his and indeed all the best farm machinery needful for his purposes was acquired. Unlike many of the Indians he kept his machinery with great care, never allowing it to lie out in the weather to rust. Drills, corn-shellers, fanning-mills, and feed-choppers are in as good order today as thirty years ago, save the natural wear on paint and edge. His son Sherman, who ran the farm after grandfather's death, was careful with the old tools.

Perhaps this love of good farming and good farm tools gave him his interest in the "Iroquois Agricultural Society," the fair association, of which he was an officer for many years, sometimes as president and other times as secretary. It was a great exhibition in his day, and the whites came from miles around to see the "Indian fair." Wagons and horses were literally lined along the fences for two miles and on either side of the road. Grandfather had an eye for business. He had a blacksmith shop on his farm which as I have said adjoined the fair grounds.

Beside being clerk of the nation, United States interpreter, census agent, marshal of the nation, orator, agriculturist and civil engineer, my grandfather was the drum major of the Seneca Indian Silver Cornet Band. He was a versatile and useful citizen of the Seneca Republic. Like his other brother Ely, he never could completely accept civilization's teachings or wholly neglect the philosophy of his fathers. Seeing true virtue in each, according to his mood he argued for each. Many Indians have this same characteristic and often appear vacillating and uncertain in judgment when in reality the quality is merely the involuntary mental struggle between hereditary impressions and proclivities and those acquired. Until civilization crushes out all of the old instincts, or wisdom brings with it a strongly balanced judgment, Indians will ever be at moral sea; for character, point of view, methods and philosophy, like religion, may be historical and ethnic. In the ethnological sense would it not be difficult for an Englishman to rebuild his whole mental and moral nature on the teachings of Buddha and to imitate the manners and philosophy of the Hindoos? Equally difficult is it for the Indian to base his concepts of legal procedure and social relations on the civic outgrowths of the Norman and Saxon people, or acquire a religion that was nursed by the Hebrews, educated by the Romans and converted by the Anglo-Saxons and readjusted to "modern" economic notions. There ever will be confusion, until in the course of cosmic alchemy all bloods revert to an original strain, like Darwin's pigeons. How dreary and hideously uniform the world will be then! There will be no mental flint and steel. It will all be flint or all steel. There will be a salt and stagnant sea. Again the earth will be without form and void and all will be sea—the rivers from many valleys will have run dry and the valleys with the mountains will be submerged.

My grandfather was a tall, dignified man of five feet eleven inches, this being an inch and a half taller than Uncle Ely. Among women he was dignified but courteous, among men he was jovial and popular. His conduct and conversation was always chaste and he despised anything profane. He was ever proud of his blood and ancestry, and unlike his distinguished brother, often appeared at celebrations and historical exercises dressed in the full regalia of a Seneca chief. He so appeared at the dedication of the Mary Jemison council house at Letchworth Park in 1879, at the unveiling of the Red Jacket monuments at Canoga and Buffalo, and at the various ceremonial and adoption councils on the reservation. When taken to task for emulating his ancestors he said, "I can be as much a gentleman in the costume of my fathers as is a Scotch lord in costume celebrating his native events. Even Englishmen affect their old-time dress on old-time occasions."

As a matter of fact the curse of the Indian Wild West show has led many good persons to discourage Indians from wearing their native costumes since it seemed an indication that education had never done any good and that after all the Indian was "an irreclaimable savage."

But for memory's sake the old tomahawk, scalping-knife and flint-lock, the beaded sashes and feather cap all hung in the big sitting-room and helped the children imagine wonderful things when grandfather told his evening story about "old times." Oh those grandfather tales, of legends of his hunting, of traditions of his boyhood days! Those tales helped to mold the minds of his grandchildren.

Naturally a breeder of good horses had to have a good hostler to care for them, so grandfather had a colored "coachman," whose wife was a gypsy. The black man's name was Henry Baltimore and his wife's Mary Polo. She got mad at me once because I laughed when she stepped backward while scrubbing the porch and sat down in her mop-pail. She chased me with the mop and hit me with it, so I got wet just as she did, but she didn't laugh—she swore in Romany. Mary and Henry lived across the road in a two-story cabin and every now and then in the noisy night old John Kennedy would come from Gowanda, the trading town, and just to show his spite or knowledge of tradition would shout: "Injun fust, white man nex', dog nex', nigger lasht—Whoop." The next hostler wasn't a negro. He was George Shongo, an old Seneca, who lived in the back basement and who whittled out odd trinkets. My grandmother just kept him because he was poor and had no place to go. He could clean the stables and curry the horses, but would much rather make colored plumes from chicken feathers, or sew on fancy vests. Because he could whittle out fiddles and carve false faces, he was known as Ha-gon-so-nis, or "False-face maker." Once he used to drink rum, but my grandmother converted him to pepper tea.

Our next hostler was more of a fisherman in his brand of veracity. He was my grandmother's brother who once was a well-known horse-trainer. He had formerly worked for A. T. Stewart and for Robert Bonner. It was he, he claimed, who trained Maud S. However, he had fallen backward from his sulky and had his head kicked by the horse that followed. His mind was never normal after that time, except on horse matters. He was an expert horse doctor, fed the horses burdock leaves to keep them in prime and was useful in many other ways. His stories of his adventures were wonderful hyperboles but he told them over and over to every listener he could find. When he died and was buried in the Indian cemetery, I carved a horse on the grave-stake. His name was Seth Hoyt.

This chapter might be lengthened to include many a romance, but our aim has been only to picture in it a view of reservation environment and link it to the story of General Parker.

My grandfather died in 1892. Two brothers died the year before him, his sister Carrie died the same year, and Uncle Ely was left alone, of all the Parkers of the grandfather generation.

It was to this farm and to this brother, with his great family, that Uncle Ely so often came bringing cheer and sunshine, good stories and inspirations. It was to this farm that many distinguished men and women of a generation ago came—writers, scientists, missionaries, newspaper men, tourists, philanthropists. In this home and the Mission across the fence—in this family, of the grandfather generation—grew and were nursed the forces that did most to bring civilization to the Senecas of New York and to save their lands from the spoiler's cunning.

CHAPTER XVIII

THE BONES OF RED JACKET

In my great-grandfather's day, when Red Jacket, famished by his long journey from Buffalo village came to Tonawanda, he often stopped at William Parker's home for his evening meal and lodging. Here he could consult Blacksmith, Sos-he-o-wa and the other Tonawanda chiefs—besides Elizabeth was a Wolf and therefore he was her brother.

Ely Parker as a tiny lad, still in his babyhood, frequently saw the great Red Jacket and was taught to call him "grandfather." Not all the Tonawandas liked Red Jacket; his own debauchery, his ambition to be a sachem and the slander of Handsome Lake, the prophet, had done much to prejudice all the people against him. Red Jacket had his friends; his clansmen were compelled to give him food and shelter, but he was fully aware of the lingering hatred that existed in the hearts of many. General Parker, well knowing the hostility of the followers of Handsome Lake to Red Jacket, writes in explanation:

> Red Jacket was a chief and an orator. His extraordinary intellectual ability and power of speech made him a great chief among the Indians, but he never attained the rank of sachem, although he schemed assiduously for it, which was a fatal bar to his success, as it was a fundamental rule of the League that the office was to seek the man and not the man the office. Red Jacket's conceit that his power could override the unwritten laws of the League was a stumbling block which ultimately caused his downfall and embittered him to his dying day. He carried his trouble to Washington but a representation by the chiefs and sachems of the Senecas that he had been deposed, was no longer a chief and hence not entitled to be heard, had preceded him to Washington and when he reached there and found himself discredited and learned that the charm of his voice had lost its weight, his proud heart was lacerated and he returned to his home a broken-down man. The breach with his people was partially healed before his death, but he was a disappointed man.

Red Jacket had done much for Buffalo, but it was many years before that city awakened to its obligation. For years his bones had reposed in the little mission cemetery. For years his grave was unmarked. The first tombstone he had was erected by an actor, but vandals chipped it away for souvenirs.

In that same cemetery lay the bones of Mary Jemison, the white woman of the Genesee. In that same field of buried memories were the great heroes of the War of 1812, captains and sachems of the Senecas. There lay the noble Farmer's Brother, Captain Pollard, with his wife and child; Little Billy, one time Washington's guide; Young King, Destroy Town, Twenty Canoes, William Jacket and the renowned Governor Blacksnake. There in that cemetery were the mortal remains of the Senecas of the loved Do-aho-weh-gey, the Basswood land, as the Buffalo reserve was called.

The Senecas by vile fraud were driven from this loved spot. With bitter hearts they went, leaving the land of memories, the bones of their honored dead, and much of their own living spirit, behind. Every human sentiment was outraged by the Ogden Land Company; and unable now to revenge, the Senecas choked back their natural rage and went on to Cattaraugus, the Waters where Odors Arise, and down to the valley of the O-hi-yu, or Beautiful River, as the Allegheny country was called. Then the cemetery became a pasture where vagrant cattle roamed. The Senecas had been led to believe this sacred acre had been reserved, but it seems that the title had somehow been passed over to the land conspirators. For years after the Senecas came there to weep and to bring flowers, but as the older people passed away the cemetery was neglected.

In the year 1884 a movement was started to re-inter the remains of Red Jacket. Much interest had been created as the movement grew and General Parker was among the first to concern himself with this plan to honor his distinguished clan grandfather. In the course of events he wrote Mr. Bryant the letter quoted below:

No. 300 MULBERRY STREET, NEW YORK, May 8, 1884.

W. C. BRYANT, Esq., Buffalo, N. Y.

DEAR SIR:—Yours of the 25th ult. was duly received. I am very much obliged to Mr. Marshall for mentioning to you the circumstance of my having written him on the subject of the re-interment of Red Jacket's remains. My principal object was to obtain an assurance of the genuineness of the remains. This I did because I was informed many years ago that Red Jacket's grave had been surreptitiously opened and the bones taken therefrom into the City of Buffalo, where some few Indians, under the leadership of Daniel Two Guns, a Seneca chief, recovered them a few hours after they were taken. They were never re-interred, but were securely boxed up and secreted, first in one Indian's house and then in another. At length I saw by the papers that they were now lodged in the vault of some bank in Buffalo. I wished only to be satisfied that the remains which the Buffalo Historical Society proposed to re-inter were really those of the celebrated chief Red Jacket. That was all. Whatever views I may have entertained respecting this scheme, which is not new, is now of no consequence, for your letter advises me that the subject has been fully discussed with the survivors of the families of the departed chiefs, and also of the Council of the Seneca Nation, who have all assented to the project of re-interment and to the site selected.

I am, with respect, yours, etc.,

ELY S. PARKER.

Mr. Bryant sent to the General the following reply, which will be found of great interest, and may be considered the first authoritative statement of the matter ever made:

BUFFALO, June 25, 1884.

GEN. ELY S. PARKER:

DEAR SIR:—In 1852. Red Jacket's remains reposed in the old Mission Cemetery at East Buffalo, surrounded by those of Young King, Capt. Pollard, Destroy Town, Little Billy, Mary Jemison, and others, renowned in the later history of the Senecas. His grave was marked by a marble slab, erected by the eminent comedian, Henry Placide, but which had been chipped away to half of its original proportions by relic hunters and other vandals. The cemetery was the pasture ground for vagrant cattle, and was in a scandalous state of dilapidation and neglect. The legal title to the grounds was and still is in the possession of the Ogden Land Company, although at the time of the last treaty the Indians were led to believe that the cemetery and church grounds were excluded from its operation. At the time mentioned (1852), George Copway, the well-known Ojibwa lecturer, delivered two or more lectures in Buffalo, in the course of which he called attention to Red Jacket's neglected grave and agitated the subject of the removal of his dust to a more secure place and the erection of a suitable monument. A prominent business man, the late Wheeler Hotchkiss, who lived adjoining the cemetery, because deeply interested in the project, and he, together with Copway, assisted by an undertaker named Farwell, exhumed the remains and placed them in a new coffin, which was deposited with the bones in the cellar of the Hotchkiss residence.

There were a few Senecas still living on the Buffalo Creek Reservation, among them Moses Stevenson, Thomas Jemison, Daniel Two Guns, and others. They discovered that the old chief's grave had been violated almost simultaneously with its accomplishment. Stevenson, Two Guns, and a party of excited sympathizers among the whites, hastily gathered together and repaired to the Hotchkiss residence, where they demanded that the remains should be given up to them. The request was complied with and the bones were taken to Cattaraugus and placed in the custody of Ruth Stevenson, the favorite step-daughter of Red Jacket, and a most worthy woman. Ruth was the wife of James Stevenson, brother of Moses. Their father was a contemporary of Red Jacket and a distinguished chief. She was a sister of Daniel Two Guns. Her father, a renowned warrior and chief, fell at the battle of Chippewa, an ally of the United States.

When the demand was made by the excited multitude Hotchkiss manifested considerable perturbation at the menacing attitude of the crowd. He turned to Farwell and, indicating the place of deposit of the remains, requested that Farwell should descend into the cellar and bring up the coffin or box, which by the way, was made of red cedar and about four feet in length.

Ruth preserved the remains in her cabin for some years and finally buried them, but resolutely concealed from every living person any knowledge of the place of sepulture. Her husband was then dead and she was a childless, lone widow. As she became advanced in years it grew to be a source of anxiety to her what disposition should finally be made of these sacred relics. She consulted the Rev. Asher Wright and his wife on the subject, and concluded at length to deliver them over to the Buffalo Historical Society; which, with the approval of the Seneca Council, had undertaken to provide a permanent resting-place for the bones of that old chief and his compatriots.

I do not believe that there is any ground for doubting the identity of the remains and I think Hotchkiss and his confederates should be acquitted of any intention to do wrong. It was an implusive and ill-advised act on their part. The few articles buried with the body were found intact. The skull is in excellent preservation and is unmistakably that of Red Jacket. Eminent surgeons, who have examined it and compared it with the best portraits of Red Jacket, attest to its genuineness.

The Rev. Asher Wright was a faithful missionary among the Senecas for nearly half a century.

There was no opportunity afforded Hotchkiss and his companions to fraudulently substitute another skeleton, had they been so disposed. I knew Hotchkiss well and have his written statements of the facts. Farwell, who still lives, and is a very reputable man, says that when the remains were surrendered to the Indians the skull had (as it has now) clinging to it in places a thin crust of plaster of Paris, showing that an attempt had been made to take a cast of it, which probably was arrested by the irruption of Two Guns and his band.

I have dictated the foregoing because on re-perusal of your esteemed letter, I discovered I had not met the question which was in your mind when you wrote Mr. Marshall, and I greatly fear that I have wearied you by reciting details with which you were already familiar.

The old Mission Cemetery, I grieve to say, has been invaded by white foreigners, who are burying their dead there with a stolid indifference to every sentiment of justice or humanity.

Yours very respectfully,

WILLIAM C. BRYANT.

General Parker, in acknowledgment of the last communication, said that he had never entertained a doubt as to the identity of the remains, but was curious to know how the Indians had been induced to surrender them to the possession of the whites.

The reburial of Red Jacket and the nine Seneca chiefs was an incident in the history of Buffalo. Many of the best representatives of the Six Nations from Canada and New York were present. Hundreds of prominent citizens witnessed the funeral cortege and the ceremonies, and many came from long distances to take part in the exercises.

The principal address of the occasion was made by William C. Bryant, but an address equally significant from the standpoint of the Senecas was made by General Parker. As an example of the thoughts of his later life, we wish to quote it in full. It will assist in measuring his mind and in fathoming the depths of his Indian heart.

GENERAL PARKER'S ADDRESS AT THE TOMB OF RED JACKET

"Much has been said and written of the Iroquois people. All agree that they once owned and occupied the whole country now constituting the State of New York. They reached from the Hudson on the east to the lakes on the west, and claimed much conquered territory.

"I desire only to direct attention to one phase of their character, which in my judgment has never been brought out with sufficient force and clearness, and that is, their fidelity to their obligations and the tenacity with which they held to their allegiance when once it was pledged. More than two hundred and fifty years ago, when the Iroquois were in the zenith of their power and glory, the French made the mistake of assisting the northern Indians with whom the Iroquois were at war. They never forgot or forgave the French for the aid they gave their Indian enemies and the French were never able afterward to gain their friendship. About the same time the Holland Dutch came up the Hudson, and though perhaps they were no wiser than their French neighbors, they certainly pursued a wiser policy by securing the friendship of the Iroquois. The Indians remained true to the allegiance until the Dutch were superseded by the English, when they also transferred their allegiance to the new comers. They remained steadfast to the faith they had given, and assisted the English people to put down the rebellion of the American Colonies against the mother government.

"The colonists succeeded in gaining their independence and establishing a government to their liking, but in the treaty of peace which followed, the English entirely ignored and forgot their Indian allies, leaving them to shift for themselves. A portion of the Iroquois, under Captain Brant, followed the fortunes of the English into Canada, where they have since been well cared for by the provincial and home governments. Those who remained in the United States continued to struggle for their homes and the integrity of what they considered their ancient and just rights. The aid, however, which they had given against the cause of the American Revolution had been so strong as to leave an intense burning hostility to them in the minds of the American people, and to allay this feeling and to settle for all time the question of rights as between the Indians and the whites, General Washington was compelled to order an expedition into the Indian country of New York to break the Indian power. This expedition was under command of General Sullivan. The Indians left to themselves and bereft of promised British aid, made Sullivan's success an easy one. He drove them from their homes, destroyed and burnt their villages, cut down their cornfields and orchards, leaving the poor Indians homeless, houseless and destitute. We have been told this evening that the 'Long House' of the Iroquois had been broken. It was indeed truly broken by Sullivan's invasion. It was so completely broken that never again will the 'Long House' be reconstructed.

"The Indians sued for peace. They were now at the mercy of General Washington and the American people. A peace was granted them, and small homes allowed in the vast domains they once claimed as absolutely and wholly theirs by the highest title known among men, viz.: by the gift of God. The mercy of the American people granted them the right to occupy and cultivate certain lands until some one stronger wanted them. They hold their homes today by no other title than that of occupancy, although some Indian bands have bought and paid for the lands they reside upon the same as you, my friends have bought and paid for the farms you live upon. The Indian mind has never to this day been able to comprehend how it is that he has been compelled to buy and pay for that which has descended to him from time immemorial, and which his ancestors had taught him was the gift of the Great Spirit to him and his posterity forever. It was an anomaly in civilized law far beyond his reasoning powers.

"In the treaty of peace concluded after Sullivan's campaign the remnants of the Iroquois transferred their allegiance to the United States, and to that allegiance they have remained firm and true to this day. They stood side by side with you in the last war with Great Britain, in the defense of this frontier, and fought battles under the leadership of the able and gallant General Scott. Again the sons of the Iroquois marched shoulder to shoulder with you, your fathers, your husbands and your sons in the last great rebellion of the South, and used, with you their best endeavors to maintain the inviolability and integrity of the American Constitution, to preserve unsullied the purity of the American Flag, and to wipe out forever from every foot of American soil the curse of human slavery. Such, in brief has been their fidelity to their allegiance.

"It was during the troublous times of the American Revolution that Red Jacket's name first appears. He is mentioned as a messenger, or bearer of dispatches, or runner, for the British. He subsequently appears at the treaty of peace and at all treaties and councils of importance his name is always prominent. He was a devoted lover of his people and defender of their ancient rights. His political creed did not embrace that peculiar doctrine now so strongly believed in, that 'to the victors belong the spoils.' He did not know that the Sullivan campaign had taken from his people all the vested rights which God had given them, and when subsequently, he was made to understand that a pre-emptive title hung over the homes of his people he was amazed at the audacity of the white man's law which permitted and sanctioned the sale and transfer by one person to another of rights never owned and of properties never seen.

"From the bottom of my heart I believe that Red Jacket was a true Indian and a most thorough pagan. He used all the powers of his eloquence in opposition to the introduction of civilization and Christianity among his people. In this as in many other things he signally failed. So persistent and tenacious was he in his hostility to the white man and his ways and methods that one of his last requests is said to have been that white men should not dig his grave and that white men should not bury him. But how forcibly now comes to us the verity and strength of the saying that 'man proposes but God disposes.' Red Jacket had proposed that his remains should lie buried and undisturbed in the burial-place of his fathers. Very soon after his death the people removed from their old lands to other homes. Red Jacket's grave remained unprotected, and ere long was desecrated. God put it into the hearts of these good men of the Buffalo Historical Society to take charge of his remains, give him a decent burial in a white man's graveyard, and over his grave to erect a monument which should tell his story to all future generations.

"We have this day witnessed and participated in the culmination of their labors. But Red Jacket has been honorably reburied with solemn and ancient rites, and may his remains rest there in peace until time shall be no more. While a silent spectator of the ceremonies today, the words of the Blessed Savior forcibly presented themselves to my mind: 'The foxes have holes and the birds of the air have nests, but the son of man hath not where to lay His head.' I applied this saying to the Indian race. They have been buffeted from pillar to post. They once owned much but now have hardly anything they can call their own. While living they are not let alone, when dead they are not left unmolested.

"Members of the Buffalo Historical Society: The representatives of the Iroquois here present have imposed upon me the pleasing duty of returning to you their profound and sincere thanks for the honor you have done their people today. Mournful memories are brought to their minds in the sad ceremonies in which they have been both participants and witnesses, but their griefs are all assuaged and their tears dried up by your kindness. They will carry back to their people nothing but good words of you and yours. They again return you thanks and bid you farewell."

General Parker then exhibited the Red Jacket medal presented by order of General Washington, President in 1792. It is of silver, oval in shape, seven inches long by five inches broad. The general had dressed it in black and white wampum, the black indicating mourning and the white, peace and gladness. In the article in the *Buffalo Courier* of October 10th describing the occasion, the editor truly says:

"The production of this medal was important, because stories, like that about Red Jacket's bones, have for some time been current to the effect that this medal was exhibited out West years ago. Like Red Jacket's bones, however, it has been carefully preserved, and there is no doubt whatever of its identity."

Six years passed and a movement had grown having as its object the erection of a fitting monument to the orator of the Iroquois. General Parker consulted with sculptors and friends. His idea was to make the monument symbolic, carrying out the Indian ideas of a fitting memorial, departing as far as possible from the ordinary statue with a merely ornamental base. The thought which came to General Parker's mind was to preserve the prophetic words of the great orator, "I am an aged tree." General Parker depicted this idea in the following plan, which I find after these years in his own handwriting:

THE RED JACKET MEMORIAL.

"I am an aged tree, and can stand no longer. My leaves are fallen, my branches are withered and I am shaken by every breeze. Soon my aged trunk will be prostrate." Such are a few of the memorable words reported to have been uttered by Red Jacket to his people in his house to house farewell visits just previous to his death. They are personal in their character, the "aged tree" meaning himself, the withered branches his exhausted strength, and the fallen leaves the loss of all his children who were the pride and glory of his early manhood. While the words are so exclusively personal, to me they also speak of the expiring life of the Iroquois Confederacy. The embers of its council-fire had been extinguished, its ashes scattered to the four winds of heaven and the symbolic Long House left a mass of ruins after the expedition of General Sullivan into the Seneca country in 1779. Whether Red Jacket felt this or not, it was notwithstanding an accomplished fact when these words were spoken. The "aged tree" represented the Indian Confederacy, the birth of whose existence was unknown to the memory of man; its fallen leaves the extinguishment of its long line of brave warriors and sage counsellors; and its withered branches the disintegration of its various tribes. Red Jacket, in condoling with his special people on the consequences which would follow his approaching dissolution, was but pronouncing a requiem upon the ghost of the ancient confederacy, the refrain to which can only be sounded by its present unfortunate survivors.

It seems to me that the happy simile of the tree must have been deeply rooted in Red Jacket's mind, for upon another occasion, in referring to his family afflictions, he is reported to have said: "Red Jacket was once a great man and in favor with the Great Spirit. He was a lofty pine among the smaller trees of the forest. . . . The Great Spirit has looked upon him in anger, and the lightning has stripped the pine of its branches."

In my mind I have hastily reviewed the many incidents happening in Red Jacket's long life, and I am at present forcibly impressed that the "aged tree" is the most fitting emblem that could be placed over the spot where rest his mortal remains, because it will appropriately perpetuate the ideas he entertained of himself and at the same time properly symbolize the ending or death of the Iroquois Confederacy.

I am neither an artist nor a critic of art, but my idea of this memorial is, for the "aged tree" to stand on the pedestal solitary and alone; Red Jacket, in an oratorical pose, with four or five Indians to represent the other nations, sitting or in recumbent positions about him, to be on the front bas-relief; broken bows and arrows with broken pipes and partially buried tomahawks and other warlike implements to be on a side bas-relief; and the symbolic "Long House," in ruins, on the other side in bas-relief. The fourth side of the pedestal might be left vacant to indicate that the extinction of the Confederacy leaves a blank in the history of this country, as has happened to other tribes who have journeyed to the spirit land before them and been forgotten.

The above are mere suggestions for consideration. Any other plan equally suggestive and comprehensive will secure my cordial approval and support.

ELY S. PARKER.

N. Y., 2-13-'89.

Another plan however succeeded, and while Mrs. Harriet Maxwell Converse was raising funds in 1890, Mrs. Martha M. Huyler contributed the amount necessary for the complete monument, though it was built on entirely different lines. It stands today at the entrance of Forest Lawn Cemetery in Buffalo, a tribute to Red Jacket and Red Jacket's people.

General Parker living came once again to witness the dedication of that monument. He came once more in death, and like Red Jacket, his remains were taken from their first grave, to be reburied beneath the shadow of that monument, and by the side of the great men of his nation who had known his father.

We can not close this chapter on Red Jacket without quoting General Parker's letter, describing Red Jacket's disappointed ambition to become a Sachem of the League. He wrote:

NEW YORK, November 26, 1884.

WILLIAM C. BRYANT, Esq. Buffalo, N. Y.:

DEAR SIR:— I owe you many apologies for not before answering yours of October 25th, which was duly received, but I have had so many other things to attend to that your letter was temporarily laid aside. I will now, however, respond as briefly as I can to your inquiries respecting Red Jacket.

You say you "have always been led to believe that Red Jacket did not belong to any of the noble or aristocratic families in which the title or distinction was hereditary." Also, "was his mother of noble birth?" etc., etc.

Let me disabuse your mind of one matter in the outset. Such a thing as aristocracy, nobility, class caste or social grades was unknown among the Iroquois. A political superiority was, perhaps, given by the founders of the League to the Mohawks, Onondagas and Senecas, who were styled "brothers," and were addressed as "fathers" by the Oneidas and Cayugas, who also were "brothers" and yet "children." Nor were the Turtle, Bear and Wolf clans invested with the first attribute of nobility or aristocracy because they were also the elder brothers and cousins to the other clans. I am of the opinion that no purer and truer democracy, or a more perfect equality of social and political rights, ever existed among any people than prevailed among the Iroquois at the time of their discovery by the whites. Often at that time and since persons attained positions of prominence and power by their superior intellectual abilities or their extraordinary prowess and success on the war-path. (Conspicuous examples of this fact are Joseph Brant and Red Jacket.) Successes of this kind, however, brought only temporary and ephemeral distinction to him, his family, his relations, his clan, and perhaps, reflected some honor on his tribe. But this accidental or fatuitous distinction was not transmissible as a rightful or hereditary one, and was retained only so long as intellectual superiority, military prowess or personal bravery could be maintained by the person or family.

When declining years broke one's intellectual and physical powers some younger person immediately dropped in to fill the gap, and the old warrior or councilor fell away into obscurity. Thus it is easily seen how the hand of power and distinction could be constantly shifted from one person or family to another, and could never remain settled longer than he or they were able to upheld the qualities entitling them to the supremacy. The founders of the League may or may not have considered this question in the organization they made. They perfected a confederacy of tribes, officered by forty-eight hereditary sachems or peace men and two hereditary military sachems or chieftains. They ignored the individuality of persons (except Tododaho) and families and brought the several tribes into the closest relationship by the establishment of common clans or totemships, to whom was confided the hereditability of the League officers. It was a purely accidental circumstance that some of the clans in some of the tribes were not endowed with sachemships and that others got more than one. But because some of the clans got more than one sachem, and because a family in that clan was temporarily intrusted with the care of it, did not in consequence thereof ennoble or make the clan or family aristocratic. Bear in mind this fact: a sachemship belongs to a clan and is the property of no one family. Honorary distinctions are only assumed by the tribes or clans from the fact that the League makers gave them the rank of the elder or younger, and the family government and gradation of kinship was introduced to bring the same more readily to their comprehension, understanding and remembrance.

This idea of Indian social grades with titles is all a vain and foolish fancy of the early imaginative writers, who were educated to believe in such things; and the idea is retained, used and still disseminated by our modern susceptibles that love and adore rank and quality, and that give and place them where none is claimed. I do not deny that Royaner in the Mohawk means Lord or Master, but the same word, when applied to terrestrial or political subjects, only means Councilor. The Seneca word is Hoyarna, Councilor; Hoyarnagowar, Great Councilor. These names are applied to the League officers only, and the term "great" was added to designate them more conspicuously and distinguish them from a great body of lesser men who had forced themselves into the deliberations of the League Councilors. The term Hasanowaneh (great name) is given to this last great body of men, a body now known as chiefs. They were never provided for and, as I believe, were never contemplated by the League originators, but they subsequently came to the surface, as I have hereinbefore set forth, and forced a recognition of their existence upon the "Great Councilors," and, on account of their following and ability were provided with seats at the council board.

Red Jacket was one of these "chiefs." He was supremely and exclusively intellectual. He was a walking encyclopedia of the affairs of the Iroquois. His logical powers were nearly incontrovertible, at least to the untutored Indian generally. In his day, and to the times I am referring, the "Great Councilor's" word was his bond; it was of more weight and consequence than the word of a chief. Red Jacket knew this well, and, while he could not be made a League officer, he used every means which his wisdom and cunning could devise to make himself appear not only the foremost man of his tribe but of the League. He was ever the chosen spokesman of the Indians to the seat of government, whether state or federal. In the signing of treaties, though unsuccessfully opposing them in open council, he would secretly intrigue for a blank space at or near the head of the list of signers, with a view, as the Indians asserted, of pointing to it as evidence that he was among its early advocates, and also that he was among the first and leading men of his tribe. He was even charged with being double-faced and sometimes speaking with a forked tongue. These and many other traits, both good and bad, which he possessed, worked against him in the minds of his people, and interposed an insurmountable bar to his becoming a League officer.

After the War of 1812, whenever Red Jacket visited the Tonawanda Reservation, he made my father's house his principal home, on account of his tribal relationship to my mother, who was of the Wolf clan. My father and his brother Samuel were both intelligent men, and knew and understood the Indians well, and were also fairly versed in Indian politics. During my early youth I have heard them discuss with other Indians the matters above referred to, and while they always agreed as to the main facts, they generally differed only as to the underlying motives and intentions of Red Jacket in his various schemes.

White men visiting Indians for information usually ask specific questions, to which direct and monosyllabic answers are generally given. Seldom will an Indian go beyond a direct answer and give a general or extended reply; hence, I am not surprised that you had never heard anything respecting my statement, for as such a thing had never occurred to you, you have never thought to ask concerning it. The fact, however, remains the same, and I do not consider it derogatory of or a belittling of Red Jacket's general character. Men of mind are nearly always courageous and ambitious. Red Jacket was not an exception.

You suggest the performance on my part of an act which is simply impossible. The words sachem, sagamore, chief, king, prince, cazique, queen, princess, etc., have been promiscuously and interchangeably used by every writer on Indians ever since their discovery. I have seen three of the above terms used in one article with reference to one and the same person, showing great looseness and want of discrimination in the writer. Yourself, let me say, mention John Mt. Pleasant as "the principal hereditary sachem of the Tuscaroras." Now, my classification of Iroquois officers would be to rank the fifty original councilors as sachems, because they are the highest officers of the League. I would not use the term sagamore, because its use is almost wholly New England, and has been applied promiscuously to heads of bands, large and small, and sometimes to mere heads of families. To use other terms, such as king, prince or princess (see King Philip, King Powhattan and Princess Pocahontas), is preposterous and presumptuous, considering the total absence among these people of the paraphernalia, belonging and dignity of royalty. My classification is: League officers, fifty in numbers, "Sachems"; all others, "Chiefs." The Tuscaroras, for certain reasons, were not admitted to a perfect equality in the League. They were not granted sachemships. Hence, Mt. Pleasant is not a sachem, only a chief. His talent and character might, indeed, constitute him the head chief of his tribe, but I doubt if his successor in name would take the same rank or exercise the same influence over the tribe that he does. Besides, the sachems alone can exercise a general authority in the League, while the chief's authority is confined to their respective tribes or bands. To invent a new name now for our fifty League officers would produce endless confusion in papers and books relating to them and their affairs. The task is too herculean to undertake.

Pardon me for having been so prolix. I may also have failed to make myself understood, for I have been compelled for want of time to leave out a great deal of explanatory matter. But you are such a good Indianologist that I feel certain of your ability to comprehend me. I am, with respect,

Your obedient servant,

ELY S. PARKER.

General Parker never forgot his obligation to his people, and in all the records that remain, we find his voice raised in petition that their memory be preserved by the conquering race. His intimate knowledge of that race's history gave him material for argument. This gave strength to his pleas which in many cases were effective in bringing about action on the part of interested friends or organizations. The Geneva Historical Society brought to his attention the old burial place of the Senecas at the State Agricultural Farm near Geneva and in a memorial to the State Legislature he petitioned that it be set aside forever in memory of his nation. We therefore record his memorial as he wrote and signed it. His prayer, and that of his friends, was granted, and today the tract is set aside as State property and shall forever be unmolested by vandal hands.

MEMORIAL TO THE STATE LEGISLATURE.

To the Honorable, the Legislature of the State of New York:

I have been informed that adjoining the "New York Agricultural Experiment Station" near Geneva, N. Y., there is a certain piece of land of about three acres, which bears evidence of having once been the "Burying Place" of the Seneca Indians. This particular "Burying Place" must have been one of the many opened and used by the Senecas after their traditional dispersion from the "Great Hills" about Canandaigua Lake, and their resettlement at Ganundasaga (New-town or Geneva), and other places about Seneca Lake and west of Cayuga Lake.

It is a historical fact that the Senecas claimed the country westward from Cayuga Lake, and their villages, or castles, were more thickly placed between Lakes Cayuga and Seneca, about the smaller lakes of Canandaigua, Honeoye, Conesus and Hemlock, up and down the beautiful valley of the Genesee river and so on westward to the country of the Neutral Nation along the Niagara river and to the homes of the Eries along the southern shores of the great lake of that name. Both of these Nations were subsequently exterminated by the combined power of the Iroquois, and this gave the Senecas unlimited claim to all the country west of them to the great Mississippi, and also Western Canada. The Senecas, however, lived in the villages and castles of their original country, but roamed, *ad libitum*, to the countries north, south and west of them in pursuit of their national amusement, viz.: that of fishing, hunting and war. The earliest expeditions of the French, English and Dutch found them a happy and contented people, and from a barbaric standpoint, they were a prosperous people, for their villages were well located, their dwellings comfortable and adapted to the climate; they cultivated fields where they raised corn, beans, squashes and potatoes for their subsistence, and where besides they had apple, peach, plum and cherry trees in profusion. They also had a regular organized system of government suitable to their condition. The avarice, rivalries and cunning of the different pale-faced races by which they were being rapidly surrounded, brought them into unfortunate entangling alliances, and for the part they took against the colonies in their struggle for independence, General George Washington, in 1779, sent an armed expedition, under command of General John Sullivan, to exterminate this people and wipe them out from the face of the American continent.

General Sullivan carried out his instructions with scrupulous exactitude, destroying thousands of bushels of corn, cutting down hundreds of acres of standing corn and fruit trees at all their settlements, and burning all their villages and castles that he could find. The Indians made only a nominal resistance, but they were scattered and their national life was practically extinct after this expedition, and the few scattered remnants at once allied themselves with the people of the United States. To that allegiance they and their children have remained true to this day.

In 1812 they fought side by side with the American soldiers in repelling the invaders from the northern frontier of the United States; and in the late Rebellion they marched shoulder to shoulder with the bravest of the Union men to the defense of the glorious flag of the Stars and Stripes and to the maintenance of the doctrine that the American Union of States is one and indivisible.

But it was on the expedition of General Sullivan that burial-places adjacent to some villages were discovered and noted. Among them, one not very far from Geneva was mentioned as a sepulchre, where there then lay in full exposure the corpse of an Indian chief, or sachem, dressed in his full robes of state. This burial place, it is suggested, should be bought and cared for by the State of New York as a monument of the place where this people once dwelt. It matters very little to the people of this State, or to the undersigned, whether this be done or not; but to the historian and to future generations, it is a matter of moment, to know what people lived here, what their characteristics, what relics they have left and also what the people of this State have preserved of their predecessors before they themselves became so deeply and firmly rooted in this ancient Indian soil.

The amount required to initiate this matter is but a trifle, and to maintain it hereafter is a mere bagatelle for the great Empire State, and the honor it will confer upon a heroic pre-existing race will be a noble one. This burial plot was forcibly abandoned by the Indians more than a hundred years ago, nor is it likely that an application similar to this will ever again be presented to the Legislature of this State. The Indians, as such, have left no memorial monuments. A monument to Logan, the Cayuga, the avowed friend of the white man, put up by private enterprise in the cemetery of Auburn, N. Y., is the only death remembrance which I am aware of that any Indian has ever received in this State.

A proposition to perpetuate the memory of the Indian Demosthenes, Red Jacket, and several of his compatriot chiefs by the erection of a monument in the cemetery at Buffalo, is yet in embryo. The few surviving remnants of the Iroquois in this State will undoubtedly make suitable provisions for the protection of the grounds wherein they are at present depositing the last of their race. It is only natural and proper for people and individuals to wish to perpetuate in some manner the memories of their existence. The ancient Egyptians left to us their obelisks and pyramids, the Romans their buried cities, the Greeks their arts and literature, the English are leaving their relics in Westminster Abbey, the Americans have already planted a Washington Monument, and all that is asked here of this Legislature is the purchase, preservation and consecration of this small piece of ground, where shall remain, undisturbed from vandal hands, the dust of the Seneca dead.

Respectfully yours,

E. S. PARKER,
A Seneca Iroquois Sachem.

NEW YORK, Feb. 1, 1888.

CHAPTER XIX

THE LAST GRAND SACHEM.

The Sachem had wandered afar from his people but he could not forget them. The force of circumstances had placed him in the midst of activities of civilization as a business man competing with other men. Though he often expressed a longing for the quiet valley of the Tonawanda and the council hall of the Senecas, his obligations held him to the island of Manhattan, and in the houses of stone dedicated to business, law and government.

His city home was on Forty-second street, west of Sixth avenue, and there with his wife he entertained his many friends. He was ever sought by cultured men for his charming manner and interesting conversational ability. Yet he never dropped to the commonplace. He was not a man who could talk about the weather, merely for the sake of talking.

The General was devoted to his wife, whom he frequently described to his friends as "the one woman in all the world for me." He was with her in sickness and in health, always kind, patient and courteous. It is said, however, that he was ever dignified in her presence, never familiar or frivolous.

As his fortunes faded he took a position in the Police Department of the city, where his old friend, General Smith, was Police Commissioner. He was at one time department architect, and later, until his death, supply clerk. It was in this historic office at 300 Mulberry street that he met many distinguished men who later entered public life. Here he saw Jacob Riis, the Danish newspaper reporter, and here he worked at the side of the aggressive Theodore Roosevelt. Three hundred Mulberry street was a meeting place for many rising, aggressive men. Jacob Riis in his "Making of an American" tells of some whom he met there, and of his acquaintance with Parker:

> I suppose it was the fact that he was an Indian that first attracted me to him [writes Mr. Riis]. As the years passed we became good friends, and I loved nothing better in an idle hour than to smoke a pipe with the General in his poky little office at Police Headquarters. When, once in a while, it would happen that some of his people came down from the Reservation or from Canada, the powwow that ensued was my dear delight. He was a noble old fellow. His title was no trumpery show either. It was fairly earned on more than one bloody field with Grant's army. Parker was Grant's military secretary, and wrote the original draft of the surrender at Appomattox, which he kept to his death with great pride. It was not General Parker, however, but Donehogawa, Chief of the Senecas and the remnant of the once powerful Six Nations, and guardian of the western door of the council lodge, that appealed to me, who in my boyhood had lived with Leather-Stocking and with *Uncas* and *Chingachgook*. They had something to do with my coming here, and at last I had for a friend one of their kin. I think he felt the bond of sympathy between us and prized it, for he showed me in many silent ways that he was fond of me.

The General was ever a busy man, but somehow he always found time to visit with a friend or to write a friendly letter. At his fireside in the evening he frequently wrote long letters in answer to the innumerable questions he received. Likewise, when he could not resist the longing he would visit his old home at Tonawanda or go for a visit to his brother Nicholson at Cattaraugus. Just who all his friends were in New York the writer does not pretend to know. There were many of them, particularly army men. His friendship with Colonel Fred D. Grant was a deep and lasting one. He had known Fred as a boy and had taken him to his sister's home at Tuscarora. We only know he worked ceaselessly. His few leisure hours were either spent at home with his wife and daughter or at a friendly game of billiards, at which he was an expert player.

His health in general was good but he showed the strain of the indoor life. An injured ankle developed a chronic case of varicose veins that left an open sore for several years. He suffered much from it, though he seldom mentioned it save to very close friends. His friend Dr. Salisbury was his physician, but though famous as a surgeon he never quite cured the injured ankle and foot.

The General was often asked to write a story of his life, but he never did completely. Many things of importance he regarded as of little interest. He never wrote the story of his parents or told of his childhood acquaintance with Red Jacket save to intimate friends. He never even mentioned that his father and mother were cousins, according to the white man's way of reckoning. In the Indian system, however, each parent was of a different clan and the marriage was perfectly permissible. Fragments of his writings have been found, however, chiefly among the papers of his friend, Mrs. Harriet Maxwell Converse.

The death of his sister Carrie in 1893 was a severe shock to him. She was the only sister of the family and the two had a deep bond of sympathy between them. With her death only three members of the family remained—Levi, Nicholson and himself. Both brothers were destined to pass away during the same year. He alone remained. That same year, on June 15th, he was stricken with paralysis at his desk at police headquarters.

He was nursed back to health at his summer home in Fairfield, Conn., but he never fully recovered, although he resumed to some extent his customary labors. His battle for life was a heroic one, such as would be expected in a man so reared; but two years later he seemed on the verge of a collapse. He was granted a leave of absence by the Police Commissioner and he went to the home of his friend Arthur Brown in Fairfield. He concealed the pain he suffered—he lived by force of an indomitable will. To a friend during these last days he said: "I came down to dinner to please the ladies, but I could not eat. I think I am dying physically." He revealed his lower limbs which were black with the lifeless blood that had settled there.

A few hours passed. He lay upon his bed, with his wife and daughter Maud beside him, and thus he passed to the land of the hereafter, passed to the sky-world of his fathers. Only his Maker knew of his pain or of his battle.

His physician said afterward that his heart had beat until there was no more blood to pump, before it ceased its work.

Then the news flashed over the wires, "Donehogawa is dead." Papers issued "extras" describing his remarkable life, and bereaved friends hastened to Fairfield for their last glimpse of the sachem of the Iroquois. His own people, with his relatives, came. Colonel F. D. Grant, then Police Commissioner, expressed his genuine sorrow. "General Parker," he said, "was a brave man. He served on my father's staff with distinction and was promoted for bravery. I am not superstitious," he added, "but yesterday morning I was especially thinking of General Parker and when I heard of his death I was not surprised. He died at the moment I was thinking so intently." Mrs. Parker had telegraphed Commissioner Grant of the General's death and a newspaper reporter recorded his remark.

Members of the Loyal Legion, a detachment from Reno Post, G. A. R., and a delegation from the Society of Colonial Wars came to do the military honors due their departed brother member. His Masonic brothers were there in numbers. Among his military friends were Colonel Fred Grant and General C. T. Colles.

From the reservation came Mrs. Jacob Doctor, the daughter of his brother Levi, Frederick Ely Parker, the son of his brother Nicholson, Sachem Chauncey Abrams and Abram Moses, all representing the Tonawanda Senecas; from Cattaraugus came Sachem Chester Lay and Andrew John; from Tuscarora came Chief Elias Williams and F. L. Johnson; from the Onondagas came Daniel LaFort, President of the Six Nations, and Abram Hill, the Wampum Keeper of the Confederacy of the Nations.

Among these men—we shall not name them—were high representatives of the ancient League of the Iroquois, and members of the ancient fraternities of the Iroquois of which Do-ne-ho-ga-wa had been a member.

The funeral was conducted after the Episcopalian ritual. Upon the dead sachem's breast reposed the insignia of the Society of Colonial Wars and of the Loyal Legion. Of greater interest were the strands of sacred purple wampum that lay upon his casket, curved inward in the form of a circle, the ends touching. These were the sachemship or ho-ya-neh "horns" and in that position symbolized that his life had been completed. But this wampum is never buried, for it is a living thing, and the seal of a title. The Wampum Keeper, before the casket was taken away, turned the ends outward like the spreading horns of a ram, or the sign of Ares, in token that the name of Donehogawa lived and would be "raised" again at the *Ho-de-os-ka* of the Nation.

So, contrary to his mother's vision and her prophecy, this son of Tonawanda was buried in the land of the paleface and in the old territory of the Pequots, the ancient vassals of the Confederacy. Was it true her fancy had come to naught, like most Indian superstitions? Was it the bitterness of a sordid world of prosy fact that prevented the death cry of his clan? "*Go-weh, go-weh, go-weh;* Do-ne-ho-ga-wa is returning to his people!"

Poetic justice, the will of his people, the patriotism of the Buffalo Historical Society, came to the rescue. Do-ne-ho-ga-wa should return and the spot seen by his mother at the foot of the rainbow should fold him in its earthly embrace.

On January 20, 1897, with the consent of Mrs. Parker, the body of the General and sachem, was brought to Buffalo and reinterred at Forest Lawn Cemetery. He now lies beside his forefathers and beneath the shadow of Red Jacket's monument. There friends gathered, red and white. President Andrew Langdon and Secretary Frank H. Severance of the Historical Society were in charge of the arrangements, and with them were Dr. Joseph C. Greene, Charles J. North, and Dr. J. H. Tilden. The Loyal Legion Committee included General James E. Curtiss, Colonel James N. Granger, Colonel C. E. Walbridge, Captain T. H. Fearey, Captain E. L. Coe, Maj. L. Marcus and H. H. Marcus Among the Seneca Indians were Sachem Chauncey Abrams, William Parker, Minnie C. Parker, Mr. and Mrs. Thomas Poudry and daughter, Mr. and Mrs. Jacob Doctor, Howard Hatch, David Shanks and wife, Chas. Cloute, Benjamin Ground, Anderson Charles, Alfred Jemison, David Moses, Truman Shanks and Mr. Skeye. The remains had come from Connecticut accompanied by Mrs. Ely S. Parker and the faithful Mrs. Harriet Maxwell Converse.

Sachem Abrams, interpreted by William Parker, made the burial address in behalf of the Senecas. "The people of Do-ne-ho-ga-wa's own race," said Sachem Abrams, addressing President Langdon, "are grateful for all you have done today. It pleases us. We are much gratified to know that Do-ne-ho-ga-wa rests among his own people and not in a land of strangers."

Once more destiny, through the loyalty of military friends and the never-ceasing interest of Frank H. Severance, and the Buffalo Historical Society, called a large company to the grave-side. It was for the purpose of dedicating the grave marker, given by Reno Post, No. 44, G. A. R., of which in life General Parker was a member. The ceremony took place on Decoration Day, 1905.

A final tribute at the grave was paid by Captain Samuel H. Beckwith of Utica, an old friend and comrade of General Parker. The two had been closely, almost intimately associated during the critical campaigns about Richmond and Appomattox. Parker had been Grant's military secretary and Beckwith his cipher dispatcher.

The last prayer was given by Rev. J. Emory Fisher, the missionary at the old Cattaraugus Mission. Then in accord with the rites of the Grand Army of the Republic, Captain A. J. Smith read the memorable address of President Lincoln at Gettysburg. When the grave had been banked with flowers, Moses Shongo, a Seneca Indian, made an address in his native tongue. In closing his talk he said:

"Today the floating spirits of the unseen are among us. Would that they could give expression of appreciation, as they all were gifted in speech far more than I. But I will endeavor to speak for my people, and to say that we extend to you our most sincere and heartfelt thanks for the noble act you have done for your brothers, the redmen of the forests, the men of nature. The quiet undisturbed surroundings of this spot show that those who have gone before although no more seen, are not forgotten."

Forest Lawn Cemetery is a part of the old Granger estate, where the Indians, in the first decades of 1800, came to council and to trade. Here Elizabeth had the vision of her future son and here she had seen the signs that the medicine man interpreted to her.

"A son shall be born to you who will be distinguished among his nation as a peacemaker; he will be a wise white man, but will never desert his people, nor lay down his sachem's horns as a great chief. His name will reach from the east to the west, from the north to the south as great among his Indian family and pale-faces. His sun will rise on Indian land and set on white-man's land, yet the ancient land of his ancestors will fold him in death."

APPENDIX

APPENDIX

A VISIT TO THE PARKER HOMESTEAD

(See Introduction, page 6.)

In collecting the material which has furnished the data for this book, not a single paper or document came from the immediate estate of General Parker. His library and files must have been rich with material that would have delighted a biographer, but so far as we know the records that we should have been grateful to have, perished during the process of clearing up his estate. The records that we have came mostly from the General's reservation relatives and friends, or from official files and published articles.

Since a small boy I had been interested in the romantic story of my Great Uncle, and thus I began a collection of notes, papers, clippings and anecdotes,—in fact anything I could find relating to him. For twenty years this process went on until in 1912 it occurred to me that the material should be brought together in the form of a biography. Accordingly I again visited both the Cattaraugus and the Tonawanda reservations seeking new material. At Cattaraugus I found numerous letters and papers, some of them just thrown out into a woodshed, from whence I rescued them. It was at the Tonawanda homestead, however, that the best material was found.

Through the sympathetic interest of Laura Parker Doctor, the daughter of Levi Parker, I was able to find in the files of the General himself, left in the homestead in the days before the Civil War, many papers of exceptional value. Several visits were made and many interviews followed. Mrs. Doctor cheerfully turned over the material and, with her brother Frank, aided in many other ways.

Mrs. Doctor is the daughter of the late Levi Parker, the brother of Ely. Upon the death of General Parker she became the owner of the reservation homestead, though the General had anticipated the bestowal of this property upon his sister Caroline. She, however, died before he did, and thus the land and buildings passed to the favorite niece, who had long been a faithful helper in every emergency. Long ago she had married Chief Jacob Doctor. It was an advantageous alliance, for she, too, was an influential woman in the tribe, being the holder of the right of nominating the successor to the title of Ga-nio-dai-u or Handsome Lake. This she gave to her brother Otto who served as Sachem of the League until his death in 1914. She still preserves the strands of wampum that have been used from time immemorial in confirming the right of nomination. The house in which she now lives is the home into which William Parker and his family moved after the land across the creek passed into the hands of the whites. It has been fixed over in a modern manner which outwardly conceals its age.

The farm is situated against the reservation line and contains some of the best land on the reservation. It edges the creek on one side, contains a wood lot, fine pasturage, a pond and a good orchard. The interior is well furnished, as country homes go, and the parlor and the sitting-room furniture, of walnut and mahogany, has been kept with great care. In the book-case are the books once belonging to Ely and Nicholson, truly a splendid collection of the scientific, historical and periodical literature of the period before the Civil War. Mrs. Doctor has preserved the home, the books and the relics with a conscientious regard that is most commendable.

In this home she has instructed her nieces and nephews in the lore and the responsibilities of the family. Here she has sheltered many an orphan and homeless boy and girl and sent them forth with a new grip on life and its problems. Her husband was equally generous. To her many duties as home keeper she added that of weaver, dairy owner and poultry keeper. For many years she wove rag carpets and rugs with such matchless skill that she had little competition,—and indeed, little spare time. To her niece Carrie, or "Dollie" as she is affectionately called, she owes many comforts and from her she has received many months of help in her multifold duties.

Always an ardent church worker, she has been the church treasurer for many years and it was ever the delight of Carrie and Maisa to sit with her in the big church, and to hear "Uncle Otto," preach in the Seneca tongue. Now that Jacob, her husband, lies in the churchyard with the dust of his fathers, she runs the farm herself, though her three score and thirteen years weigh heavily upon her work-worn shoulders. Still she is a tribal authority and widely known for her good sense and her honesty.

While sitting around the fire one winter day, I asked her to tell of her early recollections,—recollections of the grandmother days. Though she was busy preparing her maple sap she consented.

"I suppose you know that my Indian name means 'Follower of the sun,'" said she. "I hope always to follow the sun,—that is, the true light that everyone should follow. But you say you want to know about the grandmother days. I can tell you some things but not all, for I have been a very busy woman and thought more about my work than about history. Still I think I can tell you something.

"My grandmother was a member of the Wolf Clan and so my father, Uncle Ely and their brothers and sister Carrie were Wolves. How well I remember my kind grandmother! She was the busiest woman I ever knew and never was quiet during the time she was awake. I often looked at her because I thought her very beautiful, very good and a lesson to me in industry.

"When Otto and I were very small, Grandmother used to take us with her when she cared for her sugar bush. She would put both of us in a great pack-basket and carry us on her back for many a mile over the rough country to the places that she visited. Sometimes when she was tired she would allow me to run along by her side, but she was very strong and though Otto and I were five and seven years old we did not seem a burden for her back.

"She had four sugar bushes, three of them her own. She tapped three hundred trees in each bush and could do the tapping very fast. She could tap all the trees before you could fix one right, so swiftly did she work. In each bush she had a bark cabin that my grandfather William had erected. These cabins were just like the ones lived in in old times and had platform beds all the way around and above. The fire was in the center on the ground and the smoke went up through a great opening in the roof. Oh, it was very nice and we liked the time when sugar was made because of the great fun we had then. I wish these times were back again, because I think the world was better then; certainly the Indians were better off for they were more industrious and better off. The door of our cabin was often nothing more than a deer skin or a buffalo robe but we kept quite warm.

"Grandmother boiled her sap in big kettles and made sugar and not syrup. When afterward we wanted syrup we would melt the sugar with a little water. The sap tubes were made of wood but sometimes Grandmother would gash the trees with an axe. Her collecting vessels were bark or log tubs and she had a great many of them that she kept piled up in her sap-houses. I liked the smell of the woods, and the smoke in the cabins was fragrant.

"At night we rolled up in fur robes and slept warm and very sound. We were not afraid because Grandmother had an ax and was a very good shot with either a gun or a bow. She always had both with her, and would shoot rabbits, coons, big birds and other game as well as any man. We got up early and Grandmother was always attending to her sap. Those were very happy days and it seems to me I never had anything to worry about.

"Now I want to tell you about her house across the Tonawanda creek near Indian Falls, or Tonawanda Falls, as they called it then.

The house was a large log building with an "ell" used for storage or as a spare bedroom. The cabin was more than 20 by 40 feet and the lower floor consisted of one great room. It had a very large fireplace in which logs were burned. We had no furniture except benches and there were plenty of these. Our dishes were of bark and wood, our forks were awls of wood and bone, our spoons were carved out of wood dyed red in hemlock root dye. Our wooden bowls were very handsome and some were carved from knots or knarls. When we ate, two benches were put together and the bark or wood bowls of meat, soup, corn-hominy and boiled bread were put on the benches. Our tablecloth, when we had any, consisted of sheets of bark, smooth side up. They were easily cleaned. Some members of the family had their own bowls, but the children had one large bowl out of which all ate, dipping in with their wooden spoons. Some were very nice spoons with carved birds and animals on the top of the handles. Grandmother always kept a large kettle of food warm by the fire and everyone who came into the house received a bowl of food. We had many visitors,—sometimes twenty. I do not know how she cared for them all. A great many Indians and some white men came to see my grandfather, William. He was a pine tree chief, and a sort of man who gave advice on laws and customs. Uncle Sam was a real chief and sat in the Council. Many a night the men sat up until two or three o'clock in the morning talking. Then they took blankets and rolled up on the floor by the fire and slept until Grandmother arose to pound the corn meal for the breakfast porridge. She had some help but insisted on doing most of the work herself.

"She slept up-stairs, and there was room for a great many people there. In the garret we had the corn stored and there was a great deal of it, because we had so many visitors. Everybody, it seems, wanted to stay at our house, and so our home became a general source of news and a place of meeting. No one ever thought of paying for food or for lodging and such was not expected.

"Grandfather had a saw mill and ten or twelve horses. He worked a great deal and sold many logs and much lumber. He hunted some down the Allegheny, but mostly we raised our own beef and pigs. I think he had to work hard to support his large family and provide for so many visitors.

"Grandmother made baskets. She made a great many of them and would take a wagon and team and sell them to the stores in the neighboring towns and villages. She made all kinds of farm baskets, household baskets and fancy baskets. Once I made some little baskets and when I went with her on a trip I sold them for three cents each. But, Grandmother could make the real Indian baskets too. Some were of corn husk and were thought valuable by the Indians. She could make burden straps or tump-lines of slippery elm and basswood bark fiber. She made very fine bead-work too and Aunt Carrie learned from her.

"My Grandmother always dressed in the old-time costume, until after awhile she had white folks' dresses. Her older clothing consisted of a beaded broadcloth skirt, an overdress covered with brooches, leggins and moccasins, but after awhile she had shoes. It was a long time until she had a hat. Her head covering was a small shawl made of a sort of wool bunting with a ribboned edge bordered with white beads. It was very pretty and I think I like such a head-throw now because my Grandmother did.

"Ely, Nick and Carrie were away at school a good deal but when they came back they used to play with us children and give us things.

"We always talked Seneca in those days and heard little English. Long before any of my uncles went to school we used to go to the church where the Baptist missionaries came to preach. This always had to have interpreters. Now this will interest you because you are writing the book about Uncle Ely:

"One Sunday the missionary preacher found that there was no interpreter. He looked everywhere to find one and after awhile he asked Grandfather if his boy could talk English and Grandfather said, 'Yes, a little.' So Ely was called, and he was then twelve years old. He was put on the pulpit stand and interpreted the sermon. Soon it was seen that he was speaking slower and still more slowly. By and bye he shut his eyes and then he fell in a faint. The effort was too much, and it was his first attempt to speak in public, and he didn't know much English. Maybe the sermon was too hard for him to explain, I do not know. After that he went away to Canada and after a time came back and went to the Mission school where he learned English more perfectly.

"When Ely grew older all the people hoped much for him and used to put on his shoulders important tasks. He had access to his father's papers and treaties and learned a great deal about the old customs. He always went to the councils and made notes which he kept. We had boxes of papers which he kept. Some are the papers I have given you for the story of his life.

"After awhile the whites bought up our land across the creek and we had to move over on this side. Grandfather built a new house which became old after the years went by and then Ely had it fixed up with clapboards and shingles. We were always afraid that we would lose our land and the people have always been worried. We thought soldiers would come and drive us off. This idea so preyed upon my mind that just a few years before the Civil War as I was crossing a stump lot I looked up, and there was a soldier with a gun. He looked at me and I stood for a moment looking at him. I thought our time had come, and then I ran to the road and told a company of women and a man what I had seen. They just petted me and said, 'We guess not.' We went through the lot later and there was no soldier there. I do not know now whether I just imagined it or not.

"There were always being held councils at which Grandfather and Ely attended. Sometime about 1852 there was a great Condoling Council at which Ely was raised to the dignity of Sachem, with the name Do-ne-ho-ga-wa. This clipping from the *Buffalo Courier* tells of this event." And Mrs. Doctor gave me the following which may be preserved here:

INDIAN COUNCIL OF THE SIX NATIONS

A Grand Council of the Confederacy of the Six Nations, to wit: The Mohawks, Oneidas, Onondagas, Cayugas, Senecas and Tuscaroras, was held at Tonawanda Friday last, for the purpose of celebrating the funeral rites of their Last Grand Sachem, John Blacksmith, deceased, and electing a Grand Sachem in his place, electing chiefs, etc.

After the council fire was kindled, the Oneidas, Cayugas and Tuscaroras advanced in double file, as chief mourners, the leaders singing the death song. After performing some ceremonies the whole band moved to the Council ground, where all the old rules and customs of the Confederacy were repeated in song. This occupied a long time,—after which the chiefs previously selected were installed, and instructed in their duties.

Ely S. Parker, (Do-ne-ho-ga-wa), was proclaimed Grand Sachem of the Six Nations. The Speaker invested him with the silver medal presented by Washington to Red Jacket, and worn by him until his death. (Mr. Parker, now in official dignity and honor at the head of the Six Nations, is an educated man of fine talents and exemplary habits, and is one of the Assistant State Engineers).

Spencer C. Parker, brother of the Grand Sachem, together with eight others, were installed as war chiefs, to fill vacancies occasioned by death; and the whole proceedings were conducted with great harmony and good feeling.

"After this council Uncle Ely was looked upon as the man who must save his people from the hands of the land stealers, as we called them, who were trying to move us west and take the reservation. After a time Ely got the Indians to organize better and secured their lands to them, and had the State pass laws guarding their interests. Ely had many great friends among the whites and knew Henry Schoolcraft and Lewis H. Morgan.

"I must tell you about Mr. Morgan. I did not see him much because my father Levi had his own home and I was a small girl, but I heard that Mr. Morgan used to come to talk over old times so that he could write a book about the Senecas. He told the old folks a good many things, and helped them in many ways. He gave my grandmother her first set of dishes, and knives and forks. We never had real cups or plates before but only wood and bark dishes and carved wood pitchers. When we had these gifts my grandfather made chairs and a table. I have that first table here in the house now.

"After awhile we heard that Uncle Ely had come back from the West to go to war, but he tried and they did not take him. After awhile they sent for him and he got ready to go. I was there and saw him on a fine black horse. He went to council and the people talked with him and asked him to stay with them, for who would be their friend if he should be killed, but he said he was determined to go and thought he would come back all right. A Batavia paper printed this account:

MEETING OF THE SENECA INDIANS

Last week a meeting of some six hundred Indians was held at the Council House on the Tonawanda Reservation to bid adieu to Ely S. Parker, their much respected and beloved chief, who has accepted a position in the U. S. Army. Mr. Parker goes as Assistant Adjutant General on General Smith's staff, in Grant's army, now before Vicksburg, for which position we know of none more fitted, being an experienced civil engineer, and having heretofore filled responsible situations under the Government in that capacity.

"After the war we did not see him much because he was very busy in Washington and in New York. His mother died during the war and old William soon after. I have this clipping for you, saved in an old pocket-book. It tells of Grandfather's death and the kind of man he was.

DEATH OF A VENERABLE SENECA CHIEF

The venerable and well known Indian chief, William Parker, died recently on the Tonawanda reservation in Genesee County.

He was the father of Captain Ely S. Parker, one of General Grant's aides, of Nicholson H. Parker, U. S. Interpreter, and of Newton Parker. Miss Caroline Parker, an estimable Indian lady, and a graduate of the State Normal School, is, we believe, his only daughter. Mr. Parker was on the war-path as scout in the War of 1812, and was disabled by a severe musket wound in the wrist at the sortie of Fort Erie. For his services and wounds he has for many years received an invalid pension from the United States Government. His wife is the niece of the celebrated Red Jacket.

William Parker was a man of commanding size, and of a noble and dignified presence. He possessed much good sense and discrimination and was noted for incorruptible honesty. He was a true man and a faithful friend and advisor of his race, and was an associate and compeer of those other honest and true chiefs, Jemmy Johnson and John Blacksmith. In the long struggles of the Tonawanda band against the Ogden Land Company, the modest, calm old Chief Parker, was always to be relied upon, and he lived to see his band owners in fee of some 8,000 acres of valuable land, and with a large surplus invested for their benefit.

"My Grandfather died in the large room in the house where I now live,—the dining room being chosen because it was large and accessible. He was buried at the side of Grandmother, and between her and Uncle Samuel in the very back of the Baptist Cemetery. And, thus, you see how the old people have gone. Our chiefs now know little of the struggles of those who spent their lives for the Tonawandas. And, as for me, I wish the old times were back again because we were happy then, very happy. The few things that I have that were owned by Uncle Ely, I want the Buffalo Historical Society to have; the relics of the old days, like the false face and the rattles I want to have placed in Albany, (in the State Museum) where Mr. Morgan and Uncle Ely sent their things, and then all can be together. When this is done my mind will be relieved of its burden and I shall have done my duty."

THE BOY WHO DARED TO TRAVEL WEST
A Legend of Grand Island

As told by Edward Cornplanter and recorded by A. C. Parker
(See Chapter II., page 15)

Ga-non-dai'-ye-o lived with his aged grand parents in the depths of a great wood. The old people were always sad but Ga-non-dai'-ye-o was never able to discover the cause, and inquiry would only bring the injunction, "Never go west!" The boy obeyed and played happily in the forest to the north and the south and the east but shunned the dark woods to the west.

At length Ga-non-dai'-ye-o began to reason upon the matter:

"Never go west," he said to himself. "Now why may not I go west? Is not west as good as east? Surely I am denied my right and shall no longer submit. I am determined to find why west is to be avoided."

Thus determined, he crept cautiously through the vine-bound underbrush and with caution advanced in a westerly direction. He kept on for some time and then, to his surprise, found himself on the borders of a large body of swift water. He looked across the broad expanse with admiration and wonder. Was this the sight his grandparents wished to deny him? "Oh, the shameful rule that forbade him this!" he thought. While he was gazing at the scene and meditating upon it, he heard a sound behind him. A pleasant voice was saying:

"Haih, Haih! Is it not a beautiful stream and wonderful too? Did you never see it before? Come, jump into my canoe and let us visit some of the inlets and isles that are found hereabouts. We will return in a short time and you will have seen sights worth talking about."

Ga-non-dai'-ye-o was charmed with the idea, and following the stranger stepped into the canoe that lay on the sandy beach of a cove. The stranger gave the canoe a shove with his paddle and sent it shooting out from the shore. With swift even strokes he carried it far out from the land.

"We shall visit a beautiful island," said the stranger.

A short distance ahead Ga-non-dai'-ye-o saw a small island in the centre of which was a dense clump of trees. It lay near a very large island. Such a charming spot was it that he wondered if it had as inhabitants men who were "*oweh*" and not ghosts. Soon the canoe grated upon the beach, and both jumping out, the stranger drew up the canoe.

"Now," said he, "look around and see what a fine place this is. Oh, you will like it,—you will like it. I do!"

Ga-non-dai'-ye-o walked upon the shore toward a tall plant that bore flowers. He stood viewing it for a few moments and then turning to follow his guide found that he had disappeared. He ran to the water to find the canoe, but to his dismay found that it too had gone. Glancing up and over the lake he saw far in the distance the canoe and the stranger, and then he realized his situation.

Heavy-hearted he dragged himself half way around the island and then walking inland for a few rods sat down dejectedly on a fallen tree. Tears filled his eyes and he moaned bitterly, "Wo-dis-tait, I am a miserable creature."

While he thus sat lamenting his fate he heard a loud whisper, "Kechuta, kechuta!"

Starting up he looked around to discover the source of the sound, but failing, sank back to his seat with a groan of pure misery.

Presently he heard the same sound, "Kechuta!" It seemed to issue from the ground at his very feet. This time he was thoroughly frightened, and again he looked about to discover, perchance, who the speaker was, but as before he failed and flinging himself upon the log began to weep violently.

"Kechuta!" came the sound again and looking down at the ground at the end of the log he noticed a white glistening spot. Poking away the sod he saw first the hollow eye sockets of a skull and then jaws full of white teeth.

"Kechuta!" said the skull, and the Ga-non-dai'-ye-o knew that the thing wished to smoke. "Dig into the sod by that knot on the log and you will find my bag and pipe." So spoke the man-reduced-to-bones.

Marveling, the boy obeyed and soon pulled out a decayed pipe-bag and a tobacco pouch. He packed the pipe-bowl full of tobacco. Then picking up a hard round stick, the size of an arrow shaft, he twisted it in his bow string, placed a pitted stone on one end and put the other end on the log. Pushing his bow backward and forward he twirled the stick with great rapidity. Soon a tiny spark ignited the wood dust and caught in a blaze on the shredded cedar bark. It was a laborious task, but Ga-non-dai'-ye-o at length had the pipe in smoking order. Leaning over he pried apart the jaws of Jis-ga, as he had named the skeleton, and pushed the pipe-stem between its teeth. Jis-ga smoked with great diligence and exclaimed, "Agwus wiu, oh how good, how I enjoy it. I've not had a smoke in a great while. Oh, I am glad you came to me! Now let me tell you a story; but first, fill my pipe again. There! Now, boy, this is an enchanted island. You are trapped, the same as I was and the same as many more have been. There is a man who lives here. There is a man who visits here and there is a man who lures men here. He who *lives* here is Sa-go-we-no-ta, a great sorcerer. He who *visits* here is On-gwe-yas, an evil ogre. Both eat men. They ate me, they ate many others, they will eat you, unless you listen closely. Before sunrise tomorrow, run to the beach where you landed and bury yourself in the sand, leaving one eye and an ear uncovered. Look and listen! No one has ever escaped; but you may if you obey me, and moreover you may overcome the island's evil spell."

The boy solemnly promised obedience and after a restless night ran to the beach and buried himself in the sand. Soon he heard the sound of singing on the water. The song grew louder and Ga-non-dai'-ye-o knew that the singer was nearing the beach. He heard the sound of the canoe as it shot up against the sand and knew that the singer had landed. He listened closely to the song and then hummed it softly to himself. The sound of footsteps neared and turning his eye he saw a man whose grim visage pronounced him a man of terrible passion. Ga-non-dai'-ye-o looked as well as he could from his hole in the sand and knew that was On-gwe-yas. At the feet of the ogre was a pack of dogs who followed him up the incline.

As On-gwe-yas stepped upon the island Sa-go-wa-no-ta sang from his den in the grove.

When On-gwe-yas reached the top of the incline he roared, "Well, where is my meal?"

"He can not be found" came the answer.

"Put your eyes in the bushes. Send the dogs after him," roared On-gwe-yas.

The search was fruitless and grumbling in rage the man returned to his canoe, threw in his dogs, and jumping in, swept his paddle through the water and sped back to mainland.

Ga-non-dai'-ye-o jumped from his place of concealment and rushed to the log where Jis-ga lay. Breathlessly he told what he had seen and heard and told how thankful he was that he had escaped being eaten.

"Smoke,—tobacco,—I wish to smoke," whispered Jis-ga, dustily. So taking an ember from the fire he had started Ga-non-dai'-ye-o lit the pipe and shoved it between the teeth of the skull. When it had finished smoking it said,

"I am glad that you have succeeded so well. It is an omen of good fortune. Now listen. Make seven dolls from dry rotten wood and make a small bow and arrow for each; then, place each doll in the top of a tree. Conceal yourself in the sand again. See what will happen."

Ga-non-dai'-ye-o did as directed and the next day when On-gwe-yas landed he grumbled loudly and vowed he would find the boy, for he was very hungry. He strode up the beach and his dogs with noses close to the ground followed the track of Ga-non-dai'-ye-o as it circled the isle. Suddenly one dog with a yelp fell, pierced with an arrow On-gwe-yas yelled in rage, and his rage increased as one after another fell dead. Snatching up the body of each he threw it upon his shoulder and going back, flung it into his canoe, and then paddled back across the lake.

Leaping from the sand Ga-non-dai'-ye-o ran back to Jis-ga and related his observations.

After Jis-ga had been satisfied with tobacco he said to Ga-non-dai'-ye-o, "Now, I will tell you more. On-gwe-yas, always fearing death, leaves his heart in his lodge. It hangs suspended over a pot of water, likewise the hearts of the dogs. When he returns he will place the dogs' hearts back within their chests and as they beat the dogs will revive. He will then remove them and return to the island on the morrow to renew his search for you. Now listen closely. Bury yourself in the sand as before and as On-gwe-yas approches the shore sing the Sa-go-we-no-ta song. On-gwe-yas will then rush up the shore, the dolls will shoot again and, while On-gwe-yas is obscured in the bushes, jump into his canoe, go directly across the water, and when you touch the shore you will find a path that leads to a lodge. Enter the lodge and destroy the hearts you find there. Then you may return to me."

The next morning Ga-non-dai'-ye-o covered himself with sand and when he heard the song of On-gwe-yas floating over the water he shouted back another song in defiance.

On-gwe-yas stopped short in his song and listened. Then he shouted back.

"Ho-yo-ho! So you have him. So, I'll be there!"

From a mound in the center of the island came a voice in pleading tones. It cried: "No, no! I did not call you. Do not come. Oh, do not!"

"Oh, no," came the mocking reply. "You can not cheat me. You have found him and wish to eat him alone."

Landing, On-gwe-yas ran toward the mound. Ga-non-dai'-ye-o jumped into the boat and with his swiftest, strongest strokes sent it gliding out over the river. Leaping to the shore he ran up a path and burst through the curtain into a lodge. A young girl was refining bear oil by boiling it in a kettle. Without stopping to greet her, Ga-non-dai'-ye-o cried:

"Give me his heart!"

"No, no, do not touch it. It is his, it is his!", remonstrated the girl in terror.

There was the sound of footsteps outside. On-gwe-yas had followed in some mysterious manner and was now at the door. Springing toward the back of the lodge, Ga-non-dai'-ye-o grasped a large beating heart. On-gwe-yas was pushing aside the curtain and now snarled in terrible rage as he saw the boy who should have been his victim holding his heart. With marvelous swiftness Ga-non-dai'-ye-o flung the heart into the pot of boiling fat. The ogre tottered; his dogs began to yelp up the trail and as Ga-non-dai'-ye-o glanced through the door between the curtain at the swaying body of On-gwe-yas, he saw their dripping bodies, red eyes and froth-laden fangs, as they leaped toward their master. On-gwe-yas trembled, and fell. Ga-non-dai'-ye-o swept the seven dogs' hearts into the scalding liquid only a moment before the ogre crashed his head into the fire, breaking the pot of oil and spilling out the hearts. On-gwe-yas was dead, and seven dogs lay before the door.

The girl who during this terrible scene had cringed in one corner, now rushed toward Ga-non-dai'-ye-o with a glad cry.

"Oh, my brother!" she cried. "You have rescued me. I am your sister who was captured. On-gwe-yas kept me as his slave. Oh, my brother, you have saved our family!"

Ga-non-dai'-ye-o hardly knew what to make of these words, but looking down at the girl saw in her his lost sister,—lost years ago. He rejoiced with her and then running back to the shore paddled swiftly to the Isle of Fears. Going up to the log he appeased his friend Jis-ga with tobacco and told his story.

"Now," said Jis-ga "you have done well. You can be of great service to me if you will obey a few more instructions; for instance, shoot that fat bear over there and place her pelt over this little mound where I am. Scold that stump and make it move away, so that you may cover the mound entirely. Then smoke!"

Ga-non-dai'-ye-o was startled as he looked up and beheld an enormously fat bear asleep, not ten steps from him. Fixing an arrow he shot and killed the beast and removed its hide. Walking up to the stump, he shouted:

"What is the matter with you? Get out of my way or I will smash you. Go on now." With the help of a kick the stump jumped backward into a clump of bushes. Placing the skin over the mound Ga-non-dai'-ye-o built a little fire and began to throw on tobacco.

The sun was hot and the oil fairly dripped from the skin into the ground.

Ga-non-dai'-ye-o became impatient. "What is the trouble with you, Jis-ga?" he called—Move lively. You are lazy. Hurry or I will leave! I can not wait all day! Hurry or I will go!"

There was a slight movement beneath the bear skin.

"Hurry now," continued the boy, "or I will pull off the skin," and, stooping down he gave it a fling. As he did so from the ground arose a company of men. All were quarreling.

"You have my legs—my fingers! You have my hands! You have my feet! My ribs—my neck,—where is my back bone? Three ribs missing—oh,—some one has my whole body— didn't have time—made us hurry—too quick—short notice! Such were the mingled cries from the strange swarm.

Before Ga-non-dai'-ye-o was as queer a company of distorted men as the sun has ever seen. Some had one long leg and one short one, some were humpbacked, some were small-bodied and large-limbed, some had heads on backward, some had no necks, some were double the wonted length; and soon each man was a sight to behold. All were angry; and fighting, disappeared into the forest, all but one. It was Jis-ga. He stepped forward and took Ga-non-dai'-ye-o by the hand and said,

"I am your brother, let us go home."

Hastening to the shore the two seated themselves in the canoe and paddled back to the lodge on the opposite bank. A meal awaited them and after eating it the boys built a great fire and burned the evil lodge.

That night the three slept in the open. The next morning the brothers and their sister tramped through the forest to the lodge of their grandparents and found the old people mourning over the loss of Ga-non-dai'-ye-o.

The old folk were exuberant with joy when they found that not only was Ga-non-dai'-ye-o well and alive, but also their other grandchildren.

The boys built a large lodge and made the days of the old people easy with soft beds, much meat and pleasant company.

Then the grandparents said, "We are old and wise, but now we know that which we did not before: It is evil to forbid a boy of resource to do or to go without a reason."

So here it ends, this ga-gah, this ancient story.

HANDSOME LAKE THE PEACE PROPHET[1]

(See Chapter II., page 18.)

One century and eighty-two years have passed since the birth of the Peace Prophet. In the wilderness village of Ganawagus on the flat lands of the Genesee this prophet was born, but the people of his time viewed the tiny unpromising babe not as a possible prophet but

---

1. Being a portion of the address delivered by A. C. Parker at the unveiling of Handsome Lake's monument, at Caledonia, 1916.

as a hopeless candidate for the highest sachemship the Seneca nation could confer upon one of its kinsmen. The child had been born into one of the noble families, the Hoyaneh of the Nation of the Great Hill. His brothers and cousins were also potential candidates for the future honor, and of all this babe was the most likely to be rejected, for he was puny and sickly. The Turtle clan took pity on him as he became a youth, and with his half brother, the Turtles took him from his Wolf Clan relatives and gave him food and training. They hung about his neck a strand of wampum and said, "So long as our arms are about you, you shall be as a tree in our midst and may not be uprooted; your blood is that of the Clan of the Wolves, but your heart shall now be the heart of the Turtles, for they love you."

Years passed by,—years of which the recorders of tradition have left no writing, and then as if to rebuke the scoffers who predicted feebleness of character, this youth, now grown to manhood, has become the idol of the Clan of Wolves. The women speak of him in their bark cabins or while in the fields. They say he is their friend and protector. The children love him for he tells them stories of the flowers and birds; his pouch is filled with nuts and maple sugar,—he is kind to children. Yet this young man is very melancholy and seems always to be mourning. He looks to the east and shakes his head; the wagon trains of the settlers marching over the Buffalo trail fill him with gloom.

Then as if to bring him good cheer, a fair maiden begs her mother to make a marriage proposal to the melancholy young man in her behalf. No bashful suitor was the maiden who was so unconscious a believer in the modern school of eugenics. She chose her mate-man, but cumbersome etiquette required that the prospective mother-in-law make the proposal. After munching the enormous boiled biscuits of the candidate-mother-in-law, the lover meditated upon the quality of food he had received, thought over the temper and character of the maiden, consulted his mother and asked her to convey the message of acceptance. Thus in time, the moody hunter was married. The clans rejoiced and (we may conjecture) many a maiden repaired in silence to the forest to weep out her heart. He had defended them and befriended them through sheer courtesy, and he loved them, not for mates but merely as women of the nation. But such was fate,—there were other and even more handsome men to ask! No more would they husk corn with this newly married stripling and coyly present him with a red ear and demand the forfeit.

The young man after his marriage became even more popular with his people, and upon the death of one of their great sachems.

indeed the greatest, the women of the noble families of the Wolf clan called upon the adopted Turtle and told him he was their choice. Then they went to the National Council and at the ceremony of condolence placed their nomination before the sachems. The men, no doubt, were astonished, for their candidate was a young man of the Hoyaneh Wolves who was mighty of muscle and skilled in the chase. But since the women held the sole power of nomination and would not nominate the man of mighty muscle, Wolf clansman though he be, there was but one course to follow. The thin young man was elected to the highest civil office in the gift of the populous Nation of the Great Hill. He was given the name-title Ga-nio-dai'yu or Skanadario, translated Handsome Lake. The people hailed him as their wisest councillor, but though he was wise in plans for calling other men to action, he was still moody and his bride failed to bring him the cheer that she had hoped.

The white men came in increasing numbers. Their settlements were everywhere, and with the wilting of the forests, farms and pastures became verdant.

The Senecas began their westward retreat. The broken nation that was left by the army of General Sullivan was an unhappy nation and even all the assurances of President Washington or of General Dearborn or of Colonel Timothy Pickering failed to make them feel secure. In the setting of every sun they saw the symbol of their national decadence. The symbol was reflected in the eyes of Handsome Lake, who had been a silent party to the signing of the Treaty of Canandaigua in 1794. Foolishly he had accepted the trader's rum, hoping to forget his sorrows. His wife had died and more rum was required; Handsome Lake renewed his mourning. Her death was a heavy blow. Then one of his two daughters died and Handsome Lake laid her away in the gravelly hillock at Canawagus. He drank more until he could not live, it seemed, without the fiery liquor. As a sachem and councillor he was failing. He was becoming an outcast; he might lose his title and awaken to disgrace. Leaving the Genesee country he moved to the banks of the Allegany and took up his abode in a solitary cabin of bark. The Indians were debauched with the brandy and rum from the Pittsburgh traders. All was anarchy; the old religion was failing, the old government of the Iroquois League was crumbling; there was a riot of superstition. The bleared eyes of the drunkard could not fail to see the misery of his people. He mourned again and sought consolation in the contents of the black bottles that the trader gave for beaver pelts. Then he became an invalid. Long tedious days he laid in his lonely cabin, hungry, thirsty,—sick unto death. The wild whoops of the carousing lumbermen reached his ears and now and then a bullet, widely fired, would whistle through his doorway, now hanging by one rawhide hinge. At length his daughter came and offered to care for him daily. Her heart was touched with pity for her father whom as a child she remembered so tender and thoughtful. Sometimes he conversed with her telling her what he thought of the things he saw. The sunlight streaming down the smoke hole caused him to think of what sunlight meant and of the maker of the sun and its light and warmth. The stars and the moon gave him food for reflection; the gusts of wind, the odor of the flowers, the songs of the birds, all gave him messages of wisdom and of comfort. Even his pain-racked body, shrunken and weak, responded to the questioning mind of the invalid and taught him philosophy. Each day, he tells us in his book of revelations[1] he hoped that the dawning wisdom and faith would restore him, for his mind was exhilarated by the inspiration of clean, sober thinking. Then, one morning, as the daughter was singing at her task of shelling beans for her husband to plant, Handsome Lake, the sachem, upon his hard couch in the cabin, dropped into a swoon and his spirit slipped away for a long journey to the sky-world. With his last feeble gasp his daughter and her husband heard him reply as if answering a summons, "Niyuh," meaning, "So be it." Just before this they had heard him rise from his bed and totter to the door. They rushed from the shed were they were working together and heard him murmuring as he staggered to the door-post. They caught him as he fell, and carried him back to his bed.

Apparently Handsome Lake was dead. The great Governor Blacksnake, (Awl Breaker) and Cornplanter were called and both bowed their heads. The sachem, they said, was dead. With loving care the daughter dressed him for burial, and the insignia of his sachemship was laid upon his breast ready to be placed about the neck of his successor. Then the mourners filled the cabin; group by group they came as the news spread. They looked at the shrunken form and it was said, "He is but a shriveled yellow skin and all his bones are dry." Four years of sickness has terminated in death, but the Awl Breaker would not believe that the sachem was passed away. His hands continually moved over the chest and limbs of the prostrate sachem as if feeling for one, only one feeble pulse-beat.

---

1. "The Code of Handsome Lake," recorded by A. C. Parker. Bulletin 163, N. Y. State Museum.

After thus searching for a sign of life Awl Breaker arose and exclaimed, "Hold back your grief, my friends and relatives. I have a sure belief that Handsome Lake yet lives." Silently Cornplanter, the leading chief of the Allegany Senecas, approached his half-brother and placed his hand over his heart. There was a warm spot there, and he knew that indeed his sachem lived. The noon came and in faith the watchers continued to await some further sign of vitality. The noon hour came and the morning dew had dried. The cool evening approached and then, quietly the quick inhalation of a breath was heard, and then the eyes of Handsome Lake opened and slowly gazed at the throng.

The Awl Breaker addressed the sachem: "My brother, are you now recovered?" he asked quietly.

In a clear low voice the mourners heard the reply, "I have faith that I have been restored."

When he had thus satisfied the fears and solicitude of his friends he spoke again: "Never have I seen such wondrous visions," he said. "Three shining messengers and a fourth I could not see, have delivered to me a mission that I must perform for the benefit of our nation."

A council was called in the morning of the next day and all were asked to drink the sweet juice of the wild strawberry as a ceremonial invocation for bodily health. Then the risen sick man, whose eyes now burned with a strange fire, told of the "four words" he had been called to condemn for the salvation of the race. The "four words" were the names of the besetting sins of the demoralized Iroquois,—*Onega*, the use of liquor; *Gutgont*, the practice of witchcraft; *Onoityeyende*, the practice of secretly poisoning enemies; and, *Yondwiniyas swayas*, the practice of birth-control. More than this, he explained the necessity of a renewed love of one's fellow men, of the responsibility for another's welfare, of the love and care of children, of the sacredness of the rites of hospitality, of chaste, clean lives, of listening to the silent voices that called men to do good,—constructive good, and of the value of peace and industry.

Handsome Lake spoke to a disheartened people who had suffered defeat, fraud and the humiliation of national weakness. The gloom of these things had darkened the minds of the nation and a dispairing people had sought forgetfulness in debauchery. Poverty and misery had come, and the mighty Senecas, broken and besotted, bled out their hearts.

A victim of such conditions, Handsome Lake the sachem stalked from the gloom as a prophet holding up as a beacon light of hope his divine message, the Gaiwiyu. He became a commanding figure, in spite of his constitutional timidity. He created a new system and gave his people something to think about, to talk about and finally a code of ethics which they were to live. His message, whether false or true from modern ways of thinking, was a creation of their own and afforded a thought nucleus about which they could cluster themselves and fasten their hopes. He claimed to be only a speaker, a proclaimer of the will of the Creator,—he made no pretense as a Messiah, and indeed, never called himself a prophet, though he was one in every sense of the word.

A revolution was created in the religious life of the people. At first his followers were few and his popularity as a sachem did not bring popularity as a prophet. He was despised, ridiculed and subjected to bodily insult and injury. Yet he persisted, overcoming the calumny of Red Jacket and the difficulties put in his path by his half-brother, Cornplanter. Within ten years a drunken nation had become sober, and not only the Seneca, but the Cayuga and the Onondaga nations had listened and cast aside the destroying drink. The message of Handsome Lake had become potent. Wars must cease, he said, and his emissaries held back the participation of his people in the wars of the western Indians, calling them from the ranks of Pontiac, of Tecumseh and of Little Turtle, The Miami. Men were to live in peaceful relationship, to be industrious and humble. The pride of the over-prosperous must cease, the poor and the incompetent were to be helped to help themselves, superstitions were to give way to the code laid down by the Heavenly Messengers.

So successful was Handsome Lake that the Quaker missionaries of 1804 have left the testimony that not one of the followers of Handsome Lake was a user of fire-water; and indeed, the whole nation refused to touch it.

Persecution at Allegany caused the Prophet and his followers to remove to Tonawanda in about 1810 or 1812. With him went his grandson Sos-he-o-wa who later became his successor. (In passing it may be well to record that Sos-he-o-wa was the grandfather of General Ely S. Parker, known to his own people as Donehogawa, the Keeper of the Western Door.) At Tonawanda the call came from the divine messengers urging him to go to the land of the Onondagas. It was the "third call," and required a parting song. Handsome Lake then remembered that the spirits had told him he would sing three songs, and the third would precede his death. Nevertheless he began his journey. He was prematurely old and the efforts at reform that he had made had drained heavily upon his nervous energy. As he took up the march overland with his faithful bodyguard he knew that the end was near. He feared that in his prophecy he had not given due prominence to the fourth and hidden messenger of the Creator, the man who appeared in the sky world and showed to him a pierced side and feet and hands pierced with nails. That thought tormented him. He reached Onondaga only to sink to the ground in melancholy. The young men strove to cheer him and arouse his spirits by a dashing game of lacrosse, but he arose and said, "The path has appeared before me, I see my journey is to commence, I shall make ready to go to the land of the Creator, for whom I have been a spokesman."

Only a few witnessed his death agony, and these pledged themselves to secrecy. An Onondaga hidden in the cabin saw the death unobserved by others and has left the tradition that Handsome Lake cried out in anguish, "I have delivered the message, there were things I should have told but I feared to tell. Good came from all I said, but greater good might have come if I had dared to preach all I was commanded." And then the spirit of the sachem and of the prophet slipped away. His spirit began its journey over the sky-trail. Four days later a shrunken body was laid away beneath the floor of the council house, the capitol building of the Six Nations' League. There were impressive ceremonies and the disciples of the New Religion were in full control of the national religion of the League of the Iroquois. Hardly a single follower of the ancient way remained,—all were either Christians or Ganiodaiyuans.

In fifteen years this man, risen as if from the dead, had transformed the religious and intellectual life of a nation. For a man who until he was 65 years of age had been a drunkard, a failure and a dying invalid, to arise after being bedridden for four years and walk forth as the spirtual preceptor of his race, is a remarkable, even a startling thing. Yet he did so, living soberly until the day when at four score years of age he was called to the happy realm of the Great Manitou to give account of his mission.

The sages of the people called together the wise elders and discussed the doctrines of Handsome Lake and chosen priests were caused to memorize all the messages of his Gai-wi-yu so that it might be preached to all the members of the Six Nations, even as the Prophet had preached. Then the wise men wrote a new stanza to the national thanksgiving hymn known as the Go-ne-o-wa, and thereafter the Indians sang:

> "The Creator willed that a chosen one
> Should reveal his wisdom to all mankind.
> And that Gaiwiyu should be expounded.
> And so he called Ganiodaiyu to him

> That all his wishes might be fulfilled.
> So Ganiodaiyu responded truly
> And proclaimed the message until he died.
> We give thee thanks for he did his duty.
> And we follow in the way he taught us
> We shall not forget, but shall remember;
> O, Thou, who doest live Above, Our Maker!
> Now the incense of thanksgiving rises,
> We shall follow Handsome Lake our Prophet!
> Gwi-yah, we praise thee with our joyful dancing!''

The years have passed and even as the veiled spirit in the Heaven world predicted, as he held up his bleeding pierced hands, the teachings of Handsome Lake are waning. Only a few hundred may be reckoned as true followers and many half believers are worse for their half belief, for they have degenerated. The environment that made a religion efficacious has passed away leaving its practice almost a mockery. The Indian's world has become the white man's world and yet the faithful few try to worship the old way, wearing store-made clothes and cooking the feasts in granite ware kettles sweetening their cakes with domino sugar, flavoring their berry juices with coal-tar products and using packing-house beef, instead of the fresh flesh of the bear. The social and economic order all about them is the white man's, not theirs. How long may they oppose their way to the overwhelming forces of modern civilization, and still exist as efficient men? How long will they seek to meet the overwhelming forces of modern requirements with the simple devices of their ancestors, who planned not for the exingencies of a rapidly changing order?

My Indian friends will answer: ''Of these things we do not inquire, we only have faith that the Great Ruler will care for us if we are faithful.'' Asked about the clothes they wear and the food they eat and the mill-board long-house in which they worship, they reply: ''All these things may be made of the white man's materials but they are outward things. Our religion is not one of clothing, of paint, or of feathers; it is a thing of the heart.'' That is the answer, it is a thing of the heart,—who can change it?

THE RELIGION OF HANDSOME LAKE
(See Chapter II., page 18.)

Here follows a translation of the speech made by Jimmy Johnson at the Grand Council of the Confederacy of Iroquois held at the Indian Village at Tonawanda, Oct. 2nd and 3rd, 1845. This speech is an abridgement of his annual speech, or rather a repetition in brief of the religious precepts pretended to have been communicated to the Iroquois from heaven.[1]

The Onondagas and Senecas, and our children the Oneidas, Cayugas and Tuscaroras, have convened here today for the purpose of listening again to the speaking of the will of the Great Spirit, as communicated to us, through his Great Prophet Ganyodyoh or Handsome Lake. We would therefore give you all a hearty welcome.

The day is far advanced and the sun is now going down. I will therefore proceed immediately to the performance of my duties. Brothers, turn your minds toward the Great Spirit, and listen with good and strict attention. First, I want all, old and young, to know how long ago it was since the Great Spirit communicated his religion to us. It is now 46 years since the Great Spirit spoke to the Indians through his Prophet, and since that time we have attempted to live faithfully. Ganyodyoh told us, he lay sick four years. He says, "I had assigned myself to the determination of the Great Spirit. I thanked Him for every ray of light which entered my cabin, proceeding from the daily sun. In the morning I meditated on the future, and expected not to see the dusk of evening. I was more faithful therefore to the discharge of my daily duties. But evening came and through the opening in the roof of my cabin I looked upon the stars which the Great Spirit has made to serve as ornaments in the heavens. Again I returned my greatful thanks to my Creator, and again resigned myself to him, expecting not to behold the light of another morning."

In this manner his sickness was prolonged for years. At one o'clock however, he says he told his daughter, very early in the morning, to request his relatives and friends to come in and see him once more, as the sensations in him predicted that something extraordinary was to befall him. The friends convened, but he was dead. A small spot directly over the heart was discovered to be warm. At nine o'clock he opened his eyes and was asked if he saw aright. But he could not speak and again closed his eyes. At noon he again revived and opened his eyes. Being asked by one near if he could see anything, he replied in the affirmative. He then was asked what he saw. He replied as follows:

"This morning a man came into my cabin, and wished me to follow him out of doors. I did not feel strong enough to do so. But I arose to go out. At the door I stumbled and fell. Three men

---

1. Translation by E. S. Parker, *verbatim* from the original manuscript.

APPENDIX

standing at the door caught me in their arms. They said, 'we have come to help you. Haste, and eat of the fruit of these branches.'

"Each one held a branch in his hand, bearing different kinds of fruits and of different colors. The men were clothed in pure white. They said that they were sent by the Great Spirit. At different times it has pleased the Great Spirit to make known His will to his people through men, but they have all proved unfaithful. He expects you to be faithful. He has heard your prayers and receives your thanks for his preservation of your life. His mind is that you shall yet live among your people many days. Tomorrow your people must convene in meeting and have a religious dance, and at noon you must go in and look upon your friends."

The people did as they were directed. At noon he entered the council room and looked upon the mass of the congregated people. He then proceeded to tell the council what the men in white had told him to say to the council. He said:

"The men spoke to me thus: 'Tell your people the will of the Great Spirit. They have sinned a great sin and have greatly trangressed against his laws in getting drunk. You sin greatly in getting drunk. The fire-waters were not made for the Indians, and it will ruin them if they continue to use them. The fire-waters were made for the white people. They are laboring men and they need some stimulant; therefore the Creator gave them the fire-waters to drink, three times a day. But they too have violated the laws and regulations given to them by their Creator. In introducing this drink among the Indians, they have committed a great sin and as a punishment they will never get to heaven. Tell your people all. Travel among them and be yourself a temperate man. Tell your people that they have committed four great sins. Too many of the Indians are proud and haughty. Repent therefore and escape the penalty. Repent in open council. If some of the people are too timid to confess and repent before the council they may speak to you (that is the Prophet) in private, saying ''I repent.'' We (the angels) will hear and forgive. Since the Creation of all things, we have always been the guardians of earth and its inhabitants. And if they can not speak to you, let them form the new resolution in the mind, that they repent and they shall see the Great Spirit. The Great Spirit did not design when he created man and woman, that women should be barren. To deprive themselves of the generative organs, therefore, is a great sin. Repent of the evil among you. Some women come into the world barren. In order, therefore, for such to fill the position designed for them, they must adopt children and love them as though they were their own. Those doing this shall see the Great Spirit. Also they may adopt orphans and bring them up in virtuous principles. This also is good in the mind of the Great Spirit. If you tie up the clothes of an orphan child, the Great Spirit will notice it and reward you for it. Universal benevolence and hospitality is good. The Great Spirit, in instituting the marriage rite, intended that the parties should love one another. It is wrong, therefore, to use O-noh-ate.[2] This practice He says is ruinous, repent and use it no more. It is the will of the Great Spirit, that husband and wife shall love one another. If they are helped with children, whenever they become of a proper age, they must marry them to an old, experienced person. If they in turn are helped with children, let them unite in offering grateful thanks to the Great Spirit when they have grand-children, they must be more thankful, for they can not make their gratitude too manifest. When a young woman becomes pregnant, it is very wrong to circulate false stories concerning her and her husband, for in so doing it may cause a separation. This in the sight of the Great Spirit, is a great wrong. Should a man leave her under such circumstances, a great punishment awaits him. In this thing the old people did right, but the Great Spirit wished to renew old things. Parents, teach your children virtuous principles. You all know how great a trouble it was to bring up your children, therefore, teach them to walk in the paths of virtue. Children, obey your parents. If you do not willingly submit to the will and requirements of your parents, you will cause them to feel bad and to shed many tears. Disobedient children are sent to hell. It is the will of the Great Spirit, that those children who disobey their parents, should repent and disobey them no more. It is wrong for a father or mother-in-law, to vex or harass a son or daughter-in-law. But they must use them as if they were their own children. When a child is born it is wrong for the father and mother of it to hold disputes over its body. The child hears and understands all that is said, and it often feels bad; and unless the parents put an end to their disputes and bitter contentions, will return to the home of the Great Spirit. Parents should exercise love towards their children. Adultery is a great sin, and the Great Spirit says, do not commit adultery. It is wrong to whip children with the rod. If you wish to correct a child, use cold water. Tell them, "I shall either sprinkle or plunge you." If the child says, 'I shall do better,' then stop.

---

2. This probably would be nothing more than excessive passionate love. The Indians say, that this is a substance and that it has such a charming power, that the person under its influence can not separate himself or herself from the charmer. It is evident that it is not a pure love, for sometimes the parties hate one another to such a degree, as to be forced to come to blows, and yet the person charmed cares nothing about it.

"It has been the custom among the Indians to mourn for the dead one year. This custom is not right. It causes the death of many children, therefore, do it no longer. Ten days mourn for the dead and no more.[3] When a person is dead, it is right and proper to make a speech over the body, telling how much loved the deceased. Great respect for the dead, among the Indians must be observed. To be a tattler or tale bearer is very wrong. It is the root of great evil. Repent and do it no longer.

"To prove the position that alcohol is ruinous, we would say: that men using the fire waters, are apt to freeze, to get drowned, to be burned to death and a great many fights arise out of it."

Jimmy Johnson says there are a great many opposers to our religion. Some oppose it, by having too great an appetite for the fire water, manufactured by the whites. Others oppose it by disbelieving the Indian religion, and embracing the religion of the whites. There is however one class, who are strong in the belief of the Indian and who have a great desire for the perpetual existence of the Indians as a Nation; and that all things among the Indians may go off with success and prosperity. The Prophet told the Indians that the angels were happy whenever they heard two friends discoursing about doing good to their fellowmen. But whenever they heard two friends differ in opinion respecting the propriety of doing good to man, and they continued to dispute, they were sorry and wished the Indians to know that this was very wrong. The Great Spirit implanted a principle in the human mind, which should incline mankind to sympathize with one another. The principle is always exercised for the good. Be firm and resolute in doing that which is good.

At one time the Angels desired the Prophet to go with them to make a visit to the home of the Evil Spirit. Together they directed their steps thitherward. Having approached to the house, they placed themselves near in order therefore that the Prophet might see the inner part of the house to a good advantage. The outer of the house was raised up. The first object that met his eye was a haggard-looking man—his sunken eyes cast upon the ground and his form nearly half consumed from the many torments he had undergone. This man was a drunkard. For just at this moment, the Evil One coming up to him and taking him by the arm, led him to the side of a great kettle containing red hot lead. Out of this kettle

---

3. It is the practice among the old Indians, to this day, upon the tenth day to call together the friends of the deceased, and then make a public disposal of whatever effects he had.

the Evil One dipped a large quantity of fiery liquid, and commanded the person whom he held by the hand to drink it for, he says, the liquid will have the same effect, as the fire-waters manufactured by the whites, and will produce precisely the same sensations. The man took of the fiery liquid, but no sooner was it taken, than he filled the air with the most horrid cries; a lambent flame and a light smoke immediately issued from his mouth. The fiery waters of earth, says the Evil One, possess the same qualities as this. Any one might as well drink red hot lead as to drink alcohol (called by the Indians fire-water).

The next object the Prophet discovered was a woman, being led by the Evil One between two great kettles. He took and plunged her into one of the kettles. Her increasing shrieks evinced that she was in great torment, for she begged the Evil One to give her some colder place, she was too hot, she was afraid that she would be consumed by the heat. He then took and plunged her into the other kettle. But in a moment her cries again filled the air. She was complaining that it was too cold. This woman, says the Prophet, was a witch; she shall always be tormented in this manner, forever and ever, at one time being plunged into boiling liquid, the next into liquid upon the point of freezing.

The next incident witnessed by the Prophet, was the calling together of a husband and wife, who when on earth were in the habit of continuously disputing and contradicting one another. Having set them near one another, the Evil Spirit commanded them to dispute with one another now, as they were accustomed to do when on earth. They indeed did commence but had not proceeded far, before their tongues began to run out, so that they could no longer talk. This the Prophet said would be the fate of such characters.

The Great Spirit has proposed a way for all to get to heaven. Therefore when any one does wrong, they must repent and put themselves in the right way immediately, for unless they do it, they may get lost.

Ganyodyoh was very particular in explaining to us the course which departed spirits were accustomed to take upon their exit from this world and entrance into another world. There was a road which led upward; in a short distance the road forked, one branch keeping a straight forward course while the other angled off in an entirely different course. At the point where the roads separated were stationed two men; one a man deputized by the Great Spirit, the other of the Evil One. Whenever a person died they took the road leading upward; having arrived at the point of the separation of the two roads, if he was a wicked person, by a motion from the man of the

Evil One, they instinctively turned into the roads leading to the abodes of the Tormentor. But if a person was good, the contrary would follow. That is, they would follow the straight path leading to the home of the Great Spirit. The straight path the Prophet said was not much traveled, while the other was completely trodden so that, he says, no grass could grow in the path. He says it sometimes happens that the judges have great difficulty in determining which road the person ought to take. For sometimes the good and bad actions are so nearly balanced that it requires some time to determine which outweighed. When persons are sent to hell, they sometimes remain there for a day, and some for a longer time. (One day in hell is one of mortal years), and atone for their sins and then passing on to heaven. But those guilty of the unpardonable sins shall never pass from hell to heaven, but should be tormented in hell forever and ever.

The Prophet was then commanded to look upon earth. He looked and behold, there was a great gathering of the people! The first object which attracted his attention, was a man naked, running through the midst of the people. Behind him followed an innumerable number of women. They followed him because he like themselves loved fire-water very much. Next came two naked women, seemingly young. Their fault was coquetry. Their punishment was in being exposed naked to the whole assembly. He saw also a woman rolling a dust sack. This woman was punished for what is commonly called a stingy woman. He also saw a man running through the midst of the people, with a large piece of meat in his hand. This was a benevolent man, willing to give to all whom chance might happen to throw into his way. The Great Spirit designed that all men like myself should be benevolent.

Again the Prophet was commanded to look towards the east. He looked and saw the smoke of a thousand distilleries using and shutting out the light of the Sun. The angels told the Prophet that when the Great Spirit became tired or weary of the existence of the earth, he should burn it. The first earth he destroyed by water, but the second he will burn with fire. This he will do on account of the wickedness of the earth's inhabitants. The Great Spirit made all good things. He made the winds and the clouds, heat and cold, but the devil made the witches, subject however to the will of the Great Spirit. At one time he attempted to kill them, but they fled into the earth. When the end of the world approaches, the witches will come out of their retreats, for the purpose of tormenting wicked people. The sun will be removed and there will be a great smoke upon earth.

All good folks then living upon earth will then leave for heaven. The wicked will perish upon earth.

The influence of Indian preachers may not always be good. "But if you (the Prophet) in any degree lose your influence among your people, if you are faithful to your religion, we (the angels) shall abide with you and comfort you. Preachers should have assistants. For his holy Prophet Ganyodyoh, the Great Spirit, raised aids." The angels said that they respected the aids of the Prophet, because they were religious officers, and not mere dignitary chiefs. "Let the assistants thank the Great Spirit when the time draws near for them to act. When they have completed, they must renew their thanks to Him. All religious officers are placed in the path that leads to heaven and if they resign their offices they put themselves out of the way and they will find more difficulty in travelling in the wrong way, but the firm and faithful will be happy in heaven. I therefore exhort all my assistants to be firm and faithful in the principles of the religion entrusted to their charge. The Indians have many songs after which they dance for amusement. These same songs will be sung by the happy in heaven. As for instance, the grand religious dance, which is performed by the Indians at all their feasts; that also will be danced in heaven and the Indians say that the Great Spirit himself will be the singer. The angels commanded the Prophet to request the Indians to convene in council upon the Tonawanda Reservation. They assured him that if he made the request the Indians would convene. When the council convened the Indians began to confess and repent before the Prophet. The Indians from Geneseo also did the same. After they had all finished some of the Indians from the east wished the Prophet to tell whether all the Indians who had confessed to him and wished to repent, had spoken from the heart. The Prophet answered that some had not. Whereupon some immediately arose and confessed that they had not spoken the feelings of their hearts, but were only testing the Prophet.

Se-gwa-an-doh-gwe (called in English, John Littlebeard) had such a great anxiety to live justly, obeying the will of the Great Spirit that at one time he requested the Prophet to ask the angels what thing he lacked. (John Littlebeard it is said was a great favorite of the Prophet and was his constant and faithful companion in all his travels among the Six Nations). The Prophet reported to Littlebeard and to the Indian in Council, that the angels said his fault was being a double-minded man. This is, he believed the Christian as well as the Pagan or Indian religion. Thus Littlebeard was made a man of no decision of character.[4]

---

4. Immediately upon the death of Ganyodyoh, Littlebeard left the ranks of Paganism and joined himself to the Christian church then established among the Indians and remained firm in the belief of that religion.

APPENDIX

The Prophet was commanded to look into the dwelling of the white man. He looked and saw fetters for binding and securing criminals, ropes for hanging murderers, and whips for subduing the disobedient and obstinate. He beheld a great variety of torturing instruments, which he said awaited the Indians if they attempted to live after the manner of the whites. Again, it is the will of the Great Spirit, that the young shall love and reverence the aged, even though they be helpless as infants—he desired that they receive good care,—that no reasonable pains be foregone which would have a tendency to increase their unhappiness upon earth. There is a great disrespect generally paid to the old people; this is not right, but the contrary should be practiced. Children must not separate themselves from their parents nor must they, when the strength of their parents begin to fail, turn them out of doors. But they must love them and be kind to them, for this is right and pleasing to the Great Spirit.

"At one time there was a difficulty among the people of the Prophet and the Prophet himself. The angels advised the Prophet to leave Allegany and that from that place he should take three steps, where he should settle himself down forever. The first step he took was to go to Tonawanda. From this place he looked to Onondaga.

"This is what Ganyodyoh used to tell us, and all has indeed happened according to his words. Chiefs, warriors, women and children continued to listen. Leave the fire-water and be a special people of the Great Spirit. We once more say to you all, touch not, nor taste the fire-water. Many are imprudent in violating the laws regulating health and these die a premature death. This again is wrong. You will do well to fill the number of your days. The Indians were once in great darkness, but have now received the light. We think that the great prevailing sin among the Indians is drunkenness, and we desire to say all we can in order to render it abhorrent to all. Rum-sellers have no flesh on their hands. They have nothing but horns. We entreat you warriors that none of you sell the fire-water."

Jimmy Johnson here observed that he believed his religion to be true and, says he: "I shall always adhere to it as the only true religion for me." Jimmy Johnson proceeds, exhorting the Indians to be moral. The Prophet used to preach that playing and dancing after the fiddle and playing cards was very wrong. The Indians must not use nor even touch them, nor must they adopt any of the gambling practices invented by the whites. The Indians themselves have dances and they can practice them innocently. The angels told the Prophet to tell the Indians that it was very wrong to sell any of the lands which the Great Spirit had made and given to the Indians for their possession and occupancy. The Great Spirit did not make it, to be the property of the old people, but for the possession of the children. Indians who persist in selling lands must expect to meet a great punishment after death.

In one of the expeditions of the Prophet into the upper regions, he chanced to meet his friend Ho-na-ya-wus, otherwise called Farmer's Brother, drawing sand. He said that from a great heap of sand, he was taking a grain of sand at a time, and although laboring continually the heap of sand did not diminish. Such, he said, would be the punishment of those continually selling lands. Like Farmer's Brother, although working incessantly at the heap of sand, yet he could not diminish its proportions, so the Indian who sells land, although he might sell continually, yet he never could dispose of all the lands. The angels are said to have advised the Indians to always act with unanimity. If they did not, the white people, seeing their divisions, would creep in among them, establishing themselves among them and finally gain complete advantage over them. Jimmy Johnson had observed saying, that all was indeed coming to pass agreeably to the words of the Prophet.

The Prophet told of the events of a future war. This the Preacher says has all happened. The Prophet said that the day would come when the white people would try hard to buy the land of the Indians. Says he: "If the Indians do not act with unanimity, they will be the sufferers." The angels told the Prophet also that such a great difficulty would come from the fact that there would be so many parties, that the angels themselves were ignorant what the final result of them would be. The Prophet was commanded to look at the Indian village situated upon the Buffalo Creek Reservation. He turned and looked, but where was it? Naught was now to be seen of the village but the decaying remnants of wigwams, which clearly evinced that sometime, many years ago, the princely lords of the soil lived there. This the Prophet predicted to happen to our people. You can all bear witness what he said should happen is coming to pass. It has been the custom among the Indians when yet living in darkness, to have a barrel of whisky whenever they had their dances. But the angels prohibited this practice and substituted for whisky, provisions. They said that the substituting of provisions would be not only agreeable to themselves, but far more pleasing to the Great Spirit. Since the Great Spirit knew that the Indians could not do without some kind of amusement therefore he orginated the idea of dancing, which he gave to the Indians for their benefit. Moreover the Prophet was commanded that whenever he preached, to preach in the forenoon and if he choose to occupy till noon. (The propriety of this seems to consist in the idea, that the early part of the day belonged specially to the living, and the latter part of the day to the dead.) For the afternoon belongs to the dead. The earth commences to produce fruit directly at the surface. "Give me, therefore," says the Great Spirit, "a thank-offering for the first fruits. (This I believe is a strawberry feast). Also give me a thank-offering at the green corn feast and at the time of harvesting or gathering of the corn, and again at the new-year's feast." All these feasts must be accompanied with their appropriate dances. Exercises to commence in the morning and to terminate at noon.

Again, the Prophet was accustomed to observe to the Indians, that if they did not free themselves from the use of strong drinks, it would occasion the spilling of much blood among them. This, says the Preacher, has all happened.

The Great Spirit made the Indians to live by the chase. But he foresaw the day when the Indians would be deprived of their hunting grounds; therefore He has said that it was not a criminal wrong to follow the example of the whites in some respects. He said that it was not wrong to build houses after the manner of the whites, to work your farms and to raise domestic animals. But an Indian could not live and be happy when he exceeded these bounds.

Jimmy Johnson then addressed a few words to the women, saying, it is a great evil among women to talk ill concerning their neighbors. On this account the Great Spirit has given the express command that women shall not talk ill concerning their neighbors, for the Great Spirit has made all Indians equal and entitled to the same privileges and immunities. Be not a respector of persons, for the Great Spirit has given a variety of gifts, to some a pretty face, to others an ugly face, to some beautiful form, to others a deformed figure, etc. Be kindly disposed one toward another. Love one another with a brotherly love, for you are all members of the same family. If a stranger wanders about your abode, welcome him to your home and be hospitable toward him. Speak kind words to him and forget not always to mention the Great Spirit in the proceeds. In the morning give thanks to the Great Spirit for the return of day and the light of the sun. At night renew your thanks to Him, that His ruling power has preserved you from harm during the day, and also that night has again come in which you may rest your wearied body. All this, the Great Spirit is pleased with, because it is right.

ELY S. PARKER'S SCHOOL DAYS
(See Chapter VI, page 74.)

An unexpected clipping reminiscent of Ely S. Parker's school days comes from the *Buffalo Express* under date of March 24, 1915. It describes Ely as a "beau Brummel," and the writer of the letter reflects the prejudice of the day against Indian blood. The letter follows:

Editor Buffalo Express:—In the year 1845 I completed my last term of school at Yates Academy, N. Y., where Ely Parker was then a student. Eventually he became chief of the Six Nations. His was a noble, commanding form, tall, erect, broad-shouldered, and his straight, coal-black hair, high cheek-bones and copper-colored complexion plainly told his origin. His genial affability won the respect of both teachers and schoolmates. No young man in school could compete with him in oratory.

When it was announced that Parker was to address the school the house was filled to its full capacity and necks craned, eager to catch every word that came from his deep, full voice, which penetrated to the farthest corner of the spacious schoolroom. He was truly a prodigy, springing from such a slow, indolent race.

Although Parker possessed many traits that were commendable, he showed lack of discretion by falling in love with one of his fairest schoolmates, who, strange to say, seemed to reciprocate his feelings, allowing him to be her escort from lectures and evening meetings. This caused quite a stir, furnishing food for gossiping ones. In time it was rumored that Parker was to take the young lady in question for a drive on the Fourth of July. Some credited the story, while others thought she, belonging to one of the most aristocratic families, would not disgrace herself and friends by riding out with an Indian. The Fourth of July came, when many were on the alert to know if the rumor was really true.

Verandas were filled with people and even the street corners, when in a measure their curiosity was rewarded, as Parker went by with a grand livery and a negro driver. It was not long ere the splendid rig came rolling by and, sure enough, Mary was sitting at the side of Parker and the darky driver in front. The young lady soon went abroad for a long vacation.

Parker now lies in a Buffalo cemetery.

Mrs. LOUISE BACHELDOR.

Rochester, March 24th, 1915.

APPENDIX

"THE AMERICAN RED MAN"[1]
(See Chapter VI, page 77.)

I am no orator as my forefathers were who now lie in their silent graves in yonder wilderness. But as you see I stand here a simple Indian, a son of the forest, a relic of the wreck of the Iroquois, a band of nations who once peopled the length and breadth of your Empire State: and if there be any present to whom the form and address of an Indian is displeasing, I speak not to them. But I speak to those, to whom real knowledge has taught that all men are made of one blood, created free and equal, entitled to the same rights and privileges, and accountable to the same God. I speak to those who can appreciate the merits of talent and intellectual worth, who are lovers of true knowledge, and who are lovers of eloquence. The topic to which I shall call your attention for a few moments is, "The People Gone."

> "The Niobe of nations, there she stands,
> Childless and crownless in her voiceless woe."

Why weep over their fate, those brave hearted hermits of the wilderness? Their destiny was accomplished, they uttered their voice, they filled up their portion of the great universe plan, their hour upon the clock of time was struck,— and they were not! Such is the law of fate, beneath whose stern mandate other nations have wrapt around themselves the solemn drapery of the sepulchre and bowed their glorious foreheads in the dust. Birthplaces of the monarch minstrel, the blind old man of Scio, and he who plucked the last laurel from the olden tree of song, what are ye? Mouldering monuments, erected by the Destroyer to show the foot-prints of the eternal world march,—the *stern, unbending, necessary law!* What speaks it? An august truth: it tells that without and within, is force, resistless force, moving spirit and matter; moves and starts onward. Under the power, man and world must be alike pushed off the stage of existence to make room for others. System rushes on system, generation on generation, and nation on nation, in everlasting battle; a fearful war, in which the defensive must ever surrender; some expiring with a low melancholy wail, and others breathing their last in a loud, warrior shout. So died the "People Gone." The forest fire shot up fiercely unto the end, and brave souls glanced defiance in the death struggle.

---

1. An address delivered during the junior year of Nicholson H. Parker at Albany State Normal School.

We have said, Why weep over their fate? Philosophical it may not be, yet humanity unseals the fountain, and the cold hearth-stone, the broken bow, and the leaf-covered grave are wet with the mourner's tear. Were this people wronged? You do not feel disposed to investigate the subject. If wronged, then wrong is the very divinity of the inevitable laws which produced their ruin. Man's feeble eye can not pierce the cloud; man's circumscribed mind can not roll away the mists which envelope the Empire of the Real. But when you dimiss this subject, another arises which you may think of much more importance, *the doing of justice* to the characters of those, whom the "law" forced you to destroy; the rescuing of their names from oblivion and the placing of them within their proper sphere in history. This is a noble duty which the world expects you to perform, and which the inherent generosity of American character should urge you to accomplish. Will you be less manly,—aye, and less philosophical too,—than the conqueror of Gaul? He chronicled the deeds of every nation which he conquered, thus according justice to them, and indirectly was taught to consider as optional with himself: besides, what prisons had he for their safe keeping?

The Indian has been called cruel. What causes had he not to make him so? His brethren carried into captivity, his wife and children bound in the chains of slavery, his fields destroyed, his hunting-grounds harried, his dwellings burnt, his wide and beautiful country wrested from his grasp, and he driven forth without home, without food, without shelter. These, these changed his nature and sometimes made the man a demon. That the red warrior often committed acts which humanity can not pardon, we confess: but yet can not the feeling heart find much in his extenuation? We hazard nothing in saying, that the whites have deeds to answer for far more bloody than the native of America. Witness Jena! attest it, St. Bartholomew! Speak out, thou Inquisition! And what of the guillotine? Where is there an Indian Atilla or an aboriginal Robespierre? History answereth not. Oh! it is very modest in you to speak of Indian cruelty! And more easy too, than effective. But we will leave this topic for one more pleasant—the intellectual character of the red man.

His mind has always been underrated. The only faculty which you have allowed him to a high extent is that of *oratory*. But we fearlessly challenge the whole white race to afford more striking instances of judgment, caution, calculation and concentration, than can be found in Powhattan, Pontiac, Tecumseh, Philip and, last though not least, Osceola. These were all generals, great generals:

APPENDIX

self-taught tacticians and military diplomats. If not, the white leaders acquired precious little glory in at last defeating them.

Among Indian warriors Powhattan holds a high and deserved station. He made himself the sole and absolute monarch of his tribe by the mere force of native genius and iron-will. The whites called him "*The Emperor.*"

There is not a character either in the staid lore of history, or the splendid pages of romance, more martial, dignified and brilliant, than the renowned Philip. Brave, merciful and talented, he is the very *beau-ideal* of the wise, the chivalrous and the good. The diplomatic talent which he displayed in all his negotiations is admitted by his enemies to have been of the first order. But if he was great in the council and powerful in the field, what words should be applied to him when he found himself deserted, the sceptre of his fathers fading away from his hands, and himself an outcast,—hunted like a wild beast, and not owning amid his whole dominions a spot whereon the weary, broken-hearted warrior might repose his weary head! And amid all this ruin, he scoffed at peace. The frame of the great soldier was sinking, but his spirit, like the noble tree of his native forest, still dared the lighting and laughed at the storm-cloud. An able writer has said: "Philip was far from being a mere barbarian in his manners and feelings. There is not an instance of his having maltreated a captive in any way—*even while the English were selling his own people as slaves abroad, or torturing and hanging them at home.*" There is a moral grandeur in his death, the result of treachery, which even the proud Corsican could not boast. Eloquently has it been said, "he fought and fell—miserably indeed, but gloriously, the avenger of his household, the worshiper of his own gods, the guardian of his own honor, a martyr for the soil which was his birthplace, and for the proud liberty which was his birthright,"

Philip of Pokanoket is among the immortal. The eloquence of Logan has been fully proved by Jefferson and Campbell. That of Decanesora is not so much known. Yet he was as vehement and imaginative.

The Indians' oratory is to be classed with the finest in the world—if sharp point, beautiful and grand imagery, and appropriate gesture are its main constitutents. Decanesora once said to a white governor, "You have almost eaten us up. Our best men are killed in this bloody war. But we forget what is past. Before this, we once threw the hatchet into the river, *but you fished it up*, and treacherously surprised our people at Cadaraqui. After that, you sent us to have our prisoners restored. Then the hatchet *was thrown up* to the sky, but you kept a string fastened to the helve and pulled it down and fell upon our people. Now we come to cover the blood from our sight, which has been shed by both parties during the war. We make the sun clean, and drive away all clouds and darkness, that we may see the light without interruption." Decanesora once answered a charge of fraud by advising the accuser to give "less credit to the rum-carriers."

Condensity is the main characteristic of Indian oratory. In this respect *Red Jacket*, as an orator, was unequaled by any Indian of his tribe, his language was beautiful and figurative, as the Indian language always is,—and delivered with the greatest ease and fluency. His gesticulation was easy, graceful and natural. His voice was distinct and clear, and he always spoke with great animation.

Red Jacket came upon the theatre of active life, when the power of his tribe had declined, and its extinction was theatened. The white man was advancing upon them with gigantic strides. The red warrior had appealed ineffectually, to arms; his cunning had failed and his strength overpowered: his foes, superior in prowess, were countless in number; and he had thrown down the tomahawk in despair. It was then that Red Jacket stood forward as a patriot, defending his nation with fearless eloquence and denouncing its enemies with fierce invective, or bitter sarcasm. He became their counsellor, their negotiator and their orator. Whatever may have been his conduct in the field, he now evinced a moral courage, as cool and sagacious as it was undaunted, and which showed a mind of too high an order to be influenced by the base sentiment of fear. The relations of the Senecas with the American people introduced questions of a new and highly interesting character, having reference to the purchase of their lands, and the introduction of Christianity and the arts. The Indians were asked not only to sell their country, but to embrace a new religion, to change their occupation and domestic habits, and to adopt a novel system of thought and action. Strange as these propositions must have seemed in themselves, they were rendered the more unpalatable when dictated by the stronger party, and accompanied by occasional acts of oppression. It was at this crisis that Red Jacket stood forward, the intrepid defender of his country, its customs, and its religion, and the unwavering opponent of all innovations. He yielded nothing to persuasion or bribery, or to menace, and never, to his last hour, remitted his exertions in what he considered the noblest purpose of his life.

An intelligent gentleman, who knew this chief intimately, in peace and war, for more than thirty years, speaks of him in the following terms: "Red Jacket was a *perfect Indian* in every respect—in costume, in his contempt of the dress of the white men, in his hatred and opposition to the missionaries, and in his attachment to and veneration for the ancient customs and traditions of his tribe."

His memory was very strong, for in a council which was held with the Senecas by Governor Tompkins of New York, a contest arose between that gentleman and Red Jacket, as to a fact connected with a treaty of many years' standing. The American agent stated one thing, the Indian chief corrected him, and insisted that the reverse of his assertion was true. "But," it was rejoined, "you have forgotten—we have it written down on paper." "The paper then tell a lie," was the confident answer; "I have it written here," continued the chief, placing his hand with dignity upon his brow. "You Yankees are born with a feather between your fingers; but your paper does not speak the truth. The Indian keeps his knowledge here; this is the book the Great Spirit gives us; it does not lie!" A reference was immediately made to the treaty in question, when to the astonishment of all present, and to the triumph of the red statesman, the document confirmed every word he had uttered.

Previous to his death, time had made such ravages on his constitution as to render him fully sensible of his approaching dissolution. He visited successively all of his most intimate friends at their cabins and conversed with them upon the condition of the nation, in the most impressive and affecting manner. He told them that he was passing away, and his councils would soon be heard no more. He would run over the history of his people from the most remote period to which his knowledge extended, and point out, which only few could do, the wrongs, the privations and the loss of character, which almost of themselves constituted that history. "I am about to leave," he said, "and when I am gone, and my warnings shall be no longer heard, or regarded, the craft and avarice of the white man will prevail. Many winters have I breasted the storm, but I am an aged tree, and can stand no longer. My leaves are fallen, my branches are withered, and I am shaken by every breeze. Soon my aged trunk will be prostrate, and the foot of the exulting foe of the Indian may be placed upon it in safety for I leave none who will be able to avenge such an indignity. Think not I mourn for myself. I go to join the spirits of my fathers, where age can not come: but my heart fails, when I think of my people, who are soon to be scattered and forgotten." These several interviews were all concluded with detailed instructions respecting his domestic affairs and his funeral.

He died on the 20th of January, 1830, at his residence near Buffalo. With him fell the spirit of his people. They gazed upon his fallen form and mused upon his prophetic warnings, until their hearts grew weary with grief. Wisely has it been said, "Thus fell the last of the Senecas."

The genius of Pontiac—or Pondiac, as he is often called—would have shown of itself that the red man could possess all the higher faculties of mind. The warrior saw his nation sinking before the English power like the blighted leaves of his own forests, beneath the desolating breath of the hurricane. His keen perception told him that a powerful disease demanded a powerful remedy. He knew that half-way measures would not answer; and like an able, cautious but heroic general, he looked around, examined his material, collected it, and at one fell swoop rolled the fires of death upon his foe.

To imagine the combination of the Ottawas, the Chippewas, the Pottawatomies, the Miamis, the Sacs, and several other tribes of the West, with a large number of the Delawares and Six Nations, was a grand conception; but the exertions which he adopted to carry it into effect, place Pontiac with the greatest and best of the earth. The mutual animosity, fears and deep-rooted prejudices of these tribes had to be overcome, their patriotism aroused and their confidence in success fully answered, before a simultaneous attack, which was his object, could be made on the British posts of St Joseph, Green Bay, Michilimackinac, Detroit, Maumee, Sandusky, Niagara and Pittsburgh. Pontiac's matchless skill in effecting his design is fully proved by a speech which he delivered before some of the tribes at the river Aux Ecorses. The attack at last was ordered. The British lost nine forts and whole garrisons were completely massacred.

Pontiac personally undertook the destruction of Detroit, but failed, owing, as many suppose, to treachery.

Pontiac, like Peter of Russia, evinced a great desire to learn the modes of English manufacture and European tactics, and absolutely offered an individual a large portion of his land, if he would convey him to England for that purpose. He is known to have issued bills of credit, and what is better, to have redeemed them.

But we can indulge in conjectures at once pleasing and philosophical. You hold up Cadmus the inventor of letters as a glorious ornament of your Caucasian race, and justly too; but has not the Indian his Cadmus?[1] What superiority have you over him? If his invention had been given a fair trial among redmen in time of peace and prosperity, who can say the epic and the lyric, the essay and the oration, the biography and the history which would have sent the name of the red man down to a future, whose heart should thrill beneath his memory, and whose tongue might hymn his praises?

---

1. George Guess, a Cherokee.

Again, these unsophisticated denizens of the unshorn forest possessed in a high degree, that noble faculty which runs like lightning fire through the world, *mind*, warming vivifying and creating until the beautiful, august and godlike, start forth in entrancing loveliness and undying grandeur; the glory of man, and the cynosure of time.

Ideality, the love of the beautiful and the grand, they produced the bard, he was God's first speaker, and drew down the life-giving flame, from the primal electric to the man receiver. Why with all their sparkling, forcible, unique imagination, did the Indian progress no farther? This may perhaps be accounted for by continuous exertion and the absolute necessity of sharpening the physical faculties which his lot demanded. But after all, had he not literature, unwritten to be sure, but effective? There are many things of service beside books. Yes, he had a literature, the literature sung in unison with the breeze as it struck its harp of the wilderness, uttered in the grave council and thrown from the burning lips of eloquence. There is another literature also; that written in marble, the poems of architecture. This literature is always the result of religion, whatever other phases it may assume. Temples we know were the first fabrics. A literature such as this the Indian did not feel in need of. He was compelled to live mostly in the open air; his nature called but little for shelter; so he made the boundless forest his worshiping place, the steadfast sky was its dome, the winds its choir, and the eternal lights of the blue infinitude its lamps. A right brave temple that, a temple which God built, and where angels might adore; a temple too with free seats.

If the superiority of the Indian mind is still doubted, I would point you to his conception of heaven with its One Divinity, the all gracious, all potent, all omniscient, eternal Great Spirit; a heaven of beauty, with its blue streams and singing birds, a heaven far superior to any other except the Christians'. Is there not intellect in the conception of this Indian heaven? Is there not beauty in the wide stretching hunting grounds with their graceful animals, emerald trees and crystal rivers, and over all the spirit of love throwing its soft splendor, like a beautiful banner woven of sunbeams? Peace! Peace everlasting! A few more years, a few more massacres, a few more sighs, and not a descendant of that people will stand upon the soil of his fathers. The very grave of the warrior will be nameless, his dust mingled almost without a memorial with the universe atoms. The tides of life will rush over the silent realms of death, and the deep sea-like voice of other generations rise where a lost people have not even left an echo. And you the arrogant, what of you? Look to the *"inevitable, necessary law, of destiny."* In three thousand years may not two nations slumber, where but only one now lies in the icy pall of unconsciousness.

GYE-WAH-GO-WA,
NICHOLSON PARKER.

"TRAITS OF INDIAN CHARACTER"[1]
(See Chapter VI, page 77.)

There is something in the character and habits of the North American native, taken in connection with the scenery amid which he was accustomed to range,—its vast lakes, boundless forests, majestic rivers and trackless plains,—that to my mind is wonderfully striking and sublime. It is said that he is formed for the wilderness as the Arab is for the desert. True, it may be, inasmuch as we find that his nature is simple and enduring, fitted to grapple with difficulties and to support privation.

There seems but little soil in his heart for the growth of the kindly virtues, and yet if you would but take the trouble to penetrate that proud stoicism and habitual taciturnity which lock up his character from casual observation you would find him linked to his fellow man of civilized life by more of those sympathies and affections than are usually ascribed to him.

It has been the lot of the unfortunate aborigines of America to be doubly wronged by the white man. They have been dispossessed of their hereditary possessions by mercenary and frequently wanton warfare; and their character has been traduced by bigoted and interested writers. The colonists often treated them like beasts of the forest; and here I shall endeavor to justify these outrages. The latter found it easier to exterminate than to civilize, the former to villify than to discriminate. The appellation *savage* and *pagan* were deemed sufficient to sanction the hostilities of both; and thus the poor wanderers of the forest were persecuted and defamed, not because they were guilty but because they were ignorant. The rights of the native have seldom been properly appreciated or respected by the white man. In peace he has been the dupe of artful traffic; in war he has been regarded as a ferocious animal, whose life or death was a question of mere precaution and convenience. Man is cruelly wasteful of life when his own safety is endangered

---

1. An oration by Nicholson H. Parker, delivered at Canandaigua, March 7-8, 1853, in a lecture course covering two evenings. Copied from the original manuscript.

and he is sheltered by impunity; and no mercy is to be expected of him when he feels the sting of the reptile and is conscious of the power to destroy. The same prejudices which were indulged thus early, exist in common circulation at the present day. Certain learned societies, it is true, with laudable diligence, have endeavored to investigate and record the real character and manners of the Indian race; the American government, too, has wisely and humanely exerted itself to inculcate a friendly and forbearing spirit toward them, and to protect them from fraud and injustice.

The current opinion of Indian character, however, is too apt to be formed from the miserable hoards that infest the frontiers and hang on the skirts of the settlements. These are too commonly composed of degenerate beings, corrupted and enfeebled by its "civilization."

That proud independence that once formed the main pillar of native virtue has been shaken down and the whole moral fabric lies in ruins. Their spirits are humiliated and debased by a sense of inferiority, and thus courage is cowed and daunted by the superior knowledge and power of their enlightened neighbors. Society has advanced upon them like one of those withering airs that sometimes breathe desolation over a whole region of fertility. It has enervated their strength, and multiplied their diseases and superinduced upon their original barbarity the low vices of artificial life. It has given them a thousand superfluous wants, whilst it has diminished the means of mere existence. It has often driven before it the animals of the chase, who fly from the sound of the axe and the smoke of the settlement, to seek refuge in the depths of the remoter forests and yet untrodden wilds. Thus do you often find the Indians on your frontiers to be mere wrecks and remnants of once powerful tribes who have lingered in the vicinity of settlements and sink into precarious and vagabond existence. Poverty, repining and hopeless outlook, cankers of the mind unknown in savage life,—corrode their spirits and blight every free and noble quality of their natures. They have become drunken, indolent, thievish, feeble and pusillanimous. They loiter like vagrants about your settlements, among spacious dwellings replete with elaborate comforts, which only render them sensible of the comparative wretchedness of their own condition. Luxury spreads its ample board before their eyes; but they are excluded from the banquet. Plenty revels over the fields; the whole wilderness has blossomed into a garden, but they feel as reptiles that infest it.

How different was their state, while yet the undisturbed lords of the soil! Their wants were few and the means of gratification within their reach. They saw everyone around them sharing the same lot, enduring the same hardships, feeding on the same aliments, arrayed in the same rude garments. No roof then rose but was then open to the homeless stranger; no smoke curled among the trees, but he was welcome to sit down by its fire and join the hunter in his repast. "For," says an old historian of New England, "their life is so void of care, and they are so loving also, that they make use of those things they enjoy as common goods, and are therein so compassionate, that rather than one should starve through want, they would starve all. Thus do they pass their time merrily, not regarding your pomp, but are better contented with their own, which some men esteem so meanly of." Such were the Indians whilst in the pride and the energy of their primitive natures: they resemble those wild plants that thrive best in the shades of their native forests, but shrink from the hand of cultivation and perish beneath the influence of the sun.

In discussing the savage character writers have been too prone to indulge in vulgar prejudice and passionate exaggeration instead of the candid temper of true philosopher. They have not sufficiently considered the peculiar circumstances in which the Indians have been placed, and the peculiar principles under which they have been educated. No being acts more rigidly from rule than the Indian. His whole conduct is regulated according to some general maxims early implanted in his mind. The moral laws that govern him, are, to be sure, but few; but then he conforms to them all. The white man abounds in laws of religion, morals and manners, but how many does he violate! A frequent ground of accusation against the Indians is their disregard of treaties, and the treachery and wantonness with which in times of peace they will suddenly fly to hostilities. The intercourse of the white men with the Indians, however, is too apt to be cold, distrustful, oppressive and insulting. They seldom treat with that confidence and frankness which are indispensable to real friendship; nor is sufficient caution observed not to offend against those feelings of pride or superstition, which often prompt the Indian to hostility quicker than mere consideration of interest. The solitary savage feels silently but acutely. His sensibilities are not diffused over so wide a surface as those of the white man, but run in steadier and deeper channels. His pride, his affection, his superstitions are all directed towards fewer objects; but the wounds inflicted on them are proportionately severe, and furnish motives of hostility which you cannot sufficiently appreciate. Where a community is also limited in number and forms one great patriarchal family, as in an Indian tribe, the injury of an individual is the injury of the whole, and the sentiment of vengeance, is almost instantaneously diffused. One council fire is sufficient for the discussion and the arrangement of a plan of hostilities. Here all the fighting men and sages assemble. Eloquence and superstition combine to influence the minds of the warriors. The orators awaken their martial powers and ardour, and they are wrought up to a kind of religious desperation by the visions of the prophet and dreamer.

An instance of one of these sudden exasperations arising from a motive peculiar to the Indian character is extant in an old record of the early settlement of Massachusetts. The planters of Plymouth had defaced the monuments of the dead at Passonagessit and had plundered the grave of the sachem's mother of some skins with which it had been decorated. The Indians are remarkable for the reverence which they entertain for the sepulchers of their kindred. Tribes that have passed generations exiled from the abodes of their ancestors, when again by chance they have been traveling in the vicinity, have been known to turn aside from the highway, and, guided by wonderfully accurate tradition, have crossed the country for miles to some tumulus, buried perhaps in woods, where the bones of their tribesmen were anciently deposited, and there have passed hours in silent meditation. Influenced by this sublime and holy feeling, the sachem whose mother's tomb had been violated, gathered his men together and addressed them in the following beautifully simple and pathetic harangue, a curious specimen of Indian eloquence, and an affecting instance of filial piety in a savage:

"When last the glorious light of all the sky was underneath this globe, and birds grew silent, I began as my custom is to take repose. Before mine eyes were fast closed, methought I saw a vision at which my spirit was much troubled; and, trembling at the doleful sight, a spirit cried aloud; 'Behold, my son, whom I have cherished, see the breasts that gave thee suck, the hands that lapped thee warm and fed thee oft! Canst thou forget to take revenge on those wild people who have defaced my monument in a despiteful manner, disdaining our antiquities and honourable customs? See now, the sachem's grave lies like the common people defaced by an ignoble race. Thy mother doth complain and implores aid against this thievish people who have newly intruded on our land. If this be suffered I shall not rest quiet in my everlasting habitation.' This said the spirit, and I all in a sweat, not able scarce to speak, began to get some strength, and recollected my spirits that were fled and determined to demand your council and assistance."

I have adduced this anecdote at some length, as it tends to show how these sudden acts of hostility which have been attributed to caprice and perfidy, may often arise from deep and generous motives, which inattention to Indian character and customs prevents your properly appreciating.

Another ground of violent outcry against the Indians is their barbarity to the vanquished. This had its origin partly in policy and partly in superstition. The tribes, though sometimes nations, were never so formidable in numbers but that the loss of several warriors was sensibly felt. This was particularly the case when they had frequently been engaged in warfare; and many an instance occurs in Indian history where a tribe that had long been formidable to its neighbors, has been broken up and driven away by the capture and massacre of its principal fighting men. There was a strong temptation, therefore, to the victor to be merciless; not so much to gratify any cruel revenge, as to provide for security. The Indians had also a superstitious belief, frequent among barbarous nations and prevalent also among the ancients, that the manes of their friends who had fallen in battle were soothed by the blood of captives. The prisoners, however, who are not thus sacrificed, are adopted into their families in place of the slain, and are treated with the confidence and the affection of relatives and friends; nay, so hospitable and tender is their entertainment that when the alternative is offered them, they will often prefer to remain with their adopted brethren, rather that return to their homes and the friends of their youth.[2]

The cruelty of the Indians toward their prisoners has been heightened since the colonization of the whites. What was formerly compliance with policy and superstition has broadened into a gratification of vengeance. They cannot but be sensible that the white men are the usurpers of their ancient domains, the cause of their degradation and the gradual destroyers of their race. They go forth to battle smarting with injuries and indignities which they have individually suffered, and they are driven to madness and despair by the wide spreading desolation and overwhelming ruin of European warfare. The whites have too frequently sent them an example of violence, by burning their villages and laying waste to their slender means of subsistence; and yet *they* wonder that savages do not show moderation and magnanimity toward those who have left them nothing but mere existence and wretchedness.

You stigmatize the Indians also as cowardly and treacherous, because they use stratagem in warfare in preference to open force;

---

2. An Indian once captured, who consents to adoption by his victorious foe, considers himself, and is considered by his own tribe, as legally dead. Once adopted by his conquerors, he forswears his birth-tribe, considers himself divorced from his wife and family, and henceforth pledged loyalty to the tribe of his adoption, marrying and rearing another family. The captive who was tortured by his enemy considered it an honor and felt that he was not to be demeaned by being forced to forsake his own tribe and the principles for which it fought. Thus, his death song was one of defiance and of insult to his foes, while it extolled the virtues and prowess of his own people.—A.C.P.

but in this they are justified by their rude code of honor. They are early taught that stratagem is praiseworthy; the bravest warrior thinks it no disgrace to lurk in silence and take every advantage of his foe, and he triumphs in the superior craft and sagacity by which he has been enabled to surprise and destroy an enemy. Indeed, man is naturally more prone to subtility than open valor, owing to his physical weakness in comparison with other animals. They are endowed with natural powers of defense; with horns, with tusks, with hoofs, with talons; but man has to depend upon his superior sagacity. In all his encounters with these his proper enemies, he resorts to stratagem and when he perversely turns his hostility against his fellow man, he at first continues his subtle mode of warfare.

The natural principle of war is to do the most harm to our enemy with the least harm to ourselves, and this, of course, is to be effected by stratagem. That chivalrous courage that induces you to despise the suggestions of prudence and to rush into the face of certain danger, is the offspring of polite society, and produced by education. It is honorable because it is in fact the triumph of lofty sentiment over an instinctive repugnance to pain, and over the yearnings after personal ease and security, (which society has condemned as ignoble). It is kept alive by pride and the fear of shame; and thus the dread of real evil is overcome by imagination. It has been cherished and stimulated also by various means. It has been the theme of spirit stirring song and chivalrous story. The poet and the minstrel have delighted to shed around it the splendors of fiction, and even the historian has forgotten the sober gravity of narration and broken forth into enthusiastic rhapsody in its praise. Triumphs and gorgeous pageants have been its reward; monuments, on which art has exhausted its skill, and opulence its treasures, have been erected to perpetuate a nation's gratitude and admiration. Thus artificially excited courage has arisen to an extraordinary and fictitious degree of heroism; and, arrayed in all the glorious "pomp and circumstance of war," this turbulent quality has even been able to eclipse many of those quiet virtues which silently ennoble the human character, and swell the tide of human happiness.

But if courage intrinsically consists in the defiance of danger and pain, the life of the Indian is a continual exhibition of it. He lives in a state of perpetual hostility and risk. Peril and adventure are congenial to his nature; or rather seem necessary to arouse his faculties and to give an interest to his existence. Surrounded by hostile tribes, whose mode of warfare is by ambush and surprisal, he is always prepared for fight and lives with his weapons in his hands. As the ship careens in fearful singleness through the solitudes of the ocean; as the bird mingles among clouds and storms, and wings its way, a mere speck across the pathless air; so the Indian holds his course, silent, solitary, but undaunted through the boundless bosom of the wilderness.

His expeditions may vie in distance and danger with the pilgrimage of the devotee or the crusade of the knight errant. He traverses vast forests, exposed to the hazards of lonely sickness, of lurking enemies, and passing famine. Stormy lakes, those great inland seas, are no obstacles to his wanderings; in his light canoe of bark, he sports like a feather on their waves, and darts with the swiftness of an arrow down the roaring rapids of the rivers. His very subsistence is snatched from the midst of toil and peril. He gains his food by the hardships and dangers of the chase; he wraps himself in the spoils of the bear, the panther, and the buffalo; and he sleeps among the thunders of the cataract. No hero of ancient or modern days surpasses the Indian in his lofty contempt of death, and the fortitude with which he sustains its cruelest affliction. Indeed you here behold him rising superior to the white man in consequence of his peculiar education. The latter rushes to glorious death at the cannon's mouth; the former calmly contemplates its approach and triumphantly endures it amidst the varied torments or surrounding foes and the protracted agonies of fire. He even takes pride in taunting his persecutors and in provoking their ingenuity of torture; and as the devouring flames prey on his very vitals and the flesh shrinks from the sinews, he raises his last song of triumph, breathing the defiance of an unconquered heart, and in invoking the spirits of his fathers to witness that he dies without a groan.

Notwithstanding the obloquy with which the early historians have overshadowed the characters of the unfortunate natives, some bright gleams occasionally break through to a degree of melancholy luster on their memories. Facts are occasionally to be met with in the rude annals of the eastern provinces, which though recorded with the coloring of prejudice and bigotry, yet speak for themselves, and will be dwelt upon with applause and sympathy when prejudice shall have passed away.

In one of the homely narratives of the Indian wars in New England there is a touching account of the desolation carried into the tribe of the Pequot Indians. Humanity shrinks at the cold-blooded detail of indiscriminate butchery. In one place we read of the surprise of an Indian fort at night, when the wigwams were wrapped in flames and the miserable inhabitants shot down and slain in attempting to escape,—"all being despatched and ended in the course of an hour." After a series of similar transactions—

APPENDIX

INDIAN HISTORICAL LECTURES,

BY
GA-I-WAH-GO-WA.

This talented young Indian, a descendent of the Iroquois, will give two select Lectures, on the

HISTORY OF HIS RACE,

Their Manners, Customs, National Festivities, Costumes, Literature, and Religion, to the citizens of CANANDAIGUA, in the

SEMINARY HALL,
ON
MONDAY AND TUESDAY EVENINGS,
The 7th and 8th of March, 1853.

GA-I-WAH-GO-WA, is a brother of DO-NIH-HO-GA-WAH, or Ely S. Parker, of Rochester, N. Y., who is Head Chief of the Six Nations, and recently acknowledged as such by Gov. Seymour, and is a distinguished Civil Engineer in the Government service. Ga-i-wah-go-wa, (Nicholas H. Parker) is a fine specimen of the able Aborigines of this country. He possesses testimonials of a thorough education, and native powers of eloquence, and will not fail to interest any intelligent audience, that may listen to his delineation of Indian History, Character and Traditions.

The Lectures will be delivered in full Indian costume.

Lectures to commence at 7 1-2 o'clock.
Admission 12 1-2 Cents.

Printed at the Ontario Messenger Office, Canandaigua.

POSTER OF LECTURE BY NICHOLSON H. PARKER, 1853

"our soldiers," as the historian piously observes, "being resolved by God's assistance to make a final destruction of them"—the unhappy savages were hunted from their homes and fortresses and pursued with fire and sword, a scanty but gallant band, the sad remnants of the Pequot warriors took refuge in a swamp. Burning with indignation and rendered sullen by despair, with hearts bursting with grief at the destruction of their tribe, and spirits galled and sore at the fancied ignominy of their defeat, they refused to ask their lives at the hands of an insulting foe, and preferred death to submission. As the night drew on they were surrounded in their dismal retreat so as to render escape impracticable. Thus situated, their enemy "plied them with shot all the time, by which means many were killed and buried in the mire." In the darkness and fog that preceded the dawn of day, some few broke through the besiegers and escaped into the woods. "The rest were left to the conquerors, of which many were killed in the swamp like sullen dogs who would rather in their self willedness and madness, sit still and be shot to pieces than implore mercy." When the day broke upon this handful of forlorn but dauntless spirits, the soldiers, we are told, entering the swamp, "saw several heaps of them sitting close together upon whom they discharged their pieces, laden with ten or twelve pistol bullets at a time, putting their muzzles of their pieces under the boughs within a few yards of them; so as beside these that were found dead, many more were killed and sunk in the mire, and never were mindful more of friend or foe."

Can anyone read this unvarnished tale without admiring the stern resolution, the unbending pride, the loftiness of spirit that seemed to nerve the hearts of these self-taught heroes and raise them above the instinctive feelings of human nature? When the Gauls laid waste the city of Rome they found the Senators clothed in their robes and seated with stern tranquility in their curule chairs; in this manner they suffered death without resistance or even supplication. Such conduct was in them applauded as noble and magnanimous; in the hapless Indians it was reviled as obstinate and sullen. How truly are you the dupes of show and circumstance! How different is virtue clothed in purple and enthroned in state, from virtue naked and destitute, and perishing in obscurity in a wilderness!

But I forbear to dwell on these gloomy pictures. The eastern tribes have long since disappeared; the forest that sheltered them has been laid low and scarce any traces of them remain in the thickly settled states of New England, excepting here and there the Indian name of a village or stream. And such, sooner or later, must be the fate of these other tribes who have occasionally been inveigled from

APPENDIX

their forests to mingle in the wars of white men. A little while, and they will go the way that their brethren have gone before. The few hordes that still linger about the shores of Huron and Superior and the tributary waters of the Mississippi will share the fate of those tribes that spread over Massachusetts and Connecticut and bordered along the proud banks of the Hudson; of that gigantic race said to have existed on the borders of the Susquehanna; of those various nations that flourished about the Potomac and Rappahannock and that peopled the forests of the vast valley of Shenandoah. They will vanish like the vapor from the face of the earth; their very history will be lost in forgetfulness, and "places that now know them will know them no more forever!" Or, if perchance some dubious memorial of them should survive, it may be in the romantic dreams of the poet, to people in imagination his glades and groves, like the fauns and satyrs and sylvan deities of antiquity. But should he venture upon the dark story of their wrongs and wretchedness, should he tell how they were invaded, corrupted, despoiled, driven from their abodes and sepulchers of their fathers, hunted like wild beasts about the earth and sent down with violence and butchery to the grave, posterity will either turn with horror and incredulity from the tale or blush with indignation at the inhumanity of their forefathers.

"We are driven back," said an old warrior, "until we can retreat no further; our hatchets are broken, our bows are snapped, our fires are extinguished. A little longer and the white man will cease to persecute us, for we shall cease to exist!"

"INDIAN DANCES AND THEIR INFLUENCE"[1]
(See Chapter VI, page 77.)

With the red race at large dancing is regarded as a thanksgiving ceremonial acceptable in itself to the Great Spirit, *Ha-wen-ni-yuh*, and they are also taught to regard it as a divine art, designed for their pleasure and His worship.

It is cherished as one of the most suitable modes of social intercourse between the sexes, but more especially as the instrumentality for arousing patriotic excitement and keeping alive the spirit of the nation. Popular enthusiasm breaks forth in this form and these dances arise as a spontaneous product of the Indian mind.

---

1. A portion of a lecture by Nicholson H. Parker.

With their wild music of songs and rattles, their diversities of step and attitude, their grace of motion and their spirit-stirring associations, they contain within themselves both a picture and a realization of savage life.

The first impressive emotions of which the Indian youth is conscious is kindled by the dance, the first impulses of patriotism, the earliest dreams of ambition, are aroused by their inspiring influences. In their patriotic religious and social dances, into which they are properly divided, resides the soul of Indian life. The dance serves as a mighty bond by which they are united, it stimulates to deeds of daring and feeds the patriotic flame. It exercises an overpowering influence in arousing Indian spirit and in forming the Indian character, and hence is of vast importance to them. The great tenacity with which the Indians hold on to their dances furnishes conclusive evidence of the mighty hold they have upon the affections of the people. When these attractions and peculiarities are neutralized they will virtually cease to be Indians.

A mourning council of Genesee was held in 1846 to raise up sachems. There were about 600 Iroquois present representing all of the Six Nations. On the second day the Great Feather Dance was performed by a select band of Onondaga and Seneca dancers. A white gentleman (Lewis H. Morgan) who was present and witnessed it remarked that he then for the first time realized the magical influence which these dances have upon the Indians. "It was impossible even for the spectators," he says, "to resist the general enthusiasm."

It was remarked to Abraham La Fort, an educated Onondaga sachem, that they would be Indians forever if they held to these dances. He replied that he knew it and that for that reason he would be the last to give them up.

The War Dance and the Great Feather Dance are the two great performances of the Iroquois. One has a patriotic and the other a religious character, yet at the same time both are costume dances. They are performed by a select band of from fifteen to thirty who are distinguished for their power of endurance and of activity. Of the two the War Dance stands prominent. It is the dance for enlistment on perilous expeditions, as it is the dance that precedes the departure of the war party and with which their return is celebrated; of adopting captives and for the entertainment of guests, and hence is the first to be taught the young.

In the War Dance the attitudes are those of the violent passions and hence are not very graceful. In this dance may be seen at the same time or instant one in the attitude of attack, another of the defense; one drawing the bow, another striking with the war club; others listening and others striking the foe. Notwithstanding that the dance elicits the manifestation of the passions, with uncouth attitudes and contortions of countenance, still the wild music, the supple activity, the rattles of the dance, make a scene of no ordinary interest.

In the ceremony they group themselves within a circular area, standing strictly together. The singers commence their songs, beating time upon their drums, and the dancers make the floors resound with agile foot. Each war song lasts about two minutes, followed with an interval of about the same length. These war songs are verses or measured sentences. The war whoop always precedes each song. It is given by the leader and answered by the band. A description of this thrilling outbreak of human voices is out of the power of language to express.

In this dance any one is at liberty to make a speech at any stage of the dance. His desire is manifested by a rap, at the sound of which the dance ceases and all is silent until the message is delivered. Then comes the war whoop, the response by the band, followed again by the music and the dance.

All who make speeches on these occasions are expected to make a present to the dancers at the close of their speech. In this way they give variety and great amusement. The speeches are generally short, being only a few words or sentences at most. They may be a patriotic ebulition of feeling, or witticism, or an exhortation. Some are welcomed with jeers, some with rounds of applause and some with solemnity.

As an illustration of this part of the amusement I will give one, two or more specimens as they occurred at a war dance within my memory.

At the close of a time, a rap was made by Hah-sgwih-sa-ooh, a jolly chief who was very fond of fire-water. He spoke as follows:

"Friends and relatives: I am much pleased with the dance and hope that it will continue to be well sustained. I return my thanks to the war dancers for the spirit with which they perform their duty. I wish them all prosperity and long life. If any one should look at me they will find that I keep my eyes fixed upon the dancers; and, furthermore that I have a good eye, so much so that one would think I wore glasses. I take from my pocket a shilling for the dancers."

He gave them the money. The war whoop, the music and the dance were resumed. At its end Sha-do-wa-noh rapped and made a reply to the other as follows:

"Friends and relatives: We have just heard some one on the other side of the house announce that he has an eye so bright that one would think he wore spectacles. But as he has a pair of red eyes, we must I suppose, conclude that he means red spectacles."

He then gave tobacco to the dancers. The hit upon the infirmity of the first speaker was received with rounds of applause, after which the dance went on as usual.

Among the dancers was a warrior of herculean proportions, so much so that he might with propriety be called a giant. He furnished the theme for the next speech which was by Hah-sa-no-a-deh, as follows:

"Friends and relatives: I admire the ease and grace with which Sha-go-a-o-gwus, manages his wonderful proportions. He has every reason to be proud of his size and dignity. I propose to give him a present of two plugs of tobacco, supposing that it will be sufficient for one quid."

After the merriment had subsided and the next dance was over, the giant replied:

"Friends and relatives: I return my thanks to Hah-sa-no-a-deh, for his present. I assure him that my intellectual capacity corresponds very justly with my physical dimensions. I hope that my brother will publish my fame from the rising to the setting sun."

Thus they proceeded with speeches and replies, till finally a speech of more serious cast was made by Da-geh-sa-deh, a distinguished chief, in which he said:

"Friends and relatives: We have reason to glory in the achievements of our ancestors. I behold with sadness the present declining state of our noble race. Once, warlike yell and painted hand were the terror of the white man. Then our fathers were strong and their power was felt and acknowledged far and wide over the American continent. But we have been reduced and broken by the cunning and rapacity of the white race. We are now compelled to crave as a blessing that we may be allowed to live upon our own lands, to cultivate our own fields, to drink from our own spring and to mingle our bones with those of our fathers. Many winters ago our wise ancestors predicted that a great monster with white eyes would come from the east and as he advanced would consume the land. This monster is the white race and the prediction is near its fulfilment. They (our ancestors) advised their children when they became weak to plant a tree with four roots, branching to North, the South, the East and the West; and then collecting under its shade to dwell together in unity and harmony. This tree I propose shall be at this very spot. Here we will gather, here we will live and here we will die."

These specimens will give some idea of the manner of conducting a war dance and its variety of entertainments.

Next in public estimation is the Great Feather Dance. It is a religious dance being consecrated to the worship of the Great Spirit. It is performed by a select band of from fifteen to thirty or more in full costume, and is used chiefly at religious festivals and on the most important occasions of Indian life. It is the most graceful, splendid and impressive of all the dances, requiring more flexibility of person, more gracefulness of action and greater power of endurance than any other dance. Herein is a kind of climax of the dancing art, at least in Indian life, and it may be seriously questioned if a figure can be found even in civilized life which will fully compare with this in those particulars which make up a graceful and spirited dance.

The music is furnished by two singers seated in the center of the room, each using a rattle. It consists of songs, or measured verses of about two minutes in length; these are religious songs in which they praise Ha-wen-e-yuh or the Great Spirit for His many blessings in nature or supplicate His continued mercy.

The rattles are made of turtle shell and are used to beat time to the songs as an accompaniment.

In some respects this dance is like the first, viz., the singing ceases at short intervals, the dance is suspended and the performers walk around the common center to the beat of the rattles at half time. Soon another song commences, the rattles quicken the time and the dance is renewed.

Sometimes in the middle of the song there is a change in the beat of time and the music, accompanied by a slight cessation of the dance, after which it becomes more animated than before. Thus it goes on with its variety of undulations.

The leader, standing at the head of the column, opens the dance, followed by those behind. Now they advance slowly around the room and as they dance, gesture with their arms and place their bodies in a great variety of positions. They do not seek to portray the violent passions, but only the gentle and graceful.

Each foot in succession is raised from two to six inches from the floor and the heel brought down with great force as often as the rattles beat. Sometimes one foot is brought down two or three times before alternating with the others. When it is remembered that the rattles beat two or three times a second and the feet must keep time with that, you get a little idea of the surprising activity of the dance. The stamping of the foot upon the floor answers the double purpose of shaking the knee rattles on the costume and of adding to the noise and animation of the dance.

The dancers are generally naked to the waist except the ornaments upon the neck and arms, by which means they not only add to the picturesqueness of the performers but are better fitted for their herculean exertions which are so severe that the vapor of sweat makes a literal smoke from their backs before they are through. In this way they seek to test each other's powers of endurance, and it is not uncommon for some to yield to their utter exhaustion and retire from their dance before it is finished. When one distinguishes himself for a spirited and graceful performance he is called out by the spectators and placed at the head of the band. In this way several changes frequently occur during the dance.

The women join in this dance if they choose but they enter by themselves at the foot of the column and in their ordinary dress. Their step is entirely unlike that of the male. They move sidewise, simply raising themselves alternately upon each foot from heel to toe and then bringing down the heel upon the floor at each beat of the rattle, keeping pace with the slowly advancing column. The females in the dance are both quiet and graceful.

The war dance is usually performed in the evening and is only employed on important occasions or at domestic councils of unusual interest. Fifteen make a full company but frequently twenty-five or thirty engage in this dance.

After the cares of the day are laid aside and as the shades of night set in, preparations begin for the dance. The people are attracted to the council house in great numbers to witness this popular entertainment. They quietly wait for the coming of the dancers who make their arrangements in another house, appointing their leaders and singers, arraying themselves in their costumes, painting and decorating, superintended by the Keeper of the Faith.

Keepers of the Faith are what you might call managers at a ball, only with them it is an hereditary office, supposed by them to have been appointed by the Great Spirit, to attend and see that all regulations of His Divine will are executed. Hence it is the duty of the Keeper of the Faith, when a dance of any character is on foot, but more especially when it is of a religious character, to see that all regulations are strictly observed.

The war whoop now and then breaks in the stillness of the night, informing the waiting multitude that they are forthcoming.

During this preparation a Keeper of the Faith engages the attention of the people by addressing them on the nature, object and importance of this dance.

Now nearer the war whoop rings through the air, announcing the approach of the dancers. Headed by their leader and marching in single file to the beat of the drum they approach the council house. As they come up the crowd gives way, the leader crosses the threshold followed by his decorated band and immediately the dance is opened. They group themselves within a circular area, standing thick together. The singers commence the war song, beating time upon their drums, and the dancers make the floor resound with agile foot.

It is quite impossible to give a perfect description of the step and attitude of these dancers. With the whites I observe the dancing is entirely on the tip-toe of the foot, with rapid change of position and but slight changes of attitude. But with the Iroquois it is very different. With them it is chiefly upon the heel with slow changes of positions and rapid changes of attitude. The heel is raised and brought down with great quickness and force in order to keep time to the beat of the drum, to make noise and to shake the knee rattles, all of which add pomp and circumstance to the occasion.

The shuffle dance is executed in a peculiar manner by alternately moving one foot slightly forward of the other, but neither at any time leaving the ground or floor. The advance movement is quite rapid, and the elderly women make very graceful movement with their hands, arms and heads, keeping the body stiff and erect.

The dance for the dead is executed by the women alone, with the exception of the men songsters whom the women have selected. For some reason this dance at one time was required to be commenced in the middle of the afternoon, terminating at twilight. Subsequently it commenced at dusk and ended at midnight. Later yet it commenced at any time after dark and continued until the dawn of the next morning. The two men songsters commenced the song, the women all joining in the chorus, accompanying the same with a slow-snake-like forward motion of the feet, the body erect and quite rigid. The feast is a duty and not to be partaken by women in certain peculiar conditions. These feasts, owing to their mournful character, were not often held but they were regarded as essential to the peace and quiet of the departed spirits. The feast, like all others, was composed of hominy or cracked corn, boiled with meat, hulled or whole Seneca corn, boiled with meat, and Seneca corn bread, plain or mixed with dried berries.

The Death Dance can only be called by the female Keepers of the Faith, approved by the male members of the order.

The dances are nearly always accompanied and closed by a feast and can be given by any one either by day or night. They are often credited to unweaned infants, though the dance is selected and the feast provided by the mother. Sick persons are frequently the promoters of the dances and feasts, and will join in some one dance if able to walk, and if not are led around by some kind friend.

The dances and feasts are held solely and purely for social purposes and innocent pleasure, and are always enjoyed alike by the young and old of both sexes.

There are a few special dances which are not common property and therefore cannot be ordered by individuals; such for instance as the Grand Feather Dance.

A LETTER FROM ELY S. PARKER TO HIS PEOPLE EXPLAINING THE NEW LAW DRAFTED FOR THEIR BENEFIT AND PROTECTION.

(See Chapter X)

March 4, 1861.

DEAR FATHER:

I send you my communication to the Indians at Tonawanda concerning our doings at Albany. I have had no time to copy it or to put it into better shape, but I think it embodies everything I want to say to the Indians.

The letter must be carefully studied either by Newton or Caroline before it is read to the Council. The matter requires much thought and consideration. In my humble opinion it is a very good thing for the Indians and I hope that they will conclude to enjoy its benefits.

Upon my return I find that my work has accumulated and requires my immediate attention, hence the delay in writing to you.

Spring is beginning to open upon us and my work will soon begin to increase materially. In a few days I am going down the river about 300 miles and shall be absent about two weeks. My health is very good and I trust you and the family are well.

From your son,

ELY S. PARKER.

WM. PARKER, ESQ.,
　　Indian Chief,
　　Tonawanda Ind. Res.
　　　New York.

APPENDIX   287

DUBUQUE, Mch. 2nd, 1861.

To the CHIEFS AND PEOPLE OF THE TONAWANDA BAND
        OF SENECA INDIANS:—

I send you greeting, and invoke the Great Spirit that it may be His will that this, my communication, may reach you and find you all enjoying health and prosperity. As for myself, the Great Spirit has looked kindly upon me, and I am in good health.

Some time since you delegated me to go to Albany, N. Y., and conjointly with Mr. Martindale, to go before the Legislature and ask for the enactment of such laws as in our opinion we might conceive to be for the benefit and welfare of our Band at Tonawanda. I am now about to report to you what we did.

And first let me say, that I regretted very much my inability to visit you, and looking upon you all to have made my report verbally. But I was under orders from Washington to return here by a certain day, which compelled me to pass you by.

I will now, in as few words as possible, relate to you what we did. When I left here I had no definite idea of the particular things our friend Mr. Martindale had upon his mind and in which he desired my assistance in your behalf. When I reached Rochester he gave me an insight into his views. He was engaged in Court and could not at once proceed to Albany. I went on myself to Albany with a view of ascertaining the Legislative feeling respecting the Indians. I found a very friendly feeling and so wrote to Mr. Martindale. He came to Albany, reaching that place on the morning of the 20th February. He brought with him a bill partially prepared embodying all the legislation which was deemed necessary for the protection and improvement of the Tonawanda Band of Senecas. We examined this together, and after agreeing upon every point, he went the same day (20th) to New York, leaving me to put everything in shape to present for the action of the Legislature.

I will now tell you what it was, and after I have gone through with what we have asked the Lawmakers at Albany to do for us, I will then give the main reasons that influenced us in this matter.

We have asked to become a Law providing for the election by the Tonawanda Band of Senecas of three Peacemakers, one Treasurer, one clerk and one marshal (constable). All male Indians, members of said band over the age of 20 years to be entitled to vote. The Peacemakers are to be selected from among the chiefs, and they have duties enjoined upon them similar to the civil duties enjoined upon justices of the peace by white people. They are to hear and determine upon all difficulties between Indians arising from trespass, violations of contracts or agreements and other wrongs committed, where the damages claimed do not exceed one hundred dollars. Where the amount in controversy exceeds one hundred dollars, one Indian may sue another in the courts of the State in the same manner and with like effect as controversies between white men. These Peacemakers have jurisdiction only in difficulties between Indians. If any Indian refuses to pay any judgment determined against by the Peacemakers in favor of another Indian, he may be sued upon the judgment before any justice of the peace in the county and the judgment collected in the same manner as from a white man. The Peacemakers will receive a salary not exceeding fifty dollars a year, payable semi-annually.

The clerk will keep records of all elections, and the proceedings of all councils held by the Chiefs and Peacemakers. He will receive a salary not exceeding fifty dollars a year.

The Treasurer will keep all moneys belonging to the Band, paying them out only by order of a council of chiefs. He is required to give security for the faithful performance of his duties, and will receive such compensation as the chiefs may determine.

We have asked that the share of the Tonawanda Band of Senecas of the State annuity be hereafter paid directly to the Treasurer of said Band of Indians.

In the law we prohibit white men from buying timber, wood, ties, staves, shingles, bark or plaster from any Indian or Indians, if taken from lands unoccupied by any individual Indian, and recognized as the common property of the Band.

The law provides that any Indian of said Band may select a piece of land not fenced in and not occupied by any other Indian after describing it and obtaining the consent of the Chiefs in council assembled. The chiefs are required to base their consent to such appropriation of land by any Indian upon just and equitable ground, having always in view the interests of such as may come after us (that is, posterity). The decision and description must be entered by the clerk in a book kept for that purpose.

We prohibited all white persons from leasing lands of any Indian, or working Indian lands upon shares.

An Indian having a piece of ground allotted to him, in clearing it up for cultivation may sell any wood, timber, ties, staves, shingles, bark or plaster that he may find on his ground, but he shall not have this privilege upon any land recognized as the joint or common property of the Band. (Laying out and making roads.)

Such, my people, are the general provisions of the law, which our friend and counsellor Mr. Martindale and myself have asked the Legislature at Albany to enact for us.

And now, listen further, and I will give you a few general reasons that have influenced us in taking this course:

First then, I want you all to bear in mind, that we struggled for over 20 years, against the determined policy of land speculators to drive us from our Tonawanda homes. There were times in the history of the struggle when we seemed to be enveloped in utter darkness, and our wise men were lost in doubt what to do. We had no friends to advise us, and our own people, and our relations by blood, turned against us. Amid all this perplexity and when it appeared morally certain that we must be driven out of our Tonawanda homes and despoiled and robbed of our lands, we found friends in Verplanck and Martindale. By their ingenuity they interposed legal obstacles, preventing the immediate execution of the treaties which hung over our heads. Mr. Martindale was an honest man, and he proved a true friend to us. He made our interests his own, and prosecuted our views of our rights, until at length it resulted in securing to us permanent homes at Tonawanda. We no longer have a pre-emption right laying upon our lands. The lands we have now we own from the surface to the center and from the surface as high as the heavens. Our old men used to say, that our right to our lands lay only upon the surface, but now we can say that we own it to the center. Having acquired such a strong hold upon our ground, it was then considered, in what other matters did your interests require protection and in what manner could your improvement be permanently secured or advanced.

Mr. Martindale is a wise man. He has a great love for the Tonawandas. He respects their chiefs and all the people. But during the time he has labored for them he has seen that although a chief is held in esteem by his people, he is not obeyed by them. He has seen and understood that although a chief in olden times might have had great power with his people, association with, and the adoption to a slight extent by the Indians of the habits of the pale faces, have enlarged the ideas of the people, their eyes have been partially opened so that they can see somewhat for themselves, and that the chieftains' influence and usefulness have been materially circumscribed. He has seen a community at Tonawanda pretending to have a government and yet has no power to enforce or execute its will. This was a fault, in the government of any community, that needed to be remedied. The law does this. The chiefs are not curtailed in the exercise of any of their ancient rights or usages, but three men are selected from their number, who should be wise and discreet men, to be styled Peacemakers, by whom and through whom, power should be exercised to see that among the Indians right is maintained and wrongs remedied. These men will be selected annually, so that if you get a bad minded man, he can do great injury, and when you get a good man you should continue him in office and secure the benefits of his wisdom.

As the Indians improve and gather around them property of all kinds, they will begin to esteem their property as does a white man. He will feel that he has made it by hard labor, and sometimes he will want protection for this property, and if he needs it, it is right that he should have it. When he puts in a crop of wheat or oats or corn, or beans or potatoes, he will not want it destroyed by his neighbors' cattle, and if they should break in and do him damage it is right he should be paid for it. If one Indian makes a purchase of another Indian of anything and does not pay, or borrows money or any other thing and returns it not, or makes a contract and does not keep his word, it is right that there should be a power somewhere to regulate such matters, and to see that justice is done. A trespass may be committed upon another enclosure, or some other wrong may be done, in all which cases, the Peacemakers are made the arbiters and judges of the rights to be enforced or the wrongs to be abated. When a very great wrong is done, and the damages claimed exceed the sum that can be awarded by the Peacemakers then only can a suit be maintained before a Justice of the Peace. Such in brief are the duties of the Peacemakers, and I trust that you will agree that such offices are necessary in the present improved condition of the Tonawanda Band, and I shall further expect, that when this becomes a law, you will cheerfully aid in giving it a trial, for it has no other object than your own good and prosperity.

Another important change proposed for your good is in reference to the timber upon your lands. You all know that once we had very good timber upon the Tonawanda Reservation. We had large and tall pines, plenty of whitewood, walnut, ash, basswood, oaks, hemlock and chestnut. We had plenty of all kinds of wood, with which to build a house and make good fences. All this has been either sold by the Indians or stolen by bad white men. It has never done the Indian any good. It has not made the Tonawandas one cent richer. They are still very poor, and their timber is nearly all gone. They have hardly enough left to make good rails for fences.

They have no timber left fit to be manufactured into material for good houses. They have only enough left to serve them for firewood. We, therefore, prohibit all white men from buying timber in any shape from Indians, because we think the Indians need it all. If they do not want it now, the time is coming when they will require it. It may be cheap now, but by and by timber will become scarce and it will be valuable. It is sincerely hoped that upon this point you will be convinced, that to adopt this policy is for your good and that you will follow it.

Again, another point. Your friends will rejoice with you, that you have got so much land that is yours from the surface to the center. They think you ought to make good use of this and that you ought to be very rich. You have very good lands. But you cultivate only a very small portion of it. You let your lands to white people and you get very small profits. This is not right. We want you to cultivate your own lands. The profits to you will be very much greater than to let your lands to the white people. It will be difficult at first for the Indians to work all their improved or fenced lands, but they must get accustomed to it and then they will make their improvements larger and larger. Unless the Indians work their own lands, and cultivate a great deal more than they have heretofore done, they will be very foolish for owning so much waste and wild land. All we want, is to have the Indians work and receive the rich increase of their own lands. White men must not come in and take away the fat of your lands. You are not prohibited from having white men work for you but you are not to let your lands to them or cultivate your lands with them on shares. When you think this over carefully, I think that you will agree with your friends, that your adoption of this course will be a wise one, and of lasting benefit to your children.

The law proposes to give the chiefs authority to lay out roads and make ample regulations and provisions for working them. They will also be empowered to make proper rules respecting line fences or division lines between neighbors. No one can object to this because it is very proper and right. There is no wrong in it.

To carry out all the provisions of this contemplated law, it is provided that the District Attorney of Genesee County shall be the attorney and counsellor of the Tonawanda Band of Seneca Indians. He will be paid by the State. It will be his duty to prosecute all white persons who violate the wise provisions of the law to give you advice whenever required and to settle all difficulties between Indians when in his power and do all he can for your good.

These are the general provisions of a law which your friend Martindale and myself have asked the Legislature of New York to enact for your benefit. We do not contemplate that you will ever become citizens of the United States, or that you will ever want to be such. And therefore we have guarded your lands in such a manner that you and your children may always enjoy the fruits and benefits of it. We know that in your present improved conditions, your change in mode of life, the circumstances and influences that surround you upon all sides, the simple laws that governed your fathers 50 or 100 years ago, are not adapted to your present condition. And therefore without abolishing your ancient form of government which you understand so well, we have only asked for some new rules to give new vitality and efficiency to your government and materially enhance your prosperity. This is right, for no community can exist and prosper unless in its government it has executive power to enforce good order and obedience to its mandates. By this Law, you will be placed in a position that your prosperity will depend upon your own wisdom and exertions. You should all submit to it, and endeavor to make yourselves the richest and happiest Indian community in the State of New York. You must live as good neighbors and help one another. You must lay aside all quarrels, jealousies and envious feelings, and strive and labor all together to make yourselves happy and comfortable. When you help yourselves, you will find plenty of friends who will help you along.

THE SACHEM AT CHATTANOOGA
(See Chapter X.)

HEADQUARTERS MILITARY DIVISION OF THE MISSISSIPPI,
IN THE FIELD.

CHATTANOOGA, TENN., Nov. 21st, 1863.

MY DEAR SISTER:—It is now two or three days since I received your last letter written at home and mailed from Batavia. That makes the third or fourth letter I have received from you since I left home. I am thankful to hear from you at all and therefore I do not complain. The home news generally gave me great pleasure, particularly that relating to father's gradual recovery. Ever since you wrote of his failing health, his extreme sickness, and the despair of the doctor to save him, I have been quite wretched in feeling. Your news has almost wholly relieved my mind.

Of course my letter informing you of my own misfortunes has been received. I am not well yet, but I am constantly on duty and

APPENDIX

this may be one reason why I do not recover more rapidly. I am slightly disappointed about our crops at home, but I rather think that it is more probable that we have been as well favored as our neighbors. Most of our crops are good and we should be very thankful that the Good Spirit has been so kind to us.

I met with quite an accident today. I lent my horse to an officer to go across the river a few miles, and in coming home, as he was crossing the bridge, the horse jumped into the river and was drowned. This makes for me an investment of $150 in this miserable country.

You may like particularly to know just where I am and just what kind of a country it is, and the character of the people who occupy it. Well, if you will look upon a map of the U. S., up in the northwest corner of the state of Georgia, you will see a town marked Chattanooga. It is not in Georgia, but in Tennessee, three miles from the state line and only a few miles from the northeast corner of the state of Alabama. The range of the Cumberland mountains pass through here. It is nothing more than a continuation of the Allegheny range of mountains and of course very much like them. Father and old Sam both know a great deal about those mountains. The Tennessee river passes through this range of mountains at this point. And here we are among these mountains and our army lies on both sides of the river, which has in some places a flat upon one or both sides. The rebel army are south, east and west of us. In fact they almost surround us. If you understood topography, I would make you a topographical map of this particular section and let you study it. However, I will give you a little idea of my present home.

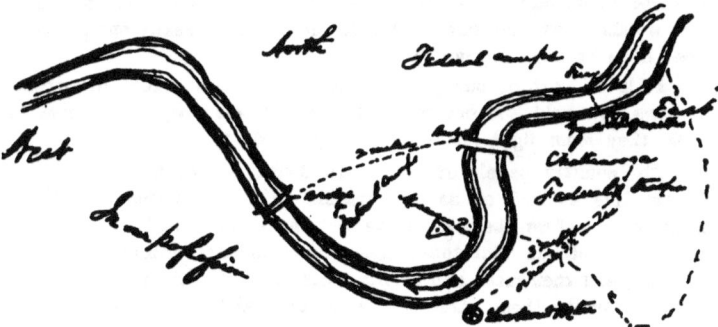

You may get a slight idea from this of the place we occupy. Our troops are in Chattanooga and the rebels are all around us on the south side from river to river. Commencing at Lookout Mountain, their lines extend around until they strike the river again away above, not so far however but that our pickets can talk with the rebel pickets. It is very hilly, of course, like all mountainous country and the summits of the mountains are almost inaccessible. The rebels have a great many troops, estimated at 60,000. They fire at us every day with cannon from the top of Lookout Mountain which hangs over our city one-half mile above the plain we occupy. Our guns are on Moccasin Point, about 1200 feet below the big guns on Lookout Mountain, and yet our guns reach them at that high elevation. No day passes that the cannons are not engaged.

Since we came here there has been one little battle fought, in which 500 or 600 men may have been killed. In two or three days a great battle will probably be fought if the enemy does not run away from us. It would have been fought today but we could not get ready. I have had so much to do that I had almost forgotten to write to you. I have known for some days that a great battle was pending, but as I have to do all the writing, I was given no time to think of anything else but my work. And now that the fight is postponed for a day at least, I concluded to write you. When the great battle is over I will write you again. The battle will be fought on our side by about 60.000 troops and we suppose the rebels number nearly the same. We intend to thrash them soundly and give the rebellion such a blow as to stagger its longer continuance in this region. General Grant feels confident of success, and so do we all. Many lives will be lost but no one who goes into battle ever thinks that he is the one to be victimized. General Bragg has a great habit of running away when he thinks the enemy opposed to him is his superior in strength. We are afraid that he will do this now and that we shall have had our trouble for nothing, for really our preparations have been on a grand scale.

It is no part of our program to relinquish one foot of ground that we now hold and occupy; and if the rebels propose to drive us back, they must fight most desperately to do it.

The country people of the entire South, so far as I have seen, do not live as well or as comfortable as the Tonawanda Indians. They may, before the war broke out, have had plenty to eat and been well clothed. But today many of them have nothing but corn, and now and then meat and seldom potatoes. Wheat bread is almost unknown among them. Our troops are obliged to feed a great many of the whites who have not left their homes and joined the seceders. The negroes, once slaves, of course are all with us and are our servants for pay. The country houses are built of logs, generally round logs and chinked up, but very often entirely open, that is, without chinks. Any Indian house is better and more comfortable and cleaner. Their clothes are home-made and of a color they call butternut. The men wear butternut pants and coats, and the women coarse homespun dresses very much like our old-fashioned flannel, usually called domestic flannel. They do not wear hoops because such articles to be had must come from the North. I am now writing only of the whites who have not left their homes upon the approach of our army. Most of the houses throughout the country are deserted or abandoned. O Carrie! this is a most desolate country, and no human being can realize or comprehend the dreadful devastation and horrors created by war, until they have been in its track.

From Louisville, in Kentucky, south for about 100 miles, the original appearance of the country is pretty well preserved. The people occupy their houses and are apparently quietly pursuing agricultural employments. Their fences are good and you see fine crops growing and cattle, horses, hogs and sheep grazing in the pastures. You then begin to come into a desolated, devastated and burnt district, and the further south you go the more like a desert it looks. You see lone chimneys standing where once may have been a fine mansion; there are no longer any fences around their once highly-cultivated fields. Rank weeds now grow all over the land. Probably there is not now one acre cultivated, where before the war there were 100 acres. Every village or collection of houses we come to is deserted. Nobody but negroes live in them. The windows are all out and the fine mahogany and rosewood furniture now forms the ornaments of negro cabins. The fine dresses that white ladies once bedecked themselves with, now hang shabbily upon the ungainly figure of some huge, dilapidated negro wench.

We occupy Chattanooga and we have no southern whites among us, except the poor "white trash," and they are so poor that they can hardly speak the English language. Oh! it is really a pitiful sight to see these people suffering to the extent they are. A blind infatuation that by and by we are going to withdraw our troops from their country and relinquish the country, and consent to a separation of the American Union, makes them endure all this suffering and humiliation. Sometimes our troops come upon these people so suddenly that they have only time to escape with what they can carry on their backs, leaving their comfortable houses for our poor soldiers to luxuriate in.

We are now having Indian summer weather. It is very delightful and pleasant. In a few days will commence our winter weather which lasts until about January, and in March and April we have another rainy spell. We are here in the ancient homes of the Cherokees, and our present quarters are only about twelve miles from Jno. Ross' old home. By and by, as I see more of the South, I will give you another history of it. My letter has reached its seventh page. I do not think you will find time to read it, and I will close, hoping that the Great Spirit may protect you all, and keep us all safe until by His kind providence we are permitted again to see each other.

From your brother,
ELY S. PARKER.

MISS CARRIE G. PARKER.

HOW THE QUAKERS FOUGHT A LAND CONSPIRACY

A history of the great land operations was so much the history of the New York Iroquois during these years that a correct account of the Odgen Land Company is necessary to the understanding of the tribal situation in which Ely S. Parker was a prominent actor.

Soon after the close of the War for Independence the State of Massachusetts laid formal claim to a large tract of land lying west of the Genesee river. After a dispute between the authorities of New York and of Massachusetts, a compromise was effected. Massachusetts ceded to New York all her right and title to the sovereignty and jurisdiction of these lands and New York ceded to Massachusetts, and her granters, to their heirs and assigns, the pre-emptive rights of all the lands occupied by the Six Nations Indians and embraced in the disputed tract. This affected only the Tuscaroras and Senecas.

This pre-emptive right was only the right to purchase these lands when the Indians wished of their own free will and accord to sell as corporate nations. Dissolution of the tribe or the tribe's refusal would make impossible a transaction.

Massachusetts in 1791 sold her interest in this land to the Holland Land Company, which in turn sold it to David Ogden. This act gave rise to the Ogden Land Company. By shrewd schemes this company laid plot for the purchase of the title from the Indians.

By legitimate purchase certain lands were conveyed to purchasers in 1794, 1797 and in 1802, which was the date of the Phelps, Bronson and Jones purchase. Again in 1823 there was the Gregg and Gibson purchase. All these sales were made openly and under the joint supervision of the Federal Government and representatives of the state of Massachusetts.

Schemes were put in motion and as early as 1818 we find the beginning of fraudulent work. Certain reputed agents of two small bands of New York Indians, the Oneidas and Brothertowns, applied for permission to purchase with their own means and upon their own account of the Green Bay, Wisconsin, Menominies, a tract of land.

Then later, in 1838, began a high-handed scheme for the removal of the New York Indians. The Senecas were dismayed at the powers arrayed against them, but rallied their strong men and looked about them for friends. The plan was to stimulate a desire among the Indians "to go West" and there to organize emigration parties or bands.

In this crisis the Quakers became the active defenders of the Iroquois. They had early manifested a benevolent interest in the Indians about them. Far from regarding them as did other colonists, the Quakers pursued a policy of unselfish service. If a thing was right with them it should be done. Compensation or reward was not considered. Neither was power, money, land or influence sought. Their policy at first puzzled the natives who could scarcely believe that the whites who appeared so avaricious could manifest any degree of altruism.

In 1796 Cornplanter asked the Philadelphia Quakers to educate three children, among them his son Henry. Five years later we find a Quaker mission among the Oneidas and Tuscaroras. There seemed to be no special effort on the part of the Quakers to force the Indians to accept the religion of the white men, nor indeed to seek to have the Indians accept their own creed. The Quakers simply taught manual industry such as milling, spinning, cooking and agriculture. With that they taught the rudiments of elementary school subjects. The religion that they taught was expressed almost solely in action. There was no attempt to rush in and with angry outbursts condemn all that the Indian natively believed.

In 1799 the Indians grew suspicious of the motives of such unheard-of white men and began to suspect after all that there were ulterior motives. The Quakers then quietly withdrew.

Just the year before, however, in 1798, a mission had been established at Allegany and later as will be shown one was planted at Cattarangus.

Here they remained undisturbed through the second war with Great Britain, though six hundred of the Iroquois enlisted as United States regulars. During this period the Quakers are said to have averted an epidemic of small-pox by vaccinating one thousand Indians. Another early mission was among the broken tribes from northeastern Pennsylvania, Connecticut and Massachusetts. These were known as the Stockbridges and Brothertowns who lived among the Oneidas. This mission was established in 1807 but afterwards abandoned. The Indians at Oneida had sadly fallen victims to the trader's rum.

In reply to the entreaties of one of the early missionaries the famous Red Jacket exclaimed: "You have got our country from us but you are not satisfied,—you want to force our religion from us. We understand your religion is written in a great book. If it was intended for us as well as for you why did not the Great Spirit give it to us, but not only to us but why did he not give it to our forefathers? You say there is but one way to worship the Great Spirit. If there is one religion why do you white people dispute about it so much? Why are you not all agreed? You can all read the Book.

"We also have a religion which was given us by our forefathers and has been handed down to us, their children. We worship in that way. It teaches us to be thankful for all the favors we received, to love each other and be united. We never quarrel about religion.

"Brothers, we have been told that you have been preaching near here. These people are our neighbors. We know them and will wait a little while and see what effect your preaching will have upon them; if we find it does them good—makes them more honest and less disposed to cheat Indians, we will then consider what you have said to us."

At another time Red Jacket replied to the missionaries, denying that the contact of the Indians with the whites had improved the Indians. "Thus you see," he said, "that our attempts to pattern after your example makes the Great Spirit angry—He does not crown your exertions."

Such was the temper of the man, Red Jacket, when the strength of manhood governed his mental action and when he yet had some faint confidence in the power of his people to hold their own. How different in tone are the utterances of his old age! The feebleness of his race bit into his spirit and he exclaims, "I am about to leave you, and my warning voice will no longer be heard or regarded; the craft of the white man will prevail. I am an aged tree and can stand no longer. My leaves are fallen and my branches are withered and I am shaken by every breeze. Soon my aged trunk will be prostrate and the foot of the exulting foe of the Indians may be placed upon it with safety; for there is none who will be able to avenge such an insult. Think not that I mourn for myself. I go to join the spirits of my fathers where age and suffering cannot come, but my heart fails when I think of my people who are so soon to be scattered, destroyed and forgotten.''

It is then that Red Jacket thought of the Friends who have ever been faithful. Into his distressed mind came the hope that they might intercede for his people and protect them from their enemies. The traditions of his fathers has told of the strange white men who actually did as they promised and conquered by kindness. Thus it was that in 1827 Red Jacket went to the city of New York and attended the yearly meeting of the Quakers and to entreat them to take his people under their care and to give them the type of civilization that was best, to educate the young men and to teach industry and agriculture. More particularly, no doubt, he was anxious that a just people should reside among his own and protect them from the greed of the unscrupulous land speculator. The matter was considered by the Friends and they informed him that inasmuch as the Friends had a mission at Onondaga they could not see their way clear to undertake a mission to the Senecas, that they would seek, however, for some means by which his prayer might be granted.

Nearly two years passed by and the anxiety of Red Jacket increased. On January 20th he wrote to the Society of Friends of the city of New York: ''At the treaty of Philadelphia with William Penn and the Six Nations, we considered William Penn a friend to us; he did not wish to cheat us out of our lands but was disposed to pay us a fair value for them. Since that time the Society of Friends have treated us kindly. They have never shown a disposition to wrong us out of our lands, but they have seemed to wish to cultivate friendship with us.'' In the next paragraph he states, ''There are at present six thousand of our people and upwards who wish that Society to send a suitable person among us.''

Again he was disappointed but was invited to confer with a committee of three and explain the situation. This conference resulted in a visit in 1830. They met on the Buffalo creek reservation where the council was presided over by fourteen chiefs and more than two hundred of the people. From Buffalo the committee proceeded to Cattaraugus. As a result of this visitation the Committee drew up a report in which they stated: ''At a General Council in which both the Christian and pagan parties were present the Indians appeared very grateful for this attention on the part of the Friends, stating that they believed that the Great Spirit had put it into the hearts of the children of William Penn to thus visit them.''

The Indians set aside a farm tract at Cattaraugus in the very heart of the pagan settlement and a residence was erected. Two hundred acres were laid out and seventy cleared and fenced. In 1833 the school was opened and there was an average attendance of twenty-five children. From that time on the farm, school and mission was given into the charge of the Genesee yearly meeting who labored faithfully for five years. Early in the year 1838 the Quaker missionaries discovered that their Seneca charges were suffering from a great deal of excitement and were charging that there was a movement on foot to rob them of every foot of land they owned in the state of New York. It appears that a council had been held near Buffalo in which a minority of the chiefs had signed away all four reservations. It was feared by the Senecas that the Federal Government would fail to heed the great remonstrance sent forth by the members of the tribe and the loyal chiefs and the infamous treaty would be ratified and they sent to destruction.

Inquiry revealed that it was the settled policy of the Government to remove every tribe and send them to the west of the Mississippi river. The Quakers were on the alert in an instant and the Senecas made desperate, frightened appeals to the various meetings for assistance in averting the loss of their ancestral domain and escaping the sure death that awaited them if they were forced west into the unsettled regions.

Early in the history of the English colonies Massachusetts had claimed ownership of Western New York and after the Revolution had relinquished its pre-emptive claims to the Ogden Land Company.

Western New York was one of the finest pieces of agricultural land in the Middle Atlantic States. It was a garden spot and its great possibilities even in 1838 made it a sought-for region. The Indians held great tracts of this land. It was among the most fertile in all Western New York, for they had been shrewd enough to retain the fertile flats and rich tracts adjacent to and lying upon four great streams of water—Buffalo creek, Tonawanda creek, Cattaraugus creek and the Allegheny river. Here was a prize worth winning. There was money in it. Money,—gold for the asking, fortunes, if it could be obtained. The Indians held it. The Ogden Land Company wanted it and the gold it would produce. What matter if that gold were sweated from the blood of men and women? What matter if men were corrupted by bribery? That land must be obtained. It seemed fortunate that the "settled policy of the Government was to remove the Indian west of the Mississippi!" It then only remained to seduce the Indians there who had been assured by solemn compact that they might stay as long as they desired.

APPENDIX

The agents of the Land Company went among the Indians. Thousands of dollars were spent in concocting a scheme by which it could be signed away. Sixteen Senecas chiefs out of eighty-one were bribed by amount varying from one to five thousand dollars.[1] They were in turn to corrupt other chiefs and get their signatures. The story is a shocking one. The Quakers investigated. They could not be bribed or their opinions prejudiced. A moderate people were they and yet from the records of their own investigation we read, "... *the committee became thoroughly satisfied of the revolting fact that in order to drive these poor Indians from their lands deception and fraud had been practiced to an extent perhaps without parallel in the dark history of oppression and wrong, to which the aborigines of our country have been subjected.*"

The Quakers at once began to work. They were thoroughly aroused. At once they got into communication with the Secretary of War, with the President himself and with the members of Congress.

The chiefs protested against the fraudulent treaty. Their names had been forged to it. So had thirty or forty other names. The land Company erected a council-house of their own in order that they could say the treaty was made in "open council." Chiefs were lured to Buffalo, were drugged and intoxicated. Their names appeared on the treaty. Some were awakened in the night and made to sign an unknown paper in the dark. Every sort of force was used, forgery, calumny, physical violence and bribery. It is a sickening tale and a horrible demonstration of the moral shallowness of civilization. Several times the treaty was sent back. This was the result of the remonstrance of the Quakers. The Rev. Asher Wright, the Congregational missionary, worked night and day in collecting evidence, in carrying the remonstrance and in encouraging the people to be brave.

At length the treaty was ratified. The land was no longer the Senecas'. They were to be dispossessed. Some were taken west under a certain Doctor Hugemboam. The most of these emigrants died of malarial diseases. The majority of people, however, remained in their old homes. They wished to die in the land of their fathers and resolved to cluster about their fathers' graves to be shot to death, rather than abandon what was theirs. They asked Elder Wright if they were not right in this end; he told them to embody that statement in a memorial to the President.

---

1. See the Quaker document, The Case of the Seneca Indians, Philadelphia, 1840.

In vain did the Society of Friends appeal to the conscience of the President and to the honor of the Senate. In one of their memorials a combined committee of fourteen men representing four Yearly Meetings appealed in these words:

"To contemplate the forcible removal of the Indians and the heart-rending scene that must accompany such a removal is shocking to every sentiment of justice and humanity. To see a great and powerful nation lending its aid to oppress the weak and helpless must tend to loosen the attachment of the people to their government. . . . The United States by the peculiar nature of their institutions stand conspicuously before the world. . . . May the Ruler of the Universe in His boundless mercy so direct the delegated authorities that they may be directed by the principles of justice and mercy."

All through the bitter trial it was the Quaker, Philip E. Thomas of the Baltimore Meeting and Asher Wright of the American Board of Commissioners of Foreign Missions, who carried the standards. Dr. Wright was everywhere. A university man of rare attainments, he had chosen a life in the wilds that his God might be glorified. He knew the Iroquois language perfectly, more perfectly indeed than any native. The Senecas respected him. His athletic prowess, his skill with the rifle and his knowledge of the woods excited their admiration. His zeal for their salvation inspired their reverence. Like the Quakers, he was no man to bluster in upon native ceremonies and drive out the participants. A rare man for his day, he collected their myths and legends, wrote a grammar of their language and took down the texts of their rituals. With his devoted wife he healed the sick. Neither ship fever nor small-pox frightened him or the wife who worked by his side. And his niece, Martha, as a nurse, bathed the sick, whatever the disease might be; she held the cup when there was bleeding to be done, and stripped the leeches. At one time she washed two hundred blankets that came from the settlement where yellow fever was raging. Small wonder that a tall sub-chief admired his brave nurse and teacher! He was a descendant of Handsome Lake the Prophet, the brother of the head chief of the Senecas. He married the nurse. He was Nicholson H. Parker, the brother of Ely. With Dr. Wright he translated and printed the New Testament into Seneca, and with Dr. Wright he labored for the saving of his people's home country.

Philip Thomas and Dr. Wright succeeded in effecting a settlement by which only the Buffalo creek and Tonawanda reservations were to be released, and by which Cattaraugus and Allegany were saved. But the loved Do-show-weh of their ancestral pride, the Buffalo creek reservation, was lost. Here were some of their most precious memorials. It had been a meeting place of the Six Nations. It was the home of Mary Jemison and of Red Jacket. Their fathers' bones were there.

The Buffalo Senecas were embittered. Their hearts turned from molten iron to coldest stone. They moved to Cattaraugus. They went back to the ways of their fathers. They would not permit missionaries to come and even Dr. Wright was only tolerated because they believed in his integrity.

The Buffalo Senecas settlement at Cattaraugus was upon an unfertile clay hill. That it was so mattered not; their hearts were dead. They would have nothing to do with Christianity. Today that spot is the stronghold of paganism in the form of Handsome Lake's "new religion."

The people were still agitated. Their educated leaders wished a revolution in their native government. Peter Wilson hinted at the plan in his address before the Baltimore Friends in 1848 when he said:

"Is there one here whose bosom does not heave or whose heart does not beat in unison and sympathy for the oppressed that are thus struggling to become emancipated?

"Is there one here whose philanthropic and patriotic spirit is not aroused with the thrilling tidings come over the great salt waters that millions of human beings are becoming free: that the spirit of freedom has crossed from America over the great ocean into the old world and there planted the standard of liberty?

"I am aware that my friends do not approve of war, but I know that you are the advocates of liberty. Shall the Indian then be censured because he too has become infected with the epidemic that pervades the political atmosphere in this free America? No, I trust not.

"The political agitation among my people is but the onward and upward progress in the scale of civilization and it is hoped that before long the people will arrive at the elevated position of your people, where the friends of the Indians have long desired to welcome them.

"Permit me therefore to conclude by expressing the hope that this committee, and the Society they represent, will continue their labors and care toward us until we shall become able to walk alone, and we shall have arrived at a maturity that will enable us to sustain ourselves and come to enjoy all the relations and privileges of American citizens."

The work of the Quakers and of the faithful Philip E. Thomas did not end here. The appeal of the people was too earnest. The corrupt chiefs must be ousted and a better government established.

Through the advice and help of Philip E. Thomas, of Dr. Wright, of Dr. Peter Wilson, Nathaniel Strong and Maris B. Pierce, the last three being educated Indians with college training, a revolution took place. This was in 1848. The old chiefs were ousted. No longer could they handle money belonging to the tribe. The people come into power with a constitutional government and a written code of laws. There were not enough adherents to the deposed chiefs to cause any trouble. A bloodless revolution had been successful. The allies of fraud, the betrayers of the people had been overthrown. The people were supreme. Their best men then threw every energy into constructive work.

The Tonawandas having had no part in any treaty, and being dispossessed, were in a precarious position. Without any approval on their part, despite their remonstrances, they were made a landless people. But they refused to leave the ground which they owned by every moral law. They refused to have a part in the new "Republic of the Seneca Indians" just as they had refused to abide by the decision of the "chiefs" government. So they returned to the government of their fathers of old and "raised up" the sachems who were ordained by Hiawatha and Dekanawideh with the approval of Jikonsaseh, the Mother of Nations.

GENERAL PARKER'S REPLY TO THE CHARGES AGAINST HIS ADMINISTRATION

MR. CHAIRMAN:—In asking you to consider the suggestion submitted by my friend and counsel in this investigation, General Chipman, it is proper, perhaps, that I should say a word myself. I will not attempt to go over the testimony, as that has been done by my friend, nor could I do so with any satisfaction to myself, or in any way to aid your committee, for I have not been able to attend the investigation, during its progress, and am not familiar enough with the facts of record to assist you in your examination of it. I do not know, either, that I can now add anything to what I have said under oath, in replying to questions asked me by the committee, and which I suppose were intended to cover the whole ground of the investigation.

When I entered upon the discharge of the duties of my office, I knew how sensitive the public were with regard to the administration of our Indian affairs. I knew, too, the solicitude with which Congress has always regarded that bureau of our Government service, and firmly resolved that I would administer the office to the best of my ability, and in such a manner that no taint of dishonor, at least, should ever attach to my conduct. To what extent my ability has proved equal to the duties devolved upon me, it is not becoming for me to speak. Know that I have spared no pains, no sacrifice of personal convenience and pleasure, to discharge my whole duty faithfully. I do not claim that I have made no mistakes, for that is more, I think, than can well be claimed by any public officer; but, Mr. Chairman, I do say, and I speak it in as solemn a manner as I am capable, and to this extent I have already sworn, that I have never profited pecuniarily, or indeed otherwise, by any transaction in my official capacity while I have been serving as Commissioner of Indian Affairs. I cannot know in advance how you will regard the various matters which have been made the subject of your investigation, as they affect my personal honor and official integrity; but whether they are sufficiently explained by the facts in the record or not, no view which you may take of them can change the knowledge within my own breast, that I have never sought to defraud the Government out of one penny, or have knowingly lent my aid to others with that view. There is not to be found anywhere in connection with this trial—if I may speak of it as a trial—a single transaction about which I had at the time, or until Mr. Welsh published his letter of December last, the slightest suspicion that my conduct would be inquired into. All of my official acts now before your committee, were performed in the usual routine of my official duties. I gave them no further thought afterwards than such as would naturally come up in the mind of a public officer in the casual review of his past administration. When I was, in January, suddenly called upon to explain transactions of my office, six months previous, I could only rely for explanations upon such records as happened to remain in my office, and upon such facts as I could from other sources, bring to the attention of the committee. As to the effect of these records and facts, you are to be the judges, and I leave them with you in the full belief that you will weigh them well before you condemn my action. If human testimony is to be believed, and if my sworn statements, as well as the sworn statements of others with whom I was suspected of being in complicity, are to be credited, I think I may safely leave the question of my personal honor in your hands. As to the wisdom of any particular act of mine into which you have been examining, of course your judgment and mine may differ, and as to this I can only rest upon the circumstances surrounding me at the time, and the facts in the record, tending to show whether I acted wisely or not.

You must admit, Mr. Chairman, that the matter is one of great moment to me, and while I have no right to ask at your hands any report other than that which may be the result of your own convictions, I think I have the right to ask that at the time you make it to the House of Representatives, you will also state all the material facts upon which your conclusions should rest. I do not shrink from any responsibility which I have incurred, or its just consequences, and I only ask that that body which ultimately determines upon the result of this investigation, shall have that full knowledge of my conduct which will enable them to form a correct judgment in a matter of such great importance to me.

E. S. PARKER.

HON. A. A. SARGENT,
 Chairman, etc.

Then came the defence of Parker by Gen. N. P. Chipman. Every charge was discussed in detail and met with the records of the department. A brief portion of Gen. Chipman's defence is quoted. It contains several interesting paragraphs and demonstrates that Gen. Parker was absolutely clean in all his dealings.

"General Parker interpreted the law naturally and honestly, and executed it accordingly. If he had entertained a suspicion that a different view was held by the Board of Indian Commissioners from his own, no one who knows the efforts made by him to maintain the best relations with that board would doubt that he would have brought it to their attention. I cannot help expressing the opinion that if the board itself had felt this matter to be one of consequence, and had regarded the commissioner as excluding them from any proper participation in the affairs of his office, they would have brought it to his attention. The gentlemen composing that board are not churls, nor are they cowards. They assumed their duties, and have performed them, at great personal sacrifice. They are men of standing and character.

"They could afford to speak frankly and openly with regard to all matters about which they had cause for complaint. They could not afford to conceal anything, and I do not believe they did conceal anything. Beyond the conduct of Mr. Colyer and the great interest he has shown in prosecuting this case, there is not to be found a single instance which tends to show the slightest want of confidence on the part of the board in the present Commissioner of Indian Affairs. It is certainly a little remarkable that the secretary and mouthpiece of the board, who is by law charged with the responsibility of performing certain duties in connection with the Commissioner of Indian Affairs, and between whom and himself there should be not only confidence, but the closest relations, should attend this investigation night after night, aiding the prosecutor in the accomplishment of a purpose to remove the Commissioner of Indian Affairs. I do not believe that Mr. Colyer, in such a position, indelicate and improper as it must seem to any mind to be, can be acting under the authority of the Board of Commissioners.

"But this is a divergence, Mr. Chairman, not important, and which I must beg pardon for having indulged in. The question here is, whether the Commissioner of Indian Affairs is to be censured for having discharged a duty devolved upon him by law, without consulting the board, which he did not at the time believe it was his duty under the law to do. You must in this as well as in other points connected with this investigation, give some weight to motives; and where the motive was not a bad one, and no evil consequences followed from the conduct of the officer, it certainly cannot be the duty or province of this committee to condemn.

"It is no unusual thing in private as well as in official life, and in the management of private as well as public affairs, for one man to take upon himself the responsibility of performing duties which are made incumbent upon two or more. The law which originally created this board gave them joint control over all the disbursements of the Indian Department, and yet that control was practically taken away from them by the executive order; and I do not suppose that out of the millions of dollars disbursed by the Interior Department, under that act, that the Board of Commissioners were called upon, or had an opportunity even, of participating in the disbursements of one-fiftieth part of it. That law did not require the Secretary, it is true, to consult the board, in terms; but how else could they have joint control without consultation? And if he failed to consult them or furnish them the opportunity of exercising that joint control, was he less to blame than Commissioner Parker in the subsequent law which made it his duty to consult the board? We have never heard any investigation contemplated into the conduct of the Secretary of the Interior or of the Commissioner of the Indian Affairs, under that law, nor have we ever heard of complaint being made against the President for practically annulling that clause which gave joint control.

"Mr. Chairman, if this were the first instance where an officer of the Government dared to take responsibilities in the administration of official duties, it might not be remarkable that public attention should be drawn to it; but, sir, as I run back over the last decade, and reflect upon the perils to our nation's life, which a strong hand has averted with public approval, even when the law had to be borne down and set aside, I cannot believe an honest officer, in the honest discharge of duty, well performed, will at this day be the first to suffer for his courage where he violated no law.

"We do not need to go beyond the last two or three years, or beyond the Indian service, to find examples of fearless discharge of duty in cases not unlike this.

"How long is it, Mr. Chairman, since General Sherman, in connection with the members of the Peace Commission created by Congress, incurred an expenditure without authority of law, vastly greater than was involved in that portion of Commissioner Parker's purchases, which were made under an emergency?

"How long is it since General Sherman, on a single telegram to the Governor of Montana, authorised the raising of troops, to be paid by the National Government, involving an expenditure of a million dollars, for the payment of which Congress has made provision?

"Who has had the temerity to attack General Sherman or the Peace Commission?

"Who has ever sought to arraign General Harney for feeding the same Indians for whom Commissioner Parker made provision, although General Harney, without authority of law, incurred an expenditure vastly beyond that which Commissioner Parker incurred?

"Who had dared to insinuate that General Sherman was in fraudulent collusion with contractors because he paid large prices for beef, much larger than General Parker paid? Who ever thought of bringing General Harney before a committee in Congress for paying almost three times as much for flour as Commissioner Parker did? The Indian office has been arraigned over and over again, and probably more discussion has taken place in and out of Congress upon the management of Indian affairs than upon any other, and I have yet to learn of an effort having ever been made to convict an Indian Commissioner of violation of law for making provision, as Commissioner Parker did. The necessity for sometimes resorting to open-market purchases and contracts without advertisement, has been recognized by every Administration and I think I may say every Congress. With this knowledge, and these precedents to guide him, how monstrous it is to assail Commissioner Parker upon this ground!

"If Mr. Welsh desires to keep the Indian Office free from outside rings and corrupt combinations, heaven help; but if he expects to reform our public service by wholesale charges of corruption that have no foundation except in his own fertile brain; if he hopes to reassure public confidence by destroying the faith the people have in their public servants, through the means of a vexatious and heartless pursuit of those in official position; if he hopes to engraft upon our Indian management the benign influence of the church through an unchristian method of attack; if he hopes to elevate the Indian by openly declaring, as he has, that the President has put into the office to which they look for protection, one who is but a remove from barbarism, thus stigmatizing the whole race; if he believes that the Christian people of this land are to join him in a crusade against this representative of the Indian by groundless accusations; if in short, he intends to work out certain theories of his own, under cover of Christian philanthropy, without regard to consequences, he will find he has undertaken that which will recoil fearfully upon him, and which will awaken an indignant protest from every honest heart.

"Mr. Chairman, you and others are not blind to the general results of the President's policy, so ably carried out in its details by the Indian Bureau; you have seen no Indian war desolating our border, since its inauguration; your committee of appropriations have had no millions to provide as heretofore, for large numbers of troops to avenge the murders of our frontier citizens, and repress the warlike spirit of the Indians; the dollars expended by Commissioner Parker have been units to the tens previously expended; since this trial began you have provided for additional of the warlike savages who are coming in to be fed and to acquire our habits of life, and you know the general feeling which pervades the people along the border is, that we must hold out every encouragement in the direction now being taken; you know—for you had frequent intercourse with the Commissioner,—how earnestly he has bent his energies to second the wishes of the President and Congress in this regard. Is it then too much to ask that these things be considered? At the worst, this record shows only that the Commissioner has been too bountiful in his supplies of food, although it does not appear that a pound of provisions has been wasted; at the worst, he has erred in not feeding the Indians from hand to mouth, keeping their minds full of doubt each day as to their subsistence for the next. I believe, Mr. Chairman, Commissioner Parker has no regret that he chose the course he did. By so doing he has convinced the Indians that the Government is in earnest and that it may be trusted.

"It may well be asked, what would have been the gravity of Mr. Welsh's complaint had a timid policy been pursued at the juncture we have considered, and an Indian outbreak been the result? I doubt not, he would have then held the Commissioner responsible for not doing the very thing of which he now complains.

"But, sir, a subject of this gravity is not to be judged by the cost of a few thousand pounds of beef or sacks of flour; or an accidental side of bacon, with a rib in it; or a few barrels of sugar made of molasses; or the difference between the cost of shipping goods up the Missouri River in the spring and fall; or the cent per cent bargaining by which some men amass large fortunes in cities like Philadelphia.

"Gentlemen in public positions, called upon to assume responsibilities unknown to urban merchants, learn to take broader views of affairs of state. The experience of your committee, Mr. Chairman, as public men, furnishes some guaranty that Commissioner Parker will be judged from the standpoint of statesmanship, and not that of a tradesman, who, however honest and well-meaning, may be very narrow when he comes to view subjects new to him."

A review of all the evidence resulted in clearing General Parker of any wrongdoing, greatly to the confusion of those who sought to discredit him.

SECRETARY SEWARD'S INTEREST IN THE INDIANS
(See Chapter II, Page 102)

Secretary William H. Seward had no personal enmity to Ely S. Parker in rejecting his proffered services as an engineer in the army. We have no means of explaining why the Secretary did not seek to place him in some position of authority or of usefulness, as Parker was well known in Washington circles. Perhaps Mr. Seward only reflected the feeling of the time that the struggle was between the whites only.

In justice to Secretary Seward we present the editorial from the *New York Mirror* given below. It indicates his very deep friendship for the New York Indians. The clipping is from General Parker's scrap book—one that he made before he entered the army. The editorial follows:

THE SIX NATIONS

Mr. Seward will receive the thanks of all friends of justice and humanity for his successful resistance of the attempt made in the Senate on Thursday night to pass a bill removing the remains of the Confederated Iroquois of this State from their ancient seats to new and strange abodes in the far West. It was a barbarous proposition, uncalled for by any public necessity, and prompted solely by speculative avarice. There have been for many years unscrupulous white men regarding with greedy eyes the valuable lands of the Indians in Central and Western New York, and monstrous frauds have been resorted to, without shame or remorse, to displace the remnants of the Six Nations from their reservations. These base efforts have hitherto been baffled. Disinterested gentlemen of the legal profession have volunteered their services in behalf of the red men, exposing in the courts with signal ability and success the villainy sought to be practised against them. It should be understood that these relics of a once powerful and most interesting Confederation are by no means savages. They have comfortable dwellings, churches, school-houses, mills and cultivated farms. Many of them differ little in education, manners or intelligence from the majority of their white neighbors. Their leading men are accomplished gentlemen. The present Chief ot the Six Nations, Mr. Ely S. Parker, a person of academical education and respectable character, is by profession a civil engineer, employed on the canals of the State.

Such are the people whom it has been proposed to drive away from their homes beyond the Mississippi. It is impossible that the Senate could have understood the real nature of the bill. Interested parties had no doubt taken pains to misrepresent and deceive. But Mr. Seward, with personal knowledge of the case in all its aspects, came to the rescue in a speech which would not be conquered.

The condition of the Indians in question, although comfortable and happy, is somewhat anomalous. With a creditable degree of general intelligence, and subject to the laws of the white community in the midst of which they dwell, they are neither regarded as citizens nor recognised as foreigners. Naturalization is forbidden them, and they can be endowed with the privileges of citizenship only by special act of the Legislature. But as an offset they are not taxed. On the other hand, they are incapacitated to alienate their lands without legislative permission. It would not be true to claim that, as a whole, they equal their white neighbors in industry, enterprise or progress. Their worst foe is the "fire water," to which the red man has everywhere a fatal proclivity, and which unprincipled whites are but too ready to furnish him. Some years ago an act was procured to be passed authorising the Indian occupants of a reservation in Erie County to sell, provided a majority should consent. The speculators who stood ready to purchase induced the tribe to go to Buffalo for negotiation, where they plied the poor Indians with rum until, by hook or crook, a sufficient number were got to agree. This nefarious fraud was not, however, successful, its character being exposed, and its purpose defeated, after a severe struggle, by the friends of the Indians, who refused to remain inactive spectators of the swindle.

EDITORIAL NOTES

EDITORIAL NOTES

THE KENJOCKETYS

On page 14, allusion is made to John Kenjockety. The name, in one form or another, is perhaps the oldest designation pertaining to the region of Buffalo. If, as students of Indian linguistics affirm, it is of the language of the Neutral nation, then it is a survival of a tongue spoken hereabouts—around the northern and eastern end of Lake Erie—long before it was succeeded by the Seneca. The word Erie (which the early French cartographers printed with a final accent, as though it were pronounced "E-ree-aye") is also of the Neutral or Kah-kwah tongue; but most of our local Indian names are Seneca.

"Kenjockety" has now become "Scajaquada," and is the name of a stream of some consequence to Buffalo. It helps to beautify Forest Lawn, a resting-place for the dead. It feeds Gala Water, the lake in Delaware Park, which is indeed but an artificial enlargement of its old bed. On the banks of this lake stands the home of the Buffalo Historical Society. The lower reaches of the stream, and its junction with the Niagara, are rich in historic associations. The Battle of Black Rock, in the War of 1812, was fought on its banks, and in its waters were fitted out some of the vessels of Perry's fleet, that fought and won the Battle of Lake Erie. Surely such a stream is deserving of a place and name in local annals.

The name it surely has, somewhat to excess. In an effort to discover what should be the spelling of this word, records and maps of Buffalo, of the earliest days of the village, as well as of later years of the city, have been examined, as have also numerous old treaties and early printed books. The result of the quest is indicated by the following list of spellings, all being designations of this same stream, now usually written "Scajaquada:"

Cajaquada	Conjockety	Scaicuada
Canjadaqua	Conjocquada	Scajacquada
Canjaquadie	Conjocquata	Scajaqada
Canjoequadies	Conjocquitas	Scajaquada
Congoquakuon	Conjoequta	Scajaquadda
Conjacadaqua	Conjoquada	Scajaquade
Conjacquities	Conjoquadys	Scajaquadies
Conjadaqua	Cunjoquoddy	Scajaquadys
Conjaquada	Kaiyoequadies	Scajaquoda
Conjaquadie	Kenjockety	Scajoquada
Conjaquadies	Konjockety	Scajaquaty
Conjaquadius	Sca-dhu-queddy	Scajaquodies
Conjaquady	Scadjaquada	Scajauquada
Conjaquda	Scagaquada	Scajaquady
Conjocadas	Scaghtjecitors	Scajoquady

Scajuquadus	Schajacquada	Scojockquody
Scajuquda	Schajakwatta	Scoy
Scajuquoddy	Schajaqaty	Scoy-gu-quaides
Scajuquoddys	Schajaquady	Skadockquay
Scaqucada	Schajaquadys	Shendyoughgwatte
Scaughjuhquatty	Schajaquater	Skajaquadies
Scaujaewada	Schajaquaty	Skendyoughgwatti
Scayuquoddy	Scajauquady	Sken-dyuh-gwa-dih
Schadaquaty	Schaudaquaty	Squajaquady
Schagadaquaty	Schaugadaquaty	
Schajackwady	Scoijoiquoides	

Early Buffalo settlers called the stream "Kenjockety's creek," after an Indian who had his home on its bank east of Niagara street. The Senecas called him Sga-dynh'-gwa-dih (according to O. H. Marshall), or Sken-dyough-gwat-ti (according to Missionary Asher Wright), meaning "beyond the multitude." Our modern spelling appears to be a modification of the Seneca word, rather than of the Kah-kwah or Neuter language. All the spellings, obviously, are attempts to represent in English the native pronunciation.

The earliest Kenjockety of whom we have clear record was known to Buffalo's first settlers as John. He claimed, and his Indian neighbors acknowledged, that he was no Seneca, but a Kah-kwah, his ancestors since 1650-51 presumably having lived with their Seneca conquerors. According to John Kenjockety's son Philip, the family, before the American Revolution, lived on Tonawanda island in the Niagara. Later, John lived, as above stated, on the bank of the stream that now bears his name. Still later, his cabin was opposite Farmer's Point on Buffalo creek. He was a famous hunter and—after the whites came—a famous drunkard. Returning to his cabin, after a fatal visit to Buffalo village, he died by the wayside. The date of his burial has been preserved—October 7, 1808.

He left at least three sons, Philip, George and Joseph. Philip, who was over 20 years of age when his father died, was a familiar figure in early Buffalo, and lived to a great age, his death occurring April 1, 1866. The *Courier* at that time said of him:

The aged Indian Ska-dyoh-gwa-deh, or as he was more familiarly known, Philip Kenjockety, died last Sunday afternoon at Newtown on the Cattaraugus Reservation.

Kenjockety was the oldest resident of this region. He came to "Buffalo Creek" with the Senecas soon after the Revolutionary War, when they were driven from their homes in the Genesee Valley by the devastating expedition of General Sullivan. His great-grandfather was a member of an almost mythological race—the Kah-kwahs, whose rude wigwams, tradition tells us, were once planted on the site of our beautiful city. The Kah-kwahs were exterminated by the more powerful and warlike Senecas about the year 1651, and the great-grandfather of Philip, one of the few survivors, was adopted into that nation. His grandson, John, acquired great influence in the nation, and became a chief. It was through his representation that the Senecas were induced to settle upon the banks of the Niagara when driven from the Genesee. When the whites came here they found him living near the creek that now bears his name. He died in 1808.

Philip Kenjockety was a person of wonderful vigor, and died at a very advanced age. It is generally believed that he was from 120 to 130 years old, but this estimate is probably incorrect. It is impossible to ascertain his exact age, but it is well established that he was nearly 100 years old at the time of his death. His mind was clear and his memory unusually correct, and much information about the Indians as connected with the early history of Buffalo has been lately gathered from his lips. With him has passed away one of the few remaining links between the past and the present. May his spirit find rest in the happy hunting-grounds of his fathers.

A few incidents regarding Philip Kenjockety have been preserved. One of them, recorded by William C. Bryant, in volume I, Buffalo Historical Society Publications, tells how Orlando Allen nearly put an end to Philip's career by bleeding him, in the absence of Dr. Chapin, who had been called on for this operation, which was popular among the Indians. The mighty hunter nearly died from loss of blood, and was laid up in his cabin for three months; but, it is recorded, he cherished no resentment against Mr. Allen.

In June, 1855, Philip Kenjockety was called as a witness in a suit before the Circuit Court in Buffalo, concerning the title to lands on Buffalo Creek. His testimony as reported in the Buffalo *Commercial* of June 20th was picturesque and of some historical value. He gave his age as 101 years and said that he was born near Tonawanda "and lived there till—using his own language—'he was so——high' raising his hand about three feet from the floor. The first war of which he had any recollection was a battle between the Cherokees and Senecas near the banks of the Ohio river when he was about eight years old.

"From his home in Tonawanda he went to Fort George opposite Fort Niagara and during the Revolution was engaged with the British and Senecas against the Americans. The former were driven before the Americans, and Conjockety (as the *Commercial* then spelled it) came up and settled at this place below the Salt Lick on the Buffalo Creek. He was in the engagement at Little Beardstown in 1779, when General Sullivan, after a desperate struggle, repulsed the British and Indians. He was also present at the treaty of Fort Stanwix on the Mohawk in October, 1784, for the negotiation of peace. At this treaty were also present Red Jacket and Lafayette; the former strenuously opposed burying the hatchet." After an allusion to Philip's success as a hunter in the Allegheny region of Western Pennsylvania the *Commercial* writer adds:

"This relic of antiquity has been living for a number of years on the Cattaraugus Reservation. and is today hale and hearty. His eyesight is good, his voice strong and clear for one so old, his form but little bent. A few days since he was invited to go into Coleman's Gallery to look at the excellent portrait of Tommy Jimmy, the celebrated chief of the Senecas, now dead. After looking at the picture for a moment, he turned away with the expression, 'Ugh! gone up!' and left."

It suffices merely to call attention to an obvious error in the above statement: There was no "Fort George opposite Fort Niagara" during the Revolution; neither were there any "Americans" who contended with the British on the Niagara, as is here made to appear. There is confusion here with incidents of the War of 1812.

For further statements regarding Kenjockety, the philology of the name, etc., the reader is referred to O. H. Marshall's paper, "The Niagara Frontier," Vol. II., Buffalo Historical Society Publications.

A writer whose identity is concealed rather than revealed by the signature "C," in the *Commercial Advertiser* of March 23, 1861, relates that among the customers of Alexander Douglas, Senior, a well-known trader of early days who lived at the village of Fort Erie, were the family "Skandauchguaty, now ordinarily written Conjaquady." "That the Skandauchguatys," he says, "were not only of one of the first families of Buffalo, but people of good repute, seems manifest from their ability to contract monetary obligations, the date of which proves my first proposition." He then submits copies of several "notes of hand," written in duplicate; that is, by the merchant, Alexander Douglas, in plain English, also in Indian cypher. "In the signature both united, the merchant by writing the name of the payee, the Skandauchguaty by making his mark between the Christian and the surname (if the reader will permit me to suppose an unbaptised aborigine had a Christian name)."

In illustration the following notes were shown:

Good to Alex. Douglas or order for Twenty-four Dollars and a half, for value received.

              his
           JACK X SKANDAUCHGUATY.
Bertie, April 18, 1808.   mark

Good to Alexr. Douglas or order for Three Dollars and a half, for value received.

                                  his
                         JOSEPH X SKANDAUCHGUATY.
Oct. 31st, 1807.   mark

Good to Alexr. Douglas or order for Ten Dollars and a half, for value received.

                                  his
                         GEORGE X SKANDAUCHGUATY.
Bertie, July 8th, 1807.   mark

Good to Alexr. Douglas or order for Twenty-three Dollars Six Shillings and Six Pence New York currency, for value received.

                                  his
                         PHILIP X SKANDAUCHGUATY.
October 17th, 1807.   mark

An odd feature of these notes is that each was marked with a circle, like the letter "O," for each dollar, with a straight line for each shilling and a shorter line for each sixpence; when partial payment was made—not on the above notes, but on similar notes by other Indians—endorsement was made by drawing a line through the dollar, shilling or sixpence symbol on the face of the note. The facetious author of the article here summarized adds:

"I carefully scrutinized the above evidences of debt, hoping to discover that forgetting to pay was not one of the early customs of the First Families of Buffalo, but no endorsement appears. On the other hand, by a memorandum upon one of them I discover Philip was in sufficiently good repute, as late as 1809, to obtain additional credit for 'six shillings' worth of cloth, one shilling's worth of tobacco, and twenty-seven shillings' worth of blanket' and then tried the experiment of repudiation; thus Pennsylvania and Mississippi are only imitators of a custom established by one of our First Families."

WAS THE SLOCUM CAPTIVE A PARKER ANCESTOR?
(Chapter II, page 21.)

The problem of the blood ancestry of the Parker family is rendered difficult in the face of the tradition of Frances Slocum, a Quaker girl carried into captivity by Indians in 1778. In the family traditions there is reference to the mother of William, who it is said was the daughter of the captive Slocum woman. The members of the family are by no means agreed upon this, however, for William's mother is also referred to as an Indian woman who had lived at Allegany and who with her boys followed Handsome Lake in his flight to Tonawanda.

General Parker under date of September 5th, 1891, left a memorandum concerning the tradition of the Slocum woman as follows:

"Samuel and William Parker with their mother came with Handsome Lake, when Cornplanter drove him away from Allegany, to Tonawanda, from which point he continued to disseminate the moral code he was receiving from the agents of the Great Spirit. (It is also said that there was another Parker brother, making three who came to Tonawanda, who was accidentally killed by the falling of a tree upon him.) The mother was the daughter of a captive woman whose family name was Slocum, and which family resided somewhere in Pennsylvania. The Parkers' mother was subsequently returned to her family in Pennsylvania by a Quaker named Jacobs, who was in some way connected with the Quaker Indian school established at an early day on or adjoining the Allegany Indian Reservation. The Parkers' mother was the offspring of the Slocum woman and a French officer at Fort Niagara where her Indian relatives had taken her on some of their trading expeditions. The Slocum woman did not want to leave her French husband when the Indians were ready to leave but her Indian relatives compelled her to return with them to Allegany and there the Parker mother was born. This child the mother took with her when she escaped down the Allegheny river from the Indians with Jacobs, but her two Indian uncles pursued her in their canoe and overtook them ere nightfall. They took the child back with them but permitted the Slocum woman to return to her white relatives. The child grew up among the Indians and became the Parkers' mother. She died at Tonawanda somewhere between 1820 and 1825. Her issue was three sons and two daughters, all of whom are now dead. William Parker my father, died in April, 1864 (when I was at Culpeper Court House with Grant during the war of the Rebellion). I judge that his age must have been about 75. He was in the War of 1812 and was wounded in the Battle of Chippewa near Niagara Falls. His brother Samuel died in 1879 or 1880 and was aged about 90 years."

If this account is true and the child of the Slocum captive was indeed the grandmother of Ely S. Parker, he then was three quarters Seneca and one quarter French and English. This fact would have made William and Samuel Parker ineligible to hold sachemships in the tribal organization, since descent is through the mother and the sachemships descend through the mother. However, we find that in spite of this or perhaps because there was no maternal white ancestor, Samuel Parker did become a sachem and a tribal chief of the Tonawanda band.

Colonel Parker's disappearance on the eve of his marriage occasioned many fantastic tales in the press. A Washington correspondent of the New York *Tribune* gave wide currency to the fiction that Colonel Parker dodged the proposed marriage because he already had an Indian wife and children. This being reprinted in the Buffalo *Commercial* of Dec. 19, 1867, drew forth an indignant denial by "W. K.," whose letter, printed in the *Commercial* of Dec. 26, 1867, quoted the Rev. Asher Wright: "I have been acquainted with Colonel Parker from his boyhood, and the singular persistency with which he has avoided every implication of matrimony among his own people, has won my unqualified admiration. . . . His 'Indian family' is a pure invention." The same writer undertook to trace Col. Parker's ancestry, as follows:

The family of Colonel Parker had its origin in the connection of a French officer who was stationed at Fort DuQuesne [!] when that post was occupied by the French, with a Seneca woman. The offspring of this connection was a daughter. On the withdrawal of the officer from that post, he wanted to take the child with him; of course this was strenuously objected to by the mother, and by the advice and through the assistance of her friends and family, she started with her child for the home of her parents, which was then on the Ohio river. The officer becoming aware of the flight of the mother with her child, sent a squad of soldiers in pursuit. They followed with such vigor, that the fear of being overtaken prompted the mother to commit the child to an Indian runner, who with the child bound to his back, took the direction through the unbroken forest to the principal town of the Senecas, then at Chen-is-se-o (Genesee river). He arrived in safety with the child, where in due time it was joined by the mother. The child grew to be a very beautiful girl. She was either the grandmother, or great-grandmother of Col. Parker.

In regarding Frances Slocum "and a French officer at Fort Niagara" as his possible ancestors, General Parker was obviously repeating an utterly impossible story, since there were no French officers at Fort Niagara after 1759, or Fort DuQuesne either, and Frances Slocum was not born until April, 1774. She was four years and seven months old when carried off from her Wyoming-valley home by Delaware Indians, November, 1778. But on these and other points bearing on our subject, *see* Buffalo Historical Society Publications,

Vol. IX, pp. 291-293; also, "Frances Slocum, the lost sister of Wyoming," by her grand-niece Martha Bennett Phelps. (N. Y. 1905.) It may be noted here that General Parker's Autobiography (Publications, Buf. Hist. Soc'y, Vol. VIII, p. 528) says he "was born of poor but honest Indian parents."

"A PROPHECY FULFILLED."
(Chapter IV, page 48.)

The prophecy referred to in the text, page 48, was written down by Harriet Maxwell Converse, who had the facts from Tonawanda Indians. In substance it is as follows:

About four months previous to the birth of her son Ely, Mrs. Parker entered the Council House near Indian Falls, then on the Tonawanda Reservation near Batavia, and placed herself before the national prophet as a candidate for a mystery interpretation. She related that a strange vision had been shown to her in a dream. She was in Buffalo near the Granger farm in the winter, and a heavy snow was falling. Suddenly the sky opened, the clouds were swept back by an invisible hand and she beheld a rainbow that reached from the Reservation to the Granger farm, when it was suddenly broken in the middle of the sky. From the lower side of the rainbow were strange pictures, which she recognized as resembling the signs over the little shops in Buffalo. Of course she could not read, but she noticed the characteristics of the English alphabet. The dream troubled her, and she was restless until she had consulted the prophet, who said to her: "A son will be born to you who will be distinguished among his nation as a peace-maker; he will become a white man as well as an Indian, with great learning; he will be a warrior for the pale-faces; he will be a wise white man, but will never desert his Indian people nor lay down his horns (his title as sachem) as a great Iroquois chief; his name will reach from the east to the west, the north to the south, as great among his Indian family and the pale-faces. His sun will rise on Indian land and set on the white man's land. Yet the ancient land of his ancestors will fold him in death."

GENERAL PARKER'S NAME

Mrs. Merton M. Wilner of Buffalo, a great-granddaughter of Rev. Ely Stone, some years since made inquiry of General Parker regarding his name. He sent to her the following reply:

NEW YORK, May 28, 1895.

MRS. EDITH L. WILNER, Buffalo, N. Y.

DEAR MADAM:—I take pleasure in acknowledging yours of the 9th inst. Yes, I remember the Rev. Ely Stone very well as a Baptist clergyman connected with the Indian Mission School once in operation adjoining the Tonawanda Indian Reservation. I was very young when placed at this school, and it was said that I was named after this clergyman. My father's name being "Parker," I subsequently added that of "Parker" to my name, and have borne it through life.

I am with respect,

Your Obdt. Serv't,
ELY S. PARKER.

THE MOUNTPLEASANTS

The Mountpleasant family has long been prominent in Western New York; indeed, no name among the Tuscaroras is more distinguished.

The earliest of whom we have information was John Mountpleasant, not an Indian but an Englishman, a captain in the British army during the Revolutionary War. He married an Oneida woman and was stationed at Fort Mackinac when his son was born in 1779. In 1781, the family came to the Niagara frontier, where Captain John is said to have been in command for a time at Fort Niagara. No official record of this is found. Later he was ordered to Montreal, and never returned to the Niagara. He is supposed to have been killed.

His son, John Mountpleasant 2d, also known as captain, served in the War of 1812—it is said he was with the British at Queenston Heights —married Sally Jack, a Tuscarora woman, and died in 1854.

His son, John Mountpleasant 3d, whose portrait we publish, was born in 1810 on the Tuscarora reservation. In 1827 he was elected a chief. In 1831 he married Jane Green, a daughter of his tribe. She dying, he took for second wife in 1864, the Seneca girl, Caroline G. Parker, sister of Ely S. Parker. Chief Mountpleasant, though of mixed ancestry, was representative of the best qualities of the English and the Indian. Thrifty, energetic and upright, he was held in high respect. He became a trustee of the Thomas Indian Orphan Asylum, and was a member of the Buffalo Historical Society. He owned a large farm, was noted for his hospitality and did much to elevate the standard of living among the Tuscaroras. He died May 6, 1887.

Caroline Parker Mountpleasant, who survived him, was the only girl in a family of eight children. Our author's narrative has delightfully pictured the home conditions of this remarkable family. Caroline was educated at the Normal Academy at Albany, and after her marriage with Chief Mountpleasant removed to his home on the Tuscarora reservation, where she continued to reside until her death, March 19,

1892. In a sketch written shortly after her death by her friend, Mrs. Harriet Maxwell Converse, we read:

"The late Mrs. Mountpleasant, often called 'the Queen of the Tuscaroras'—a title which she amiably ignored—was a woman of commanding presence and markedly typed as an Indian, rather inclined to their inherent haughtiness, which, though repellent to the impertinent intrusions of strangers, softened down to true hospitality and affectionate kindness to those who were her proven friends. With the self-sustained dignity which harmonized with the loftiness of her character, there was an undercurrent of the very simplicity of gentleness in her friendship, the rarity of which only those whose privilege it was to know her well, could understand.

"She was gifted with a keenness of intuition that rendered her an invaluable aid to her husband in his national affairs, and though she never interfered with the politics or governmental authority of the Tuscaroras save by a continual and firm opposition to severalty of lands, which she feared would be unjustly divided, her influence was more widely felt and powerful by reason of her moral example and charitable loyalty to her people. . . As a hostess her demeanor was the same whether entertaining 'peer or commoner,' by reason of a gentle courtesy 'to the manner born.' Flattery nor fulsome adulation could disturb the steady poise of her mind nor degenerate it into forgetfulness of her birth-pride of station as a representative of the American Indians. . . . It has been said that Mrs. Mountpleasant was 'the most remarkable woman of the Iroquois Indians.' No loftier praise could be rendered her and no kinder eulogy pronounced to her memory."

In September, 1891, while visiting her former home in the Tonawanda reservation, she was stricken with paralysis, and here, after a long illness, she died. And now comes in an interesting reminder of ancient tribal customs. At her death a delegation of leading men of the Tuscaroras visited the Tonawandas (who are Senecas) and requested the honor of her remains, that they might convey them to their own reservation; but as by the law of the Tuscaroras, who still hold the tribal rule, the clans are not permitted to be separated even by burial, she could not lie by the side of her late husband, who was a member of the Bear clan of the Tuscaroras. Her relatives of the Wolf clan of the Senecas decided it was the wisest and kindest course that she should rest by the side of her father and mother, and so it was.

The present editor may be permitted a brief allusion to his own slight acquaintance with this remarkable woman. On the occasion of his own adoption into the Seneca nation, as a member of the Snipe clan, Mrs. Mountpleasant shared in the ceremony, and at its close pinned upon his coat the ancient silver brooch which was a symbol of his new relationship.

Three ways of spelling the family name occur with perhaps equal frequency: Mt. Pleasant, Mount Pleasant and Mountpleasant. The last is preferred.

MRS. HARRIET MAXWELL CONVERSE

Our readers may welcome some further introduction to Mrs. Harriet Maxwell Converse, with whom General Parker maintained an interesting correspondence for some years, as set forth in Chapter 15 of Mr. Parker's narrative.

People who casually met Mrs. Converse and knew of her devotion to the welfare of the Indians, often asked if she were not in part of Indian blood. There was little or nothing in her personal appearance to warrant the question, but there was some warrant for it in the peculiar relations of her family to the Indians of Western New York for three generations. Her great-grandfather, Guy Maxwell, came from Scotland in 1768 and settled at Martinsburg, Va.; her grandfather, of the same name, came from Virginia into Western New York in 1792. He was an Indian trader and so won the friendship of the Indians that they adopted him. His son, Thomas Maxwell, also an Indian trader, was in turn adopted by the Senecas. Thomas was the father of Harriet, whose mother died early, and Harriet went to live with an aunt at Milan, Ohio, where she attended for a time at the same school as did Thomas Edison. In 1861, she married Franklin Converse of Westfield, Mass., a musician.

Mrs. Converse inherited from her father a considerable fortune and for some years Mr. and Mrs. Converse traveled widely in this country and abroad, and Mrs. Converse devoted herself largely to literary work. Of a poetic temperament, she wrote and published a volume or two of verse and was a welcome contributor to numerous periodicals. Her sympathetic interest becoming aroused in the welfare of the Indians, to whom she had naturally been a friend by reason of the peculiar relations of her father and grandfather, she devoted most of her time and energy in later life to studying the condition of the Reservation Indians, in working in their behalf, and in writing. She was especially active in opposition to the Whipple bill, the enactment of which was urged in 1891. This measure contemplated the bestowal of full citizenship on the Indians, which in the judgment of many friends of the Indians meant the abandonment of the reservation system, thus placing the unsophisticated Indian at the mercy of the land sharks and others who ever stood ready to despoil them regardless of justice. The Whipple bill was defeated and in recognition of her work and of her genuine friendship, she was adopted a member of the Seneca Nation. The following year she received the unique honor of being made a chief. This occurred at a ceremony known as the Condolence, held on the Tonawanda Reservation, September, 1891. From that time till her death, she was recognized by the Senecas and by the other tribes of the Six Nations as a fully qualified chief, authorized to look after the welfare of her adopted people. She was given the name of Gaiiwanoh, "The Watcher."

She was early led into an intimate acquaintance with General Parker, and it was in recognition of her published writings in behalf of his people that he sent her the following letter, the original of which is owned by the Buffalo Historical Society:

FAIRFIELD, Conn., Jan'y 18, 1895.

. . . I have enjoyed reading these articles very much, because they are written by one who has been much among them, knows their political and social organizations, understands their civil polity and religious beliefs and customs and can give correct dates of events. Having also been adopted and honored as chief by the people she writes about, and having been initiated by them into some of their ancient and mysterious ceremonies, enables her to give authority to her statements which no other writer can do. I am delighted that this talented person has the spirit, inclination and willingness to give her information to the general public, who I hope will appreciate her praiseworthy efforts.

ELY S. PARKER,

To "THE SNIPE," N. Y. *Iroquois Sachem.*

Mrs. Converse improved her opportunities both in Western New York and among the Grand River Indians in Canada, to collect wampum belts and other articles, now for the most part rare, illustrative of Indian life. Ultimately most of her collections, including the very valuable wampum, became the property of the State and are preserved in the State Museum at Albany.

When the Vreeland bill, which was so drawn as to force the Senecas to pay $3,000,000 for the extinguishment of the claim of the Ogden Land Company to their lands, was pending in Congress, Mrs. Converse wrote many able letters in opposition. These appeared in leading newspapers and were in some degree influential in the final defeat of the bill.

Mrs. Converse died at her home in New York City, November 18, 1903, a few weeks after the death of her husband. Her work entitles her memory to be preserved with that of two other American women noted for their interest in the Indian and devotion to his welfare. One of these, Mrs. Erminie A. Smith of Jersey City, noted for her researches in Indian languages, in the service of the United States Bureau of Ethnology, was adopted a member of the Tuscarora Nation. Mrs. Helen Hunt Jackson, whose tale of "Ramona" and whose historical work "A Century of Dishonor," made her famous the world over, is the third of this trio of American women, whom history will remember for their devotion to the cause of the Indian.

"THE TRIAL OF RED JACKET"

Allusion has been made in the foregoing narrative to the so-called trial of Red Jacket. The incident took place in 1802, on the banks of Buffalo Creek, the site, altered beyond any possible recognition, having been long included within the city limits of Buffalo. Fortunately, the scene has been perpetuated by a painting of great historical value, the work of James M. Stanley. This artist, born in Canandaigua, Jan. 17, 1814, spent his boyhood in Buffalo, and knew Red Jacket and the vicinity of Buffalo Creek when it still retained a primeval character. Stanley early devoted himself to art, for at twenty-one he was painting portraits in Detroit, having removed to Michigan in 1834. In 1837 he made Chicago his home, then removed to Galena, Ill., and in the years that followed roamed far and wide, devoting himself chiefly to his chosen subject of Indian portraiture. We find him at Fort Snelling, Minn., at that time a resort for many Western tribes. After a period during which he followed his profession in New York City, Baltimore, Philadelphia, Troy and perhaps other eastern cities, he set out in 1842 on a long tour of the wild regions beyond the Mississippi. At Fort Gibson, Arkansas, in Texas and New Mexico, he painted portraits of chiefs and warriors in full costume. He was attached to the Kearney and Emory expeditions across the Rocky Mountains, and after doing much important work for the Government, especially in California, visited Oregon, sketching native types and scenery, especially in the region of the upper Columbia. After a year in the Sandwich Islands, he returned to Washington, where he resided and worked from 1851 to 1863, after which he made Detroit his permanent home.

During his Washington residence he completed one hundred and fifty-two portraits, many of them life size, of the leading men of forty-two tribes. By travel and residence among them he had made himself beyond question a high authority on Indian life and character. This splendid collection, of inestimable value, was placed in the Smithsonian Institution, where, in 1865, it was totally destroyed by fire.

Mr. Stanley had collected for the Government a large quantity of relics and curiosities, articles illustrating aboriginal life, but the greater part of them were lost in transportation at sea.

In his later years he painted portraits of many prominent men, and was one of the founders of a gallery of paintings which was later acquired by the city of Detroit. He died in that city of heart disease, April 10, 1872.

The most important example of his work now in existence is his "Trial of Red Jacket". It is owned by his family, which, it is reported, has valued it at $30,000. For some years it has hung in the Historical

Building at Buffalo. The canvas, five feet ten inches high by nine feet two inches wide, contains the portraits of seventy-two Indians, with the costumes and ornaments of their time, shown in the various attitudes which characterize Indians in council. Among the figures towards the rear of the group appears a white man, said to be the missionary, Samuel Kirkland. In the background, under great basswoods, winds the placid Buffalo Creek.

A reproduction of this picture, fairly satisfactory, considering the great reduction in size, is herewith presented. Modern artists seldom paint in the minute, studied manner of this canvas, a chief value of which is the almost photographic record which it presents of Seneca costume, ornament and physiognomy.

The historical incident upon which the artist has founded his picture, is as follows: Cornplanter, the Chief of the Six Nations, had become jealous of the rising popularity of Red Jacket, and determined to destroy him. For this purpose he consulted with his brother, The Prophet, and the two fabricated charges of sorcery—a deadly sin with the Indians—against Red Jacket. The scene represented by the artist is the trial of the great chief upon those charges. Cornplanter is the principal figure seated at the right. Handsome Lake stands at the extreme left. Red Jacket is represented as standing in the midst of the council, in the act of delivering his great speech of three hours in his own defence. The artist paints him as turning towards Handsome Lake, with an expression of scorn and contempt, accusing him of aiming a blow at him in the dark, when he had not the manhood to meet him face to face.

The defence was so full and complete that the council at once dismissed the charges, repudiated Cornplanter's claims, and restored Red Jacket to his wonted position as a pinetree chief of the Six Nations.

THE RED JACKET MEDAL

Ely S. Parker was the last grand sachem of the Iroquois to own the so-called Red Jacket medal. It was owned successively by Red Jacket, who received it from President Washington in 1792; by James Johnson, Red Jacket's nephew, whose Seneca name was Sosawah; and after his death, by Ely S. Parker. After General Parker's death the Buffalo Historical Society bought the medal from his widow, and now holds it. Its actual ownership has been claimed by the Seneca nation, but at the time of purchase that people formally expressed the wish that the medal should be kept by the Buffalo Historical Society.

It is one of the earliest American historical medals, and, for its history, one of the most valuable. Other medals resembling it are in existence, and their possessors have from time to time claimed to have the original Red Jacket medal. These claims would not have been so strenuously asserted, in countless newspaper letters, had the writers been in possession of the facts, a summary of which follows.

Several medals of similar type were made at the United States Mint, under the direction of Dr. David Rittenhouse, from 1792 to 1795. One of them, closely resembling the Red Jacket medal, is dated 1793. As these medals were not struck, but engraved—and much of the engraving is light scratching, on thin silver—even a casual examination discovers individual differences.

The obverse (pictured herewith), shows Washington in uniform, bareheaded, facing to the right, presenting a pipe to an Indian chief, who smokes it; the Indian is standing and has a large medal suspended from his neck. On the left is a pine tree, at its foot a tomahawk; in the background a farmer plowing. Below is engraved: *George Washington, President, 1792*. The reverse shows the arms and crest of the United States on the breast of an eagle, which holds an olive branch in its right talon, a sheaf of arrows in its left, and in its beak a ribbon with the motto, *E Pluribus Unum*; above, a glory breaking through clouds surrounded by thirteen stars. The medal is oval, six and three fourths by five inches, with raised rim and ring at top.

At the Greenville treaty of 1795, between the United States and representatives of the Hurons, Delawares and other tribes, medals were given to the Indian signers which are facsimiles of the Red Jacket medal, with the date changed to 1795.

For an account of the conference in Philadelphia, March-April, 1792, at which the medal was presented to Red Jacket, the reader is referred to Stone's "Life and Times of Sa-go-ye-wat-ha, or Red Jacket," chapter four. Several other medals like it were presented, it is understood, to other Indians in 1792 and 1793.

It would be interesting to learn their present whereabouts. The Historical Society of Pennsylvania has two—the Washington, 1793, and the Greenville, Aug. 2, 1795. Another is owned by the Red Jacket Club of Canandaigua. The late George H. Harris of Rochester, in a letter to Hon. George S. Conover of Geneva, January 11, 1893, undertook to trace the history of that medal, and stated in substance that after the death of the original Indian owner—whose name is not given—the medal came into the keeping of Jasper Parrish, interpreter and government agent. He is said to have received it from Red Jacket, to whom it was delivered, after the death of the original owner, with a request that it be returned to the United States Government. In passing it on to Jasper Parrish, who was a representative of the government, Red Jacket very likely believed he was fulfilling the request. This is supposed to be the medal now in the keeping of the Red Jacket Club.

Soon after that club acquired it, when its history was under discussion General Parker addressed the following letter to his friend, Mr. Conover, widely known for his researches in New York State history.

NEW YORK, March 9, '91.

GEO. S. CONOVER, ESQ.,
Geneva, N. Y.

DEAR SIR:—Permit me to thank you sincerely and heartily for your able circular and letter, dated February, 1891, on the Washington Red Jacket Medal.

It seems that your article was written in consequence of a medal purporting to have belonged to the famous Indian orator having been presented to the Red Jacket Club at Canandaigua by Mrs. Thomas Francis Meagher, a grand-daughter of Capt. Jasper Parrish of Canandaigua, whilom interpreter for the Seneca Indians.

I saw this medal during its exhibition a short time ago at Tiffany & Co.'s jewelry store on Union Square in this city. It was labelled "The Red Jacket Medal." I took pains to assure Tiffany's people that it was not a Red Jacket Medal, nor the one he wore throughout his life, and at the same time showed them the genuine medal which is in my possession. I also took an early opportunity of writing to the Hon. Thos. Howell of Canandaigua about it, and gave it as my firm conviction that Red Jacket never wore, or owned, this medal. It is, however, a genuine Washington Indian medal, shaped and inscribed on both sides like mine, with same date, viz.: 1792. Its longest diameter is about five inches, mine is seven inches. I suggested to Mr. Howell that it would be well to advise the Club of the preceding facts. Whether he has done so or not, I am unable to say.

Perhaps it would be well for history if this medal question should now be definitely settled. But how can this be done? It is almost a century since these medals were given, and I believe nearly all of the present possessors of the Washington Indian medals have begun to trace their ownership back to Red Jacket. Besides mine and this one at Canandaigua, I hear of one being in some collection at Albany, another in the collection of the Pennsylvania Historical Society at Philadelphia, and still another in Texas.

At Red Jacket's death, in accordance with Indian custom, my medal was given by his relations, in the distribution of his personal effects, to one James Johnson, a favorite nephew of his, and at that time a young and promising chief. Johnson retained it about twenty years, and at my installation as leading Sachem of the Iroquois Confederacy in 1851, I was formally invested with it by the master of ceremonies placing it about my neck, the speaker remarking the fact that it was given by the great Washington to my tribal relative, Red Jacket, and that it was to be retained and worn as evidence of the bond of perpetual peace and friendship established and entered into between the people of the United States and the Six Nations of Indians at the time of its presentation. There were scores of chiefs and other Indians present at this ceremony who personally had known Red Jacket and were familiar with the medal, and it is not probable or supposable that they all would have been deceived as to its genuineness, or countenanced an imposition by having a bogus medal placed about my neck on so important an occasion.

I have since met many old settlers of Buffalo and vicinity, among whom I will only mention Hon. O. H. Marshall, Orlando Allen, H. B. Potter, John Ganson, Benj. Dole, Mr. Sibley, Mr. Turner (author of the "Holland Land Purchase,") who have asked me to show them the medal, and they have instantly and invariably recognised it as the one they had so often seen worn by Red Jacket, and also the bead string by which it is suspended.

The Washington medals are all inscribed alike upon both sides, varying only in size and date. Mine is a large one and dated 1792—has thirteen stars; the eagle holding thirteen arrows in one claw and an olive branch in the other.

Respectfully yours, etc.,
ELY S. PARKER,
or Do-ne-ho-ga-wa, Iroquois Sachem.

Red Jacket's own medal is said—we know not with what truth—to have been more than once put in pawn, or pledge, by him, for drink; but at any rate, its whereabouts was not lost sight of, and since the great orator's death its ownership has been as above stated.

The Cayuga chief, O-ja-geht-ti or Fish Carrier, received a similar medal from President Washington. Some thirty years or more ago, a number of Cayugas living in Canada employed a Buffalo attorney to urge a claim in their behalf for a portion of the annuity granted by the United States Government to Cayugas living in the United States. At this time they exhibited Fish Carrier's medal. Its present whereabouts have not been inquired into, but it is not unlikely that it is preserved on the Grand River reservation in Canada.

In 1902 the Sons of the Revolution had a reduced reproduction of the Red Jacket medal struck in silver. It is oval, four by three inches, with raised figures and inscription. The obverse approximates that of the original, with the added statement that it was made from the medal owned by the Buffalo Historical Society by "S. of R. 1902"—Sons of the Revolution. The reverse is blank.

IROQUOIS ADOPTION

An allusion on page 83 to the Indian ceremony of adoption recalls a custom which has existed among the Iroquois from the earliest days, and which still exists. There are many references in 17th and 18th Century records to the adoption of captives; but this was a genuine adoption, and signified permanent inclusion in the tribe and family. But even in remote days the complimentary adoption was practiced. Notable instances of this, in Western New York history, are the cases of the sons of Louis Thomas de Joncaire, an adopted captive; but his sons, never captives, were also adopted; so, under the French règime, were Chauvignerie, Longueuil, and others. Sir William Johnson was an adopted son of the Mohawks, and was raised to a chieftainship.

In the early days of Buffalo, more than one of her citizens received this complimentary expression of confidence and esteem. Among the Senecas, it has ever been a proof of friendship and trust extended only to those whites whose good-will and help they felt could be counted on. Such friends of the Indian as Orlando Allen and Orsamus H. Marshall, prominent in the earlier history of Buffalo, were no doubt adopted Senecas, though no record of their adoption has been noted. William Clement Bryant, a former prominent attorney of Buffalo, and president of the Buffalo Historical Society, was so interested in the Indians and devoted to their welfare, that he was twice adopted, once by the Senecas, and again by the Mohawks.

Among Buffalonians past and present who have been thus complimented, note can be made of the following:

BRYANT, WILLIAM CLEMENT—Adopted by the Senecas, who gave him the name Da-gis-ta-ga-na, "The Burning Fire." The Mohawks also adopted him and named him Ky-o-wil-la—its meaning is lost.

BUCK, REV. WILLIAM D.—October 16, 1862. Name bestowed, Ski-y-uck-di, "Beyond the Skies." At this time Mr. Buck was pastor of a Seneca mission church on the Cattaraugus Reservation.

BUCK, EMMA A., daughter of Rev. Wm. D. Buck, now Mrs. Emma A. Rice of Buffalo. She was adopted, same date as her father, by a Seneca family which had lost a daughter, and was named Go-wah-dox-a, "She has departed."

DOBBINS, CHARLES W.—Date and name not ascertained.

KENDALL, MRS. ADA DAVENPORT.—At Versailles, 1913. Wolf clan. Name: Gos-soh-noh-yah, "Resting in the Infinite."

MARSHALL, CHARLES D.—Data lacking.

PORTER, (GEN.) PETER BUEL.—Was for many years a chief of the Senecas by adoption.

ROOT, (GEN.) ADRIAN R.—Data lacking.

SEVERANCE, FRANK H.—Cattaraugus reservation, June 16, 1890. Snipe clan. Name: Dah-di-oh-gwat-hah, "The spreader of news," in allusion to his newspaper work.

STAPLES, GEORGE K.—June 22, 1918, at Thomas Orphan Asylum. Turtle clan. Name: Ho-don-jai-ey, "He lifts the earth."

TUCKER, GEORGE L.—June 22, 1918, at Thomas Orphan Asylum. Bear clan. Name: Huh-sque-sohn, "Hatchet-carrier."

WILSON, CHARLES R.—1885; Beaver clan. Name: "Gah-we-sah."

WILSON, ROBERT P.—Data lacking.

WALKER, (Rt. Rev.) WILLIAM D.—(Bishop of Western New York.) About 1900. Beaver clan. Name: Hor-sin-i-sas, "A hunter for names," alluding to his services among the Senecas, the enrollment of names for confirmation, etc.

WALKER, (MRS.) WILLIAM D.—1906, at Brant, on the Cattaraugus Reservation. Deer clan. Name: Weh-ooh-gwas, "One who gathers flowers from the waters."

There are perhaps other residents of Buffalo, who have received Indian adoption; but they are not numerous, for the Senecas have never cheapened the honor by bestowing it indiscriminately, and many years sometimes elapse without the performance of the adoption rites.

Three persons are always adopted at a time. Sometimes, in compliment, an Indian name is bestowed; but this is not adoption. The ceremony is explained to the writer by a Seneca friend as follows:

"An Indian friend allows his name to be given to the white. This admits to his clan. This part is executed by the mothers of the clan. The assemblage is informed of the agreement, whereupon two aged Indians take the candidate by the hand and walk with him, followed by his clan. The other clans rise and bow in reverence to the Creator, with the left hand uplifted, the right hand over the heart. The mothers clap hands in cadence with the chant sung by the old men as they lead the candidate around the council-fire, the assemblage responding, *Hae, hae*." This brings out the wholly serious and reverential character of the ancient ceremony. As now performed, the details vary according to circumstances, but always certain essentials are observed. There is always an address given, on the Cattaraugus reservation, in Seneca, stating the reasons for adoption in the particular case, the clans and persons adopting, and the name to be given; second, the welcome in which the candidate is escorted up and down the council-house, or before the assemblage, by two chiefs, the chiefs chanting and the people responding. A general greeting and exchange of gifts follow.

In June, 1918, when Messrs. Staples and Tucker, members of the Buffalo Historical Society interested in Indian welfare, were adopted, the day being rainy, the ceremony was staged in the assembly room at the Thomas Indian School; literally "staged," for under the fertile guidance of Mr. Arthur C. Parker, with the assistance of Mr. Clifford Shongo, his sister Mrs. Ray Hurd, and others, something of a melodrama was evolved, the Indians appearing in costume and the candidates narrowly escaping being scalped or burnt at the stake, perils which made their ultimate reception all the more cordial.

Of one phase of the ceremony at her adoption in 1906 Mrs. William D. Walker writes to the editor of this volume: "After having my virtues, accomplishments and qualifications duly extolled by a venerable Seneca, in the presence of many Indians and palefaces, an Indian youth and maiden dressed in complete and traditional Seneca garb, most gracefully and ceremoniously bestowed upon me two baskets of their own workmanship, very tastefully filled with flowers. The aforesaid orator then welcomed me into the Deer clan, giving me the name of Weh-ooh-gwas, meaning, 'One who gathers flowers from the waters.' Husband and wife may not belong to the same clan, tradition and morals forbid. Hence the Bishop belonged to the Beaver clan and I to the clan of the Deer."

In June, 1890, Mr. F. B. Converse, husband of Harriet Maxwell Converse, who was then a Seneca chief by adoption, Mr. James Edward Kelly, a sculptor at the time engaged on a monument to Red Jacket, and the writer, were made adoptive Senecas, at a ceremony held in the open air, under the trees of William Jones's orchard. Here benches were set in a great quadrangle, in the midst of which smoked a council-fire. At the upper end were musicians and beyond them another fire, over which a great kettle of succotash—beans and Tuscarora white corn—was boiling. The Indians took seats by clans, the Snipe, the Heron, Bear, Deer, etc., by themselves. A great throng of the younger people surrounded the central group, and the roadside was filled with wagons and carriages. There were several hundred visitors, Indians and whites together.

Among the older Senecas who shared in the exercises were Moses Stevenson of Red Jacket's family; Lester Bishop, a leader among the Christians; David Stevens and Truman Halftown, and aged Mrs. Hemlock, from Newtown, the so-called Pagan settlement; these old people held to the ancient religion of their fathers, and spoke only Seneca.

It was a privilege to meet, and is now a pleasure to recall, these "old heads," survivors of the olden time. One feeble, wrinkled woman had known Red Jacket. So had David Stevens, with whom the writer spoke, Nicholson Parker acting as interpreter. Stevens was very old in 1890, the oldest living member of the Wolf clan, which is the head clan of the Senecas. In 1848, when these people adopted the republican form of government, Stevens "lost his horns," that is, his chieftainship, was deprived of authority, but he retained to the last the dignity of his hereditary office. For many years he had been the "pagan" preacher of the tribe, a leader of the non-Christian faction and a sturdy upholder even as Red Jacket was, of the tribal traditions and customs; in short a fine, upright old conservative. He survived until December, 1899.

Andrew John, Jr., then President of the Seneca Nation, had come from Carrollton on the Allegany reservation. He was one of the most successful of Seneca politicians. Of more interest to the writer was Nicholson H. Parker, brother of General Ely S. Parker, and his sister

Mrs. Mountpleasant; the former acted as interpreter; and it was the latter who, at the close of the ceremonies, first greeted the writer in kinship, and pinned to the lapel of his coat the ancient silver brooch which he has cherished nigh 30 years.

There was music, and an introduction of the candidates by William Jones, principal host for the occasion. David Stevens made the speech of adoption and bestowed the names of each in turn. Mr. Converse became Ha-nai-ne, "The Song-maker;" Mr. Kelly, Gah-nos-qua, "The stone giant," and the writer Dah-di-oh-gwat-hah, "Spreader of News." There was the usual marching up and down; and speeches, songs and the exchange of gifts ended only when the succotash was ready and the feast began.

A yet more notable adoption on the Cattaraugus reservation was that of June 15, 1885, when a grand council was held, and Mrs. Harriet Maxwell Converse, Hon. Frederick H. Furniss of Waterloo, N. Y., and George S. Conover of Geneva, N. Y., were received in adoption. Mrs. Converse was an author whose father and grandfather had been adopted by the Indians; and all were prominent as students of Western New York history and friends of the Indian. Mr. Conover has left a graphic account of this occasion in his pamphlet entitled: "Geo. S. Conover, Genealogical-Biographical," printed at Geneva in 1885.

On the general subject of Indian adoption the reader is referred to the "Handbook of American Indians," Bureau of American Ethnology, Bulletin 30, Part I; also, Seaver's "Life of Mary Jemison," 20th ed., N. Y., 1918, pp. 331-339; and Stone's "Life and Times of Sir William Johnson," vol. I, appendix 1.

MR. ARTHUR C. PARKER'S WRITINGS

Mr. Arthur C. Parker is the author of the following volumes issued by the New York State Museum:

Excavations in an Indian village and burial site at Ripley, Chautauqua Co., N. Y.—*Bulletin* 117, 1907.

Iroquois uses of maize and other food plants.—*Bulletin* 144, 1910.

The code of Handsome Lake, the Seneca prophet.—*Bulletin* 163, 1912.

The constitution of the Five Nations.—*Bulletin* 184, 1916.

The archaeological history of New York, 1919.

Mr. Parker edited and annotated Mrs. Harriet Maxwell Converse's "Myths and Legends of the New York State Iroquois," in *New York State Museum Bulletin* 125, 1908.

Notes on the bannerstone, with some inquiries as to its purpose, Rep. Director of the State Museum, 1918.

Champlain's assault on the fortified town of the Oneidas, 1615. Rep. Director of the State Museum, 1919.

The following list, though incomplete, contains the principal contributions of Mr. Parker to periodicals and publications of societies:

Seneca medicine societies.—*Am. Anthrop.* Apr.-June, 1909.

The Seneca game of snow-snake.—*Am. Anthrop.* Apr.-June, 1909, Iroquois silversmithing.—*Am. Anthrop.* July-Sept., 1909.

The Iroquois wampums.—*Proc. N. Y. State Hist. Ass'n.* Vol. VIII. 1909.

Iroquois influence on the archaeology of the Wyoming Valley, Pa.—*Proc. Wyoming Hist. and Geolog. Soc.*, 1910.

Additional notes on Iroquois silversmithing.—*Am. Anthrop.* Apr.-June, 1911.

The league of peace.—*Southern Workman*, Oct., 1911.

The progress of the American Indian.—*Southern Workman*, Nov., 1912.

Certain Iroquois tree myths and symbols.—*Am. Anthrop.*, Oct.-Dec., 1912.

Iroquois sun myths and ceremonies.—*Am. Folk Lore Jour.*, 1912.

Squakie hill and the Senecas.—*Proc. Livingston Co. Hist. Soc.*, 1912-13.

The Seneca Indians in the War of 1812.—*N. Y. State Hist. Ass'n Rept.*, 1914.

The social elements of the Indian Problem.—*Am. Jour. Sociology,* Sept., 1916.

The origin of the Iroquois as suggested by their archaeology.—*Am. Anthrop.*, Oct.-Dec., 1916.

The tragedy of the red race.—*Quar. Jour. S. A. I.*, Vol. I, No. 4.

The legal status of the American Indian.—*Ibid.*, Vol. II, No. 3.

The awakened American Indian.—*Ibid.*, Vol. II, No. 4.

The elements of the Indian problem.—*Ibid.*, Vol. III, No. 1.

The persistence of barbarism in civilised society.—*Ibid.*, Vol. III, No. 2.

Industrial and vocational training in Indian schools.—*Ibid.*, Vol. III, No. 2.

Indian progress as shown by the Thirteenth Census.—*Ibid.*, Vol. III, No. 2.

Making Democracy safe for the Indians.—*Ibid.*, Vol. VI, No. 1.

The Indian, the country and the government.—*Am. Ind. Mag.*, Jan.-Mar., 1916.

Problems of race assimilation in America.—*Am. Ind. Mag.*, Oct.-Dec., 1916.

How flint arrowheads are made.—*Am. Ind. Mag.*, July-Sept., 1917.

The American Indians' part in the world war.—*Ibid.*

Americans in the Stone Age.—*State Service*, Oct., 1917.

A pre-historic Iroquoian site on the Reed farm, Richmond Mills, Ontario Co., N. Y.—*Researches and Trans.*, N. Y. S. Arch. Assn., Morgan Chapter, Rochester, N. Y., 1918.

Habitat groups in wax and plaster, an address before the Am. Assn. Museums.—*Museum Work*, Vol. I, No. 3, 1918.

The New York Indians in the world war.—*State Service*, Apr., 1919.

A contact period Seneca site, at Factory Hollow, Ontario Co., N. Y.—*Researches and Trans.* N. Y. S. Arch. Assn., Morgan Chapter, Rochester, N. Y., 1919.

The life of Gen. Ely S. Parker, last grand sachem of the Iroquois.—*Pubs. Buf. Hist. Soc'y*, Vol. XXIII, 1919.

MEMORANDA

For an account of the re-burial of General Ely S. Parker, by the Buffalo Historical Society, together with several of his letters and an autobiographical memoir, the reader is referred to the Publications of the Buffalo Historical Society, Vol. VIII, pp. 511-536.

For General Parker's address at the Red Jacket commemorative exercises, Music Hall, Buffalo, Oct. 9, 1884, see Buffalo Historical Society Transactions, Vol. III, pp. 41-44. This volume of Transactions is entitled "Red Jacket," and is listed as Vol. III of the Publications series.

ERRATA. P. 96, for "Miner's Lodge" read "Miners Lodge."

P. 106, line 14, for "Then came to me" read "There came to me."

P. 126, line 19, for "Custer in" read "Custer on."

INDEX

INDEX

ABRAMS, Chauncey, 224, 226.
Adoption, of L. H. Morgan, 81, of Buffalo citizens, 329, 330.
Akron, 61; lodge of Masons, 96, 105.
Albany, 100.
Albany Normal School, 92.
Albany State Normal School, 85, 92, 189.
Allegany, (see Allegheny).
Allegheny, 18, 92, 203.
Allen, Orlando, 315, 329; adoption of, 330.
Amelia Court House, 125.
American Board, Mission of, 94.
Angel and Rice, attorneys, 79.
Appomattox, 117; river, 119, 120, 122, 126, 132.
Army of Northern Virginia, 124; broken, 125, 126, 135.
Artillery, Fourth N. Y., 113; Fourth U. S., 114.
Atiwandaronk, 42.
Aurora, 75.
A-weh-hah, (WildRose), pursued, 63; died, 68; tragedy of, 69.
Awl Breaker, 247, 248.

BABCOCK, Col. O. E., 128, 129.
Bacheldor, Mrs. Louise, letter from, 262.
Badeau, Col. Adam, 119, 120.
Baltimore, Henry, 200.
Baptist Mission School, at Tonawanda, 55, 235.
Bark houses or cabins, 59.
Baskets, 234.
Batavia, larger than Buffalo in 1825, 50; Lodge, 96, 105.
Bathing, Indians, 55.
Battles of Civil War, 185.
Beckwith, Capt. Samuel H., 109, 143, 226.
Bible, translated into Seneca, 191.
Big Fire, murdered, 67.
Big Tree, treaty of, 18.
Black Hawk, 8.
Black Rock, 33, 34, 308.
Blacksmith, (John), Tonawanda chief, 4, 236.
Blacksnake, Governor, 247.
Blankets, worn by Indians, 39.
Board of Indian Commissioners, 150, 151; letter from Commissioner Parker, 151.
Bowers, Col. T. S., 110, 121, 129, 131; death of, 144.
Boyd, Gen. John N., 32.
Brady, relates incident, 110.
Brant, Joseph, 8, 27, 71; leader of Iroquois, 207, 214.
Brantford, 71.
Bread, corn, 85.
Bribery of Indians, 93.
British, 24; invade, 28, 35.

Broadhead, Daniel, 26, 54.
Brooches, Silver, 56.
Brothertowns, 71.
Brown, Arthur, 223.
Bryant, William Clement, 177, 204; letter to E. S. Parker, 204, 207; letter from E. S. Parker, 214; record by, 315; adoption of, 330.
Buck, Emma A., (Mrs. E. A. Rice, 330).
Buck, Rev. Wm. D., 330.
Buffalo Creek, 12, 325.
Buffalo *Express*, quoted, footnote, 48.
Buffalo Historical Society, viii, 204, 210, 211; patriotism of, 225, 238, 315, 316, 319, 321, 329.
Buffalo reservation, 48, 191, 205; Indians at, 205.
Buffalo, site of, 13, 14; gore, 15; fears of residents, 28; Seneca council at, 28; battle of, 34; journey to, 50; called Do-sho-wey, 51, 73, 92; in Red Jacket's time, 203; Indians' cemetery, 203, 205.
Burial place, of Senecas, 219.
Butler, George H., (Col.), 116.

CABEYO, 147.
Canada, 29, 32.
Canandaigua, 196.
Caneadea, 37.
Capitol fire, 55; tomahawk rescued from, 89.
Captives, 30.
Caste system, 215.
Caswell, Harriet, 90, 300.
Cattaraugus creek, 192.
Cattaraugus reservation, 19, 59, 64, 92, 94, 117, 192, 200, 222, 297, 299, 302, 314.
Cayuga Academy, 75; L. H. Morgan at, 80.
Cayuga lake, 74.
Cayuga tribe, win suit, 37; settlement, 74; treaty with, 75.
Cemetery, Mission, 206.
Century Company, War book, 133.
Charles, Anderson, 226.
Chatfield, Levi S., 101.
Chattanooga, 106, 109, 118; letter describing, 292.
Chavignerie, 329.
Cherokees, 34.
Chesapeake and Albemarle Canal, 93.
Chiefs, repudiated, 93.
Chiefs, Tonawanda, refuse to sell land, 70; repudiated, 93.
Chipman, Gen. N. P., defends Parker, 304, 306.
Chippewa, Battle of, 32, 205.
Chippewa Indian, 35, 71.
Church of the Epiphany, 145.
City Point, 114, 115, 116, 119, 136.
Civilization, crushes Indians, 53; how it affects Indians, 150.

Civil War, 7, 99, 105; battles of, 185.
Clark, Senator Orville, 10.
Clinton, Gov. George, 14.
Clothing worn by Iroquois, 38.
Cloute, Chas., 226.
Coe, Capt. E. L., 226.
Cold, Capt., 32.
Colles, Gen. C. T., 224.
Colonial Wars, Society of, 225.
Comanche Jack, 146.
Commissioner of Indian Affairs, 150, 154, 156, 158.
Comstock, 111.
Confederates, 120, 123, 127, 128.
Conover, George S., 327, 328.
Converse, F. B., 332.
Converse, Harriet Maxwell, (New York literary woman), letter to; records, dream of Parker's Mother, 48; Parker relates incident to, 134; letters to from Parker, 164-180; a friend of Parker's, 162; papers of, 223, 322; Biography of, 323.
Copway, George, 205.
Cornplanter, Chief, (Gyantwaka), speech to Washington, 27, 89; tomahawk, 89; petitions Quakers, 297, 313, 326.
Cornplanter, Edward, relates legend, 238.
Cornplanter, Henry, 297.
Cornplanter's Town, (Dyo-no-sa-de-ga,—Burnt Houses), 18.
Cornplanter, Young, 32.
Corps, army; sixth, 123; fifth, 123, 125.
Costume, of Iroquois, 38, not changed, 55.
Council of Confederacy, Grand, 251.
Councils of the new Confederacy of the Iroquois, founded by Morgan and Parker, 80; (see Grand Order of the Iroquois).
Creation myth, 13.
Cultivators, Nation of, (The Neutrals or Attiwandaronks), war with, 46.
Cummings, Uriah, 63, 66.
Curtiss, Gen. James E., 226.
Cusick, David, (a Tuscarora annalist), 46.
Customs, birth, 55; burial, 59.

DANCES, 82; Indian, 278-285.
Darling, Thomas, adopted, 82, 83.
Dartmouth College, 70.
De-ka-na-wi-da, (Iroquois culture hero), 10; wampum codes, 11; laws of, 71.
Dekanesora, 8, 265.
Delawares, 71, 182.
Disappearing Smoke, (Gai-yen-gwa-toh, see Old Smoke); celebrated chief, 21; raid on Wyoming, 21.
Distinguished men, met by Parker, 77.
Dobbins, C. W., 330.
Doctor, Isaac, 189, 226, 231.
Doctor, Laura, (daughter of Levi Parker), viii; 189, 224, 226, 231, 232.
Dolph, John, 61.
Do-ne-ho-ga-wa, 3, 10, 91, 93, 97, 106; name signed to letters, 170-179, 222, 225.

Douglas, Alexander, a merchant, 310.
Drake, 76.
Dutch, 207.

EDITORIAL NOTES, 311.
Elizabeth, grand-daughter of Sos-he-o-wa, (see Elizabeth Parker), descendant of Neutral Captive, 31; grand-daughter of Sos-he-o-wa, 41; married William Parker, 41; ancestry of, 42, 190.
Elmira, 162.
Elskawata, the Shawnee prophet, 25.
Ely, Christian name of E. S. Parker, how given, 320.
English colonists, 208.
Eries, (part of Huron-Iroquois stock), 12; destruction of, 17.
Essays, of Parker boys, 76, 86.
Explorers, 54.
Extermination, with Iroquois meant tribal disruption, 13, 14.

FACE POWDER, 58.
Farmer's Brother, Col., character of, 31, 321, incident of in War of 1812, 34; mentioned, 260.
Farwell, undertaker, 205.
Fearey, Capt. T. H., 226.
Feast, Seneca, 84.
Feather, as a head decoration, 58.
Fire water, 310.
Fish Carrier, 329.
Fisher, Rev. J. Emory, 227.
Five Forks, 122, 124.
Forest Lawn Cemetery, 213, 225, 227.
Fort George, battle of, 32, 34, 315.
Fort Niagara, 24; battle of, 34, 315.
Fort Stanwix treaty, 27, 311.
Fraudulent treaty, 301; defeated, 310.
Freemasonry, (see Masonry); Parker's career in, 96.

GANEODAIU, (see Handsome Lake)
Ga-nio-dai-u, (a Seneca sachem and prophet, see Handsome Lake), 18, 53, 244, 259.
Ga-o-no-geh, 16.
Ga-ont-gwut-twus, (name of Mrs. William Parker), 20; of a noble family, 20.
Garangula, 8.
Ga-wa-so-wa-neh, 18.
Genesee country, sale of, 18, 37; a garden spot, 40.
Genesee Valley, 40.
Geneva Historical Society, 218.
Gettysburg, speech of Parker at, 181; battle of, 185.
Gordian Knot, and Order, 80.
Gorget, 57.
Government schools, 75.
Grand Army of the Republic, (see also Reno Post), 177, 227.
Grand Island, 15; British occupy, 28; Senecas had interest in defense of, 30; legend of, 238.
Grand Lodge of Illinois, 96.
Grand Order of the Iroquois, 81.

INDEX

Grand River, 69, 71; Parker goes to, 72; takes Morgan to, 86, 324.
Granger Estate, 227, 315.
Granger James N., 226.
Granger, Judge Erastus, pleads with Senecas, 27.
Grant, Fred D., 148; Parker's friendship for, 222; remarks on Parker, 224.
Grant, U. S.; Parker's early acquaintance with, 96; early army career, 99; estimated by Parker, 100; called "Unconditional Surrender," 105; Parker joins, 107; humanity of, 109; saved by Parker, 111; cares for his hat, 112; anecdotes of, 113; Parker mistaken for, 115; not idol, 118; headquarters, 119; men loyal to, 120; plots against, 120; team play of, 123; stops plundering, 124; strategy, 125; letter to Lee, 125; names peace terms, 126; receives Lee's letter, 128; meets Lee at McLean house, 129; terms of surrender, 132; used oval table, 134; issued special order on surrender, 134; order to Meade, 135; anecdote of Grant's smoking, 136; greets Lee, 138; magnanimity of, 139; parole order of, 139; in danger, 142; campaign for presidency, 147; candidate for presidency, 148; appointed Parker Indian Commissioner, 150; appointed Board of Indian Commissioners, 151; as strategist, 184.
Gray Wolf, 63; killed, 64.
Great Fire, murdered, 63; (Big Fire), 67.
Green Bay, tract, 297.
Greene, Dr. Joseph C., 226.
Greenville treaty, 327.
Gregg and Gibson purchase, 296.
Griswold, Geneva H., viii.
Ground, Benjamin, 226.
Guess, George, the American Cadmus, 268.

HABBERTON, John, (*N. Y. Herald* writer), cited, 48.
Hah-sgwih-sa-ooh, speech by, 281.
Hairdressing, 55.
Hale, Horatio, (writer on Iroquois), 11.
Handsome Lake, (Ga-nio-dai-u, the Peace Prophet), a sachem, 18; a prophet, 18; goes on journey, 18; Parkers follow, 19; opposition of, 25; religion of, 53, 202; code of, 251; opposed Red Jacket, 202; address on, 244; death of, 250.
Harper's Weekly, 99, 105.
Harrington, M. Raymond, (anthropologist), with author in Oklahoma, 146.
Harris, George H., 327.
Ha-sa-no-an-da, (youth name of Ely S. Parker), 4, 88.
Hatch, Howard, (a Seneca), 226.
Hat, Iroquois, 38; cap, 57.
Heirlooms of the Iroquois, 88.
Heroes of the Indian race, 8, 10, 183.
Hiawatha, 56.

Hill, Abram, (an Indian), 224.
Hotchkiss, Wheeler, 205.
Houghton, Frederick, (teacher and archeologist), discovered Neutral site, 16.
Hoyt, Martha Ellen, married Nicholson H. Parker, vii, 94, 191.
Hoyt, Seth, (brother of Martha), 200.
Hudson, P. T., (Aide-de-Camp), 123.
Hunting, 54, 218.
Hurd, Mrs. Ray (Maud Shongo), 331.
Huron-Iroquois, (a linguistic stock), 12.
Hurons, 12, 13.
Huyler, Mrs. Martha, contributes to Red Jacket fund, 213.

INDIAN AFFAIRS, 119; corrupt administration of, 144.
Indian Bureau, 150, 305, 308, 309.
Indian Commissioner, Parker appointed, 150; report of, 153, 154, 156; President Taft on office of, 158, 316.
Indian Commissioners, Board of, appointed, 150; Parker's letter to, 151; mentioned, 307.
Indian Dances, influence of, 279.
Indian Department, (see Indian Bureau), 154, 307.
Indian Falls, 51, 315.
Indian question, 170.
Indians are different, 51; use of silver and gold, 56; women, 58; educated, 75; grateful, 85; swindled, 151; societies, 163; received whites, 183; behavior of, 216; character, 267; condition anomalous, 310.
Interior Department, 306.
Iroquois Agricultural Society, 198.
Iroquois, allies of British, 11; creation myth, 13; assail Neutrals, 13; make weapons, 31; in War of 1812, 36, 37; costumes, 38; army of, 39; go to Canada, 72; Grand Order of, 81; maxim of, 160-161; zenith of power, 209; League of, 214, social grades, 215.

JACKSON, Helen Hunt, 324.
James, Army of the, 126.
Jemison, Alfred, 226.
Jemison, Mary, (the white captive), 203; home of, 302.
Jemison, Thomas, 205.
Jesuits, 13.
Ji-gon-sa-seh, (see Ji-kon-sa-seh), Parker descendant of, 10, 44, 45; captured, 46, 56; mentioned, 304.
Jimmy, Tommy, (Seneca chief), 311.
Jo Daviess Chapter, 96.
John, Andrew, 224.
Johnson, F. L., 224.
Johnson, Jemmy (or Jimmy, or James, see also Sos-he-o-wa), prepares to succeed Handsome Lake, 41; adopted L. H. Morgan, 81; address of, 83; fount of knowledge, 87; preaches, 259, 261.
Johnson, Sir William, 22; adopted 329.
Joi-e-sey, 18.

Joncaire, Thomas de, adoption, 329.
Jo-no-es-sto-wa, (Dragon Fly), Seneca name of William Parker, 5.

KAH-GWA-ONOH, (Kah-kwas, the Neutral Nation), the Neutrals, 42, Kah-kwah, 12; 309.
Kanandesaga, (Ga-nun-da-sa-ga), the site of Geneva, 22.
Kansas, lands of Senecas, 144.
Kelly, James E., (New York sculptor) interviewed Parker, 8-9; notes on Lee's surrender, 131, 136, 137; adopted, 332.
Kendall, Mrs. A. D., 330.
Kenjockety, the name of, 313; family of, 314; philology of, 314.
Kenjockety creek, 14, 313, 314.
Kenjockety, John, (see Sken-dyuh-gwa-dih), story of, 14; death, 14; by editor, 314.
Kenjockety, Philip, 313; incident of, 315.
Kennedy, Captain John, 32.
Kieuneka, (Ga-o-no-geh), Neutral capital, 16.
Kilts, worn by the Senecas, 56.
King Hendrick, 8.
King, term wrongly used, 217.
Kirkland, Rev. Samuel, 14; defended by Old Smoke, 22; visits Spirit Lake, 59; at trial of Red Jacket, 326.
Knights Templar, 96.

LA FORT, Abraham, an Onondaga, 280.
La Fort, Daniel, 224.
Lake Erie, Battle of, 313.
Lay, Chester, (Seneca sachem), 224.
Langdon, Andrew, (President of the Buffalo Historical Society), 225, 226.
Law, difficult to enforce, 153.
League of the Iroquois, (or the Five Nations, of Iroquois Confederacy or The Long House, or the Six Nations, etc.); historians of, 11, 29; sachems of, 52; re-established, 71; fame of, 90.
League of the Iroquois, a book by L. H. Morgan, 81; produced, 88; mentioned by Parker, 214.
Lee, Gen. Robert E., 110, 118; plan to trap, 120, 122; hopes of, 125; trapped, 125; distress of, 126; illogical stand of, 126; displayed white flag, 126; message to Grant, 127; at McLean house, 129; surrender of, 129; Grant's letter to, 132; reply of Grant, 133.
Legal status of Indians, 151; 153.
Legend of Grand Island, 238.
Leggings, style of, 56.
Letchworth Park, 199.
Letchworth, William Pryor, dedicated Council House, 37.
Letters of Ely S. Parker, to brother's children, 147; to Indian Commissioners, 151; to Mrs. H. M. Converse, 164-179; to Wm. C. Bryant, 204, 214; to his father, 285; to his people, 287; to his sister, 292.

Little Beard, John, 258.
Little Beard's Town, 315.
Little Billy, address of, 29, 32.
Little Smoke, ancestor of Parkers, 21; fled to Fort Niagara, 23; character of, 23.
Little Turtle, a Miami chief, 25.
Lincoln, Abraham, 106, 119, 120, 136; assassination of, 142.
Lloyd, Herbert M., edition of Morgan's *League*, 82; foot note, 82.
Lockwood, J. T., (a veteran on Parker), 113.
Logan, 81; monument to, 220, 265.
Logan, Saul, 33.
Longueuil, 329.
Lookout Mountain, 109, 110, 293.
Long House, (symbolic name of Iroquois League), guard of, 3; extended to Lake Erie, 17, 71, 207.
Loyal Legion, 176, 224, 225, 226.
Lundy's Lane; incident in battle, 34, 35.

MARCUS, H. H., 226.
Marcus, Maj. L., 226.
Married women, (Indian), 57.
Marshall, Charles D., 330.
Marshall, Col., 129, 130, 132.
Marshall, Orsamus H., 314, 329, 330.
Martindale, a lawyer, 287; wisdom of, 289.
Masonic banquet, 97.
Masonic Chronicle, quoted, 96.
Masonic Order, Morgan excitement, 80.
Masons, 80.
Massachusetts, claim on N. Y., 296.
Maxwell, Hon. Thomas, 162, 323.
McLean house, scene of Lee's surrender, 129; scene at, 137.
Meade, Gen., 111, 118, 123, attacks Confederates, 127, 128; letter from Parker, 135.
Medal, Red Jacket's, 211, 326; history of, 326-327; letter from E. S. Parker, on, 328.
Medina, 60.
Mental Elevator, a missionary publication in Seneca, 89.
Miners Lodge, 96.
Missionary viewpoint, 85, 86.
Missionary Ridge, battle of, 109.
Mission House at Cattaraugus, 192.
Mississaga, Chippewas, 71.
Moccasins, of Senecas, 38.
Mohawks, (see Iroquois).
Morgan, Lewis Henry, (the anthropologist), vi; born at Aurora, 75; Parker's acquaintance with, 80; began study of Iroquois, 80; adopted, 81; writes "*The League of the Iroquois*," 81; called the champion of the Iroquois, 81; adoption, 82; given wampum belt, 82; read paper before N. Y. Historical Society, 86; letters on the Iroquois, 86; activities for the State Museum, 86; gathers collection, 87; produces book, 88, 237; witnessed dance, 280.

INDEX

Mother of Nations, 45; (see Ji-gon-sa-seh).
Moses, David, 226.
Moses, Sachem Abram, 224.
Mound Builders, 15.
Mountpleasants, The, 321; family of, 321; spelling of name, 322.
Mountpleasant, Caroline, (see Caroline Parker), 190, 321; death of, 322, 333.
Mountpleasant, John, 217, 321.
Murder Creek, 61.
Myrtle, Minnie, writes book, 89.

NASHVILLE, 110.
Neuters, (see Neutral Nation), 42.
Neutral-Erie wars, 14.
Neutral Nation, domain of, 12; assailed by Iroquois, 13; tales of, 15; village of, 16; descendants interested in Grand Island, 30; exterminated, 191.
New York Historical Society, Morgan reads paper before, 86.
Niagara, 12, 40.
Niagara River, 15, 36; title to bed, 37.
North, Charles J., 226.
Nye, Gen. James W., 101.

O'BAIL, *Major* Henry, leader in war of 1812, 32.
Ogden, David, 295.
Ogden, Land Claim, 70, 81, 93, 324.
Ogden Land Company, 203, 205, 295; history of, 300; accused, 301.
Old Smoke, (Old King), character of, 22.
Oneida, women in war, 33; settlement in Canada, 72.
On-gweh-o-weh, Iroquois term for themselves, 13; story of, 42, 43, 44.
Onondagas, declare war on Great Britain, 29, 214.
Orations of N. H. Parker, 263, 270, 277, 279.
Orations of Parker boys, 76.
Ontario County, 13.
Ord, Gen. E. O. C., his march, 127.
Osborn, Kate, 38.
Osceola, 8.

PAGANISM, 53.
Parker, origin of name, 21.
Parker, Albert Henry, (son of Nicholson), 192.
Parker, Arthur Caswell, vii, viii; activities of, ix; address of Handsome Lake, 244; foot note 247, 331; writings of, 333.
Parker boys, rearing, 55; school career, 74; opportunities, 76; books read by, 76.
Parker, Caroline, (see Caroline Mountpleasant), ix, 48; named Gahona, 58; at school, 74; educated in Albany, 85; beadwork, 88; surroundings of, 190; death of, 233, 237; letter from Ely, 292; named, 296.
Parker, Elizabeth, (Mrs. William Parker), ancestry, 42; beauty of, 47; vision of, 48; clan of, 48; dress of, 55; described old days, 87; described, 233; dress of, 235.

Parker, Ely Samuel, (Do-ne-ho-ga-wa), boyhood name, 4; experiences, 4; origin of Christian name, 5; unique character, 7; sachem, 7; rose to fame, 8; modesty of, 10; letter to H. M. Converse, 10; descendant of Ji-kon-sa-seh, 10; ancestry of, 11; mother's vision, 48; birth of, 50; named, 50; early teachings of, 53; cradle board of, 55; given Seneca name, 58; ran away, 69; goes to Canada, 72; drives horses, 72; taunted, 73; returns home, 73; goes to school, 74; attends Yates Academy, 74; attends Cayuga Academy, 75; messenger for Senecas, 77; guest of President, 77; admires Mrs. Polk, 77; studies law, 79; refused admission to bar, 79; attends Rensselaer Polytechnic, 79; joins canal party, 79; becomes acquainted with L. H. Morgan, 80; acts as interpreter, 84; companion of Morgan, 86; collections of, 88; superintendent of canals 91; perception of, 91; made sachem, 91; made chief engineer, 94; anecdote of, 94; strength of, 95; made superintendent, 96; love of Masonry, 96; Masonic career, 96; interest in Civil War, 99; enlistment refused, 100; oratory of, 101; estimate of Grant, 102; offers services to Secretary Seward, 102; services rejected, 103; retires to farm, 103; philosophy of, 106; Commissioned captain, 106; reported to Gen. J. E. Smith, 107; made adjutant, 108; at Vicksburg, 108; in battles, 109; illness, 110; uses whiskey, 110; temperance of, 110; saves Grant, 111; commands army, 112; as engineer, 113; appointed military secretary, 115; mistaken for Grant, 115; commissioned Colonel, 116; played billiards, 117; at headquarters, 119; talks with Lincoln, 120; dispatches of, 121, 122, 123, 124; in Appomattox campaign, 125; at McLean house, 129; drafts terms of Lee's surrender, 131; interviewed, 132; meets Lee, 133; relates Grant anecdote, 136; equipment at surrender, 138; wrote orders, 139; issued parole order, 139; serves country as an Indian, 141; becomes a citizen, 141; commissioned Brigadier General U. S. V., 142; guards Grant, 142; resigns from War Department, 143; battles he fought in, 143; tours with Grant, 144; saves Tonawanda Indians, 144; meets future wife, 145; wedding, 145; attends Indian councils, 146; appointed Commissioner of Indian Affairs, 150; policy of as Commissioner, 150; letter to Board, 151; saw needs of Indians, 153; annual report of, 153; highest goal of, 154; plots against, 155; accused, 155; trial of, 155; found without stain, 156; did not slur enemies,

Parker, Ely Samuel—*Continued*.
156; success of his administration, 157; resigned, 157; review of life of, 157; was honest, 158; honesty of, 159; integrity of, 160; his home, 160; resignation of, 159; financial affairs of, 160; letters of to Mrs. Converse, 164 to 179; influenced by Mrs. Converse, 163; autobiography of, 165; speech at Gettysburg, 181; estimate of Red Jacket, 207; idea of a memorial to Red Jacket, 212; home of in New York, 221; position of in Police Department, 221, health of, 222; stricken, 223; death of, 224; funeral of, 224-225; wampum on casket, 225; grave of, 225; retirement of, 226; his youth, 235; installed sachem, 236; goes to war, 237; school days at Yates, 262; letter explaining laws to Indians, 286; letter to sister from Chattanooga, 292; family of, 319; charges against refuted, 304; groundlessly accused, 309; incident of marriage, 319; Christian name of, 320.
Parker, Ely S., military dispatches of, 121, 122, 123, 124.
Parker, Mrs. Ely S., (Minnie Sackett), 178, 180, 224, 226.
Parker family, vii, 19; settle at Tonawanda, 20; homestead, 20; five sons in, 21; progressive, 53, 232; supposed ancestry of, 313.
Parker, Frank S., (son of Nicholson), 192.
Parker, Fred Ely, (son of Nicholson), viii, 192, 224.
Parker, Henry, (brother of William), 21.
Parker home, near Tonawanda Falls, 20; rebuilt, 20; commodious, 51; meeting place, 51; birthplace of a science, 89; visited by Red Jacket, 216; author's visit to, 231, 232.
Parker, Isaac Newton; in army, 100, 189.
Parker, Levi, 47, 84, 189, 231.
Parker, Martha Hoyt, (wife of Nicholson), v, 193.
Parker, Maud, (daughter of Ely), 180; 224.
Parker, Minnie Clark, (daughter of Nicholson), 192, 197, 226.
Parker, Nicholson Henry, (brother of Ely S.), viii, 38; named Gai-e-wah-go-wa, 58; attends school, 74; books written in home of, 89; lectured, 90; at school, 92; returned to Tonawanda, 92; married Martha Hoyt, 94; confidant of brother Ely, 117; character of, 191; his farm and home 192; description of home, 194; Seneca name of, 195; intellectual nature of, 195; lectures of, 196, 270, 278, 301; love of horses, 197; activities of, 198; manner of, 199; horses of, 200; death of, 201; son of William, 237; speech of, 263; name of, 270; speech of, 270; lecture on Indian dances, 279; work of, 302, 332.
Parker, Samuel, 19, 313, 314.
Parker, Sherman Grant, (son of Nicholson), 192.
Parker, Spencer, (brother of Ely S.), 47, 189, 236.
Parker, William, (Jo-no-es-do-wa), one of three brothers, 19; became a Baptist, 20; a hard worker, 20; knew his people, 31; enrolled, 32; returned from War of 1812, 40; owned saw mill, 40; of the Turtle Clan, 46; a hunter, 47; traded at Batavia, 50; progressive, 85; helps Morgan, 87; estimate of Grant, 100; his children, 189; a chief, 234; death of, 237; career, 238; family of 313.
Parker, William, (son of Spencer), 197, 226.
Parole, issued to Confederates, 139-140.
Peace policy, 147, 150.
Pembroke, Caroline and Nicholson Parker attend school at, 74.
Pemberton, Gen. John C., 185.
Penn, William, 298.
Pequots, 276.
Petersburg, 116, 122.
Phelps, Bronson and Jones purchase, 296.
Phelps, Martha B., 320.
Philip of Pokonoet, 8, 76, 265.
Pickering, Col. Timothy, 246.
Pierce, Maris B., 70, work of, 304.
Pittsburg, trading post at 54.
Polk, President, entertains Parker, 77.
Pollard, (Seneca Chief), 32.
Polo, Mary, (a Gipsy) 200.
Pontiac, 8, 76; genius of, 268.
Porter, Hon. Augustus, 14.
Porter, General Horace, 108, 115, 130.
Porter, Charles Talbot, a friend, 80; adopted with Morgan, 82; Morgan's friend, 82; defends customs of Indians, 86.
Porter, Gen. Peter Buel; adopted, 330.
Potomac, Army of 110, 114, 118, 135.
Poudry, Mrs. Thomas, 226.
Powhatan, 8.
Prophecy fulfilled, 320.
Prophet, The, (see Handsome Lake).
Putnam, Frederic Ward, ix.

QUAKERS fight a land conspiracy, 295; defend Senecas, 297; meet at Buffalo Creek, 299; work of, 304.
Quaker school, 300.
Queen Anne, gives a communion service, 71.
Questions relative to Indian affairs, 152.

RED JACKET, opposes Tecumseh, 25; at Detroit, 26; replies to Judge Granger, 27-28; visits Parker home, 51, 202; not popular, 202; Parker's estimate of, 202; reinterment, 203; first appearance of, 209; ignorant of legal effect of Sullivan's campaign, 210; monument proposed

Red Jacket—Continued.
for, 212; monument paid for by
Mrs. Huyler, 213; his disappointed
ambition, 214; a chief, 215; monument 225; a patriot, 266; speech of,
297; asks help of Quakers, 299;
trial of, 325; medal of, 326, 328.
Red Jacket Club, 327.
Rawlins, Gen. John A., 111, 115, 122.
Red Man, the American, an address
by N. H. Parker, 263.
Religion of Handsome Lake, manuscript account by E. S. Parker, 251.
Reno Post, G. A. R., 224, 226.
Rensselaer Polytechnic Institute;
Parker attends, 79.
Reservation life, 50-70, 89, 201.
Revolutionary War, 22, 25, 207.
Rice, Mrs. Emma A., 330.
Richmond, campaign against, 119,
Union army enters, 123.
Riis, Jacob, 221; writes of Parker, 222.
Rittenhouse, Dr. David, 327.
Roosevelt, Theodore; Parker worked
in office with, 221.
Root, Gen. Adrian R., 330.
Royal Arch, 96.

SACHEMS, poor men, 52; raised, 71;
of the Iroquois, 91; given power,
93; cannot enter battle, 100; how
term is used, 217; at Parker's
funeral, 224; elected, 236.
Sackett, Minnie, engaged to General
Parker, 146.
Salisbury, Dr., 223.
Salt Lick, on Buffalo Creek, 310.
Sashes, red worsted, 38; buckskin, 38.
Saunders, pursues Indian girl, 62.
Soajaquada, (see Kenjockety), 313.
Schenandoah, a pen name, 86.
Schoolcraft, Henry, 81, 231.
Scott, Gen., 32.
Seneca band, 198.
Seneca Castle, 18.
Senecas, left towns of conquered tribes,
14; warriors defeated Neutrals, 15;
had village at mouth of the Tonawanda, 16; traditions of Grand
Island, 17; fought for territory, 17;
remove, 18; abandon old homes, 24;
oppose Tecumseh, 26; declare war
on Great Britain, 28; participate in
war, 32; took oath, 39; deceived,
39; agriculturalists, 40; married, 41;
religion of, 52; critical stage, 53;
farmers, 54; become hunters, 54;
costume of, 55; unhappy condition,
69; confusion of, 77; dances, 84;
279; treaty with, 92; threatened, 93;
in Civil War, 103; government, 194;
in Civil war, 209; defrauded, 203;
country claimed by, 218; dominions,
219; burial place, 219; loyalty to
United States, 219; retreat, 246;
lured west, 297; of Cattaraugus, 299;
defrauded, 301.
Settlers, character of, 53.
Severance, Frank H., 225; interest of,
226; notes by, 313; adopted, 330.
Seward, William H., 102; interest in
Indians, 309.
Shanks, David, 226.

Shanks, Truman, 226.
Shawnees, 25.
Shelton house, 114.
Sheridan, Philip E., 120; orders of,
121, 125; attacked by Lee, 127;
feared treachery, 127; received
Lee's letter, 128; doubts Lee, 129.
Sherman, William T., 130.
Shikellamy, governor of conquered
tribes, 14.
Shongo, George, 200.
Shongo, Moses, 227.
Shongo, W. Clifford, assists in adoption, 331.
Silver, head band, 56; brooches, 56;
use of, 56.
Silverheels, 32.
Simcoe-Kerr, Col., a Mohawk, 37.
Six Nations, (see Iroquois), Morgan's
essay on, 86.
Skandauchquaty, Jack, 310.
Sken-dyuh-gwa-dih, (Beyond-the-multitude, or John Kenjockety, a
Neutral Indian), mentioned, 14;
protests to Governor Clinton, 14.
Skeye, Mr. 226.
Slaves, Iroquois captives made, 14.
Slocum captive, not a Parker ancestor,
317.
Slocum, Frances, 318, 319, 320.
Society of American Indians, viii;
146.
Society of Charm Holders, 60.
Society of Colonial Wars, 225.
Society of Friends, (see Quakers),
301.
Social grades of the Iroquois, 215.
Sons of the Revolution, 329.
Sos-he-o-wa, (see Jemmy Johnson),
41; succeeds Handsome Lake, 53;
wants descendants to know ancient
lore, 60, 249.
Southern army, (see Confederate
army), 119; routed, 124.
Smith, Erminie A., a writer, 324.
Smith, Capt. A. J., 227.
Smith, Gen. J. C., 96.
Smith, Gen. J. E., 107, 108.
Smoking, Grant's love of, 136.
Spies, 119.
Spirit Lake, (Divers Lake), 59; legend
of, 60.
Spottsylvania, 111; 136.
Squaw Island, 15.
Squawkie Hill, 33.
Stanley, James M., an artist, 325.
Staples, George Kelly, adopted, 330;
adoption of, 331.
State Museum, vii; Parker wampum
belt in, 3; war clubs in, 31; Morgan's
wampum belt in, 82; Morgan's
work for, 86; collections in, 98, 238.
State Library, destroyed, 89.
Stevenson, James, 205.
Stevenson, Moses, 205.
Stevenson, Ruth, 205.
Stone, Rev. Ely; Ely Parker named
for, 320.
Street, Alfred, 81.
Strong, Nathaniel, 303.
Sugar bushes, 233.

Sullivan's campaign, 212, 219.
Sullivan, Major Gen. John, raid of, 23, 24, 207, 316.
Surrender of Lee, 129; scene of, 129; incidents of, 130, 132.
Susquehanna Valley, 14.
Sweat bath, 55.

TAFT, President, William H., interview with author, 158.
Tammany, a Delaware chief, 182; lines to, 188.
Tecumseh, (a Shawnee chief), ancestry not known, 8; plan for League, 25, 26, 76.
Terms of Surrender, 130, 131; Grant's letter on, 132.
Thacher, 76.
Thomas Indian School, 192, 331.
Thomas, Philip, 193; helped Indians, 302, 304.
Timber in W. New York, 17.
Tippecanoe, 106.
Tompkins, Governor, 267.
Tonawanda Creek, 15; settlements along, 16; valley of, 17; falls, 20, 36, 51.
Tonawanda Falls, 41.
Tonawanda Indians, 47; situation, 92, 93; in fear of ejectment, 93; lands saved, 144; buy lands, 145; letter to, 286; no part in treaty, 303.
Tonawanda Reservation, set aside in 1797, 18; lose a portion of, 20, 73, 92, 99, 145, 189, 222, 323.
Tonawanda Valley, 17.
Town Destroyer, (Indian name for Washington), 27.
Townsend, E. D., 116.
Traits of Indian Character, a speech by N. H. Parker, 270.
Treaty of 1838, 92; fraudulent, 301.
Tree burials, 59.
Tree eaters, 43.
Tribes, broken, 71.
Trippe, M. F., 170.
Tucker, George L., adopted, 330.
Tuscarora Reservation, 321.
Tuscaroras, 71.
Tutelos, 71.
Two Guns, Daniel, 205.
Two Guns, Noah, 197.

UNION ARMY, 120, 122, 123, 135; closes on Lee, 127.

VALLEY LODGE, 96.
Van Buren, President Martin, 92.
Van Deventer, Peter, 61.

Vicksburg, 107, 108; Grant at, 185.
Vreeland bill, 324.

WALBRIDGE, Col. C. E., 226.
Walker, Bishop and Mrs. William D., 331.
Wampum, in State Museum, 3; meaning of, 3; Washington treaty, 28; given L. H. Morgan, 82; on Parker's coffin, 225, 231, 324.
Wampum Keeper, 224.
War of 1812, Senecas in, 26, 32; Oneidas in, 32; women in, 33; captives of Iroquois help in, 34; incidents of, 34; Iroquois were allies in, 36; estrangement of Iroquois, 37; left Senecas loyal to U. S., 39, 209, 216.
Washington, (city), 77, 79, 102, 145.
Washington, George, Iroquois grateful to, 27; treaty belt, 28; 207, 209, 219; medals of, to Indians, 326.
Welsh, William, accused Parker, 155; libeled Indian race, 155; accusation of against Parker, 305, 306.
Wenroes, 12.
West Point, 118, 133; Grant visits, 144.
White Oak road, 122.
Wilderness, Campaign in, 111, 113.
Wild Rose, (A-weh-hah), story of, 66, 68; tragedy of, 69.
Wilner, Mrs. Merton W., 320.
Wilson, C. R., 330.
Wilson, Dr. Peter, 70; interpreter, 92; becomes army surgeon, 103; speech of, 303.
Wilson, Robert P., 330.
Williams, Elias, 224.
Williams, Seth, greeted by Lee, 133.
Women in war, 23; costumes of, 57; head ornaments, 58.
Worth, Capt., 35.
Wright, Mrs. Laura M., 191, 193, 206.
Wright, Rev. Asher, (missionary to the Senecas), 191; death of, 192, 206; helped Senecas, 302, 309, 314.
Wright, W. W., interviews with Parker, 100.
Wyandots, 26.

YATES Academy, 74; mentioned, 262.
Ye-go-wa-neh, (the Great Woman, see Mother of Nations or Ji-kon-sa-seh), 45.
Young King, 21.
Youngstown, 34.

www.ingramcontent.com/pod-product-compliance
Lightning Source LLC
Chambersburg PA
CBHW081215170426
43198CB00017B/2616